THE
BiG LiE
The **Truth** about **Advertising**

British advertising is cynical, clever and witty – the best in the world. American advertising is saccharine, crass and clunky – an insult to the intelligence. Is that so? Does either work? How? An American adman who has worked in Europe for thirty years deconstructs the conventional wisdom of Adland to disclose at its heart a black hole of ignorance and deceit.

Forty years ago Vance Packard concluded his seminal exposé, The Hidden Persuaders, by questioning the morality of advertising's manipulative motivational techniques. If his concerns seem quaint now, it is because we have now surrendered to consumerism as the dominant cultural force in the world. Advertising has assumed a priestly role: to sustain its myths by promulgating falsehoods.

Yet the first Big Lie is that advertisers and their agencies know what they are doing. The second is the belief most people have that they are not influenced by advertising. Another is the contention that advertising does not have broad social effects beyond brand-switching.

This book also examines whether the seductive techniques advertisers use, such as humour, irony and celebrity endorsement, are really successful; exposes whole industries founded on falsehood; and warns of the false assumptions gathering around the new communications technology and the Internet.

In an industry which maintains strict demarcation lines between its disciplines, **CHUCK ANDERSON** has an advertising background which is probably unique. He has worked both sides of the fence: in advertising research and as a Creative Director: he has tested hundreds of campaigns for major companies and created thousands of advertisements.

He also builds his perspective from both sides of the Atlantic. An American, he worked as a copywriter for advertising agencies in New York before undertaking advertising research for Unilever in Germany. Later, he joined J. Walter Thompson in London, managing new product development. He developed this group into JWT's first subsidiary advertising agency, which had the distinction of launching "Pot Noodle" upon the British public. Later, he led a management buy-out of the company, becoming Chairman and Creative Director.

In Britain he has won an IPA Advertising Effectiveness Award for consumer goods in the only ad industry competition which is based on empirical evidence. He currently runs an independent advertising creative consultancy.

~ *Credits* ~

COVER:
© The New Yorker Collection 1998 Jack Ziegler
from cartoonbank.com. All Rights Reserved.

CONTENTS:
Hans Masereel from *The City* © DACS 2000

PART I:
© The New Yorker Collection 1997 Lee Lorenz
from cartoonbank.com. All Rights Reserved.

PART II:
© The New Yorker Collection 1994 Robert Mankoff
from cartoonbank.com. All Rights Reserved.

PART III:
© The New Yorker Collection 1992 Tom Cheney
from cartoonbank.com. All Rights Reserved.

PART IV:
© The New Yorker Collection 1986 Gahan Wilson
from cartoonbank.com. All Rights Reserved.

PART V:
© The New Yorker Collection 1993 Robert Weber
from cartoonbank.com. All Rights Reserved.

PART VI:
© The New Yorker Collection 1996 Sidney Harris
from cartoonbank.com. All Rights Reserved.

THE BiG LiE
The Truth about Advertising

CHUCK ANDERSON

Random Thoughts Limited
London

Anderson, Chuck
The Big Lie
The Truth about Advertising

British Library Cataloguing-in-Publication Data

A catalogue record for this book is available from the British Library

ISBN 0-9513573-3-6

Copyright © Random Thoughts Limited, 2000

First published in Great Britain 2000

All rights reserved. No part of this publication may be reproduced or transmitted in any form or by any means, electronic or mechanical, including photocopying, recording, or any information storage and retrieval system, without either prior permission in writing or a licence permitting restricted copying

Published by
Random Thoughts Limited
Garden Floor
12 Hill Road
London, NW8 9QG

Designed by
Jon Anderson

Edited by
Sarah Barrett

Printed in Great Britain by
Antony Rowe Limited,
Chippenham

To Julian Woolfson,
who wanted to read a sequel to "The Hidden Persuaders",
and Gerald de Groot,
who contributed his experience to Part I.

THE BiG LiE
The Truth about Advertising

---- CONTENTS ----

Preface		ix
Jesuitical Reasoning		xii

PART I "It researched well"

1	Effectiveness	The Holy Grail	3
2	Influence	Advertising isn't working	9
3	Measurement	How long is a piece of baloney?	18

PART II "Advertising never sold me anything"

4	Branding	A rose by any other name would cost a lot less	27
5	Creativity	The secret magic ingredient	37
6	Irrationality	The Kings of Misrule	45
7	Hyperbole	The Second Biggest Show on Earth?	55
8	Attention	Hello, sailor	65
9	Involvement	I can make a new man of you in just 7 days	73
10	Emotion	Gut feel	82

PART III How to tell shite from Shinola

11	Humour	A phoney thing happened on the way to the forum	91
12	Visualisation	They laughed when I sat down at the word processor	97
13	Demonstration	Seeing was believing	108
14	Endorsement	Hitch your wagon to an icon	114

15	Negativity	You gotta ac-cent-tchu-ate the positive	123
16	Tone	It ain't whatcha say, it's the way howtcha say it	131
17	Style	Does attitude wash whiter?	140
18	Deconstruction	The ironic age	149

PART IV   Masters of deception

19	Fashion	How to make a statement though completely inarticulate	161
20	Tobacco	You stick it between your lips and set fire to it? And then it kills you?	169
21	Corporate	Singing from the songsheet	179
22	Banking	I laughed all the way to the official receiver	189
23	Politics	Where there's muck, there's muck-slingers	198

PART V   Beyond the bottom line

24	Admen	The wonderful folk who brought you 'tired blood'	211
25	Unreality	Meanwhile, back in the real world	222
26	Commonweal	The do-gooders	232
27	Morality	Matters of taste	242
28	Behaviour	Monkey see, monkey do	252

PART VI   Beyond Y2K

29	Technology	The day after Doomsday	263
30	Internet	The Garden of Eden	271
31	Future	Round the bend down the yellow brick road	281

| Bibliography | 291 |
| Index | 293 |

PREFACE

MORE than forty years ago Vance Packard concluded his seminal exposé of advertising's blandishments, *The Hidden Persuaders*, with a consideration of the morality of its manipulative motivational techniques. "What is the morality", he asked:

> of encouraging housewives to be non-rational and impulsive in buying the family food?
>
> ... of playing upon hidden weaknesses and frailties – such as our anxieties, aggressive feelings, dread of nonconformity, and infantile hang-overs – to sell products?
>
> ... of manipulating small children even before they reach the age where they are legally responsible for their actions?
>
> ... of treating voters like customers, and child customers seeking father images at that?
>
> ... of exploiting our deepest sexual sensitivities and yearnings for commercial purposes?'
>
> ... of appealing for our charity by playing upon our secret desires for self-enhancement?
>
> ... of developing in the public an attitude of wastefulness towards national resources by encouraging the 'psychological obsolescence' of products already in use?
>
> ... of subordinating truth to cheerfulness in keeping the citizen posted on the state of his nation?

If these concerns seem quaint now, it is because we have now surrendered to consumerism as the dominant cultural force in the world, and the attitudes Packard feared are now the tenets of the imperial religion: New Hedonism. All the traditional cultures teach us that falsehood will eventually be destroyed by truth. Yet all around us, in public life, in the packaging of government policies, and throughout the media – in the marketing of entertainment, in the hyping of popular culture and fine art, in the fabrication of a product which is still called a *news*paper – hyperbole shades into untruth. Its dogmas are promulgated by the technique of the Big Lie, favoured by zealots since the dawn of communication and latterly adapted to mass media by Josef Goebbels. In his more judgemental era, it was labelled propaganda; now it's called public relations or lifestyle.

Yet, if these manipulators are so skilful, why is it that people so often feel that advertising is crude, tasteless, silly, irritating, condescending, irresponsible, irrelevant – in the time-honoured phrase, "an insult to my intelligence"? Partly because it is unlikely to be directed at their intelligence, partly also because most advertising is not addressed to people who read books like this, or read books at all. Yet, even when advertising is clearly aimed at you, you may often feel that it is a waste of your time, and their money. Or is it? Surely these subtle advertising people, with all the research they do, must know what they're about?

No, they do not. The people who create advertising delude themselves. Frequently it is because those practitioners who understand the principles of persuasion are not those who create and select the message. There is no general consensus on what constitutes good advertising, and little serious intellectual framework to support opinion. Of all areas of major business investment, only advertising has no accepted measurement of effectiveness. While research techniques are good at measuring what is already happening, they are poor at predicting behaviour. In mathematical models of effect, advertising expenditure is given great weight, because it is something that is easily measured. The creative factor is usually excluded, because it has proved impossible to measure it. And so, although messages which make meaningful contact can implant ideas, sway opinion, and change behaviour, most advertising content is the product of guesswork.

The managers who authorise immense expenditures on advertising do so with scant evidence that their campaigns will have any productive effect whatsoever. While a capital investment of only tens of thousands of pounds in new plant will be subject to exhaustive routines of technical specification, rigorous professional evaluation, and close financial scrutiny of its pay-out period, a television campaign for ten or a hundred times that amount will be nodded through on the basis of 'gut feel', or naive and spurious arguments. Most people who work in advertising like it that way. The result is wasteful investment on a colossal scale;

inevitably, much of it has a negative impact.

If, in the advanced industrial nations, we have not quite become the biddable zombies of George Orwell's *Nineteen Eighty-Four,* it is because the manipulators Packard feared are ignorant of the real effects of their efforts. But is it only a question of time, as more powerful technology falls into the hands of the hucksters? Not necessarily, because the new technologies will actually redress the balance of power in favour of the oppressed consumer.

Around £14 billion ($23 billion) was spent in 1998 on paid advertising in British media; globally it is a business worth £156 billion ($250 billion) annually. There are few industries in which so much money is invested with so little understanding. This book is not a quick-fix "1-minute manager" manual for those who are responsible for advertising, but through evaluating the ideas it puts forward in the light of their own experience it will provide them with a conceptual framework to appraise their own work more critically. The universal target, the consumer-citizen, can use this book to develop an essential survival skill: the identification of hypocrisy and cant. Examples are drawn principally from advertising, as the most overt, most familiar, and most controllable method of mass persuasion, from the countries in which it most advanced – Britain and America – but the principles of the Big Lie, whether you hear it from a spin doctor or a shaman, are universal.

JESUITICAL REASONING

"In choosing arguments, one must above all take account of those which affect the listener and are appropriate to his opinions, his mind, his condition and his age.

We are all attracted by the true or false appearances of that which is good, but what is good for me is not so for you. This thing may be useful to that person; this other thing may be pleasing and honourable for these people, while in different circumstances something else pleases and delights us.

As men will only let themselves be led by reasoning that accords with their feelings, this means that in addition to evidence that enlightens our minds, we must excite the passions, if the subject permits it, to undermine the will.

To this end, it would be useful to know the manners of men and the nature of movements of the soul. For every kind of cause, one must excite different passions."

Père Jouvancy, SJ, *Ratio docendi et discendi*, 1702.
His outstanding pupil was Voltaire

PART I

"It researched well"

"Ah, Harding—perhaps you can give us some input from the straight community."

CHAPTER I
THE HOLY GRAIL

Effectiveness

The time has come when advertising has, in some hands, reached the status of a science . . . Certainly no other enterprise with comparable possibilities need involve so little risk.

Claude C. Hopkins, American advertising pioneer, *Scientific Advertising*, 1923

FORTY executives sat in the darkened conference room in Camden, New Jersey. There were no women – it was 1960. You couldn't see their eyes; each man wore a pair of bright orange cardboard 3D spectacles with lenses of smoky film. They couldn't speak either, because their teeth were clenched on white lollipop sticks. Inside their mouths, instead of a sweet, a narrow ribbon of gauze was wound tightly round the end of each stick. The audience stared at a white screen on which a colour slide showed a stack of pancakes dripping with maple syrup. The projector clicked and the pancakes were replaced by a mouth-watering chocolate cake.

The man by the screen, wielding a pointer and shambling across the beam of light, was Horace Schwerin. A pioneer of advertising research, he ran a leading firm which specialised in the testing of television commercials, using a singular method of his own invention. Today he was demonstrating something new to the marketing department of the Campbell Soup Company, manufacturers of the famous canned soups and a wide range of other popular food products. It was an experiment devised by his 75-year-old father, "Pop" Schwerin, a retired Bell Telephone developmental engineer. Based on techniques used by Ivan Pavlov, the Russian physiologist, the idea was to measure the rate of salivation triggered by showing people appetising photographic images. When the lights were switched on in the conference room, the men from Campbell Soup took off their cardboard spectacles, removed the lollipop sticks from their mouths, unrolled the gauze ribbons, and solemnly counted the number of saliva stains that had penetrated through the layers.

Schwerin was using his "salivation tester" in experiments to study the reaction of adults, infants, and neurotic rats to various stimuli. If a valid measurement could be derived, it would be advertising's Holy Grail, a system of measuring the effect of food advertising not by asking people questions, but through physical measurement. If advertising could make you drool, the salivary glands couldn't lie.

Four years previously, a different physiological experiment in a New Jersey drive-in cinema had ignited a firestorm of public controversy. For six weeks, at an outdoor cinema in Fort Lee, New Jersey, a motivational research company run by James Vicary had flashed the injunctions "Drink Coca-Cola" and "Hungry? Eat Popcorn" on the screen every five seconds throughout the feature film. These messages appeared for 1/3000th of a second, calculated to be below the threshold of visual perception. The hope was that the message would nevertheless penetrate the subconscious brain. Vicary, who had already attracted attention for his studies of the eye-blink rate of female shoppers browsing through store displays, reported that the sales of cola drinks rose 18 per cent over the period of the test, and popcorn consumption went up 58 per cent. The nation which had invented advertising became alarmed about the threat of "subliminal" manipulation. It was another new word, like "brainwashed", which had been recently invented to explain why some US soldiers had rejected American values in captivity during the Korean War.

Horace Schwerin was obsessed with what he called "action measurements". To him it was patent that what people said they did, or would be likely to do, under given circumstances was burdened with so much psychological baggage as to be almost totally unreliable. During the Second World War, as an enlisted man in the US Army attached to a psychological unit, he devised a way of testing this belief. Soldiers in training camps were routinely issued with two pairs of boots, and in the interests of foot hygiene the army medical service recommended that the pairs should be worn on alternate days. For the GI, however, there was a massive disincentive: the pair he wasn't wearing had to be displayed, properly shined, beneath his cot. It was considerably more convenient to wear the same pair of boots every day, and keep the second pair on display at all times, pristine and ready for inspection.

To resolve this conflict of its own devising, the US Army resorted to advertising. Messages were broadcast in mess halls urging the GIs to change their footwear daily. To determine the influence of this propaganda, a company of soldiers which had been exposed to the messages was matched against a control group which had not. The next day, when the First Sergeants asked which men had changed their boots, every hand was raised – in both companies. One hundred per cent compliance is an unusual result in any behavioural survey, so Sgt Schwerin devised an "action measurement" to check this finding. While the soldiers were out on training, his researchers entered the barracks and chalked the soles of each pair of boots under the bunks. Following further test broadcasts, they made return visits and found that almost all of the boots under the bunks still bore chalk marks – *in both companies.* The soldiers had lied with their boots on.

After the war, the technique which Schwerin developed to test the effectiveness of radio commercials, and later television, while less absolute, recognised that self-interest is also the consumer's principal motivation. He called it "competitive preference". For decades, Schwerin conducted tests almost every weekday night in New York and other North American cities. A random sample of 300 to 400 consumers was attracted to a "preview show" in a cinema. Before the show, several tombola lotteries were held. The prizes were large supplies of various consumer products, and for each prize draw audience members were given a list of major brands in a product field and asked to tick which brand they would like to receive if they won the draw. They then saw a television programme and a few television commercials, one for each of the relevant product categories. Afterwards another series of prize draws was held, and the respondents were again asked to indicate their brand preferences in the same way as before.

Schwerin's theory was that the prize draw placed the consumer in a situation where he or she had to make a decision of some personal importance. The individual's response would be well considered, because it carried with it the prospect of penalty as well as reward; a frivolous choice could result in a large quantity of an unfavoured brand of shampoo arriving on the doorstep.

In these tests, consumers did regularly change their brand choices after a single such exposure to advertising. Schwerin's measurement of effectiveness was the difference between the percentage of respondents who chose the advertised brand before and after seeing the commercial. This figure could be compared with the results of other commercials tested for the same brand or competitive brands in the same product field, tested under the same conditions amongst different but statistically comparable audiences.

Intellectually, the technique had great appeal. While there existed plenty of measurements of various effects of advertising exposure – for example, whether people remembered seeing an advertisement, whether they recalled its message, or simply whether they liked it – Schwerin's "competitive preference" zeroed in on what most people think most advertising aims at: creating a change in consumer behaviour. There was encouraging resonance with real-life behaviour, too. The pre-choice levels, before advertising exposure, roughly resembled brand sales shares. Commercials in product fields which were known to have only loose brand allegiances, such as plastic clingfilm wraps, usually gained high preference changes, while advertisements for cigarettes, for example, where brand loyalties were known to be very strong, produced minimal shifts. And commercials for new brands with attractive new features would usually outperform the norm in any product field.

All advertising research techniques attract methodological criticism, and the Schwerin method, probably because of the scale of its ambitions, drew more than most. Complaints focused on the self-selecting nature of the audience and practical difficulties in controlling tests in the "test theatre" environment. Nevertheless the technique had certain inherent advantages. One of these was that it could demonstrate reliable results. The same commercials could be fed into Schwerin's research factory again and again under similar conditions to see whether the result could be replicated. This is a basic criterion of all scientific measurement, yet repetitive testing is flatly impossible or prohibitively expensive in most other kinds of advertising research. The Schwerin method offered practical help, too. The test commercial could be varied to evaluate various creative factors – the selling message, the style of its presentation, or its length. Or the advertisement could be held constant while its programme environment was changed. In America, commercials are shown within the context of programmes, and advertisers spend huge sums sponsoring these. As well as considering the types of viewer attracted by these programmes, the advertisers were concerned about the compatibility of the viewing environment with their brands. To help make programme choices they used Schwerin tests to explore whether, say, a commercial for Betty Crocker Cake Mix would be more or less effective in a relaxed situation comedy or a high-tension thriller.

Most advertising researchers are content with the limitations of their measurements. Mindful of how many other factors can affect a brand's success in the marketplace, such as pricing, distribution imbalances and competitive sales promotional activities, they are generally loth to venture any direct connection with sales results. Researchers usually defend their results on theoretical grounds: by measuring one or more factors which may play a part in how advertising works, they can make some sort of contribution to a judgement of an advertisement's effectiveness. Schwerin's goal was loftier and more empirical. His firm continually encouraged advertisers to test whether commercials which had earned higher "competitive preference" scores would actually produce more sales in the marketplace, through controlled market tests using different commercials in different sales regions. Successful results were presented as validation of the technique.

In the mid-1960s the quest for validation led the Schwerin Research Corporation to conduct the most ambitious attempt ever undertaken, before or since, to relate advertising test results to sales results in the marketplace. Unilever funded a nationwide study in West Germany, selected because severe federal restrictions on the value of consumer give-aways meant that sales promotion activity would be a less disruptive factor. Four major consumer product fields were studied: laundry detergents, washing-up liquids, margarine, and toothpaste. For eighteen months Schwerin tested every television commercial broadcast and every national press advertisement published on behalf of every major brand in these product fields. Some of the usual difficulties encountered in controlling "test theatre" audiences were eased in Germany. While New York audiences in the 1960s could be restive, even mutinous, in Hamburg they were docile and interested. (Once, expressing the ultimate "action measurement", a man died in a rear row; ambulance attendants entered quietly and unobtrusively removed the corpse while the show went on.) In repetitive tests, results in Germany were consistently more reliable than anywhere else.

Schwerin carried out 179 press and television advertising evaluations for 24 brands; the share of advertising expenditure by each brand in each medium was also tabulated. These key variables – test scores and spend on press and television – were compared to quarterly retail sales share movements in a multiple-regression analysis. Taken together over eighteen months, they predicted 24 per cent of all brand sales share movements in the laundry detergent field, 41 per cent for washing up liquids, 59 per cent for toothpaste and 80 per cent for margarine. Across all four fields, these measurements explained slightly under one-third of all sales behaviour, which was seen as a promising result. Significantly, if the Schwerin measurements of the effectiveness of the advertising content were disregarded, advertising expenditure alone had a much poorer, and in some cases an *inverse,* correlation to sales movements.

Today, an adaptation of Schwerin's "competitive preference" technique called "persuasion/attitude shift" is still used to test advertisements by the American firm, McCollum Spielman Worldwide, which has inherited leadership in this field, but it is just one of a basket of measurements used by this firm. In the UK, serious efforts to validate techniques with reference to sales results are out of fashion in the industry.

FORTY YEARS ON, people still worry about subliminal advertising, but usually the term is a misnomer. They generally mean irrational appeals to the emotions rather than subconscious stimuli which actually fail to cross the threshold of physiological perception. James Vicary refused to release details or statistical data from his 1956 study of subliminal effects. Despite several attempts to duplicate his cinema advertising experiment, no one was ever able to produce similar results. Apprehensions about true subliminal advertising faded, though it was not until 1974 that the Federal Communications Commission in America finally banned the technique, because "Whether effective or not, such broadcasts clearly are intended to be deceptive". Subliminal communication was dubious in any case, for the same reason that "Pop" Schwerin's taste-testing technique never bore fruit: individual thresholds of perception are different. In a 1956 BBC television experiment, some people glimpsed the hidden message while others didn't; and people salivate at different rates, too.

Research methods have not changed much over the years: they still offer to measure many different effects of advertising. Applied to the behavioural problem the US Army encountered in Fort Benning, Georgia, in 1944, all these techniques would falsely indicate, in their various ways, that soldiers change their boots every day. They do not predict behaviour. Horace Schwerin's dream of a single, validated action measurement of advertising effectiveness remains a chimera. Indeed, few advertising people seem to care much about any kind of empirical measurement of the influence of their expensive black art.

Why is that?

CHAPTER 2
ADVERTISING ISN'T WORKING

Influence

Half the money I spend on advertising is wasted. The trouble is, I don't know which half.

> The British attribute this to Lord Leverhulme, the founder of Lever Brothers, and the Americans to John Wanamaker, who founded the eponymous department store chain

ANYONE who believes that half the money he spends on advertising is wasted is an optimist. Claude C. Hopkins, who invented many successful direct-selling advertising techniques in America in the early 20th century believed the figure was 90 per cent, "because of [advertisers'] selfish purposes brazenly displayed".[1] If you drive your car across a bridge, you expect the bridge to stand up; if you buy a Hoover, you expect it to work. There are few areas of human activity – art, philosophy, and economics are the exceptions – in which there is no generally accepted measurement of functional performance. Advertising, uniquely in business, has none. As a result most of the money spent on advertising is probably wasted, and there is little accountability. Why? Because people in advertising like it that way.

Does advertising influence people? Of course it does. The evidence, though anecdotal, is incontrovertible.

In 1991, a surprise UK bestseller during the Christmas book-buying season was a heavily advertised volume on the art of fly-fishing, by J. R. Hartley. The advertising had appeared well before the work was written. The book was a copywriter's invention, the object of a sentimental search of secondhand book shops by its elderly author, a fictional figure appearing in a frequently aired Yellow Pages commercial. The advertisement was so popular it created a novelty demand for the imaginary book.

In 1994, the British soft drinks company Britvic published an advertisement warning consumers that rogue manufacturers were passing off inferior beverages under the label of its new product, Still Tango. The public was urged to report any sightings of imitation products being sold by unscrupulous traders. Those civic-minded consumers who bothered

---

[1] Claude C. Hopkins, *My Life in Advertising*, Harper, 1927.

to call the freephone number were jeered with the theme of the drink's advertising campaign, "You've been Tango'd". This stunt attracted 300,000 telephone calls. In the same year Coca-Cola's new soft drink, OK, was launched in the US with a spoof chain-letter concept. The commercials described the extraordinary things that happened to people who drank the product, or who "broke the chain". Consumers were invited to phone toll-free to recount their own unusual experiences. Three million people rang in.

Amusing larks like these cost people nothing. Can advertising get people to actually reach into their pockets? Winston Fletcher, an advertising agency chairman, believes advertising aimed at selling products is wasteful almost by definition. He once calculated that 9,500 brands each expended at least £50,000 per year on advertising in the UK, and pointed out that even an energetic consumer could probably buy no more than 400 of them.[2] His logic is dotty, since no advertiser expects *everyone* to buy every product; advertising is aimed at different individuals. But certainly there is a lot of competition tugging at the consumer's purse-strings.

When Russia first welcomed the free market, the advertising game was played with few rules on a greenfield site. One advertising campaign directed at a population not previously exposed to the capitalist advertising virus achieved spectacular success: it impoverished millions of people, damaged the credibility of the free market, and rocked a government. In 1993 and 1994 one out of every five commercials shown on television was for the MMM joint stock company. MMM offered a pot of gold to hard-strapped Russian consumers. Its shares were guaranteed to increase in value every week until the end of time. All you had to do was buy them and hold on to them for a while before reselling them, and MMM promised to buy them back. Russia's biggest TV star fronted the commercials, playing a gullible Everyman called Lyonya Golubkov, whose possessions multiplied as the campaign progressed. His early ambition – to buy his wife a new pair of boots with his MMM profits – were parlayed into a suit for himself, a car, and eventually a new flat. "In Paris?" asked his plump wife. "Why not?" responded the voice-over announcer.

Between five and ten million Russians purchased shares in MMM. Those who bought in February 1994 and held onto them as long as July found they had multiplied 68 times in value. Sergei Mavrodi, the financial wizard behind the company, became the fifth richest man in Russia.

---

[2] Winston Fletcher, *A Glittering Haze,* NTC, 1992.

His paper empire was based on a Ponzi scam, a simple fraud named after the swindler Charles Ponzi, which uses money from new investors to pay off the old. When a warning from the finance ministry set off a stampede of small investors to besiege the Moscow headquarters of the company, its share price plunged from 115,000 roubles to 1,000. Yet there was no Russian law against Ponzi schemes. Rather than collapsing in disgrace, MMM responded with another blitz of reassuring advertising. The company even issued new shares, which provoked a brisk demand. There are Russian laws against tax evasion, however, and by August Sergei Mavrodi had been clapped into prison, while a crowd of duped Russians held a wake for advertising's fictional get-rich-quick Lyonya Golubkov, burning a cardboard coffin near Moscow's Pushkin Square.

The spectacular success of MMM advertising was prosecuted in virgin advertising territory, to minds and hearts not yet hardened to advertising promises. Yet dreams beyond avarice live on in the West, too – where massive advertising for Britain's National Lottery created a whole new cultural pattern, and the British press was full of reports about inadequate people squandering their benefit grants on lottery cards rather than feeding their children.

There can be no doubt that *some advertising can have a behavioural influence* on those who are exposed to it. But whether advertising "works" depends on what one expects it do. Sometimes, to those who have not been exposed to the communications strategy, such as the intended audience, the objectives of an advertising campaign are difficult to divine. What is one to make, for example, of a 1999 poster consisting entirely of the image of a rosy-fingered dawn and the headline "Imagine what we can do tomorrow" appearing over the logo of an organisation called "The Millennium Experience". In this exhortation, who are "we"? The British nation? The people who were then constructing the Millennium Dome and for which no use "tomorrow" had yet been imagined? What was one supposed to believe, feel, or *do,* as the result of exposure to this advertisement?

Advertising campaigns can have a great many different declared objectives. Here are a few which individuals responsible for spending money on national advertising have stated in their briefings to advertising agencies:

- We've always done it
- To attract attention
- To be witty and stylish
- To amuse

- To make people like us
- To knock the opposition
- To get back at the opposition for knocking us
- To provide information
- To project our values
- To motivate our staff
- To persuade retailers to stock our products
- To keep our name before the public
- To generate free publicity
- To sell

Whatever the aim of advertising might be, it is usually impossible or impractical to demonstrate whether it has been achieved. But there is almost always an unspoken agenda as well. For advertising performs on a public stage, and the people who create, authorise, and pay for it have a great personal stake in its success. What is vitally important, for their sense of status and prospects of career advancement, is that their advertising be noticed by their peers. Above all, it must be "creative". This is a quality on which few can agree. Usually it is taken to mean that the advertisement must entertain. Or that it must be different, provocative, outrageous even. In this view a successful advertisement is one which crosses the boundary of what, by some unspecified consensus, was previously unacceptable or distasteful. Thus, to promote book readership, a 1999 press campaign showed the lower half of a youth squatting on a toilet, his underpants around his ankles and a toilet roll in the foreground.

For a canny business manager or shareholder, subjective goals like these are intolerable. They are the paymasters of the advertising industry, and they cannot begin to establish the value of their investment until they agree on its business objective. Usually they would express this as having something to do with shifting goods, or at least opinions. However, many of the best-known and most successful people who create advertising evaluate advertisements in terms of presentational criteria which have little apparent connection with its selling power. Steve Henry, Creative Partner at the UK agency Howell Henry Chaldecott Lury, believes: "In advertising we have a duty to entertain". John Hegarty, who founded the highly regarded UK advertising agency Bartle Bogle Hegarty, is also not untypical of advertising practitioners when he says: "Ninety per cent of advertising is crap, it can be dishonest, it can trivialise, it can appeal to the lowest common denominator". While dismissing some commercials, and whole product sectors such as soap powder, for being boring, he praised a contemporary ad for Heineken beer, a spoof on *Pygmalion*, on the interesting but hardly relevant grounds that "You could look at that in 100 years and understand the whole class structure of this country in less than 60 seconds".[3]

Nevertheless, the advertising industry is quick to attribute sales success to advertising, either by broad brush-stroke or specific attribution. Cause and effect are commonly linked in assertions such as these:

- BMW introduced the aggressive "Ultimate Driving Machine" advertising theme in 1979. By 1994 sales had trebled.
- Over a similar period British Airways' "World's Favourite Airline" campaign boosted its image and sales.
- Boddington's Bitter launched its stylish, ironic "Cream of Manchester" campaign in 1991. Within three years sales had trebled.
- Weeks after Wonderbra's sexy 1995 campaign went up on posters, sales went through the roof.
- In 1995, after British sales of Martini vermouth had fallen steadily for fifteen years, they grew by 10 per cent in the month following a new advertising push.

Sometimes the effect seems to be less favourable. During the early 1990s *GQ* magazine claimed that its circulation increased whenever its rival *Esquire* ran a heavy television promotion.

Very occasionally, advertising is *blamed* for marketing reverses. A high-profile 1998 campaign for Sainsbury's, featuring the very popular comedian John Cleese, in his dramatic persona as a sneering, obsessive bully, was widely attacked by financial analysts for causing a sales slump, without any evidence apart from temporal coincidence.

These effects may or may not have resulted from the advertising. Correlation is different from causation. Many factors in the marketing mix influence sales, and the time-lags between exposure and action are uncertain. But the people who publicise such conclusions are, of course, intensely self-serving. An advertising agency which handles a major ice cream account will be quick to make claims for the efficacy of its advertising during hot summers and to nominate other marketing factors during cold summers. However apocryphal, unsubstantiated or naive, such claims are enthusiastically pressed. Those seeking to find a relationship between advertising and sales – the advertising agency, the client marketing team, the chairman who approved the advertising – all have a

---

[3] *The Sunday Correspondent,* 10 December 1989.

keen personal interest in establishing the link.

Unquestionably, advertising can contribute to sales. Some of the most convincing evidence of its influence comes from the toughest arena: "selling off-the-page". In this technique, a single advertisement is literally expected to make the sale – all by itself. Thousands of different kinds of product, from herbal remedies to choice fillet steaks, are sold in this way, through coupon or telephone response or by e-mail. The people who place these advertisements know exactly which appeals work, if not always why, because the money comes in with the order. It is the purest and most convincing demonstration of the power of advertising, and the school which Claude C. Hopkins helped to found. Advertisers who depend on a less committed response, not cash with order but an enquiry, are also able to monitor closely the effect of individual advertisements by analysing returns. With the development of improved means of targeting the consumer more precisely, the technique has spread to other media – direct mail and telephone selling. Direct-response marketing, as it is now known, has become the largest growth area in advertising. Yet the sector does not attract the flower of advertising talent, who find its straightforward selling techniques primitive and uncreative.

Apart from the direct-response sector, it is unrealistic to expect advertising to close the sale all by itself, (and even there it may be building on other influences, e.g. a concurrent television campaign). Too many other factors intervene. But for most advertising, most of the time, it is reasonable to expect it to have *an influence* on the sale: to persuade people to take an interest in, consider, or possibly even predispose to buy the thing that is being advertised, to create a "sale in the mind", which, other things being equal, will contribute to a sale in the marketplace.

Advertising research has two roles: to evaluate before the appearance of a campaign the influence it is likely to have and, after it has appeared, the effect it has actually achieved. And yet, because of the uncertainty of predictive measurements and the difficulty of isolating other factors, it rarely, if ever, succeeds.

The model for good research was summarised by one of the greatest and most iconoclastic of modern scientists, Richard Feynman:

> It's a principle of scientific thought that corresponds to a kind of utter honesty. For example, if you're doing an experiment, you should report everything that you think might make it invalid – not only what you think is right about it. If you make a theory, for example, and advertise it, or put it out, then you must also put down all the facts that disagree with it, as well as those that agree with it.

Thus, when searching for a relationship or correlation *all* the available cases must be included in the analysis and there must be enough of them to make the results statistically valid. Only occasionally is convincing evidence produced about the effect of advertising which attempts to observe the elementary disciplines which would routinely be rigorously applied in any attempt to relate cause and effect in any branch of science, even the social sciences. Moreover, the industry in general does not like to expose the results of its efforts. Although there is a lot of research into particular campaigns, both before and after implementation, the findings, unlike scientific studies, are rarely published or shared in any way. And it is salutary to remember that for every campaign which may claim to have increased a brand's share of market, by definition one or more competitive advertisers must have failed. No one comes forward to establish this kind of link.

With no other generally acceptable evidence of the worth of their endeavours, advertising agencies tend to define success and compete against each other for business in terms of how many awards they have won. They do this in all seriousness. In this advertising is like arts and entertainment: the people who produce it like to give themselves awards, and are enormously impressed when they receive the praise of their peers. Thousands of advertising award competitions are held every year throughout the world, and so, as in the Red Queen's croquet match in *Through the Looking-Glass*, generally there is some prize for almost everybody. The jurors are usually rival advertising professionals, and while some of them, at another time and place, might acknowledge that advertising is supposed to have something to do with selling products, almost all such awards are based on subjective criteria which (the comments of the judges make clear) are usually impressions of originality, aesthetics, or wit. At the 1997 Design and Art Direction Awards (DADA), the UK advertising industry's equivalent of Hollywood's Oscar presentations, the jury reckoned only one television submission merited a gold award. It was not a commercial, in fact, but a sponsorship credit for a season of ITV film premieres, which superimposed the faces of deceased film stars, such as Terry Thomas and Bruce Lee, on a pair of lips noisily munching Doritos potato crisps. As one assessor explained. "It won because it was original and mould-breaking... [and] because it made all the judges in the room laugh".

In the UK there is only a single exception to this method of judging excellence by personal opinion. Since 1980 the Institute of Practitioners in Advertising (IPA), of which most advertising agencies are members, has conducted a rigorous biennial competition which is based on empirical evidence linking advertising either to sales results or attitudinal changes which might reasonably be expected to affect behaviour. It publishes case histories based on convincing statistical evidence – for example, controlled regional tests which show advertising in some areas and not in others. But these are a handful of the vast number of advertising campaigns which besiege the consumer.

In general, advertising people judge advertising the way the punters do: they know what they like. In 1987, the advertising trade magazine *Campaign* surveyed advertising and marketing people, asking them to nominate the best and worst campaigns of the past decade. This panel awarded honours to two entertaining spoofs: a Holsten Pils campaign which used innovative video mixing techniques to enable comedian Griff Rhys-Jones to interact with old movies, and a tongue-in-cheek pastiche of a popular Levi Jeans ad by Carling Black Label. They also cited a series of amusing Cinzano commercials featuring the comedian Leonard Rossiter and actress Joan Collins. Amongst the campaigns the professionals deplored were pitches by cosier celebrities whom they may have had more difficulty in identifying with: Leslie Crowther for Stork SB margarine and Jimmy Young for Ariel Automatic detergent. The opinions of the professionals generally reflected those of their intended audiences: *Campaign* magazine's weekly surveys of the commercials viewers liked produced similar results. However, there was a singular exception. The admen had nominated as one of the worst campaigns of the past ten years a new and unusual effort for Nescafé Gold Blend, which over several episodes developed a coy romance between two caffeine-addicted yuppie neighbours. Amongst ordinary viewers, however, these commercials were very popular. Nestlé attributed great success to this campaign and continued to run it for many years thereafter.

The simple 1970s television commercials in which the chief executive of Bernard Matthews plc praised his "bootiful" turkeys directly to camera are regularly cited by British advertising professionals as among the worst ever. In 2000, Bernard Matthews was provoked to respond to yet another criticism, when his ancient advertising was included in *Campaign* magazine's "Hall of Shame" of the previous century:

> My first advertisement for the turkey breast roast was one of the most successful (perhaps the most successful) new product ads to be made in the UK since the war. Sales went up by 17 times in 14 days. The commercial was so successful that we could not keep up with the demand for six months after it was shown. The ad also provided the

basis for our branding on other products with notable success – particularly with cooked poultry meat, where we sell three million packets a week of our brand and control more than 50 per cent of the market.

The IPA Advertising Effectiveness Awards competition has now attracted a database of about 600 case studies of successful campaigns, the largest collection of empirical evidence that advertising works. Yet it has been condemned by Bernard Barnett, an ad industry consultant and former editor of the *Campaign* tradesheet:

> I am fed up with the increasingly common treatment of "creativity" and "effectiveness" as antonyms. This is why the IPA Effectiveness Awards are dangerous – they increase the polarisation of both words . . . In my experience creative juries do not judge the entries on their aesthetic qualities. They judge them on how they are likely to appeal to the customer. It is true that, in the main, they award prizes to advertisements that are arresting, visible, original and persuasive, but these are the very characteristics that make them successful in the marketplace . . . I do not know of any way of quantifying the effect of a particular ad (apart from the direct response category) even though people have been trying for years to find this holy grail. Like it or not, we are stuck with judgement. Personally, I prefer it that way.[4]

Almost £1 billion is spent each year in the UK on market research. Of that, about £10 million is devoted to testing advertisements in some way. If Mr Barnett's view is correct, what on earth have the researchers been measuring all these years?

[4] *Campaign,* 24 April 1992.

CHAPTER 3

HOW LONG IS A PIECE OF BALONEY?

Measurement

Not everything that can be counted counts, and not everything that counts can be counted.

Albert Einstein, German physicist

MOST people believe that the advertisements they see are the crafted product of some sort of scientific assessment, and advertising ideas are usually sold with this phrase: "It researched well". What does that mean? At one extreme it may occasionally signify that the advertisement performed well in a laborious behavioural test such as a "single-source" investigation. In this type of research, purchasing habits may be correlated to television viewing: a compliant household is fitted out with a meter on top of the television set – perhaps even using heat sensors to determine how many people are in the room when it's on – and the family uses a scanner to record all its grocery purchases. Though empirically based, the emphasis is on the technological gimmickry; the data is often too broad to pin down specific reactions to individual commercials. And real-life techniques like these are not suitable for assessing ideas before they are turned into expensive films. More often, the palliative phrase "It researched well" refers to a methodology which is far simpler, cheaper, more convenient, and more manipulable: it means that the advertisement or the concept was shown to a number of people who made favourable comments of some kind – in a "focus group".

Like accountants appraising the productivity of the National Health Service, advertising researchers measure what they are able to measure, not necessarily what really matters. For instance, it is relatively easy to evaluate whether people are likely to have seen advertising, whether they remember seeing it, what message it conveyed, and whether they liked it. And so advertising is designed to meet these criteria. For many decades the American company Procter & Gamble used a research company called Burke based in its home town of Cincinnati, Ohio, to evaluate its television commercials. Burke's primary instrument of measurement was whether viewers could recall the selling points contained in the advertising. Even today, wherever you see them, commercials for P&G products can be identified by their emphasis on implanting copy messages. While advertisers and agencies rejoice when their efforts pass simple tests like these, there is no evidence at all that liking an advertisement or the ability to recall its content has any effect whatsoever on creating "the sale in the mind" – the disposition to buy a product or subscribe to a belief.

So, more diligent advertising researchers have developed an inventory of other tools which attempt to measure the psychological influence of advertising on consumer judgement. These efforts are handicapped by the fact that consumers are usually unwilling to admit, or may not even be aware of, the factors influencing their decisions. Straightforward declarations of "intentions to buy" are not a valid guide to actual purchase decisions. Shifts in attitudes, the tendency to agree or disagree with certain opinions, may be reliably recorded, but the contribution of these views to behaviour can rarely be conclusively demonstrated. (Relatively few advertisements are tested in any way at all; time and cost pressures restrict research to major campaigns, and not all of these.) Advertising research is fraught with methodological problems, too. In an analogy to Heisenberg's uncertainty principle, the simple act of asking questions introduces elements, such as bias for or against the interviewer, which change the situation researchers are trying to measure.

Even worldly-wise institutions which should know better have a touching faith in naive research based on what people say they may or may not do in a given set of circumstances. A 1995 leader in *The Independent* drew robust conclusions from a survey which had discovered that six out of ten people said they were ready to pay 2p in the pound income tax to boost NHS revenue, an extraordinary expression of altruism from voters generally deeply resentful of new taxes. Fortunately for the Labour Party, it was not sufficiently encouraged to include this idea in its 1996 election manifesto.

In statistical studies of advertising effectiveness, expenditure is given great weight, because it is an index of exposure to the message and something that is easily measured. Clearly, saturation techniques can make a dominant impression, even through quite meaningless advertising messages, e.g. "Heineken refreshes the parts other beers cannot reach". As David Abbott, the creative director who founded one of Britain's largest advertising agencies, Abbot Mead Vickers BBDO, put it: "On TV you can achieve results even with quite bad advertising if you spend enough on it ... 'If you throw enough pennies at the wall you make a hole in it'". The question is, what kind of "results" does he have in mind? The extent of penetration of such associations into the public mind can easily be measured. But persuasion is usually left out of the equation.

The quest has inspired the proliferation of any number of theories about "how advertising works". These range from the so-called "linear sequential models" like Starch, DAGMAR and AIDA[1], through H. E. Krugman's theory that the only thing that matters is top-of-mind ("salient") recall, to attempts to apply sophisticated theories drawn from psychology, like Martin Fishbein's, dealing with the relationship between attitudes and behaviour.[2] There is a conscientious handbook, written by the former chairman of a successful Dutch advertising agency, which summarises empirical findings of the many different things which can be measured about advertising exposure.[3] What they all have in common is the attempt to find some intermediate criterion of advertising effect on the *unproved* assumption that it is related to sales. Not only is there no proof, there is also no reason why recalling the content of an advertisement, or literally believing what it says, should in any way determine the likelihood of buying the product. Furthermore, the attempt to find one final model of the advertising process is forlorn. Advertising, like any other form of communication works in different ways, in different circumstances, and on different people. The same advertisement can even work on the same person differently depending on the circumstances – what he has just eaten, for example, and whether he enjoyed it. No wonder Raymond Chandler's private detective hero, Philip Marlowe, described playing chess with oneself as the greatest waste of intellectual energy outside of an advertising agency.

While market research techniques are good at measuring what is already happening, they are poor at predicting behaviour, for several reasons. Pre-testing cannot easily assess anything which is entirely new to consumers' experience. For competitive brands, an assessment of an advertisement's performance is only relevant if it is in comparison to other brands, yet few studies take this into account. Then there is the publicity environment of the marketplace. Anyone who could reliably predict next week's "Top Ten" records could make a small fortune.

---

[1] Starch: An advertisement must be 1. Seen, 2. Read, 3. Believed, 4. Remembered, 5. Acted upon. DAGMAR: Advertising must make the prospect 1. Aware of the brand, 2. Comprehend the product, 3. Wish to buy the product, and 4. Stir him to action. AIDA: Attention, Interest, Desire, Action.

[2] For an examination of these and other learning theories, see *The Persuaders Exposed: Advertising and Marketing, The Derivative Arts,* Gerald de Groot, Associated Business Press, 1980.

[3] *Advertising Effectiveness, findings from empirical research,* Giep Franzen, NTC Publications, 1994.

People have tried, but there is no test situation which can allow for the hype factor, the massive influence of publicity on radio, television, and the press which affects the sale of hit records.

Nevertheless, advertising research thrives. For two reasons: first, there is a great deal it can do, at every stage in the creative development, to determine whether the campaign is "on message". It can tell whether the idea is getting across (though not whether it is worth getting across) and how people react to it, and crucially, it provides everyone concerned with the creation or approval of advertising with a pseudo-scientific support for his or her decisions. This rubber crutch is a versatile and powerful weapon against opposing opinion, because few decision-makers in the industry have a real grasp of the basic principles of psychological research or statistics, or, if they do, no incentive to invoke them to limit the sweep of their judgement.

To fulfil this need, the research industry these days, and for some decades past, habitually tends to evaluate advertising on the basis of semi-structured group interviews. An interviewer guides a series of discussions, each probing chosen topics amongst homogeneous groups of six to ten individuals of the right sort – the primary target group. Where specific advertising approaches are being tested, the group will be exposed to these in rough or finished form. Properly selected and skilfully managed, these discussions can provide very useful stimulation to the development of advertising hypotheses, allowing the advertising planner or creative person to amplify intuitive thought by bouncing ideas off consumers. Researchers rigorously emphasise that such explorations are entirely qualitative in nature, and thus possess no quantitative statistical validity. Like a newspaper's rough-and-ready "*vox pop*" man-in-the-street interview on an issue of the day, they can provide insight, colour, and inspiration. But not measurement.

Nevertheless, in the way of the world, such qualitative results are invariably used to support judgement. The researchers themselves, although they know better, in the analytical reports they submit cannot refrain from using statistical terms: "most respondents felt . . .", "a majority of the sample agreed . . .", "hardly anyone thought . . .", etc. Those who take action on the basis of such reports are generally untrained in statistics and keen to support a favoured view. The combination is irresistible. In their hands the tentative, qualitative probe becomes a yardstick. This technique used to be called, unpretentiously, "small-group discussions", but some bright spark eventually reckoned that this didn't sound very authoritative. So now they are known as "focus groups", which implies a greater precision, and since this repackaging they have been generally accepted, by advertisers, journalists, politicians, and the world at large as some kind of litmus test. Only the name has changed, not the methodology; but because they are quick and cheap, and can be interpreted to produce almost any answer you want, such probes are now widely advanced by the unprincipled and the unenlightened as valid predictive research.

Gerald de Groot ran Schwerin's advertising testing operation in the UK, and later became Director of Marketing Services for Lintas, the advertising company partly owned by Unilever, and Chairman of the British Market Research Society. He believes that quantitative measurements such as Schwerin went out of favour for practical reasons. "In many product fields 'competitive preference' shifts were quite small, and it was impractical to get large enough samples to achieve statistically significant measurements. Commercial pressures prevailed in advertising research. Advertisers preferred speed to accuracy".

Some advertising research practitioners, such as the American Kevin J. Clancy, Chairman and Research Director of Yankelovich, Clancy, Shulman, are outraged by the custom of extrapolating from inadequate qualitative research:

> Focused groups (the current mania), importance ratings and gap analysis are all examples of pseudoscientific hallucinogenic drugs which inspire the cavalry generals to go crashing off into oblivion. A lot of this "research" is done among strange samples of homeless people wandering around malls, and sometimes – and this is really scary – stat types are called in to run multinomial logit regressions (or some other form of rocket science) on patently preposterous data.[4]

And from the other end of the spectrum, this *cri de coeur* from an equally outraged British copywriter, Tony Brignull, working as a creative consultant to the advertising agency D'Arcy, Masius, Benton & Bowles:

> Here we have groups of people paid to watch an approximation of your commercial. Naturally, they will be glued to it, so the first objective of advertising, "grab attention", is grabbed for you. Equally obvious, if three rubbish scripts are on the table there'll still be a winner – even if it's a loser. This explains why the breaks are still littered with dumb commercials.

---

[4] *The Coming Revolution in Advertising: Ten Developments which Will Separate Winners from Losers, Journal of Advertising Research,* February-March 1990, pp. 47-52.

Again, groups can be dominated by one strident voice. I wrote a commercial for a healthy breakfast cereal featuring Diana Dors in a silken bed saying "I never do anything because it's good for me". In research, East End ladies loved her but in the Kensington group one toffee-nosed woman said, "She looks like a prostitute to me". Guess what the next woman said, and the next. "Well, I like her?" No, they all thought she was on the game with this muesli and, when the client heard, we lost the account.

It's very hard to research a truly original idea. By definition, it won't be like other commercials and the group will split down the middle. People tend to like things they know: superior butlers, stroppy kids, adoring mothers, moody blokes, pouty girls – you've seen them a million times.[5]

In this kind of qualitative research enormous reliance tends to be placed simply on whether or not people "like the ad", as some kind of entertainment. This is fun for creative people, gives the people who are paying for the advertising a chuckle, and wins awards for the agency. Creativity is thus led away from sales effectiveness in its desire to please audiences who may or may not buy the product as a result.

Even where quantitative techniques provide valid measurements of behaviour, most people fail to understand research and are distrustful of statistics. Not surprisingly, since they are so frequently manipulated. In 1994 the head of the Government Statistical Service, Bill McLennan, expressed concern that there was little public confidence in the official unemployment statistics. Continual changes in the definition of who was out of work had prompted an inquiry by the Royal Statistical Society. Meanwhile Virginia Bottomley's frequent recitations of health service performance figures were rewarded with a Gallup Poll rating her as the most insincere of all of Britain's leading politicians. This distrust is exacerbated by the selective analysis of statistics by those with a vested interest. And the common man has a fervent disbelief in statistical probability.

So, people in advertising have a love/hate relationship with research, as an actor does with a critic. Creative people are uneasy about research and often disparaging. Some of the most highly placed habitually offer ill-considered soundbites such as: "If research was foolproof, no campaign would ever fail" and "According to research, we've got a Labour/Tory government". Yet all creative people intuitively research

---

[5] *The Guardian,* 21 December 1992.

their own experience; the difference is that the exploration is usually confined to a sample of one: oneself. Advertising researchers keep busy investigating effects which can be investigated, while leaving plenty of room for interpretation and little scope for enlightenment. Unlike scientific or academic research, there is no common effort to investigate basic questions about the psychology of advertising, and how behavioural changes occur.

No one knows for example, the answer to practical questions such as:

- As a general rule, how long should a TV commercial be? When should it be longer? Or shorter? (The industry presumes longer commercials have more value, that is, the extra time costs more.)
- Or, how big or small should a press advertisement be? (Bigger ads cost more, too.)
- Which media are most persuasive for which kind of presentations?
- Does humour work? How?
- How many times do you have to see an ad before it has an effect?
- How many times before you're sick to death of it?
- Does it matter if you're sick to death of it – or is that why it works?

Because of the competitive nature of the business there is no general funding of research, no sharing of information, and, because of its ephemeral nature, very little passing down of wisdom through the generations. And so while the ship of advertising ploughs through uncharted waters, the band plays the latest tunes.

ADVERTISING clearly can have immense effect on mass behaviour. However, because it is difficult to isolate its influence, convincing demonstrations of effect are rare. As a result there is profound disagreement about how it works, and the people who create advertising have a vested interest in preserving the mystery. That doesn't mean convincing guides do not exist. Research and experience from many fields – from psychology, physiology and sociology, from learning theory to salesmanship – provide rich instruction. The next section explores what we know about how people respond to advertising.

PART II

"Advertising never sold me anything"

"Oh, just give me a pack of whatever the guys in marketing are targeting for jerks like me."

CHAPTER 4

A ROSE BY ANY OTHER NAME WOULD COST A LOT LESS

Branding

Competing products were now more precisely similar and more unnoticeably different. This was one explanation of why modern advertising first flowered in the marketing of beers, soaps and cigarettes.

Daniel J. Boorstin, *The Image: A Guide to Pseudo-events in America, 1961*

IN THE LATE 19th century, passengers straining for their first glimpse of England from the decks of channel steamers were able to make out words painted across the white cliffs of Dover. They had arrived at a land called "Beecham's Pills".

Peddlers of pills and patent nostrums were amongst the first businessmen to appreciate the importance of brand names. They understood that the less traceable the benefit of using a product the more essential it was that its claims should be supported by a responsible identity. All the better if a scientific or medical connection could confer added credibility; one of Beecham's competitors from the freebooting era of Victorian entrepreneurs, Dr Collis Brown's tonic, still on the market, was not forced to drop the medical attribution from its brand name until 1980.

Other sectors of trade quickly followed the lead of the early medicine men, enthusiastically inventing brand names to attach to their products. It was the dawn of consumerism. Before branding, the only guarantor of the quality of a product was the person who sold it to you. You would buy your cheddar from the local farm which made the best; you could take the rotten onions back to the market stall. As ships, railways, lorries, and finally aircraft extended the limits of physical distribution, retailing systems grew more complex. The source of goods became increasingly remote. But consumers could now look to brands for an assurance of reliability. This became as important for the daily shopping-list as for expensive purchases. The brand justified the investment, and it would deliver the same experience every time. Above all, consumers, like practical businessmen, want to eliminate uncertainty. Holiday Inns built a worldwide chain of hotels on this principle, providing anxious American travellers with familiar surroundings in alien cultures, right down to the iced water, under the soothing slogan, "The best surprise is no surprise".

Branding was a prerequisite for the new patterns of retailing and the globalisation of business. In the 1950s most English people walked or took the bus to the shops, and when they got there they were served by someone standing behind a counter, often wearing an apron or a smock, and possibly a smile as well. England had 137,000 village shops then; by the 1990s there were fewer than 34,000 and people were driving miles to hypermarkets and shopping centres. Almost everything they buy is self-selected, usually with very little opportunity for assistance from sales people. Branding helps them choose.

It is now very difficult to find products which are not branded. Fresh produce has finally yielded to pre-packaging and labelling; even if you buy it at a market stall it often has a sticker to reassure you that you are buying an Israeli orange, an organically grown potato, or a banana imported by Geest. Simple, functional products have succumbed too. A few decades ago your local ironmonger would weigh out a pound of nails and let you have them in a paper bag. Today most consumers buy nails and screws at DIY warehouses in pre-packed containers, and these will carry a minor brand name. Fashion franchises have taken over the department stores: there is no longer a comprehensive department displaying skirts by size, material, design and colour; you have to roam all over the shop to make your selection, which is now influenced by less functional brand criteria. Multinational companies – even those which do not make consumer products, like ABB, the giant electrical engineering group – endeavour to present themselves as brands.

Even thought is branded: fascism, socialism, Darwinism, fundamentalism, Thatcherism, Blairism, pragmatism, new-ageism. Each of these is a handy post-it note freighted with emotional meaning which we can slap on any new idea to file it within our cognitive catalogue and thus avoid having to consider it further. By the 1980s the political label "Labour" was so encrusted with outmoded socialist doctrine that the party was unelectable under this name. As the Labour Party adviser Philip Gould said when the brand was relaunched, "New Labour is meant to be Not Labour".

The unstoppable rise of self-service retailing has concentrated buying power in remarkably few hands. Whereas major manufacturers used to have brigades of salesmen 100-strong or more roving throughout the country, now most selling is done by a few "key account" representatives at head office level. And often the buyer they sell to is their biggest competitor. Retailers' own-label brands swept in with the penetration of

American supermarkets such as Safeway into the traditional UK grocery market in the mid-1960s. Manufacturers which had poured millions of pounds into burnishing "household names" were naturally outraged when their own retail customers began to compete with them, displaying lookalike products side by side on the same shelf at a cheaper price. Some of the biggest brands, such as Kellogg's, refused to manufacture products for their retail customers, but more hard-pressed competitors broke ranks and accepted large-volume orders at a low profit margin. If not, there was always some brash newcomer willing to take a chance on the own-label market. In the early 1970s, when almost all the great mainstream brands in the British supermarket were already beset by own-label competition, a couple of likely lads in the J. Walter Thompson advertising agency identified a singular exception amongst their own roster of clients: the ubiquitous Oxo cube. The admen defected to start a company manufacturing beef extract cubes for the own-label market. As they made their rounds selling to the head offices of the supermarket chains, they were followed by the sales director of Oxo in his Jaguar, who would offer to buy up the stock the stores had just ordered. Most of them sent him packing, but Oxo's dominance was never threatened. The big brands' surest defence was the imagery their advertising had bestowed on their products over the years. Consumers generally thought own-label products were somehow inferior – certainly in status if not in quality – to a heavily advertised brand. Few, of course, would realise that the private-label goods were often made by the same companies on the same machinery which produced the advertised brand.

Own-label products flourish where brand owners overprice or fail to innovate, but big brands still control food and drink products which are purchased frequently. As in most of the world, the top-selling brand in Britain is Coca-Cola, which advertises itself as "the real thing"; nevertheless, private-label soft drinks continue to encroach, and now supply one in every five gulps. Coke had to take legal action to persuade one of its major customers, Sainsbury's, to alter the design of the familiar red-and-white lettering on its new "Classic – Original American Taste" cola drink so that it did not quite so closely resemble the original American. Insult was added by the fact that "Classic" was the name Coke had used in a disastrous attempt to launch a new formulation a few years previously. But it can be difficult for the owner of a plagiarised brand to produce the evidence needed to win a legal action, since consumers are generally reluctant to admit that they have been bamboozled.

Retail chains themselves are now amongst the largest advertisers. Significantly, their advertising has changed, too. The simple inventories of products and prices published in newspapers and paid for by a levy on the manufacturers they included have largely yielded to glossy television advertisements which invoke all the expensive arts of the big brands. The retailers themselves have become brands. In a 1998 survey British consumers said they had more trust in Marks & Spencer and Tesco than the police, the legal profession, or the government. Like the global brands they sell – Heinz, Cadbury, and Guinness – these companies have won a place in the hearts of their customers, through a powerful image projection confirmed by personal experience. For generations M&S prided itself on never having advertised; its enviable reputation had been built by word of mouth. But that was in the halcyon days before media hype. When its competitors began to seize attention, expensively, through advertising, M&S was forced to join them.

The mutation of products into brands is of vital significance and immense financial advantage not just to advertising agents and the suppliers of fast-selling consumer goods but to all industry. A product is functional: its value can be measured by its ability to fulfil a technical specification. If two rival products achieve the same specification, the choice will depend simply on which can be bought more cheaply. The value of a brand, however, is prized well beyond function. Like beauty, its value lies in the satisfaction it provides to the beholder. Research by the Monopolies and Merger Commission once concluded that the contents of a bottle of perfume retailing at £30 cost no more than £2. The rest was distribution, wholesale and retail margins. The Bic company, virtually synonymous with the ubiquitous biro, and which also made cheap lighters and razors, saw a magnificent opportunity. In 1987 it launched a range of scents almost identical to the leading brands, marketing them in plain glass phials at a fraction of the price. What the company failed to recognise until the product range failed was that what consumers were buying was not a smelly liquid but imagery.

Jeremy Bullmore, then Creative Director of JWT London, offered this discrimination between a product and a brand:

> The Model-T was a product that had to die. But the brand was Ford and the brand flourishes... An understanding of brands is found most often in markets where an objective assessment of product function is most difficult. You can measure the price and specific gravity of a beer (*Which?* has done it); but the affection of a beer drinker for his or her favourite beer is only marginally based on its price/potency relationship. If a beer is not a brand, it will never survive. Conversely, an understanding of brands is much less frequently found in developing

markets with a high technology content. The unconscious assumption is that function alone is enough: and so it may be, but only for a time.[1]

Brand power is often illogical, but it is real. Advil is an analgesic heavily advertised in British newspapers and on television; its major claim is that it comes from America. The same generic formulation, ibuprofen, is available from your GP on the national health, or you can buy it over the counter for less than half the price of Advil. Yet Advil prospers. Many patients will claim that one remedy works for them and the other does not. Aches and pains are often psychogenic and placebo tests demonstrate that suggestibility is part of the treatment, so they may well be right.

A game advertising researchers like to play with consumers is to ask them questions such as, "If Brand X were to come to life, what sort of person would it be?" People find it easy to ascribe distinctive anthropomorphic personality traits to brands, associations which are inspired by exposure to the product, its packaging and advertising. Unilever's Persil was traditionally seen as "everybody's favourite Mum" while Procter & Gamble products such as Daz and Ariel, with their hard-edged American demonstrations of competitive cleaning power, were masculine, technical, and efficient, "the man in the white coat". Such impressions are usually simplistic and directly traceable to advertisements: Coca-Cola is young, exuberant, and American, Perrier is French and elegant, Bailey's Irish Cream is warm, traditional, and Irish, BMW is efficient and Teutonic, Rémy Martin brandy is a snob. These perceptions influence product preference because they allow consumers to identify emotionally with brands.

The strongest brands are those which have been around a long time, with consistent images constantly refreshed by advertising, or those which have reputations which are rooted in reality. Motor cars are still the most important branded expression of status, and several of them have developed distinct images which are obvious to all, and hence tell us something about the signals which the people who drive them want to display to us. Few would probably disagree with perceptions such as these:

Rolls-Royce	Ostentatious
Mercedes-Benz	Prosperous
Volvo	Safe and sane

---

[1] *The Brand and Its Image Revisited, International Journal of Advertising*, 1984.

Jaguar	Assuredly British
Renault 2CV	Witty
Ferrari	Sexy
Porsche	Pushy
Mini	Cheeky
Volkswagen Beetle	Reliable Sensible
The New Beetle	Nostalgic for more sensible times

Most of these are expensive cars; the few exceptions are very distinctive automotive designs. Their images reflect genuine differences. Building a brand image for less unusual products is a much more difficult challenge. The majority of cars made for the mass markets by manufacturers such as Ford, Peugeot, Renault, Rover, and Vauxhall are not so clearly differentiated, and their images, too, are weak. Their slogans are often little more than expressions of the manufacturer's anxiety. In the 1970s Rover did have a distinctive image of British middle-class respectability. Its 1990s message, "Above all it's a Rover", was a response to the fact that the company was now owned by a German manufacturer, and beneath the bonnet it was, in fact, a Honda. The Swedish manufacturer Saab, which had built a slick, sturdy image on its aircraft association, must have discovered that consumers felt it was a bit staid, like the Volvo. In 1999 it launched a campaign featuring bizarre images, such as a pregnant athletic competitor, to make the point that Saab was "Not what you expect". If even manufacturers of motor cars, which do, after all, differ from one another in design and performance, are forced to resort to such vaporous distinctions, you can imagine the challenge confronting most other products, which come in similar jars, bottles, or boxes. Rarely is there a perceptible functional distinction; brand choice depends entirely on subjective criteria.

In the looking-glass world of marketing, people can become brands, too, in the entertainment industry. It is usually the name of the bestselling author, not the publisher, which tells you what sort of experience you may expect if you buy the book. (An exceptional publisher in Britain is Mills & Boon, which offers a consistent brand promise: a sentimental romantic story appealing to women.) Norman Mailer, commenting on the star system which drives commercial success, complained that American audiences were "incapable of confronting a book unless it is (already) successful". Faced with the bewildering stacks of choice in a modern superstore the buyer reaches for the familiar experience: between 1986 and 1996 the share of hard-cover sales accounted for by the thirty topsellers in US book shops almost doubled. Stage and film stars have always been bankable names. The star dominates the form. Content becomes irrelevant; it is simply a vehicle for the display of his or her personality. For a long time Alfred Hitchcock was perhaps the only director offering the same kind of predictability, and Hammer Films the only studio. Now many directors such as Spike Lee and Quentin Tarantino arouse distinctive expectations.

Technocrats, socialists, and the buyers of *Which?* magazine may scorn the frivolous and illusory fancies of wish-fulfilment which consumers spin around brands like cotton candy, but it is such whimsical affections that now power the engines of commerce. Brands are often the biggest assets of a business. In 1994 Bayer, the giant German chemical company, paid $1 billion for the right to use its own name. During the First World War the United States government had confiscated Bayer's American assets, including its renowned brand, Bayer aspirin, as enemy property and sold them on to an American company, Sterling Products. While the repatriation of its brand greatly strengthened Bayer's sales position in the world's largest retail pharmaceutical market, there was almost certainly a strong emotional element in the German company's enthusiasm for repossessing its long-lost American offspring. The price paid stunned investment analysts; it was twenty-three times the annual earnings of the company.

When Nestlé fastened its predatory attention on Rowntree in 1988, it was ultimately willing to pay £11 for shares nominally worth only £4. It was not Rowntree's production facilities, its distribution system, or its dominant market position which the Swiss coveted but its roster of confectionery brands: Kit-Kat, Aero, and Smarties. That same year, Rank Hovis McDougall, feeling vulnerable to a similar takeover, increased its value by £678 million at a stroke by adding to the company's accounts a valuation for its brands: Hovis, Bisto, and Mr Kipling Cakes. This sleight of hand provoked howls from the financial community, but Cadbury swiftly followed suit. The argument was that if brands are so valuable when sold, the market price should be reflected on the annual balance sheet. Grand Met transformed itself from a hotel group based on bricks and mortar to a global colossus trading in value-added labels. The prices it paid for Heublein's Smirnoff vodka and for Pillsbury, owners of Häagen-Dazs premium ice cream, included huge balance sheet valuations for these global brand names.

After a period of confusion, in 1998 the British Accounting Standards Board approved a redefinition of goodwill assets which permitted intangibles such as brands to be separately valued. In 1999 the marketing consultancy Interbrand published an analysis which, using complex formulae of its own devising, attempted to rank global brands by their balance sheet value: top of the list was the Coca-Cola name, which, they reckoned, accounted for 60 per cent of the worth of the company, or about £52 billion.

How far can a brand extend its magic halo before it's stretched out of shape? Unlike many food and drink companies, Nestlé applies its brand to all its products. The Heinz company famously spread a wholesome family umbrella image across 57 varieties of food – and then many more – but chose to present products which promote different values – Weight Watchers and HJ Heinz premium soups – as independent brands, supported with a restrained visual logo endorsement. A fascinating pastime of consumer market researchers is to evaluate new product development and business acquisition possibilities by exploring the various fields in which a well-known brand name may extend a legitimate authority – even though it may not be currently operating in that sector. In the late 1960s, Dunlop, with a monopolistic reputation for tyres, also made tennis shoes, racquets and floor-coverings in the UK. Preparing to enter the DIY adhesive market, the company was surprised when research revealed that consumers assumed that Dunlop was already one of the leading brands in the field. There was a lingering folk memory of a glue in a bicycle tyre repair kit Dunlop had once widely marketed, and the firm also sold floor tiles. Consumers had made the mental leap to general-purpose adhesives long before the marketeers had got there.

Today brand owners are more alert to the potential exploitation of their trademarks, and corporate licensing is big business. The cash-rich cigarette companies, which in the West trade in a literally dying market and are restrained by advertising restrictions everywhere, have long sought to diversify brand franchises into less sensitive markets, particularly those which enhance the brand image (see Chapter 20). In the US, Pepsi-Cola's Maxwear fashion range cashed in on the "Done it, loved it" theme from its 1994 advertising campaign, while Coors Brewing Company introduced an eclectic range of products in the belief that its beers "have come to symbolise the heritage of the American West, romance and the natural splendour associated with the Rocky Mountains". Caterpillar became as well known for rugged boots favoured by gays as its construction vehicles. But unbridled promiscuity can ruin the reputations of brands as well as people. Pierre Cardin downgraded its luxury image by applying its name to everything from umbrellas to slippers. In an act of sublime hubris Cadbury involved its UK brand in a test of strength against sensory perception by applying its name, synonymous with chocolate, to a mashed potato mix, canned meats and savoury snacks. The company later erased its name from these products. Relevance appears to play a role; nevertheless there is ample evidence that a powerful brand image can overcome a perceived lack of experience and competence in an unrelated product field. Marks & Spencer's immense assets of consumer trust allowed it to trawl its database of 3.5 million charge card holders to support a successful entry into the unit trust market in 1988. It is common values which unify activities in disparate markets, and the principle found its ultimate expression in the Virgin phenomenon, unified by the personality of a single man (See Chapter 21).

It used to take years to build major brands. Behind them were substantial companies with a long history of trading, factories, and large piles of bricks and mortar, and a reputation nourished through heavy advertising for many years. As a result they hogged space on retailers' shelves, discouraging new entrants and extracting a premium price from consumers. But it is the image which matters, and modern communications can magic that out of nothing more substantial than the whiff of the *Zeitgeist*. The Legendary Joe Bloggs Inc. Co. (world HQ: the Legendary Building, Manchester), was started in 1986 by a 32-year-old Asian entrepreneur, Shami Ahmed. He wanted a brand name which was very British. He considered Nelson, Windsor, Churchill. One of his team, a marketing naïf, disagreed, saying "It doesn't really matter, you can call them after any old Joe Bloggs". Mr Ahmed recognised that this was a very British expression, and so, when the first advertisement appeared on hoardings at Old Trafford and other televised sports venues, it simply read: "Joe Bloggs". Soon, young football fans were asking "Who the hell is Joe Bloggs?", and his company became one of the top ten jeans manufacturers in Britain.

Today, much of what people do, from eating out to holidays, is a branded experience which substitutes a blanket acceptance of received values for independent judgement. The right brand name provides instant authority. It defies logic and leaps cultural barriers. In the soukhs of Cairo, you will see labels that are passwords to Western society – Ericsson, Nokia, and Alpacino (sic) – on piles of blue jeans these entities never made.

THE CONSUMER CYCLE keeps turning. In the mid-1990s a curious shop called Muji opened branches in London offering an eclectic inventory ranging from chocolate-covered soy beans to wrist watches – all without brand names. Their pitch is that the truly avant-garde customer now eschewed the designer labels of the 1980s; the shop itself replaces them, selling anonymity as a brand. Yet by the end of the decade Muji was advertising itself. Meanwhile, far from the West End, at the Saturday market in Taunton, Somerset, shoppers still queue to buy farmhouse cheddar with a hand-written label telling them which local farm has produced it, and home-made cakes bearing the names of the women who baked them.

People relate to brands as they do to other people. The emotional stance of a brand, its philosophy towards life, exerts a powerful influence on consumer choice. Well-distributed brands with distinctive personalities enrich balance sheets like geese laying golden eggs. But where do you find the magic wand?

CHAPTER 5
THE SECRET MAGIC INGREDIENT

Creativity

Persuasion must in every case be effected: 1) by working on the emotions of the judges themselves; 2) by giving them the right impression of the speaker's character; or 3) by proving the truth of the statements made.

Aristotle

IF ADVERTISING is a hit-and-miss affair, frequently producing ineffective, or even counter-productive messages, as has been argued in the first three chapters of this book, how is the growth of powerful worldwide consumer brand franchises, as described in the previous chapter, to be explained? Effective advertising must have contributed to the early development of these brands. But once a brand has achieved a certain threshold – an omnipresent level of distribution, consumer awareness and acceptance – it is very difficult to kill it off, even through misguided advertising. Once a brand has been successfully established, the most important influence on its sales is "brand momentum", a quality which is scarcely recognised and never measured. Successful brands can be dislodged only by a significant change in the price/value relationship. For example, when consumers perceive that a cheaper own-label brand is "just as good". Or, when a marketing event alters the intrinsic consumer perception of the brand – typically the launch of a new product.

In 1950's Britain, when marketing was something housewives did on Saturday mornings with a net bag, manufacturers simply responded to imperatives arising from the demands of their production and sales departments. At that time Dunlop enjoyed total dominance of the African market for bicycle tyres. Nevertheless the company continued to innovate, and launched a superior new product, incidentally taking the opportunity to modernise the logo which appeared on the side of the tyres. The new tyres were distributed throughout the market stalls of Africa, and after a few weeks, salesmen were sent out to check on progress. While the stalls had been stripped bare of the old tyres, they were stuffed with the unsold new model. The African women who ran the stalls were distraught. "We can't sell these new tyres," was the refrain, "give us back the Jesus tyres." They meant the bearded image of the founder of Dunlop, which had been removed from the logo to modernise the image. The creative communication which had driven Dunlop's African sales for decades was entirely accidental.

Advertising agencies live and die by creative communication; that's how clients justify advertising and their choice of agencies. All advertising people agree on that, but what is creativity? Here there is no consensus, though many advertising people appear to believe it is simply something funny, unexpected, or outrageous – a man slipping on a banana-skin, or the display of a sampling of genitalia of differing maturity, as in a Benetton advertisement which was honoured at the 1993 Venice Biennale. Mathematical models of advertising effectiveness usually make no allowance for what most of us might think is fundamental: the content of the message. That is because it has proved impossible to measure its effect.

Yet, is there any reason to believe that effective techniques of mass communication are different in kind from successful individual persuasion? How does a smooth salesman sell you a suit? How does a conman convince a punter to part with his life savings? How does a bloke chat up a Judy? A pro a John? How does a Samaritan talk a depressive out of committing suicide? Instinctively, most of us can identify the tactics which are likely to succeed or fail in these circumstances.

Why should those tactics vary when you are talking to mass audiences? US President Franklin Delano Roosevelt used person-to-person appeals effectively in his "fireside chats" when the new medium of radio allowed him to talk to each member of the electorate in his own living room, John Major spoke to the individual in his "soapbox" address during his successful re-election campaign, and direct response advertisers use personal appeals to get you and me to pull out our credit cards. Why do so many mass marketers instinctively reach for a long-handled brush and a pot of poster paint instead of a fountain pen? Probably because to naive advertisers the phrase "mass communications" conjures up a mental image of a grey, undifferentiated mass of people standing in a stadium, to be addressed in the style of the 1995 press advertisement for the Datewise Worldwise lonely hearts agency which offered to help "you, the public, find true happiness".

Where large numbers are gathered together in the same place at the same time – a rally, a convention, a music-hall – immediate, visible social pressures intrude; an unruly mob is the extreme example. In such circumstances the individual can only be reached through his role as a member of the group, and a different psychology applies. But where the communication is by television, radio, print, or poster, the difference between individual and mass persuasion lies in the technical use of the medium and not the style of the message. Although appearing in media which reach millions, effective mass persuasion is not directed to masses, but to individuals. (A cinema advertisement is perhaps an exception, and paradoxically this medium reaches relatively few people in aggregate.)

Aristotle maintained that argument succeeds through emotion, reputation, and – a strange word this in the modern context – truth. He has not been proved wrong, yet in the absence of conclusive evidence other theories abound. Many advertising practitioners aim no higher than capturing attention, using hyperbole, shock, sex-tease, and humour, without any evidence that this kind of "creativity" influences brand decisions, or, indeed, a convincing rationale about how it might be expected to do so.

Certainly creativity is closely linked to humour. And it is usually described as a new way of looking at things – an unexpected juxtaposition. Arthur Koestler, who wrote about the psychological roots of creativity, contends that scientific exploration, humour, and art have a common source, which he attributes to a departure from orderly thinking: the sudden intersection of two wholly separate planes of reference, producing a new line of thought. In science the combination leads to discovery:

> The motions of the tides were known to man from time immemorial. So were the motions of the moon. But the idea to relate the two, the idea that the tides were due to the attraction of the moon, occurred, as far as we know, for the first time to a German astronomer in the seventeenth century; and when Galileo read about it, he laughed it off as an occult fancy.

In a joke, Koestler observes, the collision of frames of perception leads to a new appreciation:

> A Marquis at the court of Louis XV had unexpectedly returned from a journey and, on entering his wife's boudoir, found her in the arms of a bishop. After a moment's hesitation, the Marquis walked calmly to the window, leaned out and began going through the motions of blessing the people in the street.
> "What are you doing?" cried the anguished wife.
> "Monseigneur is performing my functions", replied the nobleman, "so I am performing his".

Koestler takes the risk of explaining his joke:

> It is the interaction between two mutually exclusive associative contexts (the logic of *quid pro quo* and the canon of sexual morality) which produces the comic effect. It compels us to perceive the situation at the same time in two self-consistent but habitually incompatible frames of reference.[1]

"Comic discovery", Koestler concludes, "is a paradox stated; scientific discovery is paradox resolved". His theory, which he termed "biassociation", explains why an invention often seems to occur out of the blue, when the mind is engaged on something else entirely. Why Nikola Tesla, strolling through a park in Budapest reciting some lines from Goethe, suddenly stopped and began to draw the concept of alternating current in the dust with a stick. How Edwin Land conceived the Polaroid process because when he was photographing his young daughter, she asked why she couldn't see her picture right away.

Owing to its ability suddenly to permit us to see things from a new angle, creativity plays a key role in mass communications. Persuasion works by reinforcing existing views or by attempting to change them. The latter demands a shift of attitude – a new way of seeing things. Its enemies are habit and convention. Where attitudes are entrenched, the challenge is enormous. As Koestler conjectures:

> To unlearn is more difficult than to learn; and it seems that the task of breaking up rigid cognitive structures and reassembling them into a new synthesis cannot, as a rule, be performed in the full daylight of the conscious, rational mind. It can only be done by reverting to those more fluid, less committed and specialized forms of thinking which normally operate in the twilight zones of awareness.[2]

He is describing how the creative individual thinks, but if Koestler's suggestive sub-rational underworld exists, it must be receptive to external influences as well as internal impulses. Effective persuasion is subversive, its strongest influences are through the irrational state; even its appeals to reason are creative: the arguments of analogy, metaphor, and hyperbole.

A sudden topsy-turvy insight can make us laugh. Particularly if it's

---

[1] Arthur Koestler, The *Act of Creation*, Hutchinson Danube Edition, 1964.
[2] *ibid.*

subversive – the man slipping on the banana-skin is more likely to raise a laugh if he's promenading with a swagger stick, wearing a top hat, and has a snooty lady on his arm. But how can the power of creativity be harnessed to sell goods and ideas? How can it be *managed*?

The advertising business is schizoid about creativity. On the one hand its trade magazine, *Campaign*, has no difficulty in periodically ranking the leading advertising agencies on this quality. It simply tots up all the prizes awarded in a selection of the many award competitions, including its own, which are held each year by self-promoting industry groups, and concocts a rating using a weighting system of its own devising. *Campaign*'s league tables of "the most creative agencies" are esteemed by those which feature in them. In its compilation covering 1994, however, the magazine puzzled as to why a "notable feature of the top creative accounts list is the absence from the top of the table of some of the IPA Effectiveness Award winners". The possibility that the two criteria – effective result and its own definition of "creativity"– might not be linked did not occur to the magazine. Instead, it came up with this hypothesis: "There seems to be a lag between the appearance of a campaign and its recognition in terms of creativity, it may be that the effectiveness winners will perform well in 1995".

Businesses which hire advertising agencies are not buying the benefit of hindsight. What they are paying for is what they expect from their other consultants and advisers: the ability to influence the future. Advertising is not a profession, but agencies nourish the cult of creativity for the same reason that doctors wear white coats, lawyers speak Latin, dons dine at High Table, and oracles lived in caves. If the worth of your opinion cannot be proved, authority can be conferred by erecting barriers which deflect dissent.

Unlike the professions, the advertising industry draws an uncompromising distinction between its high priests, the "creatives" – mostly youngish graduates of art schools – and the "suits", which is everyone else. The demarcation line is stronger than in the most bolshy trade union. Like necromancers, witch doctors and pop stars, "creatives" conceal their mystique and signify their special status through exotic dress, cabalistic communication, and eccentric behaviour. "Suits", and this of course includes all clients, have an image as responsible businessmen, which requires that they appear normal, at least in meetings; they are not encouraged to have advertising ideas. To avoid any possibility of mistaken identity the creatives avoid wearing suits. (When a JWT London team flew to Frankfurt to make a new business pitch, the creative director packed a suit for a social engagement, while the account executive ravaged his only suit during a night on the tiles. The next morning, as one was a head shorter than the other, they couldn't swap clothing, so the only solution was to switch roles for the presentation.)

If science is a creative process – and even accounting is sometimes called creative, while lying certainly is – clearly creativity is not something taught only in art schools. Is it really, as the advertising industry implies, an intuitive quality absent in most people, and possessed only by a few anointed? Obviously not. Creative responses are required in all types of business at all levels. Creativity is not a wand waved over a puzzle by a wizard. It is an integral way of thinking and begins with a creative analysis of the problem. It extends to marketing activities and the selection and use of media. Original thinking is vital to every aspect of persuasive communication and, according to Koestler's theory, may be expected from anyone who is capable of entertaining two thoughts at the same time. It's like acting: most people have some ability, but the difference between the amateur and the truly gifted is the range of parts they can play. The problem is not lack of creative instincts, but how to keep them from running amok.

The modern advertising agency was more or less invented by the firm of Carlton & Smith, founded in 1864. This firm sold space in religious publications to advertisers who told them what to put in it. Four years later they hired a 20-year-old who came up with the idea of helping the advertiser dream up ways of filling those spaces. He bought out the firm in 1878 and renamed it after himself, James Walter Thompson. For the next half-century or so, the prototypical advertising "ideas" man was an all-rounder: he dealt with the client, together they worked out the gist of the copy, the adman may even have sketched out a layout, and he placed the media. He did his research by going to the library, talking to people, or scratching his head. He used both the left and the right sides of his brain.

But as the business grew more complex, advertising followed Henry Ford's trend towards the division of labour and separated creative departments from other functions. Today, like many businesses, advertising agencies encourage a multidisciplinary approach. In a continuing debate, account executives or "handlers" represent the views of the client, a new discipline of "account planning" has been invented to interpret the needs of the target group, and the "creatives" provide the vital ignition that turns plan into idea.

Today the team concept is exalted in industry, as it is in societies both totalitarian and democratic. Elitism is politically incorrect. In advertising, the rational argument is that cross-disciplinary thinking rarely flourishes within a single individual, unless you have people like Leonardo da Vinci, Francis Bacon, Arthur Koestler, or Jonathan Miller on the payroll. Nevertheless many individuals have at least partial competence in more than one discipline – indeed, whole professions are based on the bridging ability of the generalist – journalists, architects, GPs, and barristers. None of these produce their best work in rigidly structured environments. And true creative inspiration – when it is acknowledged in the artist, the scientist, the philosopher, or the entrepreneur – often seems to be the product not of a team player but of a single determined ego.

Like everyone else, advertising agency staff genuflect to the ideal of teamwork, and people from different disciplines work together to get things done. But the crucial spur of creativity is less likely to spring from communal effort than from megalomania. Clients rarely choose advertising agencies for their management skills, while media expertise is often hived off as a separate activity. In the end, success or failure in advertising depends on creative genius. And by the rules of the game which agencies have devised, this is a personal gift, difficult to define and impossible to measure. Inevitably, this has produced a star system. In determining what the client is offered, the creative sanction is absolute. That capacity has been conferred on the "creatives" by their peers – those who bestow creative awards. The role of the "suits" is to try to ensure the game is played more or less on the right pitch, while the "creatives" keep moving the goal posts.

Though many others have an input, the inspiration for an advertisement arises from a single mind or, more usually, a closely bonded team of two in which one, the art director, is nominally responsible for the visual impression and the other, the copywriter, for the text (if any). Generally "creatives" are in their 20s or early 30s, with little experience of business outside an advertising agency. Ultimately, they are the motor which powers the advertising industry. The entire edifice of marketing, the ultimate responsibility of devising a communication which will influence consumer behaviour, devolves on them.

What are their influences? In that instant of creative insight, Koestler's intersection of unlikely planes of thought, what frames of reference do they apply? The latest experiments in communications theory? The maxims of applied psychology? The instincts of a salesman? The collected thoughts of David Ogilvy? Some "creatives" may have acquaintance of these. But the primary influences are patently three: cinema films, television entertainment programmes, and other advertisements, probably in that order.

Could a "knowledge engineer" extract advertising skill and replicate it in a computer-based robotic system, as is now being attempted in professions such as quantity surveying? No, because while creative tactics and techniques do exist, there are no measurements of their effectiveness. If a quantity surveyor gets it wrong, his building will fall down. If a "creative" is wrong, no one can prove it. What computerisation has done, however, by expanding the possibilities of visual expression, for example, is to make more impressive the process by which he makes his mistakes.

Because of the orientation of its practitioners, advertising creativity is less like scientific discovery than fashion design. It does not aim to solve problems through original thought, but by the rearrangement of familiar materials. "Originality" means inventing a new way of playing the game; "creativity", as the term is used in advertising, means reshuffling the cards of the pack.

In this it is no different from other businesses which believe that "creativity" is what they have to sell. In the film industry, television, popular music, and publishing, the demand is for facsimiles of recently successful ideas. These industries too, have little idea of what affects consumer behaviour, and so rude originality in the Koestlerian sense is as welcome as a bloodied martyr at a conclave of bishops. For businesses with deep pockets, it's a conservative commercial strategy, like betting on the favourite in every horse race. But they miss out on the long shots which pluck the rich prizes and change all the rules. Which is why you don't expect big companies to come up with big ideas.

THE TRUE ROLE OF CREATIVITY in advertising is to make that intuitive leap which defines the relationship between the brand and its user. The winning ideas may seem to come out of the blue, but they don't come at random: all successful advertisements are based on a shrewd, if often instinctive, understanding of what makes people tick. To the individual it's aimed at, the best advertising doesn't seem like advertising: it's a direct personal communication that strikes the heart of the matter, like the famous 1914 war recruitment advertisement featuring Lord Kitchener pointing directly at the passer-by and demanding "Your country needs you". (In the US, Uncle Sam was even more direct: "I want you".) You don't need a degree in marketing psychology to evaluate the arguments in the rest of this section about how persuasion works; the lessons of your own personal experience as a child, parent, employee, or lover will do nicely. Because that is what consumers are.

CHAPTER 6
THE KINGS OF MISRULE

Irrationality

Schopenhauer thought that men's actions were far less governed by premeditation and deliberate planning than they believed. Very commonly, men act in accordance with their inner strivings without realising what those strivings are, and then attempt to justify them afterwards. Anticipating Freud, Schopenhauer noted that we are frequently unaware of our true motives, and may only become conscious of what we were aiming at (or what the Will was aiming at) after we have acted and noted the results of our actions ... Jung, who read Schopenhauer in adolescence and who admitted being deeply influenced by him, begins his autobiography by writing: "My life is a story of the self-realisation of the unconscious".

Anthony Storr, Music and the Mind, 1992

IN 1978 "the Reverend" Jim Jones led more than 900 followers of his cult, the People's Temple, to the jungles of Guyana and set up Jonestown. He instructed them to drink cyanide and they did. Seventy million Chinese, members of the Falun Gong movement, believe that a mystical wheel rotates in their bellies, protecting their bodies against disease. A "Charismatic Christian" is someone who not only believes in God's omnipotence – the supernatural power to heal the sick, enrich the poor, move mountains, divide seas, and destroy or create universes – he or she also believes that, like Superman, He routinely intervenes in daily lives. Believers will testify how God preserved them from terrorists, steered them to an elusive item when shopping, or dropped a timely ten-pound note in their path. Morris Cerullo's annual London shows exploit these beliefs: his first great circus in 1992 was preceded by a come-and-see-the-miracles advertising campaign featuring smashed white sticks and dark glasses. At the beginning of this century, the "Charismatic" schism represented less than 1 per cent of the world's Christians. Today it comprises more than 25 per cent, or 400 million believers. All over the world there are religious fundamentalists who fervently believe they can make peace by force, save lives by killing, achieve redemption by sacrificing themselves. As Richard Dawkins, author of *The Selfish Gene* has observed, "The fact is any religion sounds barking mad except to those brought up in it".

The urge to find supernatural explanations for the exigencies of life is apparent in every part of our culture. The first known horoscope was cast for a child born on 29 April 410 BC. The idea that the movement of heavenly bodies helps to determine human events has been around even longer. At first, like reading from tea leaves or entrails, these were auguries on matters of state, but now millions of people turn to the astrology pages of magazines and newspapers to consult, with varying degrees of credulity, predictions affecting their personal life. Television's *X-Files* and its many imitators, and a flood of Hollywood films, are contrived around supernatural characters or situations. Millennium fever, satanic child abuse, even the magic realism of quality literature – all require a massive suspension of disbelief.

Yet many people, against all evidence, appear to have a sublime faith in metaphysics – a belief that their fate is governed by the movements of the planets, or by supernatural beings. Or that, in the face of astronomical odds, it is they who are going to win the national lottery. People often attach strong emotional faith to secular institutions which they feel have their personal interests at heart: the football club, the company, the Tory Party, the British nation. Such beliefs and actions are beyond rationality. We can conclude that such people harbour unrealisable aspiration, unreasonable hope, and an intense conviction that the immense starry void of the universe revolves around their individual destiny. There's nowt so queer as folk like these. Are any of them in your family?

Few people describe themselves as self-obsessed, intemperate, impressionable, flighty, or unreasoning. On the whole people model their self-images in heroic moulds. They like to think of themselves as altruistic, self-controlled, independent-minded, consistent, and rational. Their behaviour, they believe, is directed by reason, not by impulse, feelings, anxiety, traditional beliefs, dreams, portents, superstitions, hunches, omens, compulsions, magnetic influences, and other people. No amount of evidence will make them think otherwise, and they will rarely admit to being "sold" an idea.

The truth is otherwise. If the consumer is king, he is the King of Misrule. There is an abundance of circumstantial and scientific evidence to corroborate our susceptibility to irrational influences. And there are many reasons for it, from psychological inclinations to physiological limitations. Call it human nature.

A lot of nonsense is spouted by economists and others who approach advertising from a purely rational point of view. Free-market theory champions consumer choice on the assumption that enlightened self-interest ensures the rational behaviour of markets. However, tests by Daniel Kahneman at the University of Princeton show we do not always make self-serving choices. In one experiment, respondents were presented with £20 and offered two options: split it 50/50 or keep £18 and give away £2. The test conditions were completely anonymous: the respondents did not know with whom they were sharing, nor who was offering the choice. Yet three-quarters of them chose to split the windfall equally. Presumably these people were being true to a fair-minded self-image of themselves.

Even in terms of their own self-interest, people with money in their pockets are not unfailingly sensible about how they spend it, particularly if it's in short supply. It was for this reason that workers' wives took care to meet them at the factory gate on pay-day. In Russia today the car is the lure. Russian men must have a car, no matter if the family has to wait for furniture, clothes, holidays, even food. In all cultures in which it has been introduced motorised transport has always implied subconscious personal rewards far greater than simply getting from A to B. Ernst Dichter, who helped introduce motivational research into advertising, called this "the strategy of desire".

Blind taste tests of products habitually demonstrate that consumers' expressed taste preferences are illusory, e.g. more people will prefer the taste of a bowl of cereal when they are told it is Kellogg's than when its provenance is unknown. Their judgement of taste has been manipulated by brand imagery.

A 1999 survey concluded that one in four British adults are innumerate: they could not work out what change they should receive from two pound coins when making a £1.35 purchase. Many more are severely handicapped in dealing with more abstruse mathematical concepts. The National Lottery introduced into Britain in 1994 has been called a tax on stupidity. Around twenty-five million people, more than half the adult population, participate in it each week, spending around £2.50 on average. The odds are stacked against them more heavily than in roulette or horse racing. Numbers are chosen by hunch, by system, birthdays, even by random number-generating products sold specifically for this purpose. Few punters choose a run, say, of 1,2,3,4,5,6 as their "lucky" numbers. Yet it is as likely to win as any other combination. Their judgement is poor; tests easily demonstrate that people find it difficult to calculate probability and consistently overvalue anything that they have personally chosen, even a series of numbers. The denying response to statistical logic is emotional: "Maybe ... but just suppose you won". In 1998 the National Lottery adopted as its advertising slogan precisely this mantra of desperate hope: "Just maybe".

In his incisive book *Irrationality: The Enemy Within*,[1] Stuart Sutherland, professor of psychology at the University of Sussex, scoured the scientific literature, citing well-known experiments and others less so, to compile a dossier of seemingly mindless human behaviour. The sources which he identifies lead to the following series of conclusions.

Emotion is the most powerful force behind irrational human behaviour. Daniel Goleman, author of *Emotional Intelligence*, defines emotion as "a feeling and its distinctive thoughts, psychological and biological states and range of propensities to act".[2] Emotion seems to short-circuit the neurological system. As Pascal wrote, "The heart has its reasons that reason knows not of". Love is blind. So is anger. And fear. We all acknowledge these basic feelings and others such as sorrow, joy, guilt and disgust. You can see emotion in others. Paul Ekman of the University of California at San Francisco has demonstrated that specific facial expressions for four of them (fear, anger, sorrow, and joy) are universally recognised around the world, including preliterate people in remote cultures untouched by exposure to television and cinema.[3] You can feel emotion in yourself; it has physiological components: dry mouth, rapid heartbeat, a flushed face when someone is angered, embarrassed, or simply shy. Sexual jealousy and grief create the physical symptoms of clinical depression.

Emotional responses are frequently provoked by vivid impressions which overwhelm reasoning. It is images, rather than words, which are usually the trigger. Sutherland cites the film *Jaws*. The opening scene, supported by an ominous music track, shows an unsuspecting swimmer yanked beneath the surface of the water by an unseen force. Sutherland reports that the film kept people off the beaches in California (and doubtless elsewhere). "It has been calculated", he says "that the risk of swimmers being snapped up by a shark is very much less than the risk of their being killed in a road accident while on the way to the coast". Equally, the film *Psycho* probably kept an earlier generation of moviegoers out of the shower for some time, though that behaviour was less open to observation.

Abstract reasoning is easily bested by a concrete example, too, because the context is more accessible to us. We put more faith in the opinion of a friend in a pub, or in a single striking case, than statistics: "My

---

[1] Constable, 1992.

[2] Bloomsbury, 1996.

[3] "An Argument for the Basic Emotions", *Cognition and Emotion*, 6 (1992), p. 175.

grandfather's ninety, and he's been smoking twenty a day since he 16". The more personally we can relate to the way information is presented, the more likely we are to believe it. In this context, the size of the sample and whether it is at all representative is totally irrelevant. Sutherland points out that American women had been unmoved by government initiatives to encourage diagnostic tests for breast cancer until the wives of two national political figures, Mrs Gerald Ford and Mrs Nelson Rockefeller, contracted the disease. Personifications carry an emotional appeal. Whether they are representative or not does not matter, because most people assume that, at heart, other people are like themselves.

For instance, we all have "common sense". To the philosophers of the Enlightenment that phrase stood for the ignorance and vulgarity of the herd. The 18th-century Italian philosopher Giambattista Vico described it as "judgement without reflection, shared by an entire class, an entire nation, or the entire human race". To Somerset Maugham it appeared to be "another name for the thoughtlessness of the unthinking. It is made of the prejudices of childhood, the idiosyncrasies of individual character and the opinion of the newspapers". It is the set of shared assumptions which advertising argument calls into play. While the groundrules may vary depending on the society we live in, evolutionary psychologists, just as ordinary people do, proceed from the assumption that there *is* such a thing as human nature: people everywhere have fundamentally the same minds.

When it comes to their personal prospects, most people are determined optimists. A soldier goes into battle hoping against reason that the bullet hasn't got his name on it. In the first week of the 1996 Creutzfeldt-Jakob disease scare in Britain, consumers stopped buying beef, leaving the supermarkets holding massive stocks. Until beef was reduced to half price, when it walked off the shelves. Apparently losing one's mind and suffering a horrible death from a degenerative brain disorder was more easily contemplated at £3 than at £6 per pound. We all know people who prefer not to have a physical examination because it would reveal the true state of their health. There are occasions when all of us find it difficult to "face the truth". According to Sutherland, 95 per cent of British drivers feel they are a better than average driver, most people think they will live longer than average, and 20 per cent of patients who are told they have cancer refuse to believe it. Self-deception avoids confrontation with unpleasant facts; it governs much of our daily life in matters small and large. We are poor judges of the true causes of our own moods and emotions. We will concoct far-fetched explanations to explain circumstances which seem to conflict with our view of reality

– the exam was poorly designed, and so were the golf clubs.

This disposition contrives to encourage wishful thinking, slanting our judgement. The normal condition of the human spirit is an endearing and indefatigable sanguinity. People overestimate their chances of winning a lottery and underestimate the odds of being involved in a road accident. Smokers find evidence that smoking is harmful less credible than non-smokers do. Sutherland cites experiments which demonstrate that self-serving biases such as this can even affect the perception of pain. In the same way, despite obvious clues, something extremely unpleasant – even the existence of concentration camps – can be suppressed and avoided. We believe what we want to believe.

ADVERTISING MANIPULATES IRRATIONALITY to create consumer preferences. It starts early. The Jesuits boasted, "Give us the boy before seven and we will give you the man". The Old Testament contains the same thought. Apart from the fact that they have little disposable income, children are ideal consumers. Their uncertainty is total, their needs immediate and insatiable, their craving for peer group conformity irresistible, and they retain these early influences as adults. In some parts of the world – Sweden, Norway, and Quebec province, for example – advertisements aimed at under-12s are banned. In Britain it is controlled by the Broadcast Advertising Clearance Centre. Its guidelines stipulate that advertisements "must not encourage children to pester or make a nuisance of themselves to other people". Phrases such as "ask mummy to buy" are unacceptable. Yet, while the signs on the fruit and veg section at the supermarket may read "Selected for quality and freshness", Mum's shopping trolley is heaped with fun-food: child-sized containers of sugary drinks and sweets, salty crisps and snacks decorated with Sonic the Hedgehog, the Lion King, Mr Blobby, Power Rangers, and Thomas the Tank Engine.

A study conducted by Dr Brian Young, a psychologist at Exeter University, in the late 1990s suggests that children "catch on" to advertising very early. By the age of five, 50 per cent know what an advertisement is attempting to do; by the age of eight it's 80 per cent. But there is little direct advertising for kiddie products; they are popularised through a constant global flood of merchandising by companies which produce film or television entertainment for children, such as Disney and Warner Brothers. Even the BBC. Its pre-school programme the *Teletubbies* engendered a massive demand for merchandised items in 1997. As soon as children begin to circulate with other children outside the home, peer pressure becomes the dominating motivational force in their lives. It is a parallel world of brand values to which adults are indifferent, but which is vital to children. It is how they define themselves, in the same way the parent does by the choice of a Marlboro or a Mercedes. What matters is not what their parents say, but what the word is on the playground. A craze for yo-yos suddenly swept across Britain in 1998 without the media noticing. There are researchers who, at the risk of apprehension as presumed pederasts, patrol playgrounds armed with tape recorders and video cameras, to capture the fleeting but influential trends in children's behaviour which are of marketing significance. Long before they enter their teens children have acquired the adult custom of investing clothing and music with emotional brand properties.

As children grow into adulthood, basic childish drives may be displaced and disguised, but the urge for conformity still governs. Experimental research confirms that early impressions colour later experience not just in childhood, but throughout our lives. Although we tend to retain and believe what we have heard or seen most recently, if new evidence conflicts with our previous opinion, it will be ignored or discredited. Once a judgement is formed we cling to it like a limpet to a rock, rejecting any lines of enquiry which may prove it is wrong. People seek to confirm their judgement, not to disprove it. We read newspapers that reflect our own views. We turn the page or change the channel rather than endure an opinion we do not share. Where beliefs are strongly and publicly held, pre-existing mindsets affect the interpretation of every new observation, and contrary arguments may simply more deeply anchor our opinion. Journalists generally come equipped with received opinion – "an angle" on their story – and can rarely be diverted to a new appreciation.

Sutherland quotes Sir Francis Bacon:

> The human understanding when it has once adopted an opinion draws all things else to support and agree with it. And though there be a greater number and weight of instances to be found on the other side, yet these it either neglects and despises, or else by some distinction sets aside and rejects, in order that by this great and pernicious pre-determination the authority of its former conclusion may remain inviolate.

When this obstinacy infects whole groups of like-minded people it hardens into dogma. Man is a social animal, and there is intense pressure to conform to what his immediate peer group perceives to be correct, regardless of how improbable it may be. And because people usually choose to associate with those who have similar beliefs, these attitudes gain tremendous group reinforcement. Various experiments demonstrate that while nearly everyone denies it, people are clearly influenced by the judgement of the majority. Opinion is influenced by the fear of ostracism. It motivates gangs of hoodlums, focus groups, and prize juries. There is, of course, a rational justification for herd behaviour: if a group takes a wrong decision the individual is absolved from guilt. Social pressure is the psychological basis of fashion and of advertising's "join the bandwagon" appeals. The classic British advertising failure, the 1960s launch of Strand cigarettes with advertisements showing a solitary James Dean type lighting up with the slogan "You're never alone with a Strand", though "liked" by the public and laden with advertising awards, came to grief by misjudging the number of people who would be prepared to identify themselves as one of nature's loners.

Because the personal and social penalties of changing their views are so high, people spend a great deal of time and effort in self-justification. If a consumer has taken a decision to invest a large sum of money on a house, a car, or home improvements, he is unlikely to admit he has made a mistake. On the contrary, he will be on the lookout for any scrap of evidence which supports his decision. This explains why car advertisements attract high readership from people who are not in the market for a new car, because they have recently bought one of that make. This is why encyclopedia and double-glazing salesmen can usually confidently refer to satisfied customers. And the consumer's need for self-justification helped them make those sales in the first place. As soon as the door is opened, the householder is placed in the position of having to justify his response to himself. The skilful salesman plays on this need, asking a series of general questions which gradually back the prospect into a corner. Door-to-door salesmen typically spend hours with their prey. Along the way they sympathetically but inexorably inch their argument forward, causing the householder to restate his views in various ways. Repetition will gradually strengthen an initial disposition. Parents may have been only mildly interested in their children's education when the salesman's foot thrust through the door. Now they are fervent about it. They find it difficult to escape the escalating argument without retracting what they have said previously. Our sense of self requires us to demonstrate consistency in attitudes and behaviour. The same techniques are used in sexual seduction – if you let me touch you above the waist, why not below?

Corporate man has a strong need to appear consistent, too, a drive which periodically leads to what would seem to be easily avoidable marketing disasters. For many years after the introduction of cash machines, British banks were adamant, in the press and in the courts, that they could not be fraudulently operated, until the police advised that there are many ways the technology can be compromised. Even after the housing market had quite obviously collapsed in Britain in the late 1980s, the momentum generated by the conventional wisdom of the recent past led insurance companies such as Prudential and Norwich Union to keep piling into the market, buying up chains of estate agents at inflated prices. Within a year or so these premises were back on the market, sometimes to be repurchased at a fraction of the price by the original owners.

The need to be consistent leads to what Sutherland calls the "sunk cost error" – the irrationality of "getting your money's worth" rather than "cutting your losses". People value time as well as money in this context, and will continue to invest both resources in lost causes in order to justify their past actions. That is why the most predictive determinant of future behaviour is past behaviour. It's a far better way of pinpointing marketing targets than socioeconomic factors – sex, age, class – or sophisticated "lifestyle" categorisation – "yuppies" or "dinkies". Those who have bought by mail order in the past, or subscribed to a magazine, or donated to a charity are the most likely to do so in the future. It's for this reason that good mailing lists – "single-purpose transactional databases" – have become highly negotiable currencies.

Peer group pressure is exerted by role models. Instinctively we aim to copy their behaviour and reflect their attitudes. Our allegiance grants them credibility above other sources of information. Whatever they say is more persuasive, and not only in their obvious field of competence. Our striving for consistency creates a halo effect for "celebrities". Their salient good traits lead us to overlook failings; we expect that a person we admire is admirable in all respects. It's like falling in love. It will even impel us to abandon reason and copy deviant behaviour. Religious extremists work like this – evangelists manipulate crowd pressure, and make sure that conversions are reinforced by a very public personal declaration.

In his book, *The Trouble with Science*, Robin Dunbar, professor of psychology at Liverpool University, argues that biological evolution has simply not equipped us to think scientifically. Because we have evolved as social animals, we are good at interpersonal relationships but poor at thinking logically and objectively assessing evidence. But, probably because we are curious, we are not content to suspend judgement. We seek explication, even from the paranormal. Certainly the mass of humanity prefers hocus-pocus to hypothesis, conspiracy theory to coincidence. In all societies religion traditionally supplied metaphysical explanations for the unknown or the unlikely; now we have New Age forms claimed to be life-enhancing, some as old as the pyramids, others flavoured with scientific speculation. On the flimsiest scraps of "evidence" many intelligent, civilised people throughout the world believe in miracles, magic, flying saucers, yetis, angels and demons, talismans, and diets – because they want to believe in them. If our favourite beliefs are disproved, as when the film of the dead alien from outer space allegedly dissected by the US military establishment at the atomic proving-grounds in New Mexico in 1946 turned out to be a fake, we can easily replace that "evidence" with some other implausible theory.

Humans are different from animals because they can plan for the long term, but their animal nature finds it difficult to defer self-gratification. Emotional factors lead people to act on impulse. Self-control is not natural; it is imposed by cultural training. So advertising works best by appealing to our basic animal instincts. Nevertheless, it has to breach the cultural barriers erected by self-awareness. The last word belongs to Stuart Sutherland, who "wrote the book" on irrationality: "Persuasion works by making the improbable, even the impossible, seem to be a reasonable conclusion of our own thought processes".[4]

[4] *Irrationality.*

CHAPTER 7
THE SECOND BIGGEST SHOW ON EARTH?

Hyperbole

The titles of "humbug" and "prince of humbugs" were first applied to me by myself. I made these titles part of my "stock in trade".
Struggles and Triumphs, the autobiography of P. T. Barnum, published in 1854, was a bestseller

DO ADVERTISERS LIE?

Do politicians evade? Are government ministers economical with the truth? Do estate agents stand in front of damp patches in the wall? Would you consult a spin-doctor for a medical diagnosis?

In the 1996 Reith lectures, Professor Jean Aitchison, the Rupert Murdoch Professor of Language and Communication at Oxford University, argued:

> Humans, alongside other primates, are often called social animals. This has promoted two types of behaviour: a fondness for grooming one another, and an ability to make guesses about the mental state of others: intelligent primates can put themselves into one another's shoes, as it were. These abilities tie in with two things language is especially good at: interacting with others and influencing them ... The ultimate goal of learning to speak may be lying, or a spin-off from lying – the ability to talk convincingly about things which are absent or even non-existent. This property of language, known as displacement, is one of its great strengths.

Or, as the French statesman Charles Maurice Talleyrand-Périgord observed more succinctly, "Speech was given to man to disguise his thoughts".

Thus, the evolution of language gave *Homo sapiens sapiens* a competitive edge in the struggle for survival. He was able to communicate clearly, and he was also able to lie more effectively than other animals, which have a limited repertoire of physical signals intended to confuse. Concealing the truth is an essential skill in an intelligent social environment: it allows one to gain social acceptance and personal advantage. The reactive need to second-guess others, to find out what was really going on, must have put more pressure on developing an even bigger brain. So today, when the business Ansafone message tells us, "I'm afraid no one is available to take your call at the moment", we know that means that the staff haven't come in yet, or they've knocked off early.

The instinct to lie is human, and call it what you will, the intent of advertising is to deceive. Exaggeration is essential to advertising; it has stretched the truth for so long that the absence of reassuring hyperbole provokes more suspicion than its presence. Cards posted in a newsagent's window must describe cleaners as "reliable", prostitutes as "young" ... etc. or they will be passed over. P.T. Barnum didn't have to do any market research before deciding to call his circus nothing less than "The Greatest Show on Earth". His dazzling insight was not simply that "There's a sucker born every minute", but that the public is a willing accomplice in its own bilking. Pricing points rely on this: we know that an item (such as this book) advertised for £12.95 or £1,495 really costs £13 or £1,500. But as prospective purchasers we connive happily in the deception, and think of it as "around" £12 or £1,400. We are particularly likely to collude if an investment has been made. At Steeplechase, the famous Coney Island amusement park in New York City, one 1950s attraction came straight from the Barnum tradition. It advertised a viewing of "The Famous Californian Red Bats". These resided in a small cage in a tower at the top of a steep, narrow staircase, and could be viewed only by sacrificing a couple of precious points from your strip of entry coupons. The designers of this display knew that the file of children and adults descending the staircase would never inform those trudging upwards that what was in the cage was a pair of red baseball bats.

What happens when the willing conspiracy between buyer and seller is shattered? The price of telling the truth in business is formidable. In 1991, under various trading names, Gerald Ratner owned almost every jewellery chain in the UK. His company was the world's biggest jewellers, employing 25,000 people. In explaining his firm's spectacular rise from 3 per cent to 34 per cent of the market to an audience of 6,000 members of the Institute of Directors one day, he confided that his products were "crap". The tabloid newspapers seized on this indiscretion and the next day customers jammed his stores, wanting their money back. His employees were "gob-smacked". In less than a year the share price of the Ratner Group slumped from around £2 to under 8p and the business was trading at a loss. Gerald Ratner estimates that this remark cost his company £200-£300 million. It cost him a personal stake of around £6 million and

HYPERBOLE 57

his career as chairman of the Ratner Group.

Advertisers habitually devise elaborate constructs intended to deceive. A plain brown envelope drops through your letter box. It bears a numeric code, 095, written by hand in blue ink. And a typewritten message: "I think the enclosed survey will interest you. . . . etc". It is signed by hand in blue ink by "Linda". Above the printed name of an organisation called Consumer Research Centre her reliable Anglo-Saxon name is typewritten: Linda Harrison. The H has jumped out of line, just as it used to do in old-fashioned typewriters. The only true statement on this envelope is the typewritten message beneath: "Delivered By Hand". Despite appearances to the contrary, this specimen is one of thousands of envelopes identical apart from the address. Everything else has, in fact, been printed. "Personalised" messages like these are now common practice in direct marketing drops. The only thing remarkable about this specimen is the idea that in the closing year of the 20th century any "consumer research organisation" (for which read "advertiser") could pretend to believe that consumer research organisations still used typewriters.

Advertisers are so used to distorting facts that they find it difficult to comprehend why people are bothered about it. A 1995 Australian ad for Blackmores Active Woman Formula vitamins featured a woman identified as Caroline, who was described as an "architect, mother of three, Red Cross volunteer and recreational pilot". She was pictured wearing aviator glasses and cap, saying "People wonder how I do so much: I wonder how they do so little". The Australia Advertising Standards Council asked for it to be withdrawn, because the only true claim ascribed to the woman shown was that her name was Caroline. The head of sales and marketing for Blackmores was baffled by the decision, because he had received only a few complaints about the ad: "I don't think we've committed a moral crime or anything . . . We researched it and that ambiguity didn't come through".

The instruments of lying are the same as in any piece of propaganda: hyperbolic claims, deceptive images and misleading associations. Consider these slogans:

"We're Getting There"	British Rail, 1970s
"Securicor Cares"	Securicor, 1970s
"With the Post Office It's Sorted"	Post Office, 1995
"We Won't Fail You"	British School of Motoring, 1999

Do you believe any of these statements? Probably not entirely. Because personal experience may argue against it. But you know what they're trying to say. It may or may not be relevant to your needs. And, in an imperfect world, you may be inclined to give them the benefit of the doubt. Which may give these advertisers a slight edge the next time you consider their services.

These examples are subjective claims, subject to interpretation. But the slogan British Airways has used since 1983, "The World's Favourite Airline", is more factual and would appear to be based on some sort of objective measurement of customer satisfaction. In 1999 Virgin Atlantic tried for the third time to convince the advertising regulatory authorities that this claim is false, by maintaining that BA had won fewer industry awards than Virgin. Both airlines produced customer surveys supporting their own popularity. The Independent Television Commission and the Advertising Standards Authority rejected these as self-selecting and decided that the key factor must be simply the number of international passengers carried. They ruled that BA could continue to use the claim because, according to International Air Transport Association figures, the airline flew 28 million passengers in 1997. (The American carrier Delta Airlines flew three times as many passengers, but as most of these journeys were confined to the continental United States and there is no open access to American skies for international airlines, the regulators discounted it.) As British Airways carried more passengers than other (non-American) airlines, it had to be "the world's favourite". There was no proof that the passengers enjoyed the experience, or would not have preferred to fly with another airline had the choice been available. Nevertheless, however flawed the logic, the statement seems credible (particularly to the British), and has formed the basis of a consistent advertising strategy, hewing a line between the majestic and the pompous, for seventeen years. So now it carries even more weight. Consistent repetition of a hyperbolic claim will over time persuade consumers that there must be some truth in it. After all, "they can't just say anything they like, can they?"

Of course, "they" can. The outright lie contained in the British Airways slogan is based on deliberate semantic confusion, the "Bill Clinton defence". However, the practice of advertising prevarication does not rely merely on verbal trickery; it is psychologically pervasive. Its tools are exaggeration, oversimplification, appeals to emotional guilt and aspiration, association, and the manufactured "bandwagon" appeal.

At its simplest level, the aspirational approach always shows the dream, not the reality: an advertisement for a dry-slope skiing course doesn't illustrate its leaflet with a beginner on a green plastic surface on a dull day in Doncaster, but shows a crouching downhill racer on a shimmering alpine snow slope. Advertising is life-enhancing, and like a playful, friendly puppy, that is one of its charms.

Oversimplification is common. Apple Macintosh advertised a new 1996 computer model containing software which "takes the confusion out of the Internet and allows you to enjoy online computing within minutes. No need to . . . No need to . . . No need to . . . You simply launch eWorld, type in a few personal details and you're away*". The asterisk referred to a thick wadge of qualifying terms and conditions, including the advice that you will also need to buy a modem.

Advertisers, like speechmakers, take care to associate themselves with "good things" – motherhood, family life, patriotism – while throwing mud at the opposition. Larry Barker, Creative Director of the advertising agency BMP.DDB, offered an insight into the process in his suggestion for creating a hypothetical advertising campaign to marshal public opinion behind the House of Lords, under threat of dismemberment after the accession of the Labour government:

> You need to muddy the waters, to try and find things that make the House of Lords seem more libertarian than the Commons and distract people from the current issue . . . There's a lot of history there, and the English like their history. Do a big emotional number on it: say that it's part of our heritage and we couldn't possibly lose it. Hopefully, that will gloss over the fact that they're a bunch of old decrepit nutters. You could reverse the "thin end of the wedge" thing and say something like: "If we get rid of this, what's next? The Queen? All the things we hold dear?" You'd be looking to raise the spectre of England as a republic with a president.[1]

Since concern for the environment has swum into the consumer consciousness many advertisers have gone to great lengths to be seen to be green. A 1993 campaign by the Newspaper Publishers Association extolled the power of the press: "How else can we find out about new products that will improve our lifestyle, our health, our appearance, or our environment?" There is, of course, no product which improves the environment, only some which damage it marginally less than others. Advertisers encourage confusion, inventing definitions which sound legalistic and make objective judgement difficult. Paper products sold in Superdrug, Boots, and Sainsbury's are variously described as made from "selected waste paper", "recycled paper", "low-grade waste", and "post-

---

[1] *The Independent*, 28 July 1998.

consumer waste". Trivial associations may be expressed in a way which imply a broader benefit. An umbrella selling in Boots in the mid-1990s featured a promotional tag showing a circle of three arrows symbolising recycling. Only the small print explained the reference: "This swing tag contains 80% re-cycled material". And Tesco's Nature's Choice Organic Milk cartons were sold with the promise that "this paper container is made of wood – a re-usable natural resource". The statement is factually correct, but you can't recycle cartons which have been coated with wax.

Like lawyers and politicians, good copywriters can distract attention from flaws in an argument by the inclusion of authentic but irrelevant information. A 1999 press advertisement for a credit card, American Express Blue, showed a skier with the headline, "Do piste-taking and get paid for it". The text explained: "The credit card that gives you 1% back on everything you spend . . . so whatever you do, blue pays you to do more".

And, massively, advertisers lie by insinuating that they share the same *Weltanschauung* as the consumer. The consumer is flattered; by recognising his views, which he feels distinguishes him from the general run of humanity, advertisers ingratiate themselves with the consumer. The advertiser has become a friend with a legitimate claim to the consumer's support at the point of purchase. That was the theory behind the 1980s flood of fashionable "attitude" advertising (see Chapter 17). However, it's difficult to be convincing, as many ham-fisted advertisers painfully reveal when they aim across the generation gap at an adult's image of inscrutable youth.

Visual analogies offer more powerful opportunities for hyperbole through a process of contagion. American advertisers, particularly, like to make sure you don't miss the connection. In a magazine a golden Fabergé egg nestles in a fold of lustrous dark velvet. Beneath it a Lincoln limousine appears against a similar background of blurred motion. The headline is explicit: "Fabergé. What an egg should be. Lincoln. What a luxury car should be". An advertisement for a sportswear manufacturer associates the brand with the love of nature. A deer prances in the shallows of an unspoiled mountain lake, above the line "Wherever there's a love of outdoors you'll find Eddie Bauer". For extra authenticity, the species of deer and the location of the photograph are specified.

In 1997 the Inland Revenue had to tell UK taxpayers some bad news. From now on they would have to fill in tax forms themselves. The department introduced self-assessment with a campaign using cartoons of cuddly, balding, moustachioed businessmen in bowler hats to represent the hounds of the Inland Revenue Service. By 1999 these cuties were dressing up in silly bee costumes with tiny wings, pot bellies, and bent antennae to convey the cosy message: "Miss the 31st January deadline and you'll be stung for £100". Beer brands like to be associated with hard men, and Sheffield is known for steel. So a 1990s TV commercial for Stones Bitter, brewed in that city, began with gritty black-and-white footage of tough, sweating, goggled men labouring in the heat of the furnaces. "Sheffield Gold: when you know you've earned it," says the voice-over. As the British steel industry was now too clean and automated to provide the traditional image, the commercial was filmed in a Czech foundry.

Modern film techniques give free rein to exaggeration. In a commercial for the Solid Fuel Advisory Council, a dog, a cat, and a mouse settle down comfortably before a real coal fire – and kiss. Another featuring a child and a python sharing a hot tub was withdrawn when viewers complained.

Advertising agencies are particularly fond of the technique they call 'the big brand feel'. And not just because it's expensive. The sheer visual impact of an advertisement can generate sufficient prestige to enhance the appeal of the brand almost regardless of the message. That's why agencies recommend large ads in newspapers and like to make films in exotic locations, using big stars, large casts, and sophisticated, expensive computer technology. It's Goebbel's basic technique: the bigger the lie, the more it feeds the appetite of the gullible. It means that in the major media, heavy advertisers fight more with money than ideas.

British Airways commercials are typical of the genre. When BA wants to advertise a special offer on reduced fares, it doesn't just publish a price list of destinations. It launches a campaign which creates a vision of London spectacularly emptied of people. Suburban streets, the West End, and the City are deserted, as in a post-apocalyptic disaster movie. The lone commuter who remains howls "Where is everybody?" from the top of a building. All BA wants to tell you is that you can fly to Rio and back for £299 (under restrictive conditions, which you discover later). But the big film treatment orchestrates the simple price reduction into a momentous occasion. It's the old "bandwagon" approach, which appeals strongly to deep-rooted insecurity: everyone is doing it, so don't get left out. Similarly, British Telecom made its 1999 advertising effort to claw back customers from the grasp of price-cutting competitors seem like a mass movement with this superficial and unsubstantiated argument: "Thousands of businesses are coming back to BT every month".

The populist appeal is often very emotional: the 1970s Coca-Cola campaign promoted peace, love, understanding, and a fizzy beverage with a cast of thousands thronging hilltops and mouthing the words to "I want to teach the world to sing". The Halifax Building Society 1990s campaign massed cheery folk in various improbable constructions to form an X, and another BA commercial swept in for an aerial view of a happy horde photographed from afar, forming a smiling face. Man is a social animal, and the perspective pioneered by Cecil B. DeMille, a bird's-eye view of massed populations driven by a single purpose, exerts a powerful emotional appeal. When interpreted by a contemporary Hollywood film director, using the high-technology tools of his trade, stirring music, and a million-pound budget, you can begin to believe that this really must be the world's favourite drink/building society/airline – and that that matters.

Perhaps the biggest of all the "big-brand feel" commercials was broadcast over fifteen years ago, and it only ran once. As 1984 dawned, a single commercial, directed by Ridley Scott, who made the Hollywood blockbuster films *Blade Runner* and *Alien,* took over the centre break of America's Superbowl football telecast. An athletic woman brandishing a sledgehammer raced through a crowd of proletarians to strike a blow at a huge screen, from which an image of Big Brother pontificated. Message: because of Apple Mac, the future was not going to be like George Orwell's 1984 after all; the individual would triumph over dictatorial corporations such as IBM. The spot was seen by 43 million Americans and the press seethed with publicity before and after the event.

Advertising hyperbole is so insistent that some social observers believe it has numbed our critical faculties:

> Few today are able independently to estimate the value of anything without prompting from self-interested sources. Nothing will survive unless inflated by hyperbole and gilded with a fine coat of fraud. The quest for individual social significance is unremitting, and if you've not earned it you can affect it by verbal pomposity. When not achieved by euphemism, dignity can be projected, it is thought by quantitative means : "a great dining experience" for a great dinner "a great reading experience" for a good read.[2]

Yet there is evidence that people no longer "believe everything they see in the papers". In the United States two psychology professors, Deborah Gruenfeld and Robert Wyer Jr., showed people mock

---

[2] Paul Fussell, *BAD, or The Dumbing of America*, Summit Books, 1991.

newspaper headlines – obvious statements such as "Black Democrats Supported Jesse Jackson for President in 1988" – and asked them to rate their plausibility. The scores were all quite high. The respondents were then shown contradictory "headlines", and unsurprisingly, the original belief scores decreased significantly. But when a matched group of respondents, who had also seen the original statements, were then exposed to different headlines *confirming* the first statement, such as "Black Democrats Presently Support Jesse Jackson for President", the belief scores still dropped. The researchers concluded that communications reinforcing a previously held belief have almost the same effect as contradictory communications. Why? Because people are natural sceptics. They are able to detect a hidden agenda beneath what is being said. Why is someone telling us over and over that Jesse Jackson has the support of black Democrats? What's the game?

But like many such psychological studies, that involved only the weakest kind of communication – rational appeals to the intellect – which advertising generally eschews. As the consumer gets more and more acculturated – hip – to advertising devices, a kind of escalating arms race evolves between advertisers and consumers. The latter, even the most poorly educated, gradually "get wise" to the blandishments of the former, who must then invent more novel weapons of deception.

In advertising, as in painting, non-representational techniques are increasingly popular, because they can exaggerate expectations. The astonishing advances in film technology have created new frames of reality. In the animated short films of a generation or so ago, a solemn dog called Droopy used to turn to the audience and explain "in a cartoon film you can do anything you want". Now live action films make old animation gags seem to come true. These effects first appeared in the products of Hollywood: in an early example Meryl Streep gave a virtuoso performance by revolving her head 360°; in the 1994 film *The Mask*, an actor's eyeballs bulged out on stalks, his jaw turned into steps, and a red carpet of tongue rolled out, just as in the old Tom & Jerry cartoons. Soon commercials for a mobile phone were sliding a man's mouth across his face to demonstrate the disadvantage of phones less well designed ergonomically than their own brand, and AXA Equity & Loan was dramatising investment worries by a sleepless man literally "tied up in knots", or a woman "getting into a twist".

Computer Generated Imagery (CGI) takes a realistic photographic image, distorts it in a computer, and reassembles frames, just as cartoon animation changes individual cells, to produce a continuous lifelike action. It is destined to become the ultimate instrument of the Big Lie.

Our generation can distinguish between the fantasy of animation and the reality of photography. We are also aware of photographic trickery. And when we see Spielberg's *Tyrannosaurus rex* chase after real people, or a film actor's head expand like a balloon, we know that what we are seeing is not actually happening. Bizarre events can be compared to the reality of experience. But less obvious distortions will be undetectable. For coming generations the distinction between real moving images and imaginative constructs will be forever blurred. You can already make a film without sets, actors or cameras, simply by feeding existing film footage into a computer and tweaking it. It is perfectly possible to get Marilyn Monroe to bed Bill Clinton on television, or Stalin to endorse Stolichnaya vodka. The legal obstacles are trickier than the technology. Once these are settled, truth and myth, past and present, fact and fable all blend in the alchemist's pot. The consumer needs a new maxim: *Caveat Viditor.*

ADVERTISERS, like journalists, novelists, priests, and folk you meet in the pub, help us interpret the world. We are sceptical; we know each has his own agenda and we don't expect literal truth from them. Yet we enjoy the colour and meaning they add to everyday existence. Those who arouse our emotions by telling us the best stories, painting the best pictures, we reward with empathy.

CHAPTER 8
HELLO, SAILOR

Attention

In the mid-1970s, cryptic posters started to appear in bus shelters all over Britain. They showed a small girl and the message: "My name is Amy, I like slugs and snails". That's all. No brand name, no logo, no attribution of any kind. The posters stayed up for weeks, so someone was making a massive advertising investment. But for what purpose? Speculations in the popular press boosted casual interest into a national obsession. Finally, a press release published the results of a survey showing the high levels of recognition this poster had achieved. It also revealed the name of the lavish advertiser. Adshel, the company which owned the poster sites, had put up nonsense ads as a way demonstrating the strength of its medium; Amy was the daughter of its sales director.

THE ADVERTISING AGENTS who stand in the doorways of the strip clubs on the Reeperbahn in Hamburg wear jaunty nautical caps with shiny brims to invoke maritime tradition as they pluck at your sleeves. The girls in the doorways leading to Soho's basement venues display different credentials, but their aim is the same: to engage your interest.

All models of how advertising works must concede that the first task of an advertisement is to gain attention. Subliminal speculation apart, it seems evident that unless an advertisement is noticed it is unlikely to have an effect except upon the bank balance of the advertiser. It's not an easy task. As professional viewers-with-alarm and advertising agents keen to increase budgets are fond of pointing out, advertising messages beat about our heads each day like a rainstorm on a tin roof. And not only when you're expecting them. At breakfast you may find a message from Kellogg's on the milk bottle and another promoting BT's daytime rate on the boiled egg, the latter courtesy of a company called Eggsvertising. There are adverts on the taxi you hail and others inside when you take your seat. At the shopping centre, advertising displays keep pace with you on the escalator. Inside the supermarket you push them along on your trolley and tread on them under your feet. As you hole out on the golf course, under your ball is an ad for Glenmorangie whisky. And in the clubhouse, if you're male, as you empty your bladder your eyes fix on a message as inescapable as graffiti, though probably far less interesting.

The kinds of people who bother to count these things are always producing mind-numbing statistics such as "The average 35-year-old British adult will have seen some 150,000 different commercials – most of them half a dozen times or more".[1] In the US of Advertising a citizen only five years older will have seen a million commercials. And that's just television. The average American, it is estimated, is pelted by some 3,000 advertising messages every day. The British, apparently, are not yet so besieged. According to a 1997 report by the Henley Centre, the typical resident of these islands will see around 250 television advertisements, 350 poster sites, and 400 press ads per week. Although that's not counting the sales missives that drop through the letterbox, the telephone calls, the slogans on shopping bags.

It's not just paid-for advertising that besieges the mind, of course. Everyone wants to put in his tuppence worth. The media provide free lodgings for the commercial interests of the PR profession and self-interested pundits, arousing the angst of thinkers such as Saul Bellow:

> TV, politicians, entertainers, academics, opinion makers, porn videos, Ninja Turtles, *et cetera*. The list is tedious because it is an inventory of what is put into our heads day in, day out. Our consciousness is a staging area, a field of operations for all kinds of enterprises, which make free use of it. True, we are at liberty to think our own thoughts, but our independent ideas, such as they may be, must live with thousands of ideas and notions inculcated by influential teachers or floated by "idea men", advertisers, communications people, columnists, anchor men, *et cetera*.[2]

So why haven't we all gone ga-ga? Some observers maintain that Western PR-driven society is indeed a bit scatty, but it would seem that most of these messages are simply ignored. Evolution has provided us with a pretty efficient sensory filtration system which is attuned to our survival. Like animals prowling the jungle floor, while we are bombarded with sensory perceptions, we concentrate on those which are of self-interest. And the more immediate our needs are, the more alert we are to the signals. One doesn't take much notice of policemen, taxicabs, public lavatories, or fire exits. Except when one needs one. Manufacturers of pain relief products don't need to lure us with sophisticated advertising bombast and sleight of hand. The tiny ad placed in the corner

---

[1] Winston Fletcher, *How to Capture the Advertising High Ground*, NTC, 1994.
[2] Saul Bellow, Something *to Remember Me By*, Secker & Warburg, 1992.

of your newspaper with a simple headline such as "Haemorrhoids?" will be invisible to most people most of the time. But if you happen not to be sitting comfortably, the odds are your eye will notice it.

Another key to survival is to keep watch for the unexpected, so unusual signals are also likely to penetrate our consciousness. Even through the shutters of sleep odd noises and sensations are woven into dreams. And so there is a sixth sense which man has developed to a far greater degree than other animals: curiosity. Wonder about our world and the urge to manipulate it is instinctive in all mammals, particularly primates. It's another result of evolution. An immobile green frog in a green landscape is invisible. If it leaps, or turns red, it will be noticed. So, if a message is different from what is expected, it will be rewarded with a flicker of attention. To resolve curiosity. It is why we keep turning the pages in a banal novel, listen to *The Archers*, and like to gossip. To find out what's new. Novelty has a magnetic attraction; when we see the word "new" in an advertisement it's hard not to read just a little further. Where products themselves are new and different, they will catch the eye without the need for extravagant decoration – the first ballpoint pen, the first digital watch, the first mobile phone. But as most products are alike, the advertiser's resort is to make the communication unusual: the boring old frog turns red. The signal will be perceived, but unless you want to mate with this frog, or eat it, the perception will remain uninteresting. With repeated exposure it will become part of the background: you now know there is such a thing as a red frog; its usefulness, however, is undemonstrated and the novelty fades.

Thus, there are two ways in which advertising can penetrate the barrier of selective perception. It can be personally and immediately relevant, or it can simply be unusual. Sex appeal, advertising's favourite "come hither", has elements of both and is always a reliable head-turner. Because most advertising "creatives" feel most products are boring, they rarely try to make them personally relevant by tapping whatever inherent interest they may have. Instead, they go to absurd lengths simply to attract attention.

A tedious technique known as "teaser advertising" deliberately withholds information to arouse our curiosity. Posters are its favoured medium, because the campaign is conducted outdoors, entering unbidden into our public lives, thereby gaining both topicality and "street cred". They're something to talk about, and can generate, as "Amy" unquestionably did, that most prized advertising bonus, word-of-mouth publicity. Teaser campaigns aim to create an air of public excitement and stop traffic like a strip-tease artist. A famous one did exactly that. When the picture of an attractive girl appeared on Paris billboards in 1981 promising to take her bikini top off soon, it caused a number of car accidents. Further wing-denting occurred two days later when the same model appeared topless, with the further promise to reveal all soon. A couple of days later she did, but with her back to camera. The point of the exercise was explained by the slogan: "Avenir: the advertiser that keeps its promises". Like Adshel, Avenir owned outdoor poster sites.

More conventionally, advertisers aggravate our curiosity with visual or verbal puzzles: enigmatic messages or images which require us to supply our own solution. The thinking is that this invites the consumer to participate mentally. When the solution is revealed in a following advertisement, he feels clever and basks in his success, inspiring a warm conspiratorial relationship with the brand. After all, sharing a joke is a good way to introduce yourself to someone. Another theory might be that he finds it a pointless intrusion into his life, an irritating waste of money, and therefore, when the brand behind the trumpery is revealed, hates it.

In 1994 the letter O, plus an exclamation mark, blossomed on posters all over Britain. Was it advertising that round mint with the hole, Polo? Or Perrier, which had based previous advertising on the French word for water, "eau"? Nothing quite so exciting. Subsequent blue and green posters showed a photograph of a car with the caption, "the Omega from Vauxhall".

Advertising agencies are fond of "teaser campaigns", if for no other reason than that advertising budgets must be doubled to correct the original impression. This profligate razzmatazz may be appropriate for new car launches, which large sections of the public consider newsworthy events, but few products can claim such a high level of genuine interest. In the mid-1980s a television teaser, a short scene placed at the beginning of an advertising break, mysteriously showed two men in a derelict house. One of them said, "No one listened when they built these. What they needed were homes and not houses". Then the word "Orchard" flashed on screen. After the skein of intervening commercials, the word "Orchard" reappeared, and the two men were indeed now wandering beneath a grove of fruit trees. The revelation that they were now talking about the Midland Bank's new mortgage plan, for some unexplained reason called "Orchard", was perhaps less eagerly awaited by the general public than a sighting of Vauxhall's latest motor car.

Sometimes the riddle is too baffling. When some familiar actors appeared on TV whispering conspiratorially while the message "Have you heard the Wispa?" appeared on screen, the logical assumption was that it was a trailer for the return of the popular police drama in which they had made their names, *The Sweeney*. Viewers may have been disappointed to discover it was just the launch of another chocolate bar from Cadburys. A 1988 teaser poster for a new board game consisted of three words reversed out of black: "Where is UBI?" A woman called the game company Waddington to claim her prize, because her car number-plate was UBI. Wrong. It was not a hunt-the-number-plate competition, and the game was not made by Waddington.

Here's a teaser: which irate consumer said this about advertising teasers?

> It is such a grotesquely extravagant waste of other people's money. With some advertisements, especially those for cigarettes, you have to look at them for half an hour to guess what they are selling. I don't have the time. The only person that does is the person who makes them up. It is too clever by half. If someone tried to do that with my money, I'd kick them in the teeth.

Answer: in a rare display of intemperance, David Ogilvy, one of the most revered creative figures in the history of advertising.

Each new generation of advertising "creatives" rediscovers other desperate measures for seizing attention: the audacity of printing the advertisement sideways or upside down, silencing a radio commercial or showing a blank screen on television. The favourite tactic is to borrow interest from another source, and it can involve extraordinary contortions of reasoning. Over the headline, "How evolved is your long haul airline?" a 1994 press advertisement for South African Airways borrowed the well-known visual metaphor from T. H. Huxley's 1863 anthropological perspective on Darwinism, *Man's Place in Nature*, which shows a procession of three ape ancestors metamorphosing into the skeleton of a human being. In the SAA version, the three primitives were businessmen wrestling with heavy bags by a luggage conveyor, while the fourth strode away with a smaller case. Was the airline was going to tell us something about an improved baggage-handling service? No, the copy burbled about its culinary reputation and wine list. There was no mention of baggage-handling.

Some campaigns are based entirely on nonsequiturs. A 1998 newspaper series for the Corby trouser press pivoted on the headline: "Quote of the day from Corby". For example, "As I hurtled through space, one thought kept crossing my mind – every part of this capsule was supplied by the lowest bidder" – John Glenn. Taking up half the space of this small advertisement, this concept bore absolutely no relation to the product or the copy argument, apart from a feeble diurnal link: "Make every day a Corby trouser press day...". The company had second thoughts and abandoned this whimsy the following year for a campaign which made the straightforward point that a trouser press removes wrinkles, and thus anxieties.

A campaign seeking to raise funds for the London Zoo would seem to offer a wealth of natural emotional appeals. The 1994 advertisements chose instead to invoke a famous Monty Python sketch with the headline "Dead parrots are not funny" over an engraving of the extinct Paradise Parrot. A paintbrush guaranteed against loss of bristles might appear to possess a distinctive appeal. But the 1996 press campaign for Harris No-Loss Paint Brushes confined this promise to the strap-line beneath the logo. Attention was commanded instead by a photograph of a powerfully built man with a menacing glare wearing a kind of leotard with the logo of a slavering dog on the chest. He was not identified, but was perhaps meant to represent a gladiator in a TV game show, and he was holding a cup of tea. This visual puzzle required a headline to explain it: "You're more likely to invite him to afternoon tea than lose bristles from a No-Loss Paint Brush".

People, even ordinary people, are usually seen as more interesting than products, even extraordinary products. So they are a frequent source of borrowed interest. Pictures and short biographies of real consumers or employees are conventionally used to define the appeal of everything from scotch whisky to faceless companies like IBM. Even dull businessmen can function in this role. Usually it is the job function, rather than the personality, which carries the clout, as in the 1990s "Do you know me?" campaign by American Express, which used informal snapshots and short biographies to profile such hidden luminaries as the founder of Toys 'R' Us. In business-to-business advertisements, of course, this approach is a commonplace, as in this arena leading businessmen qualify as celebrities, the most potent form of borrowed interest.

Advertising borrows ideas from anywhere, even modern art. The artist Gillian Wearing created a 600-picture library of photographs of people whom she had stopped in the street and asked to write something on a card and hold it up. She entitled her work: *Signs that say what you want them to say and not Signs that say what someone else wants you to say*. The most salient was a prosperous-looking businessman whose placard read: "I'm desperate". In 1998 a Volkswagen television commercial appeared which played the idea for laughs: the businessman in this case held up a card saying "At weekends my name is Mandy". As few mass market consumers would be aware of the original work, this is a borrowing of technique, rather than interest, which amounts to plagiarism. Volkswagen neither gained permission nor made a payment, although Levi's, which exploited the same idea in the US, did so.

There is a simple way of establishing whether the interest in an advertisement is on loan from somewhere else. Open your weekend colour supplement, or any magazine, and cover the brand names with your hand while you look at the advertisements. Could the same idea be used just as appropriately for another brand – or even another product category? A campaign becomes a brand property only if the idea would not work with any other brand name. Most advertisements fail this test.

As "creatives" employed in the industry tend to share the same topical interests, see the same films, and pay closer attention than the general public to advertisements, fads arise and proliferate. The business often seems to be chasing its own tail, with campaigns resembling, even consciously mimicking each other. As fashions shift, so does the presentation of the brand, which conflicts with the need to maintain a consistent image. Worse, the borrowed interest, the cuckoo in the nest, may bring with it unfavourable associations which undermine the very qualities which are valued by the prospective purchaser – the ad may be arresting, but is counterproductive. This is most clearly a danger when the advertisement emphasises negative consequences (see Chapter 15).

GAINING AWARENESS is undeniably the first step towards an effective advertising presentation. Unfortunately, a very large percentage of advertisers and the agencies which create their ads take this reasoning no further. Like a drunk at a party, their entire focus is on gaining attention, without any concern for the impression they're creating. After all, you can easily measure whether an advertisement has been seen and noted. The possibility that the selling appeal may be obscured or even undermined by the presentation is ignored; in any case, that's more difficult to measure.

Yet advertisements which are personally relevant do not have to amaze, tease, shock, or entertain. In the classified advertising sector, accounting for about one-quarter of all advertising expenditure, most of the ads are composed by non-professionals. There is ready evidence that many of these advertisements work: people respond, goods are sold. Classified advertising pages are closely scanned, because people who read them are always attuned to a specific need, whether it's a job or a particular make of car. By and large, all the copywriter has to do is to present relevant information coherently.

Modern industrial society is full of distractions, and so was the jungle. Survival has always depended on distinguishing between relevant and irrelevant stimuli. Consumers become quite practised at this from an early age. Many advertising practitioners aim no higher than capturing attention, using hyperbole, shock, sex-tease, and humour, without any concern for the residual emotional effects of these tactics. Standing on your head or unbuckling your trousers may attract an audience, but however flamboyant the initial display, effective advertising must establish a personal relevance to the consumer. It does this by identifying and exploiting our anxieties.

CHAPTER 9

I CAN MAKE A NEW MAN OF YOU IN JUST 7 DAYS

Involvement

We don't see things as they are. We see things as we are.　　　　Anaïs Nin

AS THE CONSUMER strolls through the global bazaar, past hawkers, heaps of baubles, and gaudy attractions, often his mind is elsewhere, but his nervous system is alert to sensations. While many stimuli are screened out, a whiff of frying onions may set the nose quivering, the sight of a cold glass of beer may lubricate the throat. A strip show stirs the loins, but if the consumer has a headache he may head first to the drug counter. Hunger, thirst, sex, the avoidance of pain – basic biological drives demand urgent satisfaction and the appeals for these products and services are direct and easy to comprehend. Other pitchmen – the shell game manipulator, the fortune teller – are more subtle, but they too tap powerful forces. While physical needs can be sated, at least temporarily, our psychological drives of curiosity and self-regard seem to be constantly engaged in gear. Curiosity is an absolute: we always want to know which shell the bean is under. Self-esteem is a relative measure: one's status is determined in relation to a group, the need to belong to it or to dominate it. As Gore Vidal said, "It's not enough that I am successful; my best friend must fail".

Evolutionary psychologists believe that much modern human angst arises because we have never outgrown a prehistoric mentality:

> Our minds are languishing to some extent in the Palaeolithic. Our hunter-gatherer emotional demands come out in our enjoyment of open fires and picnicking and the psychological satisfaction of keeping pets or filling homes with pot plants ... Football is a compensation for the hunt, combining the elements of male bonding, adrenaline and the prospects of reward.[1]

In 1995, researchers from Georgia State University carried out re-

---

[1] Gustave Milne, *British Archaeology*, 1996.

search on two groups of men while they watched the World Cup final between Brazil and Italy. Before and after the game, which Brazil won on penalties, they took saliva samples which they analysed for testosterone, the male sex hormone associated with virility and aggression. They found that the average testosterone levels of the Brazilian fans increased by 28 per cent, while there was a 27 per cent decrease in the Italian men. The psychologists concluded, "Testosterone, and the feeling of power associated with it, increases as subjects bask in reflected glory and decreases as they experience vicarious defeat".

In the modern landscape, just as in the caves we once lived in, the overriding instinct is self-preservation. The Oxford zoologist Richard Dawkins describes a biological basis for this: the law of total genetic proliferation. Ultimately, he says, it is the survival and propagation of our DNA which matters; we are only temporary vehicles for our genes. Even our species is just a conduit. There is no logic to a gene for altruism; instinctively, we always favour Number One. Nevertheless, natural selection appears to have enabled us to benefit from social experience. Everywhere, man has created civilised social environments which work, more or less, although we need to maintain millions of offenders in prison and occasionally indulge in genocide. In his book, *The Moral Animal*, Robert Wright suggests that conflict arises because social development has outstripped the pace of natural selection. The struggle for dominance has shifted from the savannah to urban amphitheatres; while our mores and institutions have been devised for a civilised model of *Homo sapiens sapiens*, our genes are still churning out hunter-gatherers. A savage breast beats beneath the pinstriped suit. Our envies, our mating instincts, our competition for money, power, and status – all are re-enactments of the pecking-order rituals programmed aeons ago among lower life forms. We can observe these any day on our television wildlife programmes or in a farmyard. Because a female human can reproduce only once a year, while males ejaculate frequently, men have always competed for a scarce resource. Our instinctual drives mimic those of our nearest relatives, the chimpanzees. Male promiscuity and the feminine quest for the security offered by the most successful males are strategies which aim to ensure the survival of our genes.

The basic needs common to our species – for food, clothing, shelter, and sex – have natural limits imposed by our individual capacities. But they are intimately linked to psychological desires: self-esteem, our need for love and for recognition by the society we live in. In the 1950s the depth psychologist Abraham Maslow theorised that beyond these social goals there is yet another level of striving: "self-actualisation", which is our need to give a meaning to life, through spiritual activity, aesthetic achievement, creating empires, or selfless service to others. Self-actualisation is the extra carrot that motivates artists, poets, craftsmen, some demagogues and tycoons and, perhaps, some advertising people.

These desires are limitless and hierarchic. Higher levels drives cannot be indulged until all those beneath have been satisfied. The struggle to establish and maintain our self-identity is never-ending; we need constant reassurance. It is the satisfaction of these limitless desires which drives the engines of production beyond the levels necessary for subsistence, and creates a role for advertising. Like peacocks, men continue to compete for status – and available females – by means of intimidating displays, and career women are discovering ways of adapting to join the fray. A century ago, rivals duelled to preserve their honour. Today, in politics, business, and everyday life they spar with other weapons for the same reason – to save face. In offices the better-educated clash verbally. Out on the street, the less civilised demand visible manifestations of "respect". Winning these conflicts reinforces a sense of personal worth, creating both ambitious leaders and violent murderers. For the rest of us, learning to modulate our self-esteem is Nature's way of helping us to accept the ceiling of our social ambitions.

Many of our decisions – the sports young people play, the deals businessmen make, the postures politicians adopt, the friends we seek, the lovers we take, the goods we buy – are influenced by a desire to strengthen our own feelings of self-worth by signifying our status to others. In modern societies, status signifiers are a kaleidoscope of shifting incongruities. Keeping up with the Joneses is a bewildering task if you don't know where Jonesy's at. Or coming from. We extract clues from the confident images which marketing and the media push at us. There are whole emporia, from Harrods to The Body Shop, devoted entirely to products which burnish our personal image, and entire media, such as the *New Yorker*, in which every advertisement is an exercise in snob appeal. In the past, rich people knew how to behave; manners, like wealth, passed through the generations, and were so institutionalised that arrivistes were quickly enlightened. The wasteful strategies of "conspicuous consumption" which were evolved to flaunt an "invidious comparison", as identified by the American economist Thorstein Veblen in *The Theory of the Leisure Class,* were apparent to all: great mansions and lavish entertaining. The much more numerous affluent classes which have emerged in the late 20th century don't know how to be rich. Today successful men and women are uncertain about how to affirm their social position in a way which clearly distinguishes them from the less fortunate.

With increasing democratisation the strategies of "invidious comparison" have become far more complex: what you wear, where you go out to eat, which trends you are aware of, even whether you get the joke. A 1999 advertisement in the *New Yorker* for Virtual Vineyards paid obeisance to the power of social conformity (and may have set a lot of teeth on edge amongst the gullible) with the *faux* rebellious headline, "Feeling naughty? Have red wine with fish".

All advertising preys on these social anxieties. No one is immune. While his kids feel ostracised if they're wearing the wrong football strip, the striving businessman is fearful of not having the right opinions. The long-standing campaign for the *Financial Times*, "No FT . . . No comment", portrayed him squirming in embarrassment because he has failed to read the acceptable newspaper. A 1998 advertisement for *The Economist* probed social insecurities by demanding, "Would you like to find yourself sitting next to you at dinner?", while its television version showed a man luxuriating in his business class airline seat until he discovers that his conversational partner for the next few hours will be the intimidating presence of Henry Kissinger. For modern man, as for his ancestors, the danger of a bigger ape swiping your banana means you have to be careful where you sit:

> The psychological origin of inequality, as Rousseau brilliantly sketched it in the Second Discourse, comes when "solitary" man begins to assemble and finds that the strongest, the handsomest, the best dancer and the best singer get an undue share of the goods. Envy begins to show its face. In order to be like the handsomest or the most artful, the others begin to dissemble, cosmetics are used to mask the rough and the ugly, appearances begin to count for more than reality. If consumption represents the psychological competition for status, then one can say that bourgeois society is the institutionalization of envy.[2]

However artificial the social games we play, the rewards to be gained in such competitions are real, and may even have a biological effect. In a 1950s Canadian experiment, rats pressed a lever to spark electric stimulation through electrodes attached to their brains. Some pressed it thousands of times, until dropping from exhaustion. Like rats, we have a primitive section of our brain which rewards certain actions with pleasurable experiences, activities such as eating and sexual reproduction, which are too important to leave to conscious control. Some drugs

---

[2] Daniel J. Boorstin, *The Image: A Guide to Pseudo-events in America*, Atheneum, 1961.

work by hijacking this system, training brain cells to learn new behaviour. This adaptation works in the same way that pumping iron will habituate your muscle cells to make more protein and thus build up muscle bulk. Addiction is a form of adaptation. Alcoholic addiction, for example, is the result of chronic changes in the brain's circuitry effected by bombarding it with the chemical ethanol. By rewarding the unthinking primordial brain, the process circumvents the higher reasoning power of the cortex. The theory behind Alcoholics Anonymous, is that good habits, such as abstinence, become established in the same way. By habitually offering a compensating reward, such as feeling good about oneself, they chemically change the molecular structure of the brain. If this is so, is the same true of shopaholics? If the constant feel-good stimulation offered by subtle status rewards affects our brains, it explains shopping as therapy and we may conclude: consumerism is addictive.

What is the best way to communicate to this anxious bundle of primitive urges that is the human beast? Unless the recipient of the message has been deprived of free will – a helpless child, a prisoner, a soldier, or the inhabitant of a totalitarian state – a command, an injunction, or an exhortation will have little effect. Free people do not absorb dogma like dry sponges. The mind is not a blank mental slate waiting for an inscription. It is a complex web of feelings, attitudes, and prejudices. It is cluttered with received opinions and popular clichés. It is far more likely to believe, as one memory test showed, that librarians are serious than that they are pretty.

People react only to stimuli which carry personal relevance, interpret them in the light of their experience, reject those they can't use, and respond to those which tempt them. If they have already formed opinions, in the interests of personal consistency they will be minded to defend these views against contrary claims. It is hardly surprising that, apart from their possible entertainment value, the messages of most advertisements seem to be of little interest to most people most of the time.

Yet advertising can use the obstacle of pre-conditioning as a vaulting horse. The trick is to establish empathy with the intended recipient and then invite him to complete the message in a meaningful way from his own experience. The consumer enters into partial ownership of a fresh idea – and welcomes it into his credo. When the Democrats campaigned against Richard Nixon in 1962 he had already accumulated a reputation for deviousness. In his televised debates against John F. Kennedy he looked unshaven and ill at ease. Had his opponents launched a smear campaign claiming that Nixon was dishonest, they would have run head-on into entrenched attitudes, including a sense of fairness, and not just from Republicans. Still, Nixon clearly *looked* dishonest. So they circulated a photograph of the candidate appearing particularly blue-jowled and shifty with the caption: "Would you buy a used car from this man?" It was left to the voter, drawing on his past impressions – both of the candidate and of used car salesmen – to complete the message.

Personal involvement like this is fundamental to effective persuasion. Because we are so curious it is not difficult to create involvement. We love stories, we are "dying" to know how things turn out. When we hear the punchline of a joke, we laugh. Arthur Koestler attributed this reaction to the explosive release of pent-up energy created by the tension of our vicarious involvement in the situation. We share the emotional predicament of the protagonist. Koestler's marquis (Chapter 5) escaped from the bishop's affront to his masculine pride with a single bound, by leaping into another context. We jump with him, and laugh with relief.

An effective advertisement, like a good joke, trades on common assumptions, using a kind of in-group shorthand. Many successful ads seem incomprehensible to the outsider because they are precisely targeted on the perhaps somewhat arcane experiences of a particular group. If a brand is well attuned to its audience, it doesn't even have to mention its name; the consumer will fill in the blanks. Visitors to London in recent years have seen posters for two famous musicals on the backs of buses. One showed the eyes of a cat and three words: "New London Theatre". The other showed a partial face mask and "Her Majesty's Theatre". The tourists already knew what shows they wanted to see; by solving this little puzzle they played a part in reminding themselves.

Cigarette advertisements, constrained by strict prohibitions, were recognisable by a mystifying illustration appearing together with a warning against using the product. Many non-smokers would have been unable to identify the brand advertised in Britain by a picture of a red motorcycle, the only splash of colour in a bleak monochrome Kansas landscape, or a red traffic light and a skyline of the seedier part of Manhattan, or an overalled American with a sunburnt neck standing by his pick-up truck. The message had been reduced to its essential: the dominant colour used on the pack and some associated imagery – in the case of this brand, rough-and-ready, independent-minded, and American. The advertiser was hoping to arouse a sense of knowing personal involvement amongst those willing to try to solve the puzzle.

In advertising, as in chatting up, the first step is an effective introduction. The aim is to establish rapport – a mutual interest. And what most people are interested in above all else is themselves. Outside a shop in the Tottenham Court Road the Church of Scientology attracts young passers-by with a sign set up on the pavement. Religious conversion is the service on offer, but the sign does not mention it. Instead it offers a free "Personality Analysis and IQ Test". Rigid conformity is advertised by an appeal to individualism. A 1996 military recruitment poster involved the same perversion: "Do you have the strength of mind to join the Royal Marines?" We are all sensitive about our age. "Over 50?" read the headline of a small 1998 press advertisement for Saga Home Insurance. It would guarantee at least a glance from anyone of that age. (The ingratiating illustration, of course, showed a vigorous couple with dyed hair, looking about forty. Conversely, if an advertiser wants to appeal to 4-year-olds, he will show kids of 7 or 8 in his advertisements.)

While observing a crowd at an airport, Marlene Dietrich allegedly remarked to her daughter, "Look at how many ugly people there in the world. No wonder they pay *us* so much money". The admass – the people most advertisers are talking to – is not nearly so comely as a throng in an airport terminal. A more appropriate cross-section of the traditional focus of the British advertising industry, the young C_1C_2 families with rising expectations, would be the milling masses on a cross-Channel ferry. Few of them look like the people they see in television advertisements. Advertising appeals to our idealised perceptions of our own potentialities, and in this hall of elastic mirrors no image over-stretches credulity: we are taller, stronger, more attractive and confident, and forever young. Whatever the personal reality, few of us have difficulty projecting ourselves into the images which advertising sets out before us. Almost all advertising is aspirational. Models are beautiful, cars whiz down open roads or park in front of stately homes, people bounce with health and joy. If we buy those images, we flag them to others through the clothes we wear, the cigarette packs we carry, the brands we use.

Our images are self-selected to reflect our unique personality. Most people attach great importance to their individuality – their family heritage, their allergies, their star sign. However, few individuals in any culture want to stand alone for very long. Whilst insisting on our individuality, most of us, most of the time, are driven by strong pressures to conform. We have a basic need for the approval of our peers. We select our own peer group, and that's the one that matters, whether it's the kids in our class, the crowd at the golf club, or our colleagues at work. We construct our self-image to suit the expectations of these groups.

Persuasion must always appeal to that self-image. A small advertisement which appears irregularly in quality British newspapers offers a correspondence course to improve memory. It shows a photograph of a frowning but good-looking executive in his 40s, under the headline: "IQ of 145 and Can't Remember?" Far less than 1 per cent of the British population meet this criterion, yet the firm has run this advertisement in mass circulation newspapers for decades. Presumably the rest of us have little trouble identifying with genius. Another coupon response ad, from Royal Insurance, knows as surely as we do where blame always resides. Its headline: "I'm a careful driver but I keep getting hit by other drivers' mistakes".

As the consumer's perception of himself is irrational, he can have his cake and eat it too. A noble self-image can provide excuses for self-gratification. An American advertisement for a new Chevrolet swiftly twisted political correctness into self-indulgence without a trace of shame: The headline avowed, "Even in the caring, sharing '90s, you can still use a little personal space". The copy continued, "After all the time you've spent raising your sensitivity to the needs of others you could probably use some time for yourself..." The headline in a UK press ad for the sybaritic paradise Club Med stressed, "It's time you spent some time with your children", and showed a loving Dad cavorting with his young daughter. The copy went on to extol the child care facilities, while the illustration showed an empty tennis court waiting for Dad in the background.

Some advertisers risk a bare-knuckled confrontation with the self-image. Since the 1920s, when "Charles Atlas" began to run ads for body-building correspondence courses which offered you a new body in seven days, a red-blooded vein of advertising has aggressively tapped the American passion for self-improvement. As foot-in-the door encyclopedia salesmen have done for years, a 1994 press advertisement for a CD ROM, the Microsoft Encarta multimedia encyclopedia, hawked its wares with a personal challenge verging on ridicule: a little girl chirped, "C'mon Dad, tell us about Sartre and existentialism". Daks of London advertised its traditional English sports jacket by showing the conventional handsome model posing with a classic Purdey shotgun and the headline: "If you don't like it you're obviously a pheasant," clearly a play on "peasant". What are the effective limits of mockery? British self-esteem is tightly bound to class status, which is expressed through the appropriate choice of clothing. If an advertiser takes the mickey out of the conventions which underline class and classical fashion, the whole in-group comes under attack.

Nevertheless, advertisers are fond of making fun of the consumer (though less inclined to make fun of themselves). It may not be the behaviour recommended in their sales training manuals, but it's good for a laugh. In the mid-1990s the fashion turned to ridiculing aspirations. In an effort to ingratiate themselves with the presumed prejudices of their target consumers, television commercials took the form of mini-dramas poking fun at the kind of person their product was *not* intended for. The suburban middle-aged couple got a drubbing: the dreary folk who got up the noses of the liberated Maxwell House Coffee lovers, the jealous frumps who disturbed the idyll of the cavorting Häagen-Dazs ice cream lovers by banging on the ceiling with a broom handle, the mouldy oldsters whose vegetables marched out of the fridge because it was the wrong make. Audi was particularly particular. Its 1996 colour supplement campaign featured an aspirant lower-middle-class family of six in their lounge furnished to 1950s tastes, with the headline, "They don't fit in". The text made clear that it was not the size of the family the car couldn't accommodate, but their lack of adventurous style. In 1994 Volkswagen jeered at acutely felt status concerns in arch commercials fitting various of its models to social stereotypes. The economical Golf Match was paired with a fat, northern sales representative who attempted to justify to himself the value of a company car which cost only "ten measly grand".

Exploiting presumed prejudices is a dangerous business. The intended consumer may not be as opinionated as the advertiser believes, or his self-image as a fair-minded person may resent the sneering attitude of the presentation. Other consumers may identify with the reviled stereotype, yet nevertheless be in the market for the product. They will be offended, or at least highly confused. And for anyone else not immediately in the market, the advertiser is creating a reputation for gratuitous intolerance.

PERSUASION must in every case involve the self-interest of the consumer. He or she will usually define this with reference to his or her peer group. Most advertising fails because the self-interest of the advertiser patently gets in the way. And often, because the people who create and approve advertising are too self-referential, and mistakenly assume that the experiences and attitudes of the target group – particularly an alien group – say, toffs or businessmen or suburban couples – are much like their own.

Effective advertising must always appeal to the consumer not as you think he is, nor as he actually is, but as *he thinks he is*.

CHAPTER 10
GUT FEEL

Emotion

In enumerating the factors capable of making an impression on the minds of crowds, all mention of reason might be dispensed with, were it not necessary to point out the negative value of its influence ... Logical minds, accustomed to be convinced by a chain of somewhat close reasoning, cannot avoid having recourse to this mode of persuasion when addressing crowds, and the ineffectiveness of their arguments always surprises them ... The destinies of nations are elaborated at present in the heart of the masses, and no longer in the councils of princes"

Gustave le Bon, 19th-century French sociologist, in *The Crowd: A Study of the Popular Mind*

NIGHT AFTER NIGHT, at a Broadway cinema in Manhattan in the late 1950s, you could set your watch by a certain audience reaction. This was the Schwerin Research Corporation's "test theatre", where advertisements were shown within the context of the same television programme for years at a time. During this period that was a quiz show in which contestants competed for an array of extravagant prizes: entire new kitchens, luxury cars, a Chriscraft motor yacht. The audience viewed the unveiling of these riches without a murmur. But when, during a stunt, the presenter deliberately smashed an egg, a collective gasp rose from the audience. This kind of extravagance they could not handle. It is interesting to conjecture whether there would be the same effect today: is there some deep-seated atavistic feeling about an egg, the symbol of life, or was it that all the members of these audiences, or their parents, had lived through the Depression, and were emotionally disposed not to waste food?

Emotional conviction girds our strongest beliefs – prejudice, religion, love – and governs our often irrational behaviour. Attitudes harden into habits: ways of eating, drinking, smoking, exercising, and taking medication. To change behaviour you need to dissolve these attitudes, and the only solvent is emotion. Medical practitioners have found that, even when one's life is at stake, reasoned argument is of little effect. The patient must be emotionally prepared to consider change, and thereby in the final analysis, must convince himself. In their researches of addiction therapy Doctors Stephen Rollnick, Paul Kinnersley, and Nigel Stott have identified three emotional states leading to behavioural change: "pre-contemplation" (when people simply don't want to know), "contemplation" (ready to consider change) and, eventually, "action". They found that smokers and heavy drinkers advance hesitantly through these stages towards abstinence:

> Giving lifestyle advice seems to form the basis of most discussion of attempts to change behaviour. The logic of this approach seems to be that people lack information, which, if received from a respected source, is sufficiently compelling to produce change. This method can be used in a more or less authoritarian style, but it relies on an essentially paternalistic relationship. The evidence of its effectiveness is not very convincing. Success rates of [only] 5-10% are not uncommon. While some patients seem to respond to advice, most do not. Patients are not uniformly committed to receiving advice, especially if it is unsolicited and not clearly related to the presenting problem.
>
> Another limitation is that it can have a negative effect. A common experience is to find unsolicited advice being met by resistance, taking the form of a "yes, but" dialogue. In their efforts to change behaviour practitioners are likely to be general in their outlook, placing emphasis on the benefits of change, while undervaluing the personal costs. Patients [on the other hand] will look very closely at the personal implications of change and are likely to be concerned about immediate costs while discounting future benefits. Giving advice is limited in effectiveness and can readily descend into non-constructive disagreement ... a patient's motivation to change can be enhanced by using a negotiation method in which the patient, not the practitioner, articulates the benefits and costs involved.[1]

This research presents a useful analogy to consumer decisions. Advertising rarely stimulates an unrecognised ("pre-contemplation") need. However, all of us have a long list of things we are *contemplating* doing "sooner or later": start getting regular exercise, check the guttering, go to the dentist, clean out the car, plan a holiday, service the gas boiler, buy some socks, sharpen the lawnmower, make a will, find out where the umbrella's got to. Anyone, however well organised, who has a job and

---

[1] *Methods of helping patients with behaviour change,* Stephen Rollnick, Paul Kinnersley, Nigel Stott, BMJ Volume 307 17 July 1993, P.188.

children finds it difficult to shorten the list. All of these intentions, grand and petty, short-term and long-term, lodge somewhere on a conveyor belt in the mind. They are all in the "contemplation" stage. Then *something happens.* An exterior influence – a toothache, a rainstorm, a ladder in a stocking, a cold spell of weather, a money-off offer, an advertisement – pops one of them up the urgency scale to action. Sales-oriented advertising therefore strives to increase the priority of the desire which is already there. As with patients, personal emotional benefit is the engine of persuasion in negotiations with consumers, too. Factual content, if any, is necessary only to supply a rationale for justifying a decision to oneself – and to one's peers.

An emotional hook is the surest way of gaining the immediate involvement of any prospect. In 2000 the widest and fastest spreading computer virus yet swept the world. The "love bug" plunged governments, international financial institutions and telecommunications companies into disarray. What headline enticed the world's security conscious bureaucrats, civil servants and middle managers to open this electronic letter bomb? The cyber-terrorist had appropriated an emotional appeal used by successful gold-diggers throughout human history, those "three little words" long the stock in trade of those practical psychologists, the writers of popular songs: "I love you".

It is a cliché that the British repress emotion, and like most clichés, this popular belief has accreted around a kernel of truth. The people who create advertising in Britain, certainly, seem to find emotional appeals embarrassing, apart from the special case of advertising on behalf of charities. They are much more comfortable in an attitude of ironical disparagement. While American advertising wallows unashamedly in emotion, often with great impact, British advertising people generally deride such earnest efforts as soft-headed and heavy-handed. Certainly, America is a culture in which blatant appeals to emotions are less taboo, yet the great British public, as opposed to advertising people, also seems to have an insatiable appetite, not just for fast food, but for much of the warm, gooey sentiment of American culture. And, of course, the immensely popular British tabloid newspapers have always shamelessly milked vulgar emotion. Are the British ad people right, or are they simply projecting personal class-bound prejudice?

When British advertisers do venture into emotional territory they don't plunge in like the Americans, but roll their trouserlegs up and stick a toe in the water. Advertisements for British Gas in 1997 showed a white-haired old dear in her kitchen, headlined, "To my friends I'm Madge, but to the gasman I'm Bunnikins". The involved explanation revolved around a password that had been arranged between British Gas and partially sighted people who have trouble reading the identity cards the service engineers carry. The copy managed to be both prim and insinuating: "Don't worry, there's nothing improper going on".

The emotional drive for sexual success is essential to self-esteem and it is also suppressed by our society. Thus it's doubly attractive to advertisers: it arouses desire and when acknowledged in public it commands attention. A 1979 poster for Pretty Polly stockings, featuring a woman's legs with the line "When was the last time a man said you had a great pair of jeans?", caused so many accidents when it was put up at cross-roads in Ireland that it had to be taken down. But sex in advertising is a notoriously unreliable weapon, a bomb which can blow up in your face. Partly because it's so potent it can easily overwhelm any product connection you are trying to make. But also because it is the naughtiness, the smirking, rather than genuine emotional attraction, that seduces most advertising "creatives". So, sex in British advertising usually comes in the form of moist sixth-form daydreams and schoolboy sniggers. Wonderbra enraged feminists in 1995 with a poster campaign featuring busty models with headlines such as "Or are you just pleased to see me?" and "Look me in the eyes and tell me that you love me". Another proposed headline, "Have you lost your tongue?", was dropped on the grounds of bad taste. The advertiser defended this campaign by claiming the tongue was actually in cheek: the advertisements were reversing traditional roles, putting women in command and treating men as sex objects. It was a new argument to justify an ancient advertising ruse: traffic-stopping tits on public display.

Sexual appeal is relevant to the selection of female undergarments, where it actually plays a role in product selection. But because it's virtually guaranteed to swivel heads, sexual titillation and innuendo is used indiscriminately, in the most unlikely connections. In 1994 a press appearance for Sharp, using a picture of a pile of paper in the unremarkable way that office copier advertisements do, confined innuendo to the verbal. Headline: "The SD-3076. Take its top off and you'll find something that lifts and separates." Copy: "The concept of lifting and separating may be as old as the hills (Ed. surely mounds) in the women's lingerie field . . . ". The same year London buses were being promoted with a nudge-nudge: "Everyone needs something they can jump on". At the same time, a press advertisement for Air Miles showed a couple embracing on a hotel balcony, with a rumpled bed in the foreground. The punctuation-free headline adroitly combined the two British vices of prurience and one-upmanship: "free from AIR MILES a dirty weekend that'll make her THINK you're filthy rich".

On the day that the US House of Representatives voted to start impeachment proceedings against Bill Clinton as a result of the Monica Lewinsky affair, an advertisement for Iceland Stores reproduced a newspaper cutting suggesting that Bill Clinton had influenced the British government to permit genetically modified foods, under the headline "The US President doesn't care what you put in your mouth". It would have been more precise to write "...doesn't care what you eat". But that would have lost the topical sexual allusion to fellatio. To ensure the reader did not miss it, the copy added: "President Clinton may be indiscriminate about what other people put in their mouths. But we are not".

Only rarely are British advertisers more profound in exploiting the emotional appeal of sex. The name of the Scottish Widows assurance society has an obvious anthropomorphic advantage, and when the company eventually realised this by including a winsome young lady in black with a come-hither glance in all of its advertising, it not only gained enormous visual advantage in the grey vistas of financial advertising, it also plucked an atavistic chord in the emotions of its largely male and older target group: the availability of a sexually experienced young widow. In 1992 Häagen-Dazs, an American ice cream with a name famously invented to sound Scandinavian, finally took sex seriously with a series of arty press advertisements, stressing a sensuous connection between naked flesh and ice cream by featuring entwined couples dripping white dollops into each other's mouths. The company claimed a 60 per cent increase in sales and the campaign won an IPA Gold Effectiveness Award. A copycat campaign for Walls ice cream managed to include two powerful emotional triggers in the same ad: sex and children. It showed an image of a woman playfully biting the bottom of a young naked girl. This aroused emotions powerful enough to cause viewers to complain to the Independent Television Commission. Despite the advertiser's protestations that the woman was the child's mother, and the ad was based on the premise that "people have a basic instinct to 'bite' the things they love", the commission was resolute in its defence of British sensibilities, ruling that "advertisements should not portray children in a sexually provocative manner".

The charity appeal is one of the few forms of UK advertising which effectively exploits sentimental appeals; the usual ironic bent of British copywriters rarely intrudes here. It's an easy task, because the cause generally carries social approbation and there is no specific brand competition. Charity advertising often has very high impact, and has provided the launching-pad for many creative reputations. The advertisement which first brought the Saatchi brothers to general notice in the industry was their 1970s poster for the Family Planning Association, showing a young man with a swollen belly and the line: "Would you be more careful if it was you that got pregnant?" The Yellowhammer agency made its name in 1984 with its award-laden poster and cinema campaign for the animal rights group Lynx, directed by fashion photographer David Bailey, showing bleeding animal corpses and the catchline put-down, "It takes forty dumb animals to make one fur coat. But only one to wear it". Emotional appeals to our social conscience work by arousing guilt. An Interflora newspaper advertisement on the occasion of Mother's Day 1995, exercised emotional blackmail: "It's time you thought of your mum". A 1998 example was headlined: "You missed her first words. You missed her first steps. You missed her first party". Then: "Guilty?" A phone number and the promise of same-day delivery offered immediate exoneration. The relief of emotional anxiety is the business of this organisation, and so the job of its advertising is to create it.

Emotional ties like these are strong, but short. They extend only to our family, lovers, friends, and tribe – those whose opinion is important to us because they confer personal status. The criminal Harry Roberts, interviewed in 1992, after spending 26 years in jail for killing three policemen, felt no remorse, because, he said, "It wasn't like someone I knew".

More promiscuous is the affection, strongly felt in Britain, for animals, particularly little furry ones. This is accountable for the remarkable longevity of the anthropomorphic antics of the Tetley Tea chimps campaign, as old as commercial television in Britain, and the blizzard of complaints to the Independent Television Commission when a 1998 TV ad for Levi jeans despatched a rodent called Kevin to hamster heaven. The ITC imposed a late-night-only broadcast restriction and the ad was withdrawn.

THE MOST PERSUASIVE visual impressions are those which appeal directly to the senses. "Appetite appeal" is the strongest motivation for food products. Which is why "Pop" Schwerin used mouth-watering colour photographs of cakes when he wanted to measure salivation rates. Vivid images strike through the eye to arouse the senses of taste, touch and smell, provoking powerful, even visceral, reactions. There is no arguing about the effectiveness of these appeals to the senses: they evoke an observable physical response. In the cinema, they make us wince or gag or gasp. Comedies make us laugh, horror films make the scalp creep, melodrama brings tears to the eyes and porn films arouse us. Aural stimuli too, particularly music, can provoke similar reactions. Psychologist Anthony Storr points out, "Music brings about similar physical responses in different people at the same time ... Arousal manifests itself in various physiological changes, many of which can be measured".[2]

Yet, apart from food advertising, the British advertising community is strangely fastidious about blatant visceral appeals. A 1990 Ogilvy & Mather campaign for Lever Brothers' Radion detergent included a brief but unforgettable scene in which a woman smelled the armpit of a blouse and wrinkled her nose. "People sniffing shirts – truly horrible", a well-known creative director and advertising agency principal, Rupert Howell, winced in the advertising trade press. The campaign topped *Marketing* magazine's poll of "most disliked ads" – conducted amongst advertising and marketing professionals – although the new product captured 8 per cent of the ferociously competitive soap powder market in ten months.

STRONG SENSORY STIMULI affect us physically. They are the most vivid and demonstrable expressions of the emotional conviction advertising can stir. To summarise this section, effective persuasion appeals to the consumer's basic emotional instincts through the self-image, his idealised perception of himself in society, applying leverage to anxieties and prejudices to shift him to a new position. Persuasion works only if it answers the emotive demand, "What's in it for me?" While few consumers admit to being influenced by advertising, or any other initiative, they mislead themselves. Emotionally they happily conspire in their own seduction. The magic wand of advertising creates successful brands which are nothing more than wispy confections of desire and belief, insinuating into consumers' minds hopeful trust in place of empirical judgement. The role of intellectual argument is simply to provide acceptable rationalisations for deep-seated, illogical attitudes and behaviour.

How successfully do the hucksters manipulate our emotions? In the next section we examine the salient techniques used in advertising to see how ably they tap into the wellspring of brand allegiance – our deepest anxieties.

---

[2] Anthony Storr, *Music and the Mind,* HarperCollins, 1992.

PART III

How to tell shite from Shinola

"Let me see the first one again."

CHAPTER 11
A PHONEY THING HAPPENED ON THE WAY TO THE FORUM

Humour

In the beginning was the pun.　　　　　　　　　Samuel Beckett, *Murphy*

IN THE National Newspaper Campaign awards of 1995 a distinguished panel of national newspaper editors, advertising agency creative directors, and leading advertisers was unanimous in its selection of Moet & Chandon champagne for producing the best colour advertisement of the year. According to the award announcement, "They considered what makes a great colour ad. Great colour, of course. Lots of style, excellent artwork and reproduction . . . that goes without saying. But forging a strong message for a brand name as powerful as Moet & Chandon required a blend of quality graphics and memorable words". Those words were: "Should the power of the press be limited? Moet & Chandon think so". Beneath was an illustration, in the style of Mucha, showing workers pressing grapes in a vat.

If you ask any non-professional to write an advertisement, he will start by trying to think up a punning headline. So will most professionals. But if either puts together an advertisement to sell his own property – his car, his television set or his house – in a classified advertising section, it will be a model of product description. Why is this?

An astonishingly high proportion of press advertisements depend on a pun in the headline. Because it confounds expectation, the pun is hard to ignore. To our atavistic senses it's the verbal equivalent of a sudden movement in the underbrush. So it's a reliable way of catching the attention of the casual reader. You don't need it in a classified ad, because the reader is in hunter mode. He's looking for something particular and scans the columns with close attention.

Literary devices have always been particularly popular in British advertising. Rhymes are now rare, but alliteration remains common, while puns are omnipresent. Attitudes towards puns are highly subjective. They can distract or even backfire and, like farts, most people tolerate their own more than other people's. While the reader may thus disagree with the following specific examples, puns can usefully be categorised under the three Rs: routine, ridiculous, or relevant.

Routine puns are the copywriter's crutch. He has nothing to say, but it will make what he writes look like an ad. How many business-oriented ads have you seen with the limp wordplay, "We mean business"? It's the wrist-jerk reaction of the time-pressed hack confronted with an assignment from a boring business-to-business client. Similar examples of routine wordplay are:

- A 1997 poster for Nat West bank with the headline "We've just won Mortgage Magazine's Best Overall Lender" over a picture of a washing-line strung with overalls of various colours.
- A 1995 press advertisement with the headline "Time to prune the cost of home insurance" over a picture of pruning shears. The copy, after a half-hearted reference to gardens getting out of control, eventually gets around to the real story: you can save the 30 per cent broker's commission by dealing with Direct Line home insurance.
- On 1990s tube cards Abbot ale believed it a sufficient brand promise to advertise the fact, in old English script with an illuminated capital letter, that it was "Now in Abbottle".
- The first page of a 1994 double-page magazine spread showed a conventional photograph of a table set for an outdoor lunch in a Spanish landscape, with a bottle of Tio Pepe sherry over the headline "The Spanish know what's real Spain". The advertiser paid as much again for an adjacent full colour page, to add, under a picture of a sombrero, "And what's old hat".

Routine puns often lure copywriters into emphasising the negative. A press advertisement for motor car accessories supported the headline "Halford's take the load off your mind", with an illustration of a heavy load crushing the top of the driver's car. Others are simply verbal dead ends, as in "Wedgwood – wouldn't you?"

The second category, the ridiculous pun, carries a whiff of excruciating embarrassment that may well cling to the advertiser:

- A 1995 Christmas poster for the retailer Books etc: "Where Prices No Longer Reign Dear".
- A 1996 campaign in the London underground for the airline Braathens advertised its flights from Gatwick to Norway with gnomic examples such as: "Norwegian Would" and "I Did It Norway".

- A 1997 billboard for Conqueror letter paper showed a caricatured businessman in a bowler hat impaled on a paper spike. The tortured connection for this grisly presentation was: "Use our paper or on your letterhead be it".

Apart from drawing the eye, the above self-indulgences are pointless, even counter-productive in motivational terms. But some puns are relevant. By inducing the reader to solve a little puzzle, they promote involvement in the central message. Why does a small van have Mr Sam Widge painted on it? Why is a chain of petrol stations called Q8? Why did a 1996 poster for the British Heart Foundation read "Britain's number one lady-killer isn't a man"?

- A tube poster for the London to Cambridge railway line showed the usual graphic representation of a tube line linking those two cities, but without the intermediate stations. The headline was appropriate to the message: "We've pulled out all the stops".
- A 1995 press advertisement for HSBC financial services showed a picture of a tree with the line, "We've got branches in places even we've hardly heard of". A desultory pun, it had been used more meaningfully twenty years previously in a campaign for the Trustee Savings Bank with the headline "Our roots are our branches", to position the company as locally responsive.

The British fascination with the pun is, of course, not confined to advertising. It's a favourite ploy of the newspaper headline writer, and reflects a general irreverence towards and trivialisation of almost anything serious. The trailers which appear before the commercial breaks on Channel 4 News in order to direct attention towards the next news item are invariably puns, nodding and winking to mass culture. On the day Nelson Mandela was released from prison, heralding the downfall of apartheid in South Africa, this news was announced by reference to the game of Monopoly, "Get out of gaol free". In 1994, on the occasion of the kidnapping and murder of an Israeli soldier by the extremist Palestinian terrorist organisation Hamas, a strong stomach and an acquaintance with Latin were required to share the whimsy in the trailer: "Amo Hamas Amant".

Curiously, the verbal pun also appears in visual presentations, where there are far better ways of attracting attention. Many television advertisements are nothing more than an elaborated verbal pun. A mid-1990s commercial devoted thirty seconds to portraying a glamorous, leggy woman in peril, her short red dress riding up her thighs as she slid off the roof of a tall building. There was no voice-over, no explanation, until the camera revealed that it was all happening on a film set. A red Rover car drove into the final frame accompanied by the slogan, "The excitement is unreal".

Other illustrated tricks defy comprehension. A 1995 television commercial for the Visa Delta credit card was devoted to a cascade of verbal riddles. Words or syllables pronounced in the voice-over commentary were illustrated by visual puns: a sculling oar for "or", a man wearing a false wig as the announcer said "to pay". A 1990s press campaign for Pernod hijacked a convoluted cartoon feature which appeared regularly in broadsheet newspapers read by the educated classes, called "Lost Consonants" (© Graham Rawle), which pictured amusing situations suggested by such misprints. One advertisement headlined "He had been warned that Paris was full of dangerous rivers" showed a man in a Renault car stranded in flooded street surrounded by sharks' fins, to justify the pay-off line: "In Paris, you drop the 'd'." Was it really necessary to go to such lengths to ensure that the well-educated readers of these newspapers knew how to pronounce the name of this pastis, or did agency and client simply find it all a good giggle?

Starting with the use of the pun to gain attention, the idea has got abroad that advertising is supposed to be funny. Distracting, even destructive ideas are routinely introduced for the sake of a weak joke. The text of a 1999 newspaper advertisement for Le Creuset's new frying-pan offered a perfectly convincing proposition: because the bottom is ridged, food fried within it will contain less fat. The headline, too, was compelling: "The most effective way of losing weight", except that the copywriter felt it necessary to add three more words: "since the guillotine". Over the photograph of a large, empty frying-pan, the effect of this idea is revulsion.

A 1996 commercial reprised some familiar images, beginning with a girl mouthing a simulation of fellatio of the sort pioneered twenty years earlier by Cadbury's Flake – wetting her lips with her tongue, pouting, daintily removing crumbs from her lips. It was a close-up black-and-white image and her hair and make-up was from the 1960s. When the camera pulled back to reveal her bare shoulders, another cultural reference intruded: it mimicked the well-known photograph, widely published during the Profumo scandal, of the notorious prostitute Christine Keeler straddling a curvaceous Arne Jacobsen plywood chair, and so the assumption was the girl was naked. Finally, the voice-over revealed the point of this pastiche. The ad was for a brand of bread:

"The original granary – it tastes great with nothing on".

In a late 1990s commercial, again shot in moody black and white, we saw a stereotypical old-age pensioner in his mean home with his budgie, his goldfish and a set of false teeth in a jar. As he dressed for a formal wedding, in black and white, the Pete Townshend quote "Hope I die before I get old" flashed onto the screen. The action cut to the steps of a registry office, where the old geezer was with his new bride, a heavily pregnant young blonde. The meaning we'd been waiting for appeared on the screen: "Not Everything in Black and White Makes Sense". In its elaborate visualisation of simple wordplay, this commercial went to great lengths simply to remind viewers that Guinness is black and white, while associating the drink with an image it had been trying to escape for the past forty years – the downmarket tipple of destitute old people keeping warm in the corners of pubs.

Puns are a symptom. The infection is the idea that advertising has to be entertaining and funny. Even if you're selling funeral services. This has spawned a whole genre of advertising conventions which the audience expects, the "creatives" enjoy and the clients accept, or sometimes demand. The very popular notion that people have to like advertising in order for it to be effective is of relatively recent origin and by no means universally acknowledged. A great deal of classic American advertising before the Second World War was based on painful social embarrassment, e.g. "Your best friend wouldn't tell you". Incessant jingles were often extremely irritating. The advertising gurus serving clients such as Pepsi-Cola and the American Tobacco Company believed the way to gain new customers was to wear resistance down by attrition. In 1955, when commercial television first came to Britain, a great deal of American TV advertising was aggressively hard-sell. The British government was apprehensive about public reception of the new commercial service and exerted pressure on the first TV contractors to curb advertising excesses. Concern was so great that in the early years of its franchise Rediffusion commissioned the Schwerin Research Corporation to pre-test every commercial aired on the station. Although Schwerin threw in its usual measurements of effect on brand-switching behaviour, what the contractor wanted to know was simply whether viewers liked the commercial. These data were used to allay government fears, and naturally provided a direction for copywriters.

If the objective of advertising is to entertain, the practitioners have done a good job. In its 1992 survey of public attitudes towards advertising, the Advertising Association reported that three out of four people approved of and liked ads – a proportion that had grown steadily over the past twenty years. The consumer has no difficulty in evaluating advertising. He judges commercials in the same way he judges television programmes. For him a "good" ad is one which is entertaining or emotionally satisfying. That is hardly surprising. After all, the consumer has no vested interest in the more businesslike objectives of the advertisements. Media commentators take the same line. The *Independent* ventured a compilation of the "Worst Ads of All Time" in 1994. Many of them were straightforward sales pitches, enduring campaigns by personalities the writer found unappealing: former "Brain of Britain" Ted Moult pitching Everest double-glazing, TV actor Gareth Hunt selling Nescafé, the actress Nanette Newman promoting Fairy Liquid, and, inevitably, entrepreneur Bernard Matthews appearing in his own commercials for his "bootiful" turkeys (see Chapter 2). This superficial aesthetic prejudice is not surprising. What is astonishing is that professional advertising people share such views. Humorous commercials regularly top the lists in the many competitions in which the advertising industry votes itself awards. Aesthetic considerations also play an important role in their judgement of what constitutes good advertising. In public pronouncements, commercials for laundry detergents are regularly panned, because they are too blatant, or uninteresting. But the greatest sin in the creative handbook is to be uncool. The professionals are particularly scathing about anything unsophisticated, and with poor production values. The all-American Wrigley's Doublemint chewing gum commercials with their innocent boy-girl situations always produce a mocking laugh in British advertising circles.

Even in terms of identifying new trends in their own industry, the advertising professionals have poor judgement. When a new campaign promoting the Renault Clio appeared in the early 1990s, commentators in the advertising industry press found it cringe-making, criticising the sentimental humour of the character portrayals of "Nicole" and "Papa", their coy conspiracies, even the romantic Provençal setting. However, audience surveys nominated this series as the most popular car commercial on television in 1993 and again in 1994, and the advertiser was well pleased, as Renault sales almost doubled during this period. Whether the advertising had anything to do with this was unproved, but it did send the advertising agents for rival car manufacturers scrambling tardily to produce their own romantic mini-dramas.

DOUBTLESS humour can provide a suitable ambience for effective persuasion; however, many advertising professionals have clearly substituted the means as the end.

CHAPTER 12
THEY LAUGHED WHEN I SAT DOWN AT THE WORD PROCESSOR

Visualisation

I have always been suspicious of the cliché about one picture being worth a thousand words... Pictures produce impact, writing adds meaning.

Ladislas (Lucien) Aigner, photo-journalist

Dorothy Sayers's 1930s novel *Murder Must Advertise,* describes the way advertisements used to be put together. First, they were *written.* For example, like this:

> It has a wonderful winning way. It means so much. It costs so little... In it you find the happy answer to thirst. A taste thrill. A quick, wholesome little lift when you need one. It fits so naturally into a pause, from work or play, and leaves you cool and refreshed... Ready ice-cold at eight hundred thousand soda fountains and refreshment stands. Popular demand put it there. Everybody welcomes the pause that refreshes... so will you.

After he had composed his thoughts on paper, the copywriter would ask an illustrator to provide a suitable decoration. The 1930s American magazine advertisement for Coca-Cola quoted above, was accompanied by a photograph of an elegant young lady and a smiling sodajerk.

In Britain, advertising copywriters used to be graduates of the old universities, with degrees in classics – including Dorothy Sayers. They wanted to write novels and saw writing ads as something to do in the meantime. But words have to be read. They are poor transmitters of sensual experience. The development of photography, innovations in printing, and television shifted the balance irretrievably to the visual experience. The golden age of copywriting is dead. Today, Coca-Cola achieves sensory impact with an explosion of colourful images, music, and action. These communications aren't read, they happen. And the people who create them are turned on by graphics, not syntax.

While people will always read something that captures and sustains their interest, in general they read less and less. Carefully chiselled copy arguments linger on in the business press on the perhaps too hopeful assumption that busy executives read a lot – they probably do, but mostly documents, and these must have a single-page summary in the front. You can read long copy arguments on tube platforms, too, where people have time to kill. Everywhere else, inexorably, the power of the visual impression has triumphed. In medieval times the mass of people were illiterate. So stained-glass images and statuary were used to decode the Scriptures for them. Today, the comic book, action movies, television entertainment, and advertising have reverted to iconic literacy.

In the 1996 Reith lectures Professor Jean Aitchison, the Rupert Murdoch Professor of Language and Communication at Oxford University, pointed out the limitations of words: "Language is good at transferring some types of data, especially negative reports, such as 'No buses will run on Sunday', provided the speaker is telling the truth. But it's bad at other types, especially spatial information, and bad at conveying pain or emotion. It's typical of behaviour that is biologically programmed: it has evolved to deal with some things, not others, just as rabbits nibble grass but don't crack nuts".

Imagery, not words, appears to be our natural conceptual tool. A survey of forty eminent American mathematicians was undertaken in 1945 to investigate their processes of thought. Only two replied that they worked out ideas in verbal terms or algebraic symbols. All of the others thought visually. In the words of one scientist: "The words of the language as they are written or spoken do not seem to play any role in my mechanism of thought, which relies on more or less clear images of a visual and some of a muscular type". That respondent was Dr Albert Einstein.

Visual ideas stick in the memory better. While people find it difficult to remember words in isolation, they have remarkable image recall. Researchers who showed 10,000 images to people just once each, found that those people could recognise almost all of them a week later.[1] Even the simplest images can exert profound emotional power. In 1957, a series of gigantic silhouettes of black bulls began to appear on the Spanish landscape, visible from miles away. Painted on each sheet metal bull were the words "Osborne Veterano Brandy". In time 500 of them bestrode the Spanish countryside. In 1988, when a law was passed banning advertising within sight of rural highways, the advertiser simply blacked out the brand name. By that time everyone knew what brand

---

[1] L. Standing, "Learning 10,000 Pictures", *Quarterly Journal of Experimental Psychology*, 25 (1973), pp. 207-22.

the silhouettes were advertising. Now unlabelled, the huge fighting bull with its horns spearing the skyline was blacker, mysterious – a mythic icon. It was rumoured that barren couples made love in the shadow of its massive *cojones*, and in the film *Jamón Jamón* a character scaled its scaffolding to shatter them symbolically. In 1994, when the Spanish transport minister declared that the bulls must finally go, he aroused a storm of intellectual protest. Leading artists described it as a national symbol of Spanish virility. Journalists waxed lyrical: "It is the protective shadow of the fields of Spain . . . in communion with the space it occupies". The political row was eventually won by the Minister of Culture, who declared "the bull has gained an aura only exuded by works of art", and the Osborne advertising symbol was spared as a national treasure.

Successful advertising, like successful politics, depends on reducing complex ideas to simple ones. The simplification is dramatic and usually visual, e.g. the shape of a bull. Even at its best, a television commercial cannot communicate a message of any complexity. Invariably, it draws on the common shorthand of popular culture, history, and mythology, using symbols everyone recognises. Our brains were developed to respond to sensory stimuli, of which vision became the most important. Speech developed much later, while the written word is a thoroughly modern invention which is still not universal. So, people think in symbols because it's easier. Wear a beret in England and you're assumed to be a Frenchman. If you happen to be carrying a loaf of French bread, it's deemed a certainty. National stereotypes are endemic in advertising: selfish Germans hogging sunloungers, laconic Australians in wide-brimmed hats, and naive Americans in spangled trousers. Ask a Continental art director to draw an Englishman and he will produce a figure with a clipped moustache and a rolled umbrella, wearing the *chapeau melon* popularised by James and George Lock, hatters of St James's Street, 150 years ago. You'll see this figure everywhere on the Continent, in advertisements for tea, marmalade, or holidays in Britain. Brief your average British art director on a financial advertisement and his first doodle will be the same figure, although the bowler hat has been virtually extinct in the City of London since the mid-1970s. In Adland a "monster" deal inevitably suggests a visit to Dr Frankenstein's laboratory, and any mention of energy seems to require the presence of a white-shock-haired Einstein impersonator.

One of the visual impressions which attracts us most strongly is the human face and form. While it is easy to ignore a picture of an object, it is impossible not to glance at, for example, a woman's face reproduced larger than life, as in the 1999 press advertisements for Egg, a banking division of Prudential. Yet this is an exception. Take any edition of any national newspaper and examine all the pictures used to support editorial matter. At least two-thirds of them will feature the human face or figure, very often in close-up.[2] Now go through all the advertisements. The proportions will be roughly in reverse: a minority of the ads will show a person. Advertisements tend to feature products, which puts them at a disadvantage in attracting attention within the same environment. Newspaper photographers and editors tend to show people because experience tells them that they have to humanise their story. They know that readers always want to know what other people look like. Why? Recognition of friends and enemies, possible mates and potential competitors, has always been essential to survival. Experiments conducted in 1999 by Tim Valentine, professor of psychology at Goldsmiths' College, London, concluded that human capacity for facial recognition is so quickly learned, so accurate and durable, that it is a plausible substitute for passwords and PINs for use as personal authentication in systems such as automatic teller machines, computers, and the Internet.

An advertising agency art director earns his salt by creating powerful visual images. Typically, his or her overriding belief is that the objective of the advertisement is to gain attention at any price. More profound questions are of scant interest. Most of those who must approve and authorise this advertising share similar views. So, inevitably, many advertising images are irrelevant, distract from the intended message, or completely overwhelm it. Often the link between thought and illustration founders on the ambiguities of language. The British Gas campaign of 1993 and 1994, aiming to convey the idea that you can regulate a gas flame better than an electric burner, attempted to demonstrate the concept of "control". However, instead of physical precision, what it chose to illustrate in a series of vignettes was that British obsession, people exerting *social* control to gain the upper hand in confrontations with others.

In striving to make a connection at a rational level, advertisers often seem oblivious to the emotional impact of the illustrations they choose. Powerful images easily arouse anxieties which conflict with the advertiser's purpose. Absurdly, National Power, which you might expect would be exquisitely sensitive to hostile public attitudes about high-voltage

---

[2] A 1999 study by the advertising agency Publicis examined all editorial photographs appearing in nine British national newspapers over a four-week period. Eighty-nine per cent showed people.

power lines, in terms of both visual impact and suspicions about harmful radiation, chose to introduce itself on television in the 1990s with dramatic imagery derived from H. G. Wells's *War of the Worlds:* electric power pylons stalked the countryside like giant robots, emitting electric flashes from mechanical tentacles.

A television commercial promoting the former Leicester Polytechnic lifted a memorably bloodthirsty scene from a BBC wildlife programme which showed a panicky group of seals desperately flopping onto the shore to escape a voracious piebald whale, which then walloped down onto the beach in pursuit. The allegory expressed by the voice-over commentary was that these terrified seals were actually confident, and had survived because they had a university degree. Applying this kind of reasoning, arresting footage could be used to illustrate almost any argument, and some people have tried. In the 1980s a syndicated television advertising service was launched in the UK under the name TV-Link. It offered a library of secondhand commercials for hire. One showed an orang-utan apparently reacting to a voice-over by making sceptical faces. Originally made for the South Carolina Federal Bank, it had been sold to more than forty other clients in the US and elsewhere, including the German Christian Democratic Party.

The progress of wars used to be measured in sterile propaganda announcements of body counts. The Vietnam War escalated the power of visual imagery. Pictures of atrocities and dead Americans created a revulsion which stopped a war. Ever since, in trouble spots like Somalia, Haiti, Bosnia and Kosovo, real pictures in real time have shaped government policy from day to day. Language has shrunk to the caption or soundbite, vivid words which conjure up an image to touch the senses, like the phrase "the iron curtain" which Winston Churchill used to describe Soviet domination descending over Europe in his Fulton, Missouri speech of 1946. The role of words in advertising today is similar: to encapsulate a distinctive brand identity in a slogan, which is amplified by visual content: "Australians wouldn't give a XXXX for anything else", "Vorsprung durch Technik", "It's a lot less bovver than a hovver", "You've been Tango'd". And as brand differentiation has come to depend more and more on evocations of lifestyle, slogans have descended to vague inspirational Americanised exhortations such as Nike's "Just do it" or Holsten Beer's "Get real". Clients usually insist on adding slogans or "strap-lines" to their advertisements, if only to convince themselves that they are making some kind of statement. Many advertising "creatives" resist them, feeling they are corny and unsophisticated. Levi Jeans and Pepsi-Cola dispensed with slogans entirely, relying on the visual style of their commercials as a badge of identity.

The craft of the copywriter has suffered insult as well as injury. Art directors and particularly typographers, that subspecies which deals particularly with the selection of typography, have little interest in the content of words, which they rarely read. To them, what the text *looks like* is what counts. This is why so many press ads are often unreadable.

A procession of visual styles glides through the generations at a stately pace, new fashions heaving over the horizon with each change of tide of the *Zeitgeist*. The ambience is so pervasive that one can usually date advertisements to their approximate decade simply by their general appearance. The advertisements of the 1970s, flared and ballooned in innocent primary colours, came off the same drawingboards as the Beatles' *Yellow Submarine*. As the millennium approached, the industry appeared to be reviving the iconography of the 1950s: the flat, sketchy style of a Mr Magoo cartoon decorated with panels scissored from pastel-coloured oblongs and naive, curly typography. Over the decades in between, advertising art directors and typographers had been liberated, then obsessed and enslaved, by Apple Mac technology. Typographers were traditionally backroom boys obsessed with fine issues not apparent to most readers, such as the shape and spacing of letters. In the 1990s they stepped into the limelight. Inspired by the chutzpah of the designers who put together avant-garde magazines such as *Face*, they seized the opportunity to flaunt their creative skills, garnishing headlines and sprinkling visual zest throughout the text by changing the type size of some individual letters or words, putting others in a different face or colour, twisting and spinning them, enlivening the message to the point of incomprehensibility.

This explosive typography, reflecting the nervy, clashing, restless idiom of the music video, is designed to be looked at rather than read or understood. It is often defended as appealing to the fleeting concentration span of the fast-forward generation, but now contorts the advertising of even the most staid organisations. A 1990s advertisement for an insurance company, Commercial Union, was embellished with a huge initial capital occupying a full column width, to begin a meandering account of a golf course mishap in the style of *Punch* magazine. This text was entirely in italic, which is notoriously difficult to read in large swathes, and decorated with further impediments to legibility: captions running vertically, reversed white out of black, and the random insertion of boldface, all-caps, and varying typefaces. The company's slogan, "We won't make a drama out of a crisis", was precisely contradicted by the effect of this dynamic typography.

Trendy typographers also dislike conventional paragraphs, which, because they vary in length, may be awkward visually. Where they cannot eliminate continuity by reducing the copy to short individual elements, they are inclined to run all the text together in a solid, unreadable block. An Air Miles ad also dispensed with initial capitals to start new sentences, though it did not go so far as removing full stops to end them.

The argument against these self-indulgent excesses is not simply aesthetic, but physiological. Typographers frequently place paragraphs of text in blocks of dark colour, where they have to be reversed out in white. The human eye finds this extremely difficult to read. They are also often cavalier about scan, which is the length of a line across a page. The brain begins to experience difficulty in comprehension when a line contains more than fourteen to sixteen words. This is why books, apart from picture books, are printed in vertical rather than horizontal format. And why newspapers have columns, rather than simply extending the words all across the page. Serious scan-width problems are the hallmark of the amateur advertiser. You will encounter them in manifestos published by protest groups, for example, where the text may extend the full width of the newspaper. The advertiser might as well print his copy in Sanskrit, because it is impossible to try to read an over-width scan without irritation and brain-pain.

Yet impossibly wide scan also issues forth from major advertisers who employ prestigious advertising agencies. Not just in the small-text legal disclaimers at the bottom of the ad, which are not intended to be read, but in the body text, which presumably is. A 1995 advertisement for Sun Alliance had a paragraph with an average scan of twenty-two words and another for First Direct Bank had twenty-three. These communications appeared in the same issue of the *Independent*, a newspaper with a conventional column width accommodating an average of five or six words. A 1998 campaign by a consortium called "All the phone companies together" contained more than 300 words of information about changing telephone numbers. Across a ten-inch span the chosen type size generated 25 words per line. A 1999 ad for Mazda cars averaged forty-two words per line. A 1996 ad for the international airline TWA ran its text across the full width of a broadsheet page in six-point type. This resulted in an average scan of fifty-four words per line. The initial sentiment of the text, which was reversed out of red, provoking further eye-strain, was: "Your comfort is as important to us as it is to you".

If you are not convinced, try reading the next page, which while retaining the same type size, extends the scan only modestly, from an average of eleven words per line to seventeen.

The instant visual metaphor, and its handmaiden, the visually contorted written message, now dominate advertising. But in downgrading or discarding text, the motivational argument is often lost as well. Readers are only rarely exposed to a rational, reasoned argument, such as the 1998 press campaign for Timberland shoes, which used detail, demonstration, and logic in full-page advertisements to expound on what the manufacturer knows about shoes and create an assurance of authority. New generations have been brought up on television, and their attention spans have been shrunk by slam-dunk pop video presentations, psychedelic club imagery, the distressed design of pop magazines, and the kaleidoscopic imagery of MTV, the pop music TV station, which has erased the boundary between entertainment and advertising. Its content is one enormous commercial, designed to promote music. Amongst the wall-to-wall music videos and fashion and cosmetic commercials, the station ID appears: a metal butterfly lands on a book and spreads its wings, showing the MTV logo, and then a green woman flicks out her long tongue and swallows it. The people who now make TV advertising in Britain have grown up with this stuff.

In both television and press, the visual style of presentation has become the message. Sometimes there is no idea behind it which is capable of articulation. When there is, often the image is so powerful it perverts the intention of the advertiser. Some of the best-known and most applauded campaigns are in this category. Motor-car ads often fail effectively to harness their breathless romantic imagery, such as a vehicle racing in silhouette against a burning cornfield, to a brand name. Others cram so many curious, compelling or grotesque images into thirty seconds that they overwhelm the message. A shotgun blast of images cutting from lightning to polar bear to firestorm to shark actually has something to do with a beer called Grolsch. In 1995 Eurostar announced the rail connection of Britain to the Continent in a TV campaign which resisted the temptation to convey any information about this astonishing event in favour of parading bizarre science-fiction images through a train carriage. It was widely criticised as incomprehensible.

The greatest influence on "creatives" is the cinema. Most are dedicated cineastes, and they scavenge feature films for ideas. A 1990s commercial in which a series of people repeatedly filled an Ariston washing-machine was taken from an obscure Polish film. A sixty-second 1992 television commercial in which a young man wearing only Levi's jeans undertook a marathon journey from one swimming pool to another was the central idea of a recondite 1969 Burt Lancaster vehicle called *The Swimmer*. In a 1999 commercial for Miller beer, the rhythm of a squeaking bedstead

The instant visual metaphor, and its handmaiden, the visually contorted written message, now dominate advertising. But in downgrading or discarding text, the motivational argument is often lost as well. Readers are only rarely exposed to a rational, reasoned argument, such as the 1998 press campaign for Timberland shoes, which used detail, demonstration, and logic in full-page advertisements to expound on what the manufacturer knows about shoes and create an assurance of authority. New generations have been brought up on television, and their attention spans have been shrunk by slam-dunk pop video presentations, psychedelic club imagery, the distressed design of pop magazines, and the kaleidoscopic imagery of MTV, the pop music TV station, which has erased the boundary between entertainment and advertising. Its content is one enormous commercial, designed to promote music. Amongst the wall-to-wall music videos and fashion and cosmetic commercials, the station ID appears: a metal butterfly lands on a book and spreads its wings, showing the MTV logo, and then a green woman flicks out her long tongue and swallows it. The people who now make TV advertising in Britain have grown up with this stuff.

In both television and press, the visual style of presentation has become the message. Sometimes there is no idea behind it which is capable of articulation. When there is, often the image is so powerful it perverts the intention of the advertiser. Some of the best-known and most applauded campaigns are in this category. Motor-car ads often fail effectively to harness their breathless romantic imagery, such as a vehicle racing in silhouette against a burning cornfield, to a brand name. Others cram so many curious, compelling or grotesque images into thirty seconds that they overwhelm the message. A shotgun blast of images cutting from lightning to polar bear to firestorm to shark actually has something to do with a beer called Grolsch. In 1995 Eurostar announced the rail connection of Britain to the Continent in a TV campaign which resisted the temptation to convey any information about this astonishing event in favour of parading bizarre science-fiction images through a train carriage. It was widely criticised as incomprehensible.

The greatest influence on "creatives" is the cinema. Most are dedicated cineastes, and they scavenge feature films for ideas. A 1990s commercial in which a series of people repeatedly filled an Ariston washing-machine was taken from an obscure Polish film. A sixty-second 1992 television commercial in which a young man wearing only Levi's jeans undertook a marathon journey from one swimming pool to another was the central idea of a recondite 1969 Burt Lancaster vehicle called *The Swimmer*. In a 1999 commercial for Miller beer, the rhythm of a squeaking bedstead resonated in the activities of the other residents of a block of flats; the idea was taken from the cult French film *Delicatessen*. The futuristic imagery of the 1920s masterpiece *Metropolis* has been recycled for many products, from lagers to computers. Yet cinema-going is a minority popular culture: only about half of UK adults go to the cinema more than once a year; frequent attendance is heavily concentrated in the age group 7-34. Although most films end up being shown on TV, there is a time-lag for current releases, and most television viewers are unaware of recherché art house films, which means that many artfully contrived filmic references may simply escape many television viewers.

Although in 1998 press advertising still accounted for 52 per cent of all advertising revenue in the UK, and television just 28 per cent, in the onslaught of visual imagery the power of static press advertising has waned. From time to time the Newspaper Publishers' Association attempts to stem the tide with the gestures of King Canute, arguing that newsprint has longevity and can present information in depth. Its 1993 advertising headlined "What the TV ads don't tell you about shampoos" pointed out that, unlike "glossy" commercials, press ads convey product knowledge about details such as pH balance. The clinching argument, according to this campaign, was that in the usual time span of a television commercial, thirty seconds, you can only read aloud about forty-five words. Which is hardly the point. For an example of effective press advertising, the NPA had to reach thirty years into the past for David Ogilvy's famous long-copy advertisement headlined: "At 60 miles an hour the loudest noise in this new Rolls-Royce comes from the electric clock". His fact-crammed approach seems a lost art today. Yet for firms hoping to influence the selection of increasingly mystifying products such as computers, mobile phones, and digital cameras, the provision of straightforward information before purchase is as essential as good after-sales service.

Also neglected is the opportunity to create a quiet, persuasive mood through verbal imagery, for example this 1990s patch of purplish prose for the J. Peterman's catalogue, a regular advertiser in upmarket American magazines:

> He told me about her; told me more than I would have told anyone. They met on the Atlantic coast of Ireland, near Cashel Bay, at a remote hotel. She'd left her husband (a Duke the rumours said. They were almost right). She'd left a note: "Don't worry", it said. "I'll be OK", it said.

It went on in this vein for about 300 words, only two of which, "Norfolk jacket", concerned the product. But every phrase evoked the romantic snobbery which fashion advertisers trade upon.

COPYWRITERS AND ART DIRECTORS used to learn their trade working for low pay on the staff of big department stores, where they had to produce advertisements for daily newspapers and catalogues which moved goods off counters. Now they serve their apprenticeship watching television and going to the cinema. No wonder the emphasis in advertising has shifted from selling to entertainment. Yet something has been lost to the craft. Writing can create imagined images which are uniquely personal in the mind of each reader. Just as radio can. Explicit visuals cannot.

When advertisers have something really important to say, they turn to the press medium, discarding all the usual visual flummery for a straightforward announcement, in words only. That's because they don't want it to be confused with "advertising", which by implication is unrealistic, irrelevant, and unimportant. In effect, they are saying "That's enough larking about, this is serious, so now sit up and pay attention". Typical was the notice issued by Zanussi dishwashers in 1998: all-copy, a spartan layout prepared on a word processor, its only visual a diagram to show where to find the model number on the appliance, plus a telephone number for obtaining a free safety check. Within a context of hyperbolic advertisements, the stark simplicity of the product recall announcement shrieks: "Important".

Visual communication has great impact because it compresses and symbolises meaning; but it is now regularly used in advertising as a substitute for meaning.

CHAPTER 13
SEEING WAS BELIEVING

Demonstration

The little girl bounced up off the sofa and pulled it out to make a put-me-up bed. Time after time after time. Throughout the 1950s, night after night, viewers of off-peak-time television in the New York City area saw a black-and-white commercial in which the Castro Convertible sofa bed unfolded in real time. The sofas sold like hotcakes, and the girl in the commercial, Bernadette Castro, the daughter of the man who owned the company, grew up to run it.

IN TELEVISION's early days advertising people hailed the new medium because of its new power of demonstration, adding motion and sound to vision. The simple sofa bed commercial was a paradigm: the Castro Convertible is so easy to set up a 6-year-old girl can do it in less than sixty seconds. You've seen it happen with your own eyes.

So why is it you hardly ever see a demonstration commercial on British television these days? Partly it's because most brands are alike in performance, and so the emphasis has shifted to attempting other means of differentiation – expressions of brand personality and attitude. And partly it's because the British advertising community disdains the technique, and all direct selling techniques, as unsubtle, hence uncool. They're *trying too hard* to sell the product. The few demonstration commercials which filtered on to our screens in the 1990s tended to be low-budget productions by fringe advertisers, or American derivatives, such as the Head and Shoulders anti-dandruff shampoo split-screen test comparison, which had been on television screens since Bernadette Castro was a tot. Even this campaign was moved to gently mock the genre, by using the new technology to split the presenter himself in half, while two different girls shampooed him with different brands of shampoo.

The power of simple demonstration is that it makes its point with absolute clarity and economy. A 1995 press advertisement for British Meat showed two plates, one with plain cottage cheese and the other with a grilled pork leg steak and the headline, "Which one has the lower fat level?" It is of course the pork steak. A Sony press ad for a mobile telephone so small it could fit inside a box of cook's matches simply showed it nestling inside one with the title: Telephone Box. To emphasise build-quality a 1992 commercial for Nissan heaved the car out of an aeroplane. A 1999 public safety commercial showed in three easy steps how a fireman safely puts out a chip-pan fire, and also powerfully demonstrated why – when the voice-over narrator was revealed as a woman with a face disfigured by burns.

These are exceptions. When a distinctive new product or service does comes along that really should be demonstrated, admen often seem to have forgotten how to do it. When Vauxhall introduced a truly revolutionary "dual fuel" system for the 1998 Motor Show, a range of cars with two fuel tanks which allowed the driver to switch between petrol and natural gas, it did so in long-copy press advertisements without illustrations (as there were only 100 or locations in the UK where you could fill your tank with natural gas, it was more of PR stunt than a serious commercial undertaking).

While straightforward product demonstration remains a stalwart performer in the arena where the test is to actually sell goods right this minute – the televised shopping channels – more sophisticated advertisers, bound by less stringent and less measurable criteria, have the budgets to indulge in subtlety. The difference between the two approaches was exemplified in 1995 when two competing airlines presented the same idea: both now offered passengers more space in business class. British Airways invoked fashionable production values, freighted with misplaced symbolism, illustrating a verbal pun by showing a spaceman lumbering about the interior of the aircraft. The Virgin Airlines commercial simply showed a seated passenger stretching out her legs, with the comment: "If your toes touch the seat in front you're on the wrong plane". It was something which, like Bernadette Castro, you could test for yourself.

While generally disdaining straightforward demonstration, advertising art directors, like many creative artists, are receptive to its cousin, visual analogy. This is Arthur Koestler's theory of creative intelligence in graphic form: what else does this shape or colour remind you of? As Pablo Picasso put it, "A green parrot is also a green salad. He who makes it only a green parrot diminishes its reality".

Visual analogy distorts fact through simile. It is the simple thought behind a great deal of what has been accepted as transcendental modern art, such as Magritte's umbrellas descending as raindrops and Dali's red lobster telephone. It is also the inspiration of kitsch art: teapots presented as country cottages or a watch-face using Mickey Mouse to point the hours. The line between the two is hard to draw, as the avant-garde Italian designer Samuel Mazza demonstrated when he commissioned riffs on the theme of the brassiere from contemporary artists and designers. His exhibition included bras with aeroplane propellers on the nipples, bras as edible sweets, flowerpots, Fiat head lamps, plumber's plungers, globes of the earth, bras with electric switches, bathroom taps sprouting from brass hemispheres, inflated rubber gloves, and 192 other conceits.

Visual analogy is the thought behind a great deal of humour, too. Much of the attraction of the cartoon *The Flintstones* lay in the ingenious Stone Age inventions: the woolly mammoth's trunk as a lawn sprinkler, the gramophone using the beak of a living bird as its needle. It's fundamental to the art of the mime and the Marx Brothers.

From its beginnings, advertising has often been based on laboured visual interpretations of wordplay. A 1994 magazine ad for a pen called the Parker Sonnet showed us the pen and an attractive oriental female violinist. It needed a headline to explain the connection: "Born to perform. Just like a Parker", and it needed text to explain why she is oriental: "The Ambre lacquer is a genuine Chinese lacquer". But visual analogy doesn't need to be explained in words. The campaign which launched the 1993 Nissan Micra dramatised the shape of the car with simple line drawings which looked like bubble-cars drawn by children. It was the shape the manufacturer wanted to get across: not a typical aggressive car, but different, round, and cute.

Visual analogy is a gift for art directors. When they can persuade an advertiser to attempt to "own" a shape or a colour, the advertising message is reduced to a simple mnemonic device, and the rest is money for old rope. The mid-1990s campaign for the Halifax Building Society centred on the letter "X". A series of expensive commercials filled television screens with determinedly cheerful cross-sections of the British ABC_1C_2 population clambering over each other to form various structures of that shape. In the UK alone, Pepsi-Cola spent £330 million in 1996 on Project Blue – their decision to change their cans from red, white, and blue to blue. This earth-shaking event required the repainting of Concord and printing an issue of the Daily Mirror on blue paper.

There is a beverage which, by legal requirement, has no distinctive colour, aroma, or taste. Apart from its packaging, there is no way a consumer can tell one brand from another. How do you sell the distilled liquor vodka? A traditional response is to search for some characteristic of the production process, which though neither meaningful nor distinctive in itself could be stressed as a brand property – in the words of Rosser Reeves, a "Unique Selling Proposition". One American brand of vodka, Cristall, has been promoted as the vodka which is filtered twice through quartz crystals. Other vodkas are made the same way. Whether quartz filtration is, in fact, a better method of producing vodka than using sand or charcoal is a moot point; certainly the person who drinks the product would not know. What matters in this tactic is to produce an apparent difference which can provide a focus for the presentation of the brand and, to the consumer, a rationale for preferring it. To pre-empt a common fact in this way is a time-worn deception; in the 1980s Harp lager tried and failed to revive its flagging fortunes with the claim that it was "precision-brewed", while sixty years earlier the USP for an American beer was that its bottles were "steam-cleaned", a precaution required in all bottling processes.

Absolut vodka, one of the great American marketing successes of the 1980s, chose a less logical route in its advertising. In 1979 it entered a market in which nine out of ten bottles of premium vodka sold had the name Stoli on the label. By the end of the decade Stoli's share had reduced to two bottles out of ten, while Absolut dominated the market. In one sense, its press advertising campaign was a throwback: the brand as hero. The early examples were reasonably conventional booze ads, simply an illustration of a clear glass bottle with a somewhat unusual short-necked shape with the word Absolut underneath. Plus a good deal of copy about Swedish tradition written on the bottle in fine lettering. Later headlines used the brand name as a modifier: "Absolut Perfection", "Absolut Hollywood". Absolutely simple and obvious. As the decade progressed, the campaign distilled to its essence, abandoning the real bottle for surreal impressions in which the shape of the bottle became the point of brand distinction. A typical advertisement showed the bottle shape imposed on a computer circuit board with the headline "Absolut Intelligence" and a few words about making a logical choice. An advertisement relating to the 1994 Olympics showed an overhead view of Atlanta airport presented as a – just recognisable – bottle shape with the two words "Absolut Atlanta". Finally, even the word Absolut was dropped. Absolut ads imposed the now familiar shape on almost anything – the Brooklyn Bridge or a beehive hairdo. The impression which long-lasting campaigns like this succeed in achieving may not seem like very much: they have simply converted a word into a graphic mnemonic – a kind of visual shorthand for the brand. But because it is a picture, it will now be remembered, and the stylish photographs and the media in which they appear bestow overtones of snob appeal. In the battle for consumer preference for a product which is tasteless, odourless, and with absolutely no physical brand distinction, these two factors may well be enough. By relentless concentration on this core idea in prestigious upmarket publications, Absolut vodka established itself as a "badge" product. The consumer reward was not the effect of the drink, but the opportunity to show off one's sophistication. You drank and, importantly, served Absolut because it was the one to drink and serve. Just as you wore an Armani suit, drove a Porsche, and perhaps wore a Porsche wristwatch and sunglasses as well.

In advertising as elsewhere, innovation spawns imitators who transpose the original idea to less appropriate environments, often torturing it to breaking-point. A 1999 press campaign for Ruddles County beer showed a hayrick rolled into the shape of a can with a tab opener. A reasonable tactic, perhaps, for a beer presenting itself as "Country born and brewed". A 1994 Michelob campaign seemed less appropriate. Does it matter that you could, if you wanted to, carve a bottle of beer out of wood on a lathe? Does a bottle of beer really resemble what appears to be an industrial-size spool of cotton with brown thread where the beer usually is and gold thread where the neck label is? Does either ad justify the slogan "a subtle quality"? Do they mean anything at all?

VISUAL ANALOGIES are valued because they can attract attention and create a memorable look for the brand. Advertisers rarely seem to consider their more powerful effect: the adverse associations they can produce. The most obvious are very powerful gut reactions provoked when illustrations tamper with food; literally they leave a bad taste in the mouth. Another advertisement in the Michelob campaign showed the bottle as an illuminated glass base filled with an oily liquid with nasty free-form bits suspended in it. The line "Are you missing something subtle?" pointed readers to the deduction that this was a representation of a 1960s lava lamp. The advertiser may have been missing something rather more obvious. A 1992 American colour advertisement for Maker's Mark bourbon showed the liquor on the rocks, but in an ice cream sundae glass topped with a twirling pyramid of whipped cream and a maraschino cherry, an assault on the stomachs of whisky drinkers and ice-cream fanciers alike.

A 1990s press campaign for Boddington's beer won considerable acclaim in advertising circles for its irreverent approach to traditional beer advertising. However, it sent very confusing taste signals, such as a glass of beer with the foam on top whipped into the kind of frothy ice cream sold from travelling vans. But what was going through the mind of the art director who showed a glass of beer riddled with holes to resemble an Emmental cheese? The answer came in the slogan which completed the ad: "The Cream of Manchester". Cream is a dairy product. So is cheese. Get it? Or do you get the impression that this beer tastes like cheese? Worse was to come. The creamy head of this beer can also be contrived into an oily quiff, with a steel comb laid alongside just it in case you miss the point.

In 1995 the Covent Garden Soup Company replaced the usual steaming bowl of appetising soup with a photograph of its sticky remains in an unwashed bowl, a gnawed crust of bread and four spoons. This was intended to illustrate the idea that soup can be served for all four courses. Marks & Spencer reprised the anti-taste appeal approach in its 1999 press campaign showing only the sticky remains of its seafood terrine and chocolate dessert. Or, you may prefer old man's sweat and dandruff on your sausages. A bizarre 1994 press advertisement introduced "the Famous Porkinson Banger, the first sausage from an internationally renowned photographer". It showed an elderly man who wore on his thinning scalp a crown of fat sausages dangling down his naked chest and looped around his neck like a turban. Referred to as "Parks" in the copy, he was apparently the distinguished fashion photographer Norman Parkinson, and this picture was an attempt to satirise what is beyond satire: the fashion photograph – at whatever cost to readers' stomachs.

The new technology makes it easy to create the impossible. A 1994 television commercial featured a team of all-time Manchester United soccer greats. A contemporary star, Ryan Giggs, scored a goal after passes between ancestral team-mates from the past fifty years, such as Denis Law, Bobby Charlton, and George Best. Each frame of black-and-white film was manipulated so that it would appear they were all playing together in the same stadium, and hand-coloured to match the contemporary red strip and white ball. Its production consumed 600 hours of computer work and cost £1 million, which may seem a lot, as only Ryan Giggs wore a strip advertising Reebok. However, for the price paid to the copyright owners of the film footage, the brand purloined the tacit endorsement of the other players, too. The remaining ten members of this dream team never wore Reebok boots; the great goals scored by Law, Best, and Charlton were booted in by Adidas.

Visual demonstration carries conviction only if it appears to be really happening. Ever since the invention of photography, despots, cranks, and opportunists have sought to deceive by airbrushing people and events in and out of reality. How long will such techniques as visual analogy continue to arrest attention? Now that literally anything can be made to seem to happen, viewers will become increasingly confused about the dividing line between the real and virtual world. For a while this may seem to give the advertiser added powers; in the long run consumers may become less willing to extend credibility to anything they see.

CHAPTER 14
HITCH YOUR WAGON TO AN ICON

Endorsement

A famous 1960s photograph shows Jackie Kennedy laughing while her infant son John-John playfully tries to tug a pearl necklace over her head. The pearls are fake and the necklace has no intrinsic value. Three decades later, when Sotheby's planned its 1996 auction of the personal effects of the late Jackie Onassis, this piece of costume jewellery was estimated at $500 to $700. It went for $211,500. Sotheby's had estimated the total sale would fetch four million dollars. It realised forty million.

CELEBRITIES add commercial value to anything they rub up against, for two reasons. Firstly, they lend extrinsic interest, or "glamour" to the ordinary. Some advertisers exploit this with crude directness. A 1994 American advertisement in upmarket magazines began: "The Duchess of Windsor Wore this Pin", and the text declared, "Now you can wear it too... If made of real gems, this pin would cost over $10,000. But like the Duchess of Windsor, you can own this authentic Kenneth Jay Lane panther pin for just $49.95". More profoundly, celebrities increase worth because they have come to represent certain values in the public mind. By personifying these, they become brands themselves, summarising and simplifying complex ideas which they symbolise more vividly and more persuasively than any intellectual articulation. John Wayne's swagger says more about the he-man values of America's frontier heritage than volumes of political speeches. And, as the *New York Times* commented about the prices paid for the keepsakes of Jackie Onassis, "They are not selling things. They are selling yesterday, when the world was young".

People seem to have an insatiable interest in anyone who has been touched by the fleeting spotlight of publicity: those whose greatest attribute is topicality. Why do we find them so interesting? Perhaps because today we live not in hierarchical communities, but in increasingly separate worlds. Our status is known to our friends, family and colleagues. But if we want to impress others outside this intimate circle, we have to invoke symbols with which they are familiar. Celebrities are the lingua franca.

In his 1961 book, *The Image,* professor of sociology Daniel J. Boorstin memorably characterised a celebrity as "a person who is known for his well-knownness" (later sharpened, doubtless by a media professional, into "famous for being famous"). His inspiration itself came from an advertisement – for a book called *The Celebrity Register*, a listing which the copy described as "the 'names' who, once made news, [who] now make news by themselves". Boorstin distinguishes between the celebrity and the genuine hero, who has achieved something significant, such as Charles Lindbergh:

> The hero is made by folklore, sacred texts, and history books, but the celebrity is the creature of gossip, of public opinion, of magazines, newspapers, and the ephemeral images of movie and television screen. The passage of time, which creates and establishes the hero, destroys the celebrity. One is made, the other unmade, by repetition. The celebrity is born in the daily papers and never loses the mark of his fleeting origin.[1]

The dissociation of fame from achievement reached its apotheosis with the invention of supermodels: people whose value depends on how well they reflect contemporary aesthetic ideals when wearing a costume. Nor is heroism expected from members of the British royal family, who are famous by virtue of having been born. Even minor royals carry great cachet in America, where the former Duchess of York has endorsed cranberry juice and a range of diet products. Is her fame less deserved than that of Eleanor Roosevelt, who in 1928 lent her photograph to an advertisement for Simmons mattresses? At the conclusion of a century in which popular media have fudged the line between fact and fiction, Boorstin's distinction is a difficult one. The leaders of the two great world powers in the 1980s were surely engaged in seriously useful activities. Yet movie actor Ronald Reagan had been the genial spokesman for the General Electric Company ("Progress is our most important product") and Chesterfield cigarettes ("They satisfy") in the 1950s, long before he was selected to play a similar role for his nation. Less credible was the part played by his former adversary, the last leader of the Soviet Union, in a 1997 commercial. Mikhail Gorbachev thought it was worth debasing his reputation as an ex-world leader for, reportedly, the best part of $1 million, to feature in a skit set in his country where a debate on his contribution to the Russian political economy was settled by a female supporter who declared, "Because of him we have things like Pizza Hut".

---

[1] Daniel J. Boorstin, The *Image: A Guide to Pseudo-events in America,* Atheneum, 1961.

Many politicians who have established vivid reputations have become advertising endorsers. In 1997 alone, Nigel Lawson, Ken Livingstone, Denis Healey, and George Bush joined Gorbachev as television hucksters. Celebrities sprout wherever the limelight lingers: in politics, sport, entertainment, high society, and increasingly, the media which present these activities.

Why would the health insurance plan HSA employ a minor celebrity, Olympic Gold Medal rowing champion Steve Redgrave, in its 1998 posters, simply to point out that he's a customer? Yes, he looks brimming with good health, but what's the connection? Often there is none. Being well known, celebrities are assumed to be successful, and they bestow a halo of success on anything in which they partake. Magazines have long known that the best way to boost sales is to feature a celebrity on the cover. (They can afford to because legally the rights to a negative belong to the photographer, not the celebrity.)

At the peak of their fame very popular celebrities can sell almost anything. In postwar Britain the face of cricketing star Denis Compton, though not particularly handsome, beamed down from hoardings everywhere. His record-breaking performance as batsman brightened a drab, rationed world, and so one slogan read "Men people look to – use Brylcreem". Compton was a totem of broad general appeal, embodying a kind of latter-day royal warrant. Exclusive shops like Asprey gained endorsement for their goods "by appointment to His Majesty King George VI", but the man on the Clapham omnibus deferred to the king of sport. Compton was paid £200 per year for the use of his reputation. By the early 1990s, Coca-Cola and Pepsi-Cola were fuelling the soft-drink wars by lavishing millions of pounds on celebrity endorsements. Pepsi recruited Michael J. Fox, Tina Turner, and Michael Jackson. Coca-Cola retaliated with Jerry Hall and Elton John. At the height of his fame the latter was known to be so expensive that his sponsorship of Diet Coke dispelled rumours that the company might discontinue that variant of the product.

Celebrities are rarely seen as whole human beings, but as shorthand caricatures. Sometimes their appeal can be encapsulated in a simple vivid image or catchphrase: Charlie Chaplin's bowler hat and cane and bow-legged walk, Mae West's "Come up and see me sometime". These are the equivalent of a brand's trademark or slogan. Audiences do not want to see their personalities develop. They demand more and more of the same. Advertisers want to use them because of what they represent, not to offer anything strikingly new. And so celebrities quickly become typecast: each fresh appearance reinforces the same image. While superstars may have a somewhat elastic appeal, every celebrity has a particular area of greatest perceived competence.

A new type of liquid shaving-cream in a tiny bottle sold at a high price had a claim which invited disbelief: you only need to use a few, almost invisible drops. To gain credibility, England rugby captain Will Carling was used to endorse the product, not only because rugby players are macho, but because, as they let their whiskers grow before matches, they know about tough stubble too. A new kind of fundraising charge card launched by the Charities Aid Foundation used as its spokesman James Fox, an actor less famous for his acting than the fact that he dropped out of the profession in the 1970s to join a monastic order. Though Americans don't easily identify with losers, the pharmaceutical company Pfizer made an astute choice when it selected Bob Dole, the unsuccessful 1996 Republican presidential candidate, to front a 1999 American advertisement aiming to dispel the embarrassing stigma surrounding erectile dysfunction. Bob Dole, vanquished by the priapic Bill Clinton, had publicly admitted to this problem, and although the product wasn't mentioned in this apparently high-minded appeal, Pfizer markets Viagra.

But celebrities are often used more clumsily. A 1998 press ad for the Citroën Xsar interspersed photographs of the car and supermodel Claudia Schiffer under the headline, "What gives Claudia Schiffer confidence?" The copy drew analogies between her construction and that of the car. "Could it be her body? ... Could it be her side profile? ... Or could it be her rear?" And even, though this was an unlikely allusion for a scrawny supermodel, "Could it be her airbags?"

Comedians are popular endorsers; they have broad appeal and their performances have established a singularity of character. Leslie Nielsen, the star of the dumbed-down *Airplane* and *Naked Gun* films, was perhaps an appropriate selection for the Red Rock cider commercials which won awards in the mid-1990s, because his irreverent, zany antics formed the whole basis of the appeal of the brand. But the pratfall can be a pitfall. The anarchic qualities of the comic are not always in sympathy with the personality of serious brands. Whenever Rowan Atkinson appeared in a commercial, the audience instantly recognised the supercilious anti-hero of *Blackadder* and the nasty, accident-prone *Mr Bean*. Through the one-upmanship humour of his long-standing campaign for Barclaycard in the 1980s and 1990s, the bank wilfully associated itself with a character whose arrogant and venal schemes always ended in ignominious failure. These advertisements were very popular, but what was the effect on the bank's image? Equally, George Cole, the actor who had achieved fame playing a devious conman, Arthur Daley, in the highly popular TV series

Minder, seemed an odd choice of front-man for the financial products of the 1990s Leeds Building Society. The much-loved 1970s campaign for Cinzano, which attempted to position the brand as a more sophisticated tipple, gained its laughs by using the comic actor Leonard Rossiter to portray the Cinzano-drinker as a smarmy oaf who spills the drink over his crotch, though the balance was perhaps retrieved by casting the sophisticated Joan Collins against him.

Celebrity endorsement loses its sparkle if it is perceived as personal aggrandisement or an attempt to revive fading popularity. It can self-destruct if the personality later fails to live up to the public image or offends public decency. In the US, rankings of celebrity appeal are published regularly. Burt Reynolds was one of the nation's favourites until 1994, when he dropped off the list completely after publicly suggesting to his estranged wife that they settle an alimony dispute by taking lie-detector tests to discover who had committed adultery first. In 1992 Sony signed a contract worth billions to hire Michael Jackson, who commanded the hearts and minds of hundreds of millions of fans all over the world. But the mojo stopped working for Michael two years later, when a court action in the US brought his sexual habits to public attention, and the sponsor dropped him.

Promiscuity devalues the currency of celebrity. The managers of instant marketing creations like the Spice Girls, mindful of pop music's short product lifecycle, slap their names on as many products as they can as quickly as they can. In contrast, as the most highly prized (and priced) celebrity endorser of the 1990s, the American basketball player Michael Jordan, carefully chose the brands he associated with, such as McDonalds and Coca-Cola, while rejecting others, and so acquired an all-American symbolism, thus adding a new facet to his glory.

"Celebrity brands" short-cut the lengthy process of building up brand value by cashing in on the perceived personal qualities of the celebrity. Success is not automatic: amongst those who have tried and failed to convert their image into a branded product are Julio Iglesias, Sophia Loren, Cher, Bjorn Borg, Michael Jackson, Joan Collins, and Princess Stephanie of Monaco. However, when personality and product are well matched, the brand promise is clear and powerful. Film star Paul Newman has successfully marketed salad dressing and other food products under his own name since 1982. The rationale is that his friends liked the sauces he served at dinner parties so much that they wanted to buy them, which fits well with his easy-going, home-loving image. Prince Charles licenses a range of biscuits called The Prince of Wales Duchy Originals. Perfume is the most attractive field for personality brands, because it is sold exclusively on glamour. The more closely the star is involved, the greater the chances of success. Elizabeth Taylor's brand, White Diamonds, succeeded because of her willingness to make personal appearances at department stores.

When a celebrity is so closely associated with a product, it takes on all his or her attributes, for better or worse. Celebrity brands can crumple as quickly as they flower. Helmsley Hotels were established by Mrs Helmsley, a wealthy New Yorker of considerable *chutzpah,* and their advertisements traded on her fastidious attention to detail for the comfort of her guests. After her famously indiscreet public remark, "Only poor people pay taxes", she was sent to prison for income tax evasion in the early 1990s. Many companies might have considered changing the name of the hotels. But the Helmsley chain reasoned these events had only burnished her reputation for bloody-minded intransigence. Mrs Helmsley no longer appeared in the advertisements but her spirit lived on. To anyone unacquainted with her history they would have been incomprehensible. The new headline read, "Say what you will, she runs a helluva hotel". The copy reassured readers that "details are constantly polished, perfect and inspected to make sure we always satisfy you. And you-know-who". The only mention of the tyrant in question appeared in small print: "While Mrs. Helmsley doesn't personally operate or manage the Helmsley hotels, the high standards she has set are meticulously kept".

Advertisers sometimes attempt to avoid real-life problems by creating fictional celebrities. "Beatie", the Jewish mama played by Maureen Lipman, was invented by British Telecom (BT) in the 1980s. In BT's playlets based on Jewish stereotypes she became one of advertising most recognisable characters. While "Beatie" was immensely popular, not everyone thought these characterisations were harmless fun, her role began to overwhelm the commercial message, and she was eventually replaced in 1993 by advertisements with less edge. Or, as BT's marketing director put it, "The character has become too strong and it's impossible to use that vehicle subtly now".

Where the fictional creation is the name used for the brand it has a much longer useful life than a mere human, and its image will have to adapt to evolving consumer attitudes. Aunt Jemima was the invention of a Missouri businessman who created a self-raising pancake mix in 1889. He borrowed the brand name from a popular vaudeville song of the era, and decorated his packaging with a jolly smiling "mammy" wearing a red bandanna. When he sold out to the Quaker Oats company, it continued the theme. Copywriters, of course, wrote in her idiom, as in this 1918 advertisement in the *Ladies' Home Journal*: "Yo' know how de men folks an de young folks all loves my tasty pancakes, an' you can make dem fo' dem jiffy quick, an jus' right every time, wid my magic-ready-mix". In the 1960s the company began to react to attacks against this stereotype by black power leaders. Aunt Jemima's bust and hips deflated and she acquired a more stylish headband. By 1989 she had gone on a crash diet and binned the bandanna altogether in favour of a perm and a pair of pearl earrings, the uniform of the American middle-class "Mom" of any colour. In 1995 the image was personified by Gladys Knight, the 1960s soul artist, now singing jingles while making breakfast for her grandchildren. This transformation generated a whole new wave of protests from African-Americans, an ethnic group unrecognised at the time Aunt Jemima was conceived. They demanded, unsuccessfully, that she be finally be dismissed from the scullery, along with Uncle Ben, the venerable image of a courtly black manservant used to promote rice.

America's General Mills Company handled the transition more subtly. Betty Crocker is the mythical figure invented in 1920 to lend her name to a range of cake mixes. She was represented on packaging and in national magazines by illustrations of the archetypal mature American housewife. As popular radio stations were local, several different voice artists were use to portray Betty Crocker with the appropriate accent in each region. When national television arrived in the 1950s it presented General Mills with a dilemma. Several candidates were screen-tested to select one woman with whom the whole nation could identify. Because by this time Betty Crocker was a true celebrity. Only one third of American women deduced that she was an actress; another third thought she was a real, living person; and the rest were illogical: they realised she was only a representation of Betty Crocker, but nevertheless felt somehow she must be more than just an actress. The wishful reasoning was along these lines: "If there isn't a real, live person called Betty Crocker, there probably is someone very much like that, who would say something like that, and I would believe her". It is this cognitive dissonance which the company exploits. Betty Crocker was white, of course, and this too became an issue. Forty years on, when the Betty Crocker brand was seventy-five years old, General Mills staged a promotion in which women of all ethnic groups were asked to send in photos of themselves. Seventy-five were selected and fused by computer into a politically correct image of Betty Crocker for the 1990s.

Expert status can be conferred on whole groups of individuals. The successful international brand Fisherman's Friend doesn't advertise much, but the package shows fishermen wearing oilskins, and we all believe a fisherman should know about sore throats. However, he would be of little credibility for relieving period pains. To maintain credulity, endorsers must stay within their perceived roles. When Victor Kiam, the man who bought the Remington company, and later Ronson, urged us to try his products, his self-interest was apparent. But we could accept his word, with all the normal caveats we might apply to the exhortations of the enthusiastic businessman. For people in other roles, disinterest is important. Scientists have a reputation for scrupulous accuracy. However, as soon as one appears in an advertisement, he is tainted – a kind of ethical Heisenberg principle. The perception is that advertising traffics in dishonesty. Thus the appearance of Professor Steve Jones, evolutionary geneticist at University College London, in a mood of controlled hysteria in a futuristic car commercial, while increasing his celebrity quotient, may well have unsettled viewers who knew of his reputation, and certainly could not have done a great deal to enhance his own standing within his profession.

In 1961, Daniel J. Boorstin claimed that the celebrity was always an ephemeral contemporary. He was on shaky ground even then. The appeal of nostalgia was a well-known advertising device, and photographs of long-dead icons of stage and screen could be used to invoke glamour. The power of celebrities outlasts death; indeed, the best celebrities are dead celebrities. The usage fees are lower, and their image is frozen in time; being dead, they can do nothing to tarnish it. In 1997 the Gap campaign reminded us that maverick male sex symbols as diverse as Humphrey Bogart, Pablo Picasso, Gene Kelly, Steve McQueen, James Dean, Allen Ginsberg, and Ernest Hemingway wore khakis (though Gap wasn't around when they did). Hemingway has become an industry, as his estate has licensed furniture which he did not design, fountain pens he did not use, and *The Hemingway Cookbook*, which he did not write. The new technology combines old film footage with new, bringing long-dead film stars back to life to strut their stuff for commerce again. In 1994 Elton John jammed with the shades of Humphrey Bogart, Jimmy Cagney, and Louis Armstrong for Diet Coke, while Steve McQueen drove once more over the hills of San Francisco hills in a new Ford Puma. In 1997 Marilyn Monroe was still promoting Chanel No. 5, while Fred Astaire was a pitchman for Dirt Devil vacuum cleaners. Eighteen years after his murder, the spirit of John Lennon was invoked to plug One2One mobile phones when DJ Chris Evans was plummeted onto the mattress Lennon had shared with Yoko Ono in his famous weeklong 1969 "bed-in" peace protest. In 1999 the living comedian Stephen Fry hosted a dinner party for a number of famous celluloid phantoms in a television commercial for After Eight mints.

A perfectly targeted 1998 television commercial for the Ford Cougar demonstrated the emotional power of the well-chosen celebrity. Its hero, the 62-year-old American actor Dennis Hopper, did not have to say a word, because the entire commercial was built on cultural references shared by the intended audience, people near his own generation. He drove the car down a desert highway to the sound of the 1960s anthem "Born to be Wild" by Steppenwolf. An apparition grew out of the heat haze behind – a shaggy drop-out in a battered cowboy hat astride a souped-up motorbike. It was, of course, the 33-year-old Dennis Hopper, in footage lifted from *Easy Rider*, the seminal road movie he had made with Peter Fonda in 1969. Through the easy magic of electronic imagery, the two personifications drove side by side – mature, quizzical Dennis in his snappy charcoal suit and his flaky younger self. At a lunch stop, the waitress flirted with the older Dennis, ignoring hippy Dennis at the next table. Back on the road, the older Dennis accelerated away with a grin, leaving the image of his hippy past dwindling in the rear-screen mirror. Maturity wins the contest with youth, with a strong whiff of nostalgia. For those who recognise the responsibilities of maturity but still yearn for the youthful independence of the open road, the Ford Cougar hit the mark.

CELEBRITY "TESTIMONIALS" can be wickedly influential. They are effective because we happily defer judgement to celebrities. Our infatuation is an abdication of responsibility. There is no freedom of choice where one is in thrall to another personality – living or dead, real or fictional.

CHAPTER 15
YOU GOTTA AC-CENT-TCHU-ATE THE POSITIVE

Negativity

You gotta acc-cent-tchu-ate the positive,
E-lim-in-ate the negative
And don't mess with Mister In-between.

Popular 1940s song lyrics by Johnny Mercer

NO ONE pays as much attention to advertising as the people who make it, and they focus particularly on rival brands. Advertisers are hypersensitive, and quick to defend their brand against an attack which the intended public often has hardly taken on board. Face-saving retaliation becomes the overwhelming reason for advertising. This takes the form of "knocking copy", which was a feature of the "cola wars". A 1995 television commercial appeared to be lifted intact from the troubled dreams of the advertising executives of the Coca-Cola company. It showed a family drinking the brand as they drove through a sunny landscape, before plunging into a thick band of fog, and entering a nightmarish supermarket where automata tried to sell them an anonymous brand of cola. A voice boomed, "Not all colas are the same", and the family left in disgust, re-emerging into the sunshine, to resume drinking "the real thing". Pepsi-Cola retaliated with a television commercial showing rapper M. C. Hammer, the epitome of cool, being given a Coke by mistake, and slipping into a kitsch rendition of the song "Feelings". Another simulated a psychological trial: over a period of time, one chimp was given Pepsi to drink, another drank Coke. The Coke-drinking chimp learned how to fit pegs into the right-shaped holes, while the Pepsi-drinker lounged on the beach surrounded by beautiful women.

These squabbles, in which competitors project their anxieties onto an indifferent public, always run the risk of simply reminding consumers of whatever they already know about the rival brand. Direct comparisons to "brand X" or "another leading brand" are more common in the US, with its more functional approach to advertising. Until 1994, when a new Trade Marks Act became law, it was illegal to refer to a competitor's trademark in UK advertising, though there were exceptions, such as the motor car sector, which arose from tacit industry-wide understandings. The new legislation allowed companies to use the registered trademark of a rival "in accordance with honest practices". This removed the matter from the legal arena to the adjudication of the Advertising Standards Authority.

"Knocking copy" is often an expression of corporate pique – the advertiser has been outraged by a competitor's claim or action, and girds himself to seek retribution. When Reebok aired its "dream team" commercial falsely implying that the great Manchester United footballers of the past had worn its boots, its aggrieved competitor struck back with a poster maintaining that eight of the eleven had worn Adidas. It was erected in only one location: in Bolton, Lancashire, opposite Reebok's headquarters. Advertisers sometimes get swept up in a downward spiral of retaliation to the general mystification of consumers. A press advertisement showed a can of the Australian-originating Castlemaine XXXX lager squashing a spider, with the copy: "Australians wouldn't give a XXXX for A.N. Other lager. (So that's that rumour squashed.)" This was in response to a recent TV commercial by Carling Black Label, which featured Australian references and an animated spider, and if you hadn't seen that, the Castlemaine ad was incomprehensible.

A storm of alarm swept through British households in 1994 when the two soap powder giants, Procter & Gamble and Lever Brothers, which normally produced predictably reassuring commercials on television, turned the public press into a battleground over independent tests which claimed that concentrated powders caused damage to fabrics. Persil ran full-page defensive ads. Ariel responded by using exactly the same full-page layout, headline style, text typeface, and an almost identical model with a similar colourful patterned blouse, except that this one was in tatters, to demonstrate why it "does not contain the 'Accelerator' but some new powders do". In their zeal to destroy each other's credibility, competitive brands can easily lose sight of the reality that consumers are rarely forced to select between brand X or Y, but have a whole range of other options.

Not just "knocking copy" but a very large proportion of routine advertising is expressed in the negative. A common approach for office equipment manufacturers, for example, is to portray administrative bedlam with a headline such as "Running an office needn't be a nightmare if you choose [brand name]". This provides the opportunity to dramatise the nightmare, with an image, say, of Dracula, rather than trying to illustrate the prosaic benefits of a piece of office equipment.

NEGATIVITY

Accentuating the negative is such a popular approach it amounts to an advertising convention.

CLAIM: travelling as a passenger on our freighters you can expect luxurious comfort.
CREATIVE SOLUTION: a cartoon showing people crowded into a floating sardine tin.
(Might not this 1998 American press advertisement for Ivaran Lines also arouse concerns about the seaworthiness of its ships?)

CLAIM: if you use our credit card your purchases are insured.
CREATIVE SOLUTION: a shopper staggering under a falling tower of packages.
(Could this 1998 TV commercial for Barclaycard also stir fears about credit cards tempting one to profligacy?)

CLAIM: if you bank with us, we'll give you a 48-hour overdraft, without quibble.
CREATIVE SOLUTION: an enlarged photograph of a scorpion, its claws menacing and its stinging tail raised to attack, with the headline "No stings attached".
(Would this 1996 press ad for Barclays Bank reinforce images of grasping banks?)

CLAIM: our new car offers you all the extras, without qualification.
CREATIVE SOLUTION: a photograph of the car surrounded by gaping metal man-traps, with the headline: "All the trappings, none of the traps".
(Would this 1996 press ad for Volvo remind prospective purchasers of car dealers' dodgy practices?)

CLAIM: it is simple to join our new telephone service.
CREATIVE SOLUTION: a cartoon of a man talking on the phone, while viewing his front garden being destroyed by a JCB, with the caption: "And I've dug up my front garden to save time for when they lay the cables".
(Would this 1996 press campaign for Mercury arouse the very fears about disruption it seeks to allay?)

CLAIM: when you have an insurance claim, our help line lessens domestic trauma by providing you with a reliable local tradesman

within four hours, day or night.
CREATIVE SOLUTION: a cartoon of two housewives wearing gas-masks while chatting over the garden fence. Caption: "Sorry, Mrs D, our septic tank's leaking".
(Did this 1995 press advertisement for Royal Insurance do justice to a quite extraordinary consumer promise?)

CLAIM: your employee healthcare programme is safe in our hands.
CREATIVE SOLUTION: photograph of a 1920s telephone switchboard and operator, with the headline: "Worry about your company's technology, but don't worry about your company healthcare".
(Did this 1995 press campaign for Guardian Health arouse irrelevant anxieties?)

CLAIM: Your investment with us carries an absolutely guaranteed return.
CREATIVE SOLUTION: a cartoon shows a fishing tackle box next to a jaw-shaped gap at the end of a quay. There is a ripple in the water showing where the angler has disappeared.
(Would this 1994 campaign for National Savings. exacerbate the fears of inexperienced investors?)

CLAIM: we use only pure fresh-pressed English apples in our cider.
The creative solution raises a question about a different kind of purity: it's a cartoon treatment of a bullet firing through an apple, to remove a loathsome green worm.
(Would this 1995 press advertising campaign for Scrumpy Jack Cider arouse unpleasant taste associations?)

CLAIM: our PEP investments carry no hidden charges.
CREATIVE SOLUTION: a cartoon of a dog, hidden round a corner, trailing a mouse in front of a cat, with the headline: "PEP charges. We've absolutely nothing to hide".
(Would this mid-1990s press advertisement for Stewart Ivory and Company associate the firm with the dubious traders in the field?).

CLAIM: if you use our credit card you will earn a discount off a new Ford car.
CREATIVE SOLUTION: photograph of a popular comedian famous for wrinkling his nose, distastefully contemplating a handful of sparking leads from an old Ford.

(Did this 1994 press campaign for Barclaycard denigrate the performance of the car on offer?)

CLAIM: we offer a sympathetic service to companies which want to borrow capital.
CREATIVE SOLUTION: faceless, animated Giacometti-style stick figures wander aimlessly through a threatening Alphaville city, with a voice-over reassurance that there is a company which will accommodate the commercial borrower.
(Would this 1987 television commercial for the Royal Bank of Scotland confirm images of impersonal financial institutions?)

CLAIM: our tyres will give you better control of your vehicle.
CREATIVE SOLUTION: photograph of a powerful black male sprinter teetering in an awkward high starting position because he is wearing ladies' high-heeled shoes, with the headline, "Power is nothing without control".
(Would this mid-1990s press and poster campaign for Pirelli tyres suggest the brand is both perverse and precarious?)

CLAIM: this car model comes with air conditioning as standard.
CREATIVE SOLUTION: photograph of a sweltering traffic jam.
(Many cars offer air conditioning. Is this 1999 press advertisement for the Peugeot 306 recalling the worst drawbacks of motoring a good way to sell cars, to say nothing of this particular marque?)

The instinct for the negative is so ingrained in advertising "creatives" that even where a perfectly good opportunity exists to tell a positive story, black humour is preferred. A 1999 press campaign for the One2One cellphone network compared the number of words you could say for a given price on the four competitive telecom services. Four consecutive headlines pointed out that while Vodafone, for example, would only allow one to say "Jack, I took the car in for a service like you asked...", only One2One would give one the whole scenario: "Jack, I took the car in for a service like you asked but on the way the brakes failed, I jumped a red light and, whilst avoiding two old age pensioners, ploughed into a brand new Rolls Royce... your dad's brand new Rolls Royce". Subscribers could thus confidently rely on One2One to bring them bad news.

Some advertisers do not balk at associating their wares with images of personal injury and death. A 1995 comic strip ad for the Nationwide

Building Society showed a car crashing into a tree with a big WHAAM! The argument: "Geoff was distracted by the incredibly low rates". An ad for the National Dairy Council laid out 200 bones of a human skeleton, including the skull, in a colour press advertisement which aimed to play on other advertising with the statement "Milk refreshes the parts other drinks cannot reach". In its early 1990s poster campaign Toshiba used a double negative. It showed a queue of office workers waiting to use an office copier to illustrate the claim, "You won't have to wait an eternity to use a Toshiba copier". At the end of the queue was a human skeleton. A 1995 television commercial for the Abbey National Building Society showed a man diving off a sloop anchored in sparkling sunlit waters. But menace was betrayed by ominous music, a barking dog, and a dark shape glimpsed in the water – all references to the horror film *Jaws*. The looming shape turned out to be his female companion, a scuba diver. They embraced over the strap-line: "It won't cost you an arm and a leg".

In a series of late 1990s television commercials parodying the TV drama *The Singing Detective*, the financial advisers Allied Dunbar found humour in the worst fears of their middle-management customers: losing their jobs and their lives. In one vignette a man in a washroom overheard colleagues gossiping that he was about to be sacked; in another, when a patient on an operating table heard the surgeons saying he had a serious, chronic problem, he rose like Lazarus and burst into song. The press advertisements, though equally macabre, were serious in tone. One headlined "Every two minutes someone dies of heart disease" showed the view from a grave with the vicar reading from his prayer book and mourning relatives framed against the blue sky. The company's quite positive slogan, "For the life you don't yet know", seemed particularly inapt for this treatment. The simple intent of all of this drama was to get across the idea: "Financial plans should adapt, to help you cope with the unexpected". Yet the frivolous insensitivity of this company's presentation betrayed its remoteness from its customers. To this firm of financial advisers personal tragedy is a statistical "lifestyle event". Only from that emotional distance could it be viewed as a joking matter.

ALL EFFECTIVE ADVERTISING TRADES ON ANXIETIES. Negative images stir them; positive images resolve them by evoking the rewards of success, happiness, and status in warm emotional terms. Why does the creative instinct favour the negative? Irony, of course, demands it. And it's always easier to dramatise a negative situation than a positive result. Frustration, danger, disaster – these threats compel attention, and are the basis of much humour. The man struck by a car turns our heads, the man walking down the street in the ordinary way does not. So, much advertising is built upon the negative consequences of not using the product. Often these are so vividly conveyed that there is a danger that the negative impression will stick to the brand. To redirect this negative thrust into a positive preference for the advertised brand requires a powerful counter-reaction, a kind of persuasive ju-jitsu. But in a thirty-second commercial it is virtually impossible to distance the message from a vivid initial negative impression, and that is what clings in the mind.

The early classics of advertising were always careful to achieve this balance, often through "before-and-after" photographs or stories. In defence of the negative approach, "creatives" sometimes cite the famous American 1960s Volkswagen Beetle advertisement, which simply showed the car over a one-word headline: "Lemon". But this unusual headline compelled readership, and it was balanced by lengthy copy which revealed that this car had been rejected from the Volkswagen production line because of a minor blemish detected by one of the firm's 3,389 obsessive quality control inspectors. And this was just one in a serious of reputation-building advertisements which included the equally famous powerful positive appeal: "Did you ever wonder how the snowplow driver gets to work?" The mid-1990s TV campaign for Volkswagen was still trading on this reputation, reciting a series of unreliable lifestyle experiences, balanced only by the strap line: "If only everything in life was as reliable as a VW". This type of disenchanted presentation, popular in many product fields, requires a reputation as strong as Volkswagen's to balance it, and does nothing to enhance that reputation.

The business of many charities is to change attitudes towards suffering; to arouse sympathy their first instinct is to dramatise it. And so campaigns aiming to reverse prejudices are always in danger of reinforcing them. A 1998 full-page newspaper advertisement showed a whitewashed window finger-painted with several inflammatory headlines: "Open door policy for bogus refugees", "We're being swamped by crime waves of immigrants", "Refugees blamed for housing shortages", "Why do we let in this army of spongers?" These outbursts would have prompted a lot of head-nodding amongst conservative-minded readers who failed to notice the artfully scrawled logo of the Refugee Council near the foot of the window, or neglected to proceed as far as the clever riposte in the text: "Next time you read about 'bogus refugees with false passports' read between the lies".

"Charity fatigue", the feeling people have that they are continually being asked to pour money into sink-holes, is compounded by the incessant parade of negative images which charities use to arouse guilt.

Amnesty International has contributed its share of shocking impressions of human atrocity and confinement. In 1998, however, it shifted to a more balanced treatment: a press campaign showing photographs of former prisoners who had been released. The camera focused on their hands, and the copy emphasised that while prisoners' hands are bound, free people can take action. These portraits faced another page describing cases currently under investigation and containing ten blank lines to suggest that readers write to appeal for a prisoner's release. This charity thus offered a double reward to prospective donors: positive proof that it could achieve results and a mechanism for personal involvement.

This is a rare exception. The creative instinct is to dramatise the negative. That's playing with dynamite, and few advertisers manage to deflect the blast of the explosion away from themselves.

CHAPTER 16

IT AIN'T WHATCHA SAY, IT'S THE WAY HOWTCHA SAY IT

Tone

"Say, I'm going in a-swimming, I am. Don't you wish you could?" But of course you'd druther work – wouldn't you? Course you would!"
Tom contemplated the boy a bit, and said: "What do you call work?"
"Why ain't that work?"
Tom resumed his whitewashing, and answered carelessly: "Well, maybe it is, and maybe it ain't. All I know is, it suits Tom Sawyer".
"Oh come now, you don't mean to let on that you like it?"
The brush continued to move.
"Like it? Well, I don't see why I oughtn't to like it. Does a boy get a chance to whitewash a fence every day?"
That put the thing in a new light. Ben stopped nibbling his apple.

Mark Twain, The Adventures of Tom Sawyer

TOM SAWYER, like many modern advertising men, believed that the best way to persuade someone of something was to hide the act of persuasion. More traditional advertisers argue that if the presentation is too oblique, the intended buyer may miss the point entirely. Ben might well have said, "You are a lucky sod, Tom. I'm off to the swimming hole".

Should advertising by straightforward or allusive? On this issue, the Atlantic seems to be a great divide. The British usually characterise American advertising as too obvious and hard-selling, while American admen visiting Britain are astonished by the whimsical indirection of British advertising. These are generalisations; after all, the Americans invented the allusive "mood" commercial, and downmarket British retail advertising is little different from American examples. Nevertheless, the transatlantic difference in attitude is real. Clearly, Britons and Americans are not different species; the successful transference of so many American ways of satisfying consumer demands to Britain – from McDonald's to Toys 'R' Us – testifies to that. But cultural considerations do have an influence on how consumers see themselves, and therefore help determine the right tone of voice for the sales approach.

Major advertising agencies on the whole are rather good at working out the "message" – what impressions must be made to improve the attractiveness of the brand. Consumer research, effectively employed and intelligently analysed, can tell them what people need to know, believe, and feel in order to commit to a brand preference. These ideas are set out in a formulation, generally known as the communications strategy.

Sometimes advertisers think that is the end of the process; they simply produce a literal statement of what they would like people to believe. Promoters of port wine, clearly reacting to research which showed its market was ageing, produced a poster for the 1998 Christmas season asserting the opposite: "You don't have to have white hair to drink it". The Stilton cheese promotion council doubtless commissioned similar research. The argument of its 1999 Christmas poster campaign was: "Who says Stilton's only enjoyed by old men with a glass of port?" Simply showing young people gleefully consuming these products, as both campaigns did, will not change ingrained behaviour patterns.

A 1999 advertisement for the Mitsubishi Carisma took a literal approach to the car as status symbol, with its headline "What does your car say ABOUT YOU? IDENTIFY YOURSELF". The bones of the research report also stuck out of the TV campaign British Airways used to introduce its new Club Class "cradle seat" in 1996. You could almost hear the motivational researcher intoning something along the lines of, "When he's travelling on a long haul flight, the hard-driving businessman wants to be pampered, cocooned, revert to infancy, and have caring female cabin staff tuck him up for the night". The resulting commercial showed a businessman's adult face bizarrely grafted onto a baby in nappies, cradled in his mother's arms in a 1940s nursery. This literal translation of the "communications strategy" ignores a fundamental consideration: whether or not the research analysis is correct, will businessmen accept having their infantile yearnings exposed when they sit down to watch the News at Ten, or talk about it the next day with their colleagues?

In advertising, as in any kind of communication, the way you say something, the body language, and the overtones, is often more important than what you're saying. The social environment of this and every advertisement is determined by four factors: the product field (air travel), the medium (television news programmes), the brand (British Airways), and the nature of the consumer (self-esteem of the businessman). All of these influence the way in which the message is perceived. And each has its own set of conventions. The *mood* of the message, as well as its content, must be consistent with the way these forces interact.

OF THESE FOUR environmental influences – the product field, the medium, the consumer, and the brand – advertisers are keenly sensitive to only one: they are usually well aware of what surroundings are appropriate and inappropriate to their own brand image. It may seem perverse for a manufacturer to launch a lawsuit against a retailer which starts selling a lot of its brand, but that is what happened when the Superdrug retailing chain began stocking Givenchy perfumes. Superdrug had got its supplies from pirate wholesalers, and Givenchy sued, because it felt the brand's presence in this discount chemist chain would cheapen its image. Becoming an authorised perfume retailer is an involved process requiring satisfactory completion of a detailed questionnaire, the submission of photographs of sales assistants and a promise not to taint the scent by selling it within fifty feet of a food counter. The European Commission approved a distribution agreement which restricted sales to shops appropriate for upmarket fragrances. When both Superdrug and Tesco complained to the Office of Fair Trading in 1993, the Monopolies and Mergers Commission found against their claim that Chanel, Givenchy, and Yves St Laurent had unfairly declined to accept them as retailers and had put pressure on glossy magazines to refuse Superdrug advertisements offering their brands. In effect the commission determined that it can be in the public interest to preserve a system which keeps prices artificially high.

Not just retail shops, but even consumers can be seen to be the wrong sort for the brand image. While motor car marques such as Honda and Toyota are more popular among older consumers because of their reliability, the aspirational advertising for these brands never features people of their age. Many products traditionally associated with the youth market – soft drinks, jeans, and beauty and cosmetic brands – are now bought by a much larger and older constituency. Yet brands like Levis, Pepsi, and Nike are relentless in their advertising efforts to preserve their street cred amongst teenage consumers. Advertisements always reflect the image of the customers the manufacturer *would like to have*, rather than showing those who may actually buy the brand, as suggested in this advertising anecdote:

> An obese man waddled down the concourse at Newark Airport, a soiled, slogan-splattered T-shirt stretched over his enormous belly. Coming the other way was a well-dressed executive with a briefcase. He walked up to the fat man and said, "I'd like that T-shirt to add to my

collection". For fifty dollars the fat man took it off his back. The businessman, who was the American distributor of Absolut Vodka, folded it carefully into his briefcase, and walked away to phone his office and tell them to stop selling Absolut Vodka T-shirts.[1]

If the wrong kind of retailers and consumers can detract from the brand image, so can advertising communications which are at odds with the conventions of the product field. Air carriers are aware, for example, that the most important anxiety affecting their customers is too highly charged ever to be mentioned explicitly: safety. Yet advertisers often fail to comprehend that what may be an excellent way of selling an impulse treat like a sweet, for example zany humour, is not an appropriate method of persuading people to buy, say, life insurance.

Advertising analysts often attempt to categorise advertising appeals by the price of the goods involved, e.g. light-hearted ads are okay for cheap items, like tea, while high-ticket purchases, such as cars, require a more serious approach. A more useful classification lies in the emotional anxieties surrounding the product. By this yardstick, there are three broad classes of goods which seem to demand a particular style or tone of voice.

- Self-indulgent/frivolous products: cheap treats like tea, sweets, and snacks, but also fashion, which can be very expensive. In this category, almost anything goes. Advertising can be irreverent, outré, silly, it doesn't matter. The only motivation is to have a good time, to satisfy an impulse, and facts get in the way. The 1993 campaign for Häagen-Dazs ice-cream broke new ground by showing the naked intertwined bodies of consumers enjoying the product. By adding stylish, voluptuous sex to conventional taste appeal the advertising joined two kinds of sensory indulgence, and justified a higher price.

- Self-expression products: cigarettes and drinks, which can be low-priced, but also cosmetics and jewellery and the retailers who sell them, as well as cars, all of which are expensive, The most valued element of a gift purchased at Asprey is the labelled box it comes in. Self-esteem is paramount here, and the presentation must never damage it. (When's the last time you saw a funny send-up in a perfume commercial?)

---

[1] Paraphrased from Carl Hamilton, *Absolut: Biography of a Bottle*, Texere, 2000.

- Serious products/services – banking, financial services, politics, portrayals of business in general, etc. All of these involve money, where caution and probity are the watchwords. Presentations must be conservative. (Would you trust a financial adviser whose ambition is to be the life of the party?)

Fourthly, an advertising presentation must be appropriate to its medium. Some obvious physical factors affect how ideas are received in each. Size, for example. When a client sees his new television commercial for the first time, advertising agencies take care to show it on a large screen in a viewing room, where it will seem more impressive than on a television monitor. The advertisements we see in cinemas are more commanding for this reason. Roadside posters, which whiz by in a flash, are only suitable for a vivid instant impression, usually graphic. They are the quintessence of advertising; an axiom in the trade is that if you can't reduce an advertising concept to an outdoor poster, with one image and a few words, it isn't an advertising idea. However, posters which appear on the wall across the tracks in the underground or inside public transport have captive audiences with little else to do. Unlike newspaper readers they can't even turn the page and so these media lend themselves to discursive verbal argument.

There are important psychological considerations, too. These derive from the ambient circumstances. Most media exposures are relatively private and intimate. Television advertising takes place in the home usually, often in the presence of children, and its conventions are those which surround the hearth. In this setting there are restrictions which are peculiar to advertising: displays of nudity and bad language, for example, are forbidden, although commonplace in the surrounding programme material. Reading is an intimate experience, and so different rules apply. Whilst newspapers are very public media, magazines are a more private world in which embarrassing topics, such as piles and tampons, can be discreetly discussed. Magazines are often chosen to reflect personal enthusiasms, and can build up an emotional relationship with the reader, a chief selling-point belaboured by magazine space salesmen. With the advent of television, radio listening was displaced as a family activity, and has become a generally private experience. Its primary characteristic is that it's instant – topical and ephemeral. Cinema advertising is unique: the only occasion on which one is intensively focused on advertising together with a crowd of strangers in a public place.

All advertisements borrow authority from the medium in which they appear. Anything published – no matter how silly – gains some credibility.

Even the most vulgar of the tabloid newspapers carries the advantage of topicality and confers the authority of the printed word. New clothing designers achieve acceptability by advertising in the pages of *Vogue* and Absolut Vodka ads acquired panache by being published in the snobby American weekly, the *New Yorker*. Orson Welles's radio production of H. G. Wells's *War of the Worlds* would not have caused mass hysteria if he had chosen to make it as a movie. It famously caused panic in jittery pre-Second World War America because radio then was the primary medium for fast-breaking news.

Some advertisements are deliberately crafted to take account of the environment in which they will appear. "Have you got anything smaller, Guv?" is a meaningless headline for a cigar anywhere except on the taxi card in which it appeared. "Kill your speed" was the theme of the 1995 UK road safety campaign. It still lingers at some safety black spots throughout the country, where it acquires a strong emotive force, because the word "kill" is unusual in the context of the British countryside, and the road is precisely the "point of purchase" for this selling idea.

Outdoor advertising is different. It confronts us in the street – a public place – where public conventions apply. This is why people found the realistic photographs on the posters of the clothing retailer Benetton, such as the one of a newborn baby, streaked with blood and vernix, so shocking. They would be less offensive in a magazine, and unremarkable in the context, say, of the *British Medical Journal*. Which is precisely why this advertiser chose to use the most public medium – for its shock value. Many outdoor signs, from traffic notices to "keep off the grass" notices, are instructions regulating public behaviour. These stimuli are not surrounded by an artificial media environment; they are real. No media experience is as topical and as realistic as the one which takes place in the street. An American visitor to Britain in the mid-1960s thought the two words which appeared on posters everywhere at the time represented a type of "big brother" campaign sponsored by the government to maintain public morale in a period of economic crisis. "Take Courage" was, in fact, an exhortation to drink a brand of British beer.

The famous 1914 war recruitment advertisement featuring Lord Kitchener (Uncle Sam in the US) gained enormous force because it appeared in the public arena. A young man would find it hard to ignore unless he were wearing a uniform. It was felt to be so successful that the same theme was recycled in both countries for the next world war. Similar social pressures strengthened the celebrated 1979 Conservative Party poster featuring a familiar street scene, a dole queue, over the headline, "Labour isn't working". Political parties, with their tradition of public rallies, have always understood the importance of advertising in the public arena. The Tories, in the past, were particularly favoured by the fact that most of the best poster sites were block-booked long-term by tobacco companies, which could be persuaded to release them to a party which they felt would support their interests. Politicians soon came to appreciate how much spin-off publicity a poster could generate. During political campaigns, new outdoor posters are now regularly unveiled by leading politicians for the benefit of press and television journalists, who dutifully reproduce the photo opportunity. For the price of hiring a few poster sites, or even one, for a brief period, the party gains extensive nationwide exposure in other media. Other advertisers have cottoned on to this game, where advertising blurs into press management. A 1998 poster for the charity Age Concern featured an attractive woman with big breasts in a bra, over the headline, "The first thing some people notice is her age". Because the youthful-looking 56-year-old model had a colourful personal history the charity counted on provoking a lot of tabloid-style journalism. It put the poster on one mobile hoarding and attracted several hundred inches of coverage in the national press and ten hours of broadcasting coverage. Putting aside the moral question of whether substituting prurience and sexism for ageism may be counted an advance, the charity made a good publicity investment.

Because posters have the unique ability to challenge private attitudes in public, they are hard for the passer-by to ignore. For this reason they are often chosen to draw public attention to provocative advertising in questionable taste (see Chapter 27). Apart from that, advertising agencies generally fail to exploit the emotional context of the medium, and prefer to focus its stopping power on cryptic allusions and riddles. Cigarette brands such as Silk Cut and Benson & Hedges started this surreal fashion in the late 1970s, as advertising restrictions forced them to say and show less and less. Hutchison Telecom launched Orange, a new mobile phone service with solitary words reversed out of black: "Laugh". "Cry". "Talk". "Listen". These tied into a complementary television commercial which was not greatly more forthcoming. Advertising for the *Economist* news magazine introduced a minimalist white-out-of-red format in 1988 with cryptic wordplay, e.g. the words "Attracts magnates". Other serious publications, the *Financial Times* and the *Telegraph*, quickly imitated this style.

Radio used to be promoted as the ultimate creative medium, because its dramas are played out in the theatre of the mind, where anything is possible. The classic example peddled by radio time salesmen was the American comic Stan Freberg's audio simulation of filling Lake

Michigan with hot chocolate and dumping whipped cream into it from a B52 bomber, while an ICBM popped the maraschino cherry on top. The punch line was "Let them try that on television". Today television could visualise that, and any other unlikely exaggeration, though there's a loss of audience involvement as the imagination plays no part. Although they can have a lot of fun with it, radio is unpopular with "creatives" because most of them are spawned by art colleges, and they have little interest in the non-visual. It's also hard to win acclaim for radio work. Because it's non-visual, ephemeral, and cheap, it won't be reviewed in the advertising trade press.

As they appear within the context of so much light, witless entertainment, the tradition that radio commercials are supposed to be funny has become ingrained. The response of the "creatives" is conditioned: they seem to find it impossible to handle radio advertising without trying to get a laugh. So, when the seriously sexy Häagen-Dazs television and press ads were "adapted" to radio, it could only be done through subversion: the radio campaign mocked the core idea of selling ice-cream through sex. The real creative potential of radio as an advertising medium, its quiet one-to-one intimacy, is largely neglected. It's not a stage, like TV, more like a counselling room. It harnesses the power of the imagination, and, of course, that most powerful emotional force, music.

Few adults in Britain can hear "Air on a G-String" without thinking of Hamlet cigars and relaxation, nor "Going Home" without conjuring up a nostalgic picture of a northern town and Hovis bread. Yet it took a long time for the British advertising industry to appreciate the emotional valence of music, both classic and popular. The simple trick, of course, is to match the desired emotion to the mood of the music. Nevertheless, it's a trick often missed, because usually the selection is made not on the character of the music but because the title or the lyrics are appropriate. So "Up on the Roof", a hymn of urban ghetto escapism, was used in a British Airways television commercial to describe a different kind of upward mobility: the delights which awaited the traveller upstairs in Club Class. The racial theme tune "(Say it Loud) I'm Black and Proud" was borrowed to describe a cup of espresso coffee. While it's fashionable to decry this custom as vandalising the icons of popular culture, it is the advertisers who run the risk by trying to redirect the appeal of such powerful feelings. Million-selling pop records like "I Heard it on the Grapevine", "Stand by Me", or "When a Man Loves a Woman" carry a lot of emotional baggage. If they're not relevant to the emotional mood of the sales pitch, it will be overwhelmed.

Advertisements which strike the right tone of voice for the brand and its environment powerfully assist their impact. Too often, however, as agencies slavishly follow the latest adfashion, the tone is inappropriate. The presentation must be internally consistent. Misplaced accents garble the message or cloud the impression. This affects both visual and aural elements. The upmarket Nikko hotels chain aimed for a distinctive style in its American advertising, using dark thick-lined drawings in the style of the painter Edward Hopper, an artist indelibly associated with an atmosphere of seedy hopelessness. A campaign aiming to broaden the appeal of the Victoria & Albert Museum as "an ace caff with a nice museum attached" counteracted its demotic appeal by using the sublimely plummy voice of art critic Brian Sewell to deliver this observation.

Over the past couple of decades, conceptions about how advertising works have moved away from specific claims of performance towards associating brands with the right kind of feelings. The ultimate expression of reliance on "tone of voice" is the total abandonment of an explicit message. This new phase in advertising began in Britain on 28 October 1991, with the first commercial sponsorship of a TV drama. The distributor of Croft Port associated its name with the immensely popular drama series *Rumpole of the Bailey*. The company bought the privilege of book-ending each episode with a five-second animated sequence showing a shadowy bottle of Croft Port transforming first into the sculpture of Liberty on top of the Old Bailey and then into a caricature of Leo McKern, who played the part of the slovenly, cantankerous, claret-snorting barrister. The bibulous Rumpole, of course, offered a natural connection with port, though perhaps not quite the youthful image most alcoholic beverages, even port, seek these days. Yet the marketing manager for the brand felt his outlay of £300,000 was well justified, "We've calculated that to get us the same exposure through commercials would cost us closer to £1m". This advertiser was happy to abandon control over his message. In his calculations he made no allowance for the "effect" a television commercial might have had, as opposed to the values generated by the Rumpole association. This is the embarrassing but logical conclusion which advertising agencies must face because they have abandoned any coherent efforts to establish the true effectiveness of their contribution.

WHILE IT'S NO SUBSTITUTE for an idea, the manner of delivery is essential for the favourable reception of a message. Four factors determine the right tone of voice for an advertising message: the nature of the consumer, the product field, the brand, and the medium in which the message appears. In effective advertising, all work in harmony.

CHAPTER 17
DOES ATTITUDE WASH WHITER?

Style

My revolution is aimed at the so-called harmony of the page, which is contrary to flux and reflux, the leaps and burst of style that run through the page. On the same page, therefore we will use three or four colours of ink, or even 20 different typefaces if necessary. For example: italics for a series of similar or swift sensations, boldface for violent onomatopoeias and so on".

Emilio Filippo Tommaso Marinetti. *"Futurist Manifesto", Milan, 1899*

ONE OF THE APOLOGIES ritually trotted out in the defence of advertising is that it presents useful information. That is indeed how advertising began 200 years ago, with utilitarian purposes such as the announcements of the sailing times of ships. Yet the first thought of any agency starting to work for a retail account nowadays is to advise the client to undertake an image-building campaign to replace those boring full-page informational advertisements listing its wares and prices. It's a suggestion that many in the client organisation will resist, because it's contrary to their experience; they know an attractive price offer, a "loss leader", can bring people into the shop. The argument is between the kind of attitudes which may cause consumers to favour the retailer over the long term versus the immediate effect of short-term measures, which may cheapen those impressions.

There is an imperative to let the consumer know exactly what is on offer and how to get it, but the overriding appeal is emotional. Successful advertising turns on finding the right balance between information and image, as in the placards in Soho doorways:

> Young Blonde Model
> [Insert evocative name here, e.g. Monique, not Mary.]
> 1st Floor Upstairs
> Come on up.
> [Vertical arrow]

Today, with the exception of classified advertising, which is not intended to have a mass effect, the informative content of most advertising is minimal. This is particularly true of television, where a new word had to be coined for a special aberrant type of long-winded commercial which does aim to inform – the "infomercial". In many advertisements, where information would appear to be essential to effective persuasion, the advertiser forsakes the task. Frequently, he embarks on a broader agenda: telling people how to live. The rapidly evolving, highly technological global village has burst the parochial bonds of school, family, and church. Movies, television, and advertising are now the arbiters of mores for the emerging consumer classes all over the world. It's a permissive, entertainment-oriented society. Responsive to desires rather than directives, brand culture represents the ultimate triumph of manner over matter: lifestyle.

A golden rule of good communication holds that the artifice used to present an idea should be transparent. The design of the communication should be invisible, allowing the idea to pass straight through to the receiver. Today in advertising, the opposite idea holds sway: because products are similar, the design *is* the distinguishing message. The Absolut Vodka campaign (see Chapter 13) aimed neither to communicate information nor to dramatise nor to entertain. It presented *the style of the advertising itself* as its Unique Selling Proposition: any product which strikes such an attitude must itself be truly wonderful. By 1999 the brand felt confident enough to dispense altogether with its core idea, the bottle shape, in its American advertising, and simply linked the name to the essence of an experience. Under the headline "Absolut Memphis", an illustration showed a pair of legs rocking and a microphone stand teetering in front of a curtain. On the feet were blue suede shoes. This was king-of-the-hill advertising with a breathtaking hubris worthy of a high-spending cigarette brand. There was no indication whatsoever of what product was being advertised, except for the statutory information supplied in the small type beneath, acknowledging the permission of Elvis Presley Enterprises to use this image.

The earlier examples of the simple and stylish Absolut vodka campaign have been described as "art as advertising", and indeed the company has fostered that image by sponsoring exhibitions of works featuring its bottle, commissioned from artists such as Chris Ofili and Keith Haring. Many people who earn their living by it do view advertising as a form of art. Illustrations of classical and modern masterpieces have always been a favoured means of lending prestige to pompous corporate presentations, and artists of reputation have sometimes strayed into Adland: Andy Warhol, whose oeuvre is a parody of marketing, once made an ad for Polaroid, and the 1960s minimalist artist

Sol Le Witt designed packaging for Nina Ricci. Throughout the 1980s and 1990s, as advertising strove to heighten visual imagery and art stooped to examine cultural artefacts, the two were bound to bump heads. Conceptual artist Damien Hirst and TV commercials director Tony Kaye found they were performing in the same theatre of the absurd. Hirst was discovered and promoted by the archetypal adman and modern-art enthusiast Charles Saatchi, who commissioned a fourteen-foot shark suspended in formaldehyde for exhibition in his St John's Wood gallery. Tony Kaye was also an exhibitionist. He once described himself in a full-page newspaper advertisement as "the greatest British film director since Hitchcock". In 1993 the Dunlop tyre company spent half a million pounds indulging his conceit of an extended journey involving hazards such as a silver-coated bogeyman with black eyes romping with witches in a bizarre desert landscape to dramatise its slogan, "Tested for the unexpected". Whatever the intentions of the advertiser in expressing this unextraordinary claim, the director's aims were clear: he picketed outside the Tate Gallery, trying to persuade that national institution to put his commercial on view. A year later, while demanding £750,000 from Saatchi & Saatchi in a legal dispute over a commercial he made for British Airways, Tony Kaye kept controversial publicity bubbling by commissioning Damien Hirst to direct a commercial for the Meat and Livestock Commission. Hirst, whose works by that time famously included a dead sheep, pigs sawn in half, and a skinned cow's head covered in maggots, regarded advertising as just another medium: "I don't think there's a big difference between what I've been doing and this. Commercials have to be visually compelling with a bit of shock value". Like advertising, Hirst's modus operandi is the pillaging of cultural symbols. "What I like about adverts", he has explained, "is that you can rip anything off".

Advertising pre-empts as argument not only visual design, but also Noel Coward's concept of "Design for Living". It reprocesses attitudes towards life, turning them into "theatre". Gesture supplants thought, drama overwhelms information, emotion replaces understanding. "Relationship marketing" is the currently fashionable term for this approach. It's not what the product *does* that matters, but what rewards you draw from it. The marketing men of the 1990s have rediscovered the truisms unearthed by the pioneer of motivational research, Ernst Dichter, applying them to the confusion of choices laid before today's consumer. Advertising takes on the role of behavioural, even spiritual, counsellor: you should want to be this kind of person, who uses this sort of product. You are what you consume. Lifestyle advertising is just another way of displaying badges and selling status.

In 1960, lager accounted for 1 per cent of British beer sales, and was usually served in a half-pint glass, with a splash of lime juice, to a woman. Thirty years later, more than half of the beer sold in Britain was lager. Brand advertising had achieved an immense shift in attitudes amongst younger men, establishing lager as the real lad's drink. In converting a generation, lager advertisers borrowed the "lifestyle" approach pioneered by beverages such as Coca-Cola and Pepsi-Cola. They exploited "attitude" – which sought to establish differences not between the brands, but in the assumed *weltanschauung* of differentiated consumer groups. A flood of machismo icons of pub culture dominated television screens. Early examples such as Skol Lager's "Skolar" series were crudely sexist: a Skol drinker counted out a large number of cans for himself, so that he had enough left over to "give Samantha one". A new catchline was coined for manly performance: "I bet he drinks Carling's Black Label". Hofmeister's swaggering, beer-swilling, snooker-playing, bird-pulling "George the Bear" was a role model for public house mores, a teddy with attitude. Aggressive Australian brands such as Castlemaine XXXX and Fosters upped the stakes with romantic images of hard-boiled reactionaries of the outback.

Massive expenditure ensured that lager advertising entered popular culture; advertising agencies came to the view that the point of lager advertising was simply to be a social catalyst – to get talked about in pubs. Britain converted to lager, but by the mid-1980s, the variations of manly image were blurring. When Holsten Pils finally abandoned its 1980s campaign in which comedian Griff Rhys-Jones was inserted into old film footage to play opposite tough-talking men such as Humphrey Bogart, its marketing director was ingenuously apologetic: " 'Old Movies' was a star campaign; everyone from 18-year-olds to grannies loved it. But it was proving very difficult to get people to listen to what the ads actually said".

The distinctions between brands on the general theme of laddishness had virtually dissolved. When advertising "creatives" discovered computer gadgetry – "Harry" and Paintbox, photo-animation, model animation, pixellation, and digital edit – these effects became the ideas. A 1991 sixty-second television commercial showed a man wearing a chequered suit and carrying a hammer, wandering in a surreal world of many doors. Weird objects passed by, a moving eye in a walking picture frame, a clockwork mechanism also holding a hammer. The voice-over informed us that our hero was looking for something. Entering a room with a chequered floor, he encountered a huge animated bar of music and – the first clue to the product – another ambling picture frame containing a man drinking a beer, before emerging into a party scene with a few intercut glimpses of a glass of beer and finally the logo for McEwan's lager. The agency account planner explained that the chequered motifs were visual reference to draughts and hence draught beer, while the bar of music was a pun on a place where you drink. "It's basically about him not being able to find things he likes and building things to his own liking ... There is a sense that when it's you and your mates you live by your own rules". The cult director whom the agency hired to make the commercial was less confident: "I'm not quite sure what's on the brewer's mind ... On the whole I wouldn't have associated heavy beer drinking with my sort of films. But maybe that's what they do – go and get tanked up and watch art movies". By the end of the century lagers were aiming to identify themselves with casual attitudes towards sexual behaviour in miniature soap opera episodes. A 1999 Castlemaine XXXX television commercial, set to the sound track, "Your Cheating Heart" developed the proposition that it was okay to make love to your best friend's wife, but not to accept his last can of cold beer from her.

"Attitude" as an expression of a brand's personality is an elaboration of a brand's tone of voice – identifying closely with the outlook and aspirations of the members of the target group, so as to become accepted as part of their life. If you read their perceptions right – and that's a big if – it seems to engage involvement. But essentially it's a dead end. Because any brand can do it, it's not a unique property. And street cred fashions are fickle. Because attitudes change, a product which is nothing but an expression of empathy can go out of fashion quickly. It takes enormous resources to continuously update a brand personality – and perhaps only the superbrands like Coke and Pepsi can do it.

ADVERTISING LAGS CULTURAL CHANGE rather than leads it, but it's quick to sniff nascent social trends and exploit them for commercial purpose. While it can spread change fast, popularising new models for behaviour, there is no evidence that advertising can invent culture. In any event that is beyond its remit; advertisers do not like to take chances on the unknown. Advertising "creatives" are closely in touch with popular visual culture, and as new themes appear – in the cinema or television – are quick to borrow interest by adapting the latest theme to commercial interests. Advertising is highly ephemeral, because by the definition of avant-garde, by the time a new fashion is reflected in the mass media it is passé. That's why when you leaf through the newspapers of yesteryear, you find your eye wandering to the advertisements. They freeze a moment in time: the anxieties, the aspirations, the collective symbolism of the day.

The ruthless competitive spirit of the wheeler-dealers of the international business community captured in 1980s films like *Wall Street* was quickly emulated as normative behaviour in television commercials. The extra cost of flying British Airways Club Class was justified on the premise that a comfortable journey would allow the sharp-witted business executive to put one over on his associates. His female counterpart, the hard-driving power-dressed young woman who specialised in puncturing male egos, appeared in countless others. In a Volkswagen Golf commercial, she celebrated her divorce, incidentally mocking an old dear who thought the occasion was a wedding – pensioners are well out of the target group for the Golf – to contrive a situation for the slogan, "If only everything in life was as reliable as Volkswagen". Because Japanese car manufacturers had to overcome old prejudices about cheap oriental imports, advertising for Toyota in the 1990s attached the brand to spiritual qualities of the Japanese work ethic, evoked by a Japanese ideogram and statement of philosophy. The 1994 launch of the Hyundai faced an additional handicap: it was made in Korea. The television advertising showed conventional cultural images: traditional buildings, Korean people, blossoms, underpinned by a confrontational voice-track: "Even deeply held prejudice can be removed by knowledge and experience". By purchasing a Hyundai, therefore, people who wanted cheap transport could defend their brand decision as an expression of an enlightened world-view.

As the 1990s released a flood of sentimental Hollywood films about characters getting back into touch with their real selves, advertising dutifully reaffirmed family values. An American magazine campaign launched in 1992 for Drambuie liquor played on the angst of "thirtysomethings": an exhausted young Santa Claus crashed out by the Christmas tree alongside the milk and cookies left out for his visit, with the headline, "Oh no! I'm becoming my father!" In advertisements for family cars, the role model was now self-actualised and responsible. The young businessman in a 1992 British commercial ignored the temptations offered by the sexy sirens at his firm because he only had eyes for his wife, two children, and his Volkswagen Passat with its anti-lock brakes, catalytic converter, and engine running on lead-free petrol. A Volvo campaign in America presented a classroom "show-and-tell" session in which kids explained how they know their daddy loved them: "My daddy loves me because he bought me a toy airplane", said one. "My daddy loves me because he bought me a doll's house", said another. The third trumped those with "My daddy loves me because he bought a Volvo".

UNIFORMITY DRIVES PROFIT, while people seek distinctiveness. As branding is about conformity, the technique of the Big Lie is to assert the opposite: its themes are independence, self-realisation, rebellion, and alienation. The soft drink Tango provides youngsters with the opportunity to identify with zany dysfunction, while Adidas and Nike trainers are for self-reliant youth. The 1996 television ads for the Peugeot 406, a prosaic family car, suggested that its purchase would enable you to "search for the hero inside yourself". An American magazine advertisement with the headline, "Do you dream in Sony?" addressed the maverick lurking inside the consumer of mass market entertainment:

> fantasy is just another word
> for fearless *there will always be*
> *a place in the world for rebels*
> the key to creativity is yanking
> convention inside out

Youthful protest is often seen as a kind of materialist backlash, a reluctance to use branded products as badges. In fact it is simply the substitution of one generation's tokens for those of another. Youth feels it is "anti-advertising", so a 1993 advertiser aiming at teenagers created a commercial which, like a rampaging cuckoo in a warbler's next, suddenly hijacked pastiche commercials apparently advertising other products, erupting in a frenzy of video static and zoomy graphics to plug Sega computer games.

In *The White Negro*, Norman Mailer developed the idea that black consciousness, leaching into white culture, would foment a revolution against the institutions of capitalism. But marketing fashioned the symbols of protest into products, and advertising co-opted rebellion as an identity badge. Subversion became a communications strategy. The social and political expressions of the white hipster stars of the 1960s counter-culture were sucked up by the advertising hoover and regurgitated as commercials. Waves of dissidence arising from the gutters were restyled as marketing fads: Generation X, the New Beats, the MTV Generation. Tony Kaye employed the iconoclastic Velvet Underground track *Venus in Furs* in his Dunlop tyre commercial. Janis Joplin's sour ballad satirising the acquisitive society, "Oh Lord, won't you buy me a Mercedes-Benz?", was employed without a hint of irony in 1995 to sell – Mercedes-Benz motor cars. (Janis herself owned a Porsche.) Revolution became a lifestyle; preaching rebellion became the role of the consumer goods manufacturer. To inherit the mantle of reformers such as Gandhi, Miles Davis, and Picasso it was only necessary to "Think Different" and buy an Apple Macintosh instead of a personal computer. Mailer's vision was faulty; it was the argument of the philosopher Herbert Marcuse which prevailed: radical impulses have been suborned by business and transformed into new instruments of conformity.[1] Marketing has absorbed the shot hurled by the counterculture, beaten it into trinkets, and sold it back to the dispossessed: the Sex Pistols perform for Levis, Allen Ginsberg models Gap. Why does it work? Perhaps because, for most people, what rebellion is about is not changing the world for the benefit of mankind, but to create a brighter patch for one's self.

As Goebbels knew, a cardinal tactic of propaganda is to promote bonding within groups by targeting outsiders for derision. In Britain "anorak" (a windbreaker) is a contemporary term of abuse for eccentrics, i.e. people who are truly independent-minded. A mid-1990s television commercial showed a man wearing an anorak describing how he had constructed his model of the Empire State Building. "Five years, six months in the making ... 76,478 matches, each individually stained ... ". Suddenly, as in a Monty Python skit, a giant foot smashed his dream to pieces. It was wearing BK-branded trainers.

Because they focus on rebellion, the aspirations of youth are superficially different from adults, but underneath the motivations are the same. If you find the right nerve to press, youth are indeed more susceptible than adults because, feeling their way uncertainly to maturity, they have more anxiety. While craving individualism as a means of self-expression, and wanting to be seen to be cool (indifferent to adult values), they have a desperate need to conform to those of their own peer group. Young people are highly aware of advertising as a cultural influence, and will steal posters from bus shelters and hoardings which touch their sensibilities and post them on their bedroom walls alongside those of other heroes: Malcolm X, Martin Luther King, Che Guevara, and Take That. These become cult classics because the youth are in the market for the attitudes they express, though that does not necessarily mean they will buy the products which ally themselves to these ideas. (The traffic in icons moves both ways; advertising influences pop culture too. The 1996 television campaign for Levi's jeans catapulted its sound track, "Spaceman", by a new pop group called Babylon Zoo, to the top of the UK charts. In 1999 a series of British Gas commercials featuring

---

[1] Herbert Marcuse, *One Dimensional Man*, Routledge & Kegan Paul, 1964.

the over-protective mother of a gormless son inspired a BBC comedy programme, *Mrs Merton and Malcolm*).

OVER THE PAST TWO CENTURIES the character of advertising has advanced from the provision of essential information, such as announcements of ships' sailing times, through the application of social pressures, to the assertion of product claims, to associations with borrowed values, to now simply association with a point of view or attitude towards life: almost anything will do, from the idiotic pronouncements of the dysfunctional cartoon character "Reg" in the Embassy Regal cigarette advertisements to the lofty ideals explored by Benetton. The drive towards minimalism was fostered by the creative response to the increasing restrictions on cigarette advertising. Because it was so prominent, and because innuendo is easier than thought, the empty content of cigarette advertising was mimicked by other advertisers who neither had the need to be so evasive nor the massive resources necessary to make the tactic work. The style of advertising presentation is now so essential to the brand message that new campaigns are promoted as media events. When Guinness launched a new television campaign in 1994 which involved seeing fantastic worlds in a pint of stout, it advertised its launch in the national press, and other brands have since followed suit.

Facts are now irrelevant to much advertising. Today brands seek to distinguish themselves by projecting an attitude or association which they believe will ingratiate them with their intended consumers, like a youth worker wearing a baseball cap back to front. Even a highly technical product with performance differentials, such as a mobile phone, is now advertised as a way of making a personal statement. A 1998 TV commercial for Siemens provided no brand information whatsoever; it focused entirely on the fashion designer Jean-Paul Gaultier, who had designed a dress with a pocket for a mobile phone. Towards the end of the 20th century, like modern-art, there seemed to be nowhere else for advertising to go, except to self-destruct. Which is what happened next.

CHAPTER 18
THE IRONIC AGE

Deconstruction

We tend to be subjected day after day to the most all-pervading cynicism about almost every aspect of our national life. Nothing ever seems right. There is a persistent current that flows along undermining the integrity and motives of individuals, organisations and institutions.

Prince Charles, 1994

"ADVERTISING IS LEGALISED LYING". This statement, a quotation from H. G. Wells, appeared in bold black-and-white on posters all over British high streets in 1996. A warning from a government watchdog? A protest by a concerned civic group? No, it was a new advertising campaign for Guinness. Like modern art, self-critical and absorbed with sensation, advertising appeared to have finally self-destructed in a tailspin of irony.

Verbal irony is saying the opposite of what you mean, for humorous or emphatic effect. Procedural irony is an action which achieves the opposite of what you intended. Irony is a noun commonly qualified as "bitter" or "cutting". Among its many synonyms are satire, sarcasm, ridicule, derision, mockery, scoffing, and sniggering. Irony does not create, it carps. It is the scold of aspiration, the scion of disappointment. Its ungenerous handmaiden is cynicism. All in all, it seems a strange attitude for a salesman.

Many have recognised a special British sense of ironic humour. It has a distinguished pedigree, with forebears such as Dean Swift and Charles Dickens, and modern exemplars such as the deadpan deliveries of characters in plays by Harold Pinter. Conservative writers have dedicated many passionate paragraphs to deploring the British penchant for mockery. Auberon Waugh has described his countrymen as "mean, envious, full of rancour, hatred, and bogus self-righteousness", and the Archbishop of Canterbury, in his 1992 Christmas morning sermon, lamented, "We are becoming a people ready to scoff . . . [known for] an uncharacteristic meanness of spirit". Martin Amis ascribed this unpleasant national trait to "the sullenness of post-greatness".

According to most critics of this savour, the rot set in during the permissive 1960s, when genuine heroes of the past began to be supplanted by role models thrown up by popular culture. With the Beatles, a Great Cult of Youth emerged. Ignorance and lack of qualification were no longer an obstacle to success and immediate satisfactions replaced deferred achievement. And so, in the mid-20th-century social revolution the weapon of the disenfranchised was not the pikestaff but mockery. It was used to assault the traditional totems of civilised authority: intellect, epistemology, aestheticism, mores, and standards and the institutions behind them – the government, the Church, the Establishment.

British advertising agencies began to produce arch, self-aware, and often very funny advertisements which attracted the admiration of their peers throughout Europe at international prize festivals, and were often ineptly imitated by advertising agencies on the Continent. The view widely maintained in British advertising circles was that the mentality of the British audience is somehow especially attuned to cynicism: through heavy exposure to media, consumers have become as sophisticated as the practitioners are themselves about advertising. Claims of superiority can be advanced to this hip constituency only if they are expressed tongue-in-cheek. Even factual statements will be rejected without this knowing gloss. Advertisers who show they share viewers' disillusionment with hackneyed advertising techniques break through the TV screen to the real world. Consumers, the logic goes, will reward them by becoming involved with the brand.

Ironical statement, the British "cultural mass"[1] believe, is lost on gauche Americans. This is a shallow judgement of the nation which produced Ambrose Bierce and Mark Twain as well as the caustic television show *Rowan and Martin's Laugh-In,* extremely popular in Britain in the late 1960s. A more likely analysis is that Americans are more at ease with commerce. They have no hang-ups about selling or being sold to. They make funny commercials too, but the humour does not generally depend on denigrating the practice of salesmanship. In the lexicon of free enterprise, with its emphasis on thrift, self-reliance, perseverance, innovation, and ruthlessness, there is no entry for bemused irony. British advertising, because it abandons classic principles of persuasion for the limp, knowing gibe, simply bewilders most American professionals.

The young Britons who create advertisements are well attuned to popular culture, and, like the young designers who dragged street cred onto the catwalk, they have opened advertising agency doors to the

---

[1] The American sociologist Daniel Bell uses the term "cultural mass" to describe the elitist, self-referential group of people who work in the media and are thus in a position to influence cultural trends (*The Cultural Contradictions of Capitalism,* BasicBooks, 1976).

irreverence of alternative comedy. In both industries, what began as pavement movements were adopted by mainstream commerce. During the 1990s sarcasm spread well beyond its natural home in the youth market. Advertisements addressed to every kind of target group now delivered their messages with a nudge and a wink; there was a mocking smirk in every voice-over, the pot at the end of every rainbow had to turn out to be a crock of shit.

Advertising for British lagers became almost incomprehensible. Holsten Pils introduced American film star Jeff Goldblum to make gnomic statements directly to camera. Carlsberg deconstructed advertising with enigmatic posters depicting rhubarb, a red herring, and a bull. A commercial for Tennent's Pilsner showed two men walking into a pub with an odd gait and ordering beers in weird, tape-manipulated voices. "It tastes a bit different", said one. The barman replied, in a demoniac manner, "But do you know why? Czechoslovakian yeast!" This was an adman's insider joke – sending up the traditional "Unique Selling Proposition". "It's almost meaningless", admitted the creative director of the advertising agency, "But you cannot be didactic. You can't say: 'drink this, it's good.'"

Postmodernism ransacked the past to recycle old ideas, dipped in irony, as new. This requires a lot less creative energy; familiarity provides an easy hook to audience involvement, and the author is absolved of the risk and responsibility of proposing a new idea. The term art critics like to use for re-presenting old images in new arrangements is "recontextualising". The art lies in why the artist made his choices, a joke or insight which the viewer is challenged to share. Originality became deeply unfashionable. Given Salvador Dali's generous legacy of whimsical juxtapositions, there was little more originality to be expressed in any case. Postmodern artists have continued with variations on the themes, extending the techniques of the meaningful collage with the aid of photocopying machines, videos, CD-ROMs and facilities for exploring their own bodily functions and memorialising their own emissions. The formula is that of the spin doctor: wrest the element out of its original setting, then change its meaning by inserting it into another which is absurd, anachronistic, or personalised. The content is irrelevant; attitude is everything. But is a Union Jack on a Carnaby Street wastebasket daring and provocative art, or simply a predictable joke in poor taste?

Television viewing, reinforced by the relentless preoccupation of the popular press with the medium, is the most widely shared cultural experience, and so many recycled advertising ideas were drawn from the medium in which commercials appeared. In 1988 Guinness refreshed its enigmatic series of commercials featuring the Dutch actor Rutger Hauer with a pastiche of the 1960s science-fiction programme *The Twilight Zone*, then enjoying revived trash cult status. In 1994 an imported Australian lager, Tooheys, lampooned chat-show formats. Continuing media introspection led to parodies of parodies: a 1994 TV campaign for the *News of the World* featured a deranged news reader delivering mock bulletins in a take-off of a BBC satirical programme called *The Day Today*.

Feature films were appropriated for every type of product, not just those aimed at children, youth, or consumers, but also those appealing to investors, opinion-leaders, and the City. In a late 1980s commercial for the soft drink Tango, a childlike figure in a red plastic mackintosh turned out be a female dwarf who assaulted another character with a knife, mimicking the climax of Nicholas Roeg's 1970s film *Don't Look Now*. In 1996 Findus Lean Cuisine borrowed the leading character from the film *Shirley Valentine*, the Nissan Micra did a take-off of *9½ Weeks*, and Peugeot reprised both *Thelma and Louise*, whose heroines drive off a cliff, and *The Great Escape*, in which Steve McQueen bounces his motorbike over the barbed wire of a concentration camp. That year's model of the Ford Fiesta was presented as the vehicle in which to break free from the pastel lollipop world of suburbia drawn from the film *Edward Scissorhands*, because the car was "not for the small-minded". Even the repellent images of the ruthless gangsters in *Reservoir Dogs* and the cannibal murderer Hannibal Lecter of *Silence of the Lambs* were invoked to promote products as unlikely as margarine spread and tampons. To make sense of a 1994 commercial promoting the conglomerate Hanson, shot in black-and-white, you would have to know that in the coda of Orson Welles's 53-year-old cinema masterpiece, *Citizen Kane*, the dying newspaper magnate uttered a last word, "Rosebud". In this case, it was a dying investor, and the word was "Hanson", the company he wished he'd owned.

From its earliest days, long before the practice was known as "deconstructing", broadcast advertising was prone to poke fun at itself: the announcer fluffing his lines, the slide-show appearing upside down. The strategy behind such japes was flattery: by taking the audience behind the scenes and showing the magic tricks, the advertiser deferred to its cleverness. In the time-honoured ploy of the hustler, the "mark" could be taken in by suggesting he was too smart to be taken in. Top celebrities such as the renowned American radio comics Bob & Ray could even assume the privilege of gently mocking the product. Bob Hope made a career of it. But such personalities were well established as product spokesmen. High priests in the temple of commerce were permitted to make irreverent remarks, because their audiences knew they were only kidding. Deep down, they belonged to the company store, heart and soul. When British ironists turned their attention to debunking the style of advertising presentations, they, too, began by gently poking fun. The 1970s advertisements for "Vladivar Vodka brewed in (V)Warrington" were based on the conceit of a non-Russian vodka. Phileas Fogg snacks, from the same era, were "manufactured in Consett" (a British Nowheresville) and admonished viewers to "Pay attention". When British comedian Bob Monkhouse declared in his commercial for Sekonda Watches that "time is money" because he was being paid £1,000 a second for his endorsement, and when his fellow comic Jack Dee, infuriated by clichés of advertising production, stalked off the set of his commercial only to be lured back by a bag of gold, they were following the script of the old-time American radio trouper Jack Benny, charming consumers with their venality.

However, the British were soon dismantling conventional advertising root and branch. In 1991 a new telephone company, Mercury, launched a massive multimedia campaign featuring an invented spokesperson called Mr Grayson and his chum Cholmondley-Warner, both played by the popular television comedian Harry Enfield. The black and white television commercials were painstaking spoofs of the wooden style of 1940s Ministry of Information films, including, on television, the deliberate simulation of scratched old film, and on radio, scratchy sound. Although the ads nominally attempted to put across specific information, e.g. how to use the curious new pastel-coloured telephone boxes which had suddenly sprouted on British pavements, the faux-authoritarian characterisation of the spokesman dominated the presentation. The campaign won plaudits from the advertising industry and gained loads of free press publicity. Yet Mr Grayson habitually represented attitudes not necessarily beneficial to multinational companies, e.g. xenophobia. To get across the idea that you could use Mercury services from abroad, his foil was a French artist wearing a beret in Montmartre. Mr Grayson's message: "Beware. Johnnies abroad often can't speak English ... Yes, leave improvements in telecommunications to us at Mercury, Gaston, while you get on with making your excellent range of 365 cheeses for which your country is justly famous".

Imprisoned in a sardonic, unsympathetic characterisation, Mercury's flexibility of presentation was compromised. When British Telecom dropped its rates, Mercury could only reply by carping, through Mr Grayson's press ads: "WARNING! DON'T BE BAMBOOZLED by a rival's befuddling statistics – which cause FROWNS. MERCURY are the kind company who gentlemanly GUARANTEE better savings on UK long distance and international calls from your home. Which makes them SMART as PAINT". Or smartass, threatened, and unsporting, perhaps, in the view of their audience.

Mercury's payphones never made money, and in 1994 its 2,700 post-modern phone boxes were uprooted. At the end of that year, Mercury announced 2,500 job losses. Mr Grayson and his pal Cholmondley-Warner were among them. In noting the dismissal, a company spokesman gave this clue to the campaign's objectives: "Harry Enfield was tremendously successful in getting a lot of people to take notice. What we have achieved has been done with a fifth of BT's ad budget. His ads won a lot of awards". But had they influenced consumer behaviour?

From parodies of presentation styles, advertising "creatives" went on to poke fun at specific commercials. A series of Daz commercials used the comedian Danny Baker to send up traditional expectations of laundry detergent advertising. A Hamlet cigar ad spoofed the famous Andrews toilet tissue puppy. In a celebrated 1980s commercial for Levi's, a young lad had flouted propriety and influenced fashion trends by taking his jeans off in a launderette. A decade later, the scene was replayed in a lager commercial, to illustrate the punchline, "I bet he drinks Carling Black Label". The campaign for this beer guyed a whole series of well-known advertisements, including the Christmas perennial, the Old Spice aftershave surfer, and even presented its own compilations of "those commercials you liked best". In 1994 it took aim at another lager, Foster's "Mad Max" campaign, itself derived from a 1970s film. Foster's sidestepped by sending up the sensuous advertising for Häagen-Dazs ice-cream.

In 1994 British Rail Intercity ran a commercial which was a pastiche of a clutch of current commercials for cars such as Vauxhall, Renault, Peugeot, and Citroën, using the same characters and situations, with gags about the lower fuel consumption of train transport. Was this a serious attempt to attempt to stop people driving or just an irresistible joke? In the creaky 1995 advertisements for Wrigley's Doublemint chewing gum, girls still wondered where their clean-cut beaux might be taking them on a date, and worried about onions on their breath. A contemporaneous campaign by Haitai gum sent up the dated all-American image of its competitor. Its countercultural scenario simulated a 1950s public information film in which "straight arrow" FBI agents rounded up bankers, soldiers and cheerleaders – because they were chewing Haitai, promoted as "thoroughly un-American gum". A milestone down this cul-de-sac was reached in 1994 when Holsten Pils lager commercials employed Denis Leary, a misogynist American comedian, to trample advertising clichés and then sweep away a selection of bottled lagers for being "full of shit".

Advertising's progress from aspiration to denigration is neatly encapsulated by comparing the 1990s ads for Martini with those of the 1960s and 1970s. The earlier commercials showed aspirational images of beautiful young people cavorting on ski-slopes and wafting aloft in hot-air balloons. In 1995 a Martini commercial lampooned its own heritage. When a moody Jean-Paul Belmondo lookalike who had been eyeing a blonde sexpot left a café she rose to follow him, snagging her tight knitted dress, which unravelled as she walked to show us she wasn't wearing any knickers. There is a second agenda to advertising like this: the likelihood that this controversial shot will be publicised in the tabloid newspapers and that the sardonic script will be guyed in television comedy routines. But it's a short term strategy. While it makes a big splash, it will be unlikely to have the staying power of the original themes of success, played straight, which lasted for two decades.

Had consumers stopped having aspirations? In 1996 the sports shoe company Nike was claiming in its advertisements, "We don't sell dreams, we sell shoes". And a laid-back press ad for Sprite was saying, "It's not an image, it's a drink". These campaigns appeared in hip magazines aimed at young people under 30, who are assumed to be cynical and media-wise, and were created by cynical and media-wise advertising people, mostly under 30. Richard Benson, editor of *The Face,* reckoned his cool readers could be swayed only by underground cultural movements: "The 1990s has seen the death of aspiration. Rather than pick products that are sold to them, the youth market seeks out trash pop culture. Advertising has to work with this . . . [through] appeals to the antipathy of the enlightened consumer".

This is the strategy of exclusion. Those who share the gnosis are permitted to feel superior and privileged. This is intended to form a bond between the advertiser and consumer. It is the same strategy as that of a group of 9-year-olds banding together to form a club with secret passwords, or of Freemasonry, with its occult rituals. But elitism is a dangerous attitude for a mass-marketed product. To decode counter-cultural advertisements requires an intimacy with pop culture which may not be as widespread as their creators assume. It can become a closed world if you've not been paying a great deal of attention. Practitioners of the ironic strategy have a difficult line to tread. Their advertising has to be dumb enough not to exclude any potential buyer, but wise enough not to make its audience ashamed of the dumbness. For those of us who have not attended the creative briefing, the line between advertising cliché and excoriating irony is sometimes difficult to detect.

A full-page ad from the usually staid advertiser the Halifax Building Society, with the headline, "Our mortgages are as individual as you are", showed a rather odd-looking young couple wearing 1970s gear in their home, which was decorated in the same style. Was it taking the mickey out of them or not? In 1998, women in a focus group were perplexed by a Salon Selectives shampoo commercial which parodied the genre. "The women took it literally", regretted the J. Walter Thompson advertising agency; "they didn't realise that the absurd big hair was a joke". There was industry disagreement about a Ferrero Rocher commercial, a laboured portrayal of glamorous Eurotrash society stereotypes at an ambassadorial party. Devised by the manufacturer's in-house advertising agency, it was shot in England in 1987 for use on the Continent and not released on British television screens until 1993. UK advertising critics found it hard to decide whether it was a serious presentation of sophisticated tastes for the masses or a knowing send-up aimed at the cognoscenti of media culture. (The chocolate itself takes itself very seriously – gold-foil wrapped at a premium price for special gift occasions.) In the advertising trade press, respected advertising professionals described it as a brilliant ironic pastiche. John Lloyd, who had produced a previous campaign for Ferrero, disagreed: "We might think the ad is a joke, but for an Italian audience it looks genuinely sophisticated... We have a serious ad culture over here. People understand all the genres... they [Ferrero] do this ludicrous stuff at a cocktail party, which I'm sure they think people are meant to take seriously – and people laugh at it for the wrong reasons. They think it's utterly naff". In these appraisals, whether the audience could tell the difference was never at issue.

It's all great fun for the creatives who fall about at their cleverness in the viewing rooms and the "cultural mass", fattened by the 30,000 young Britons who graduate with a degree in media studies each year. They conjecture that the television commercial which successfully introduced a product called Shake and Vac in 1983, in which a singing housewife pranced about her home maniacally deodorising her carpet, was not serious, but artful parody. They gleefully deconstruct advertising clichés in presentations such as the 1999 television campaign for the new Egg credit card, which showed a stereotypical young family on a storybook village green. Aspirational illusions were systematically trashed. The wife said, "Of course, we're not really the ideal married couple – in fact in real life I can't stand him". The husband replied, "I tell you, if I was straight,

I wouldn't touch her with a bargepole", before flinging the baby to the ground because it's only a "hideous doll". But does the family in the shellsuits on the cross-Channel ferry share the same perspective? And if they buy the joke, will they buy the brand? Is irony a sales technique?

The American reaction to anti-aspirational attitudes was to defuse them by wrapping them, like a fractious child, in a warm comfort blanket. A 1998 press ad for a new Volvo carried the headline "We don't believe in conspicuous consumption. But it's sure going to be hard to hide this". Beneath was the usual voluptuous shot of a luxurious interior swathed in white leather.

Irony ridicules aspiration, limits expectation. Cynicism may have been the mood of sections of the British public under the austerity government of Clement Atlee, but does it hold true in today's society, which apes so many American ambitions, from upward mobility to out-of-town shopping? You don't see irony in perfume ads. And can you imagine the Japanese, who flock to buy Aquascutum mackintoshes and Gucci handbags, going for it? The Broadway playwright George S. Kaufman once observed, "Satire is what closes Saturday night". Is advertising parody what flops on Saturday morning at the checkout?

IRONY IS THE ARMOUR of the insecure, who fear being exposed to ridicule. It is not surprising, therefore, that the young, who are the least experienced with and therefore most threatened by life, are the most desperate to conform to what their peer group thinks is "cool". Rejecting the values of their elders and not yet having had the opportunity to learn from life experience, they borrow attitudes from the media, which may be obtained without involvement and at no personal risk. Being "cool" is an expression of solidarity which is beyond criticism; anyone who tries to think originally is ostracised. It converts the weaknesses of youth – ignorance, inability and isolation – into anti-social expressions of power. Its price is the anxiety of constant vigilance, to keep abreast of the blurring pace of shifting fashions.

As an exploitation of dissidence, advertising irony cleverly penetrates the tinplate armour of some youthful target groups to manipulate their craving for conformity. But in the tail-chasing way of the industry, it has been widely misapplied against less appropriate targets. Corporate irony, which ridicules the very thing that it is selling – and ridicules the act of selling, too – is self-defeating.

Irony requires no self-exposure, no manifesto, no commitment. It scorns principles of any kind. It's the nihilist ethos of the trenches, making sardonic wisecracks as a shield against fear. There's a difference between scepticism, a natural and healthy consumer attitude, and cynicism, which is funking emotional commitment. Detachment is easy. What is difficult is to defend something you believe in, even at the risk of being uncool. Emotion takes this risk. It grows out of belief in an idea or a person. It creates involvement. Without it, the consumer remains outside the message, untouched and uninvolved.

To summarise this section, once brands were built on "Unique Selling Propositions"; now they seek to distinguish themselves through expressions of common attitudes, striking poses they believe will resonate with their intended consumer. But the self-referential nature of those who create advertising leads them into self-deception. Assuming that the attitudes of their target groups are much like their own, they talk to themselves, and succumb to self-indulgent distractions such as puns, sexual allusions, or irony. Being camp places them beyond criticism.

Advertising techniques are thus often widely misapplied; yet artfully employed they can exploit our deepest anxieties. Over the decades, the flawed apparatus of advertising has fostered the growth of entire industries based firmly on falsehood. Five of these edifices are examined in the next section.

PART IV

Masters of deception

"Not eating your Cheezies, Miller?"

CHAPTER 19

HOW TO MAKE A STATEMENT THOUGH COMPLETELY INARTICULATE

Fashion

Fashion is only for people who don't know who they are. Quentin Crisp

FASHION is fleeting; style is lasting. If you've got style, you don't need fashion. In theory, observers of the fashion scene tell us, if a teenage girl were sufficiently self-actualised to wear her granny's housecoat to a hip-hop rave, and cool enough to bring it off, the next week all the ravers would be dressed as Mrs Mop. (Remember granny glasses?) But few of us are self-confident enough to abandon the display which identifies us. Just as few people would have had the courage to walk the streets of 1930s Soho as a flamboyant cross-dresser, as Quentin Crisp did. Because the more usual result of eccentric behaviour is ostracism by the peer group. Otherwise men wouldn't wear suits to the office and jeans at the weekend. As change occurs, society responds by ritualising it: to wear a suit to the office on Friday, at a company which has adopted a Friday dress-down policy, is equally unthinkable. In practice, acceptance of new fashions depends on the status of the innovator. Only the king could get away with wearing no clothes. Today the princes and princesses of popular culture wield that kind of power, their techniques of display proselytised and their status reconfirmed by the courtiers of the media. The merchants of advertising, hovering as ever on the verges of any new source of empowerment, are quick to clothe old ideas in new garments.

The need to conform is a powerful drive. Cultural movements which promise simple, complete answers to social problems thrive, from new religions to fashion magazines. They allow us to resolve fearfulness and insecurity without the labour of exercising independent judgement. Fashion commentators tell the teenage girl what to wear, whom to go out with, why she's upset, how to deal with sex. They tell her mother the same. In 1999 women were putting their names on waiting-lists in London's smart shops for the privilege of shelling out over £1,000 for a small sausage-shaped handbag with a distinctive logo: the Fendi baguette was the "must-have" badge of the season. In recent years, men and boys have succumbed to similar influences.

Department stores used to encourage individual choice by grouping garments together. There was a corsetry department, haberdashery and suits, available for inspection, each in its own area. Today these items appear all over the store, so if you aim to make a functional choice through comparison, it's a nightmarish task. That's because department stores, which advertise very little, have realised that most of their customers now shop for "designer labels" which advertise a great deal. We have chosen to become label victims, because it's easier, and safer for our self-esteem, than venturing an independent evaluation. An important part of the appeal is that labels advertise our status, turning us into walking hoardings flaunting the brand name.

The mass marketing of fashion began with the glamour of Hollywood stars, ceaselessly invoked as female role models. In the 1920s Clara Bow showed her knees and millions of flappers raised their hemlines. In 1930 the studio photographer on the set of *Hell's Angels* highlighted the glow of actress Jean Harlow's blonde hair with a spotlight, and MGM's publicists invented the phrase "platinum blonde". Before that film was released most hairdressers were reluctant to apply bleach, but afterwards, according to her biography, "beauty parlors in every major city were overwhelmed, as tens of thousands of women demanded platinum".

Hollywood showed women how they were supposed to look, and how to behave. Waves of fashion stimulated women to adopt Marlene Dietrich's eyebrows, Joan Crawford's squared shoulders, Jane Russell's pointed breasts, Greta Garbo's cheekbones, Paulette Goddard's pert sophistication, Marilyn Monroe's wanton vulnerability. The glamour machine could persuade women to do almost anything: bob their hair, shave their armpits, pluck their eyebrows, pad their shoulders, wear trousers. Advertising testimonials from Hollywood stars, and the society ladies who imitated them, promised to fulfil adolescent daydreams via everything from shampooing to smoking. Men were not invulnerable to such impressions. Clark Gable was single-handedly responsible for a decline in the sale of undershirts when he stripped off his shirt and appeared bare-chested in a film, and for the effective demise of the traditional industry of Danbury, Connecticut when he went hatless. The new reality of the permissive generations of the 1960s and 1970s threw up more attainable role models, until Madonna returned to glamour, with her sadistic, ironic interpretation of the old Hollywood values, while other pop stars encouraged women to shave their heads.

Celebrity testimonials are still ubiquitous in fashion advertisements, though now the selection of role models is eclectic. Glossy magazines are the medium of choice. The mannequins which feature in them have emerged from anonymity to become supermodels, making the transition from objective example to subjective endorser. The mid-1990s campaign for the retail chain Gap included writers and philosophers, as well as actors, in its roll-call of personality endorsers. The portrayal of the garment was incidental. The idea, captured in moody black-and-white photographs by leading impressionists such as Annie Leibowitz, was that the choice of apparel somehow captured the soul of the personality. An American advertisement featuring the druggy philosopher Timothy Leary shortly before his death was a portrait photograph of his head and shoulders, where the $34 chambray shirt he wore, though distinctively patterned, was barely identifiable. Added to your wardrobe, it was a magic cloak which could enhance your own perception of yourself. A 1998 advertisement for the American retailer Paul Stuart ran this copy beneath a photograph of a smart but ordinary-looking woman wearing a coat and trousers: "Create a picture perfect image of yourself. This savvy New York museum administrator understands that she too is always on display. With an inherent appreciation of the uniqueness of creativity, she reflects her own sense of style in our olive superfine covert wool ensemble..."

But fashion ads rarely need to be so explicit. Usually they leave the reader to imagine the world of privilege she seeks to inhabit. In an advertisement for designer Giorgio Armani it was deemed sufficient to add just three words to a black-and-white close-up of a well-known young lady wearing sunglasses. Two of them were "Giorgio Armani", and the third the name of the lady in question. Photographs for fashion labels are often generic impressions identifiable as a clothing advertisement only by a barely visible hem or shoulder strap.

The power of visual imagery now dominant throughout advertising was first recognised and perfected in fashion. High-fashion photographers instinctively knew that they were not portraying a garment, but a mood of fantasy. Models were placed in unlikely, even surrealistic situations. Advertising simply picked up the lead. The American Banana Republic retail chain promotes its back-to-nature style with a wistful picture of a modern Eve by an apple tree. An Emporio Armani ad poses an equally wispy model wearing a black and white pinstripe cloak and trousers in front of the business end of a huge semi-trailer. Its message: butch but vulnerable. Neither illustration needs words.

From mood imagery it was a short step to attitude, and the fashion industry took it first. There was always a good reason for the vacant expression of fashion models: photographers knew that a vibrant human personality would disrupt the mood of ethereal fantasy, and models knew that smiling created wrinkles. But the mood soured. Now models scowled, sulked, eyeballed us belligerently, or hung their heads in listless despair. We saw less and less of the clothing, more and more exposed flesh. A 1996 American ad for Docker's trousers by Levi Strauss laid it on the line. It showed a burly black man, bald, stripped to the waist, wearing only what one presumes is the product on a city street, with three nerdish-looking types wearing conventional suits and white shirts and ties, looking at him disapprovingly. One holds up a handwritten sign which reads, "To those who have completely missed the point, independence is an economic term. For everyone else, it's a way of life. – The Mission, Chap. 2 p. 18". The only other text in the ad is the advice that you can pick up a copy of the aforesaid document at your Docker's dealer, listed below.

In Britain, attitude was adopted as the not-quite-so-unique selling proposition of several brands of jeans and trainers. Commercials for brands such as Levis and Nike consistently won creative awards. Bartle Bogle Hegarty's 1985 commercials for Levis established a formula: an insouciant hero indifferent to social constraints, and a strip scene. In one he took a bath in his Levis. In another he took them off in a launderette. In a third a 14-year-old girl stripped to wriggle into her absent boy friend's jeans. Allegedly these efforts revitalised a flagging demand for denim, also boosting competitive brands, such as Lee, which did not advertise. Imitators followed in droves. The British manufacturer Pepe attached an enigmatic one-world *Weltanschauung* to its jeans in a 1988 commercial which featured flickering Super-8 footage of a Hopi Indian rain dance, before cutting to a pubescent European youth and an American Indian girl sheltering from a downpour in a shop doorway. The lame connection was contained in the slogan: "Pepe Clothing – Worlds Apart".

Inevitably, commercials for jeans returned to their American origins. In a Wrangler ad the hero demonstrated his rejection of society by quitting his yellow cab in a mid-Manhattan gridlock to clamber over stalled traffic to his goal. A Levis commercial was set in a hectic Wall Street financial trading room, where, as the script synopsis enthused, "out of the lift emerges a cool-looking motor-cyclist wearing sunglasses, leather jacket, denim shirt and Red Tab 501s, riding a gleaming Harley Davidson". He steered his machine between the computer terminals and flung a pair of jeans on to the desk of an attractive female trader. She dropped her skirt, and the jaws of her shocked colleagues, to wriggle into the jeans. In the last shot, she was riding pillion into the setting sun over the 59th Street bridge.

In the logic of advertising, the way to protest against materialistic values is to go out and buy something. A 1995 cinema commercial for Pepe jeans substituted adolescent angst for teenage dreams: a disillusioned youth drove off in his father's Mercedes and hung it from a crane in the shadow of Canary Wharf tower. While trashing a badge product of one generation, the young hero promoted another: life's a drag, so chill out with a new pair of jeans.

As mass market retailers such as Gap and Next began to fill the pages of magazines with images as sophisticated as the editorial content, in order to distinguish themselves from the ruck, the haute couture fashion houses were driven to ever more extreme, less explicit, more allusive devices. Rather than showing clothes, the emphasis was on projecting the innovative spirit of the designer and his label. Facing a conventional model across the page we see a black-and-white portrait of a bald, moustachioed man wearing a pair of ladies' sandals. This was top designer Franco Moschino's way of selling his shoe collection. Another monochrome ad showed two bare-chested body builders. Only the waistband of Jean Paul Gaultier's new jeans was visible. Comme Des Garçons showed no clothes at all – just two girls back-to-back, laughing, with braces on their teeth. The press handout explained they "represent vitality and energy". This aid was not available to the general reader, who may easily miss the point of cryptic ads aimed at the cognoscenti.

In his film *Pret à Porter* Robert Altman satirised the minimalist approach when a couturière on the brink of bankruptcy made a desperate gesture: her models walked down the runway naked. It was not so far-fetched. A 1998 issue of *Dutch,* a tiny European style magazine with an influential international circulation, caught the attention of America's important fashion newspaper *Women's Wear Daily* when it published 83 continuous pages of black-and-white nude pictures by Mikael Jansson, a Swedish photographer. Each picture, without showing any clothing, was intended to represent the essence of a particular designer. Editor-in-chief Matthias Vriens matched the photos to the brands: "Some of the pairings are obvious, such as the feet in water with the shoe label Cesare Paciott; others less so. The Missoni picture features girls with plaited hair. The plaits represent Missoni's knitting. Fendi, (known for fur coats) was also obvious. There was a little fur available there, on the pudendum". According to Cristina Ortiz, the designer from the French house Lanvin, the symbolisation of her label as a bare-breasted girl covered in goose-pimples was spot on: "I wasn't shocked at all . . . I think it is the Lanvin woman, sensual but not aggressive".

Of course, all the famous couture houses which have survived are now big business. Christian Dior is owned by the luxury goods giant Louis Vuitton Moët Hennessy. LMVH also owns Louis Vuitton, Givenchy, Kenzo. Guerlain, Céline, Le Bon Marché (Paris), Christian Lacroix, and Sephora cosmetics as well as most of the champagne labels James Bond would have found agreeable. The reality is that the market for haute couture does not exist; there are fewer than 1,000 women in the world who can afford it. The famous designer names have prospered by extending their exotic appeal from the tiny international group of heiresses, dictators' concubines, and trophy wives who buy exclusive gowns to mass market products. You can buy their neck-scarves, their sunglasses, their lipstick, their perfumes and creams, and stick them in their handbag with its indiscreet logo. The hoopla of the famous international fashion weeks in Paris, Milan, and London is aimed not at sales, but at publicity. At the 1998 Paris event the dresses shown by new designers such as Viktor & Rolf were not for sale. "We could sell thirty pieces a season, but we refuse to, because we don't have the structure". Designers do not hope to recoup the cost of creating a couture collection. They appear at these shows to gain acceptability and generate publicity for their ready-to-wear lines. A fashion house has to pay nearly £20,000 for one full-colour double-page spread in British Vogue. The publicity surrounding a couture show, with its invited cast of movie stars, fashion editors, and supermodels, replayed in the press and on television, is a cannier investment. That's why there is intense competition to *give away* couture gowns to Hollywood stars scheduled to appear on stage at the annual Academy Awards. Not to create a market for £10,000 gowns, but to peddle stockings at £2.99 a pair and cellulite cream at £29.95 a jar under the same name.

In the hothouse atmosphere of fashion the exceptional iconoclastic advertisement has an air of wilting desperation. A 1994 ad for a brand of jeans called Everlast was a whinge. With its logo as the only illustrative device, the copy read: "Taking a bunch of plastic-looking models, putting them in ridiculous outfits and photographing them in places no one really goes. Is that fashion? Activewear by U.S. Classic Inc. are the real thing and everyone else's sportswear is about having some sort of attitude".

Fashion advertisers also generally avoid a humorous perspective; it is imprudent to poke fun in a product sector where consumer pretensions are so close to laughable. The ironic posture is ludicrous. "Ellesse is more" read the headline in an introspective 1997 parody of a press fashion advertisement. The copy began, "Pair fishnets with boat shoes and you've got the perfect sole for sole (look I'm really sorry)". It went on to list all the apparel which did not appear in a long shot showing two figures just barely visible in a rowboat on a misty mountain lake, and which was "unavailable in Misty Buff, Lambsblood and Unripe Prune", and concluded with production credits: "Words, locations, continuity & worm-charming: Jack O'Falltrades. The Ellesse team stayed at home as it's only a stock shot from a photo library anyway..." In 1995 Levis took the bold stroke of satirising its own scenarios of rebellious youth. As a licence to indulge in lavatorial humour, it used a non-realistic technique, Claymation, a way of animating three-dimensional figures popularised by the *Wallace and Gromit* films. A scatological spoof of an adolescent "rescue-the-fair-damsel" scenario involved crapping pigeons, an old man squatting on a toilet, and a neon sign for the "Schmitt Hotel" in which the letter "m" was missing. Preparing to enjoy his sexual reward in the toilet, to the consternation of its occupant, the hero took off his jeans in homage to the brand's famous "Launderette" commercial. The rescued damsel went berserk, thrashing her big hair about and grinning insanely. Her tongue hung out and she fell to her knees before him in ecstasy. Soberly assessed, it overspecified the fantasy.

Deviant experiments such as these are unlikely to make much headway. In this world of wishful fulfilment there is no place for dissidents. The boy who pointed his finger at the naked king will have been apprehended by the thought police. Has a salesman ever sold you a suit by taking the mick?

Rationality has no relevance in this emotional marketplace. In 1999 the Department of Trade and Industry championed consumer choice by backing retailers such as Tesco and Asda in their struggle to win the right to sell designer labels such as Levi's jeans, Pringle sweaters, and Calvin Klein underwear at discount prices. These retailers argued that restrictive practices, sanctioned by the European Court of Justice, meant that consumers were paying up to 70 per cent more than they ought to. Tesco sponsored a test case in the courts "to bring better value to our customers". But price is only one side of the fashion equation; how long would consumers bestow extra value on the Calvin Klein label if they found it displayed in Tesco at cheap prices next to the nylon shirts? What is the value of diamonds if beaches are made of them?

Fashion and its sister siren, cosmetics, indulge our fantasies by offering a simple panacea to our dissatisfactions: we can become somebody else. Both allow us to believe we have shifted the image we see in our mirror closer to our self-image. Shirley Polykoff, a New York copywriter who ended up running her own agency, wrote enduring headlines which offered self-transformation to millions of women. For Miss Clairol, the first effective hair colour lightener, introduced in 1956, she wrote: "Does she or doesn't she? Only her hairdresser knows for sure", for Clairol's Nice 'n Easy shampoo-in hair colour: "The closer he gets, the better you look", and for Lady Clairol's platinum bleach: "Is it true that blondes have more fun?" and "If I've only one life to live let me live it as a blonde". In the 1970s L'Oréal Preference hair colourant responded with another justification for self-realisation created by another female copywriter, Ilon Specht: "Because I'm worth it". Between the 1950s and the 1970s the number of American women colouring their hair rose from 7 per cent to over 40 per cent. In 1997 L'Oréal adopted "Because I'm worth it" as a corporate slogan embracing all their products, and an astonishing 71 per cent of American women now link that battle cry to the L'Oreal brand.

FASHION is the ultimate triumph of style over substance. Expressing your individuality is its USP. "It isn't me, somehow" is the way we reject a style. Yet fashion forces us to conform. To identify ourselves as part of a group we belong to, aspire to belong to, or to be taken for. Always avant-garde, the slick emptiness of fashion advertising has now set the tone for aspirational advertising of all kinds, from toiletries to booze to motor cars.

CHAPTER 20

YOU STICK IT BETWEEN YOUR LIPS AND SET FIRE TO IT? AND THEN IT KILLS YOU?

Tobacco

In the United States in 1949 the National Broadcasting Company launched the "Camel News Caravan", a 15-minute television programme fronted by the eminent newscaster John Cameron Swayze. The sponsors laid down certain ground rules. Cigars were considered a competitive product, so no news footage could be shown of anyone smoking one – with the exception of Winston Churchill, who was granted a special dispensation. Filmed shots which showed "No Smoking" signs in the background were strictly forbidden.

EVERY KID always knew you shouldn't smoke if you wanted to be an athlete. And everyone could hear a smoker's cough. Even cigarette advertisements admitted there was a problem. A typical American example from the 1930s showed a glamorous woman puffing away over the headline: "20,679 physicians say LUCKIES are less irritating". The copy explained, "Toasting removes dangerous irritants that cause throat irritation and coughing".

But other doctors could see inside the lungs. In 1964 the Surgeon-General's office of the United States established the link between smoking and lung cancer. Yet, in a country which had made the movies which glamorised smoking throughout the world, where former President Ronald Reagan once advertised Chesterfields wearing a cowboy suit, and which still subsidised its tobacco farmers because of the export value of their crop, regulation was an uphill struggle. The strategy of the tobacco companies was consistent denial. Their argument was that there was no incontrovertible proof, which gave smokers, who were unable to give up one of the world's most addictive substances, the answer they wanted to hear. At the same time the tobacco industry fostered "independent" research aimed at disinformation and launched filter cigarettes, which appeared to be safer but were no less dangerous. And, reaching into bottomless pockets it fought every legal action tenaciously. Tobacco companies never paid a penny in damages until 1999 when they disgorged $206 billion to 46 American states, the largest legal settlement in the history of the world, to avoid being sued for the medical costs of treating smokers. Yet, apart from the Ligget Group, the smallest manufacturer, the industry refused to comply with new codes forbidding the use of cartoon characters in advertisements, which the Federal Drug Administration asserts are deliberate attempts to hook children.

The youth market is critical for cigarette manufacturers because the users of their products do not live as long as other people. In Britain half of all regular cigarette smokers are eventually killed by their habit. Eighty-two per cent of smokers begin as teenagers, and advertising to children is a good investment. Thirty per cent of those who experiment with cigarettes become regular smokers. And, on average, an adolescent who smokes at least 100 cigarettes has committed to 16-20 years of addicted smoking before he will be able to quit. In 1999 one in three 15-year-old girls were smoking regularly in Britain, on the increase for the first time in 25 years.[1]

How advertising people rose to the challenge of persuading youth to acquire a deadly habit was revealed in a strategic advertising planning document dating from 1975 which surfaced in a legal action against British American Tobacco in 1999. The Ted Bates agency presented proposals to the BAT subsidiary Brown & Williamson for its Viceroy brand which aimed to convert non-smokers and smokers of competitive brands. In order to avoid confronting smokers with "the fact that they are illogical, irrational and stupid", the recommendation was to present cigarette smoking as an initiation into the adult world.

> In the young smoker's mind, a cigarette falls into the same category with wine, beer, shaving, wearing a bra (or purposely not wearing one), a declaration of independence and striving for self-identity... Present the cigarette as part of the illicit pleasure category of products and activities... touch on the basic symbols of growing-up, the maturity process. To the best of your ability (considering some legal constraints) relate the cigarette to pot, wine, beer, sex, etc.

Commenting on the litigation, a B&W spokesman passed the buck: "We eventually fired Ted Bates & Co".

---

[1] Statistics are extracted from the *Journal of the American Medical Association*, 1989 (a paper by Willard Manning) and 1996; John Pierce of the University of California, San Diego in the *Milbank Quarterly*, 1992; and the *British Medical Journal*, 1994.

The tobacco companies' classic defence of advertising, and its common sense rebuttal, were efficiently summarised in an exchange of letters in the *Guardian* in 1992:

> The reason the tobacco companies do not "save themselves a bob or two" (letters February 14) is the same as why petrol companies do not save themselves a bob or two by ceasing to advertise and why soap manufacturers don't do the same. The fact is that all such manufacturers spend money on advertising to encourage customers to switch brands, not to increase total consumption.
> Sir Frank Rogers, Deputy Chairman of the *Daily Telegraph,* chairman of the Newspaper Publishers' Association and of the European Publishers Council

> We must be grateful to Sir Frank Rogers for his explanation that "manufacturers spend money on advertising to encourage customers to switch brands, not to increase total consumption" (letters February 19). We can now understand why the privatised utilities spend so much of their vast profits on advertising. Were it not for Beattie's amusing routines I might be sending messages by pigeon post; the water companies dissuade me from filling my kettle from my ornamental fish pond; but for those cosy electricity adverts I would be using candles, and highly paid American stars are needed to induce me to switch on the gas rather than search the shores for driftwood to burn.
> Gwenda Sanders, Folkestone, Kent

Advertising agencies were able to justify their work for tobacco companies only on the grounds that it was ineffective; that is, it could not create peer group pressure on young minds. Unlike the ads created for soft drinks, sweets, snacks, clothing, video games, toys, trainers and the rest, by which the same people earned their bread. Cigarette advertising, for some reason, was invisible to non-smokers or the young. With the accuracy claimed for laser-guided missiles, advertising messages targeted only existing smokers over age 25; new recruits could pick up the habit only from their example.

These assertions were contrary to the experience of virgin markets. In the late 1980s the US government negotiated trade agreements which permitted American cigarettes to be sold in Japan, South Korea, Taiwan, and Thailand in competition with state-owned tobacco monopolies. Because established smokers rarely change brands, manufacturers sought to attract young non-smokers and, particularly, to emancipate women from the social strictures against smoking, as they had in the United

States in the 1920s.

As a condition of a 1987 trade agreement, cigarette advertising was introduced into Taiwan for the first time. Advertisers were unhampered by the advertising taboos of the West: they could use attractive young role models, and a fag jutted once more from the weather-beaten lips of the Marlboro cowboy. Although American cigarettes were far more expensive, within six years smoking amongst high-school students rose from 26 to 48 per cent for boys, and from 1 to 20 per cent for girls. When American tobacco advertising assaulted Japan that same year, the domestic monopoly retaliated with a new brand called Dean, after James Dean, and another called Misty, aimed at young women. Within a year cigarette expenditure on television had risen from the fortieth largest product category to second, and smoking by women and teenagers soared. A year after the South Korean market was breached the smoking rate for male teenagers rose from 18 to 30 per cent, and for young girls from 2 to 9 per cent. By the mid-1990s Asia was in the grip of a smoking epidemic, as Britain had been in the 1930s.

The advertising of tobacco products was finally banned in Britain in the closing days of the 20th century. Television advertising had been outlawed in 1965. Over the intervening thirty-five years, tobacco advertising in other media was increasingly restricted. It could not show people who appeared to be under 25, nor attractive models; it could not glamorise smoking nor encourage people to smoke. In short, it should be as ineffective as possible. The advertising response to these interim measures is instructive: it suggests how the ban on advertising will also be compromised.

In 1977 cinema-goers were mystified by a cinema commercial in which the camera spun through impressions of dazzling sunshine and glittering wealth before coming to rest on a glowing pack of cigarettes: Benson & Hedges Gold. By the early 1980s gold-tinged press and poster advertisements were omitting the brand name altogether. Without the obligatory black-and-white government health warning there would have been no clue to the advertiser. The puzzle begged involvement and the solution was simple-minded: B&H = gold = status. These enigmatic advertisements reaped a golden harvest of advertising awards, unleashing a flood of copycat advertising. A cigarette was the first to subvert advertising itself. In the early 1980s posters appeared whinging, "We're not allowed to tell you anything about Winston cigarettes, so here is a tart leaning on a bar", and showed a picture of a jam tart resting on an iron bar. Another, with the conclusion "... so here's a walk in the Black Forest", showed a Chinese wok buried in a gateau.

In 1984 Charles Saatchi, whose agency had flourished on the reputation of its early anti-smoking campaigns for the Health Authority, had a creative inspiration on the level of a pictogram: the brand Silk Cut could best be embedded in the national consciousness by showing a piece of rent silk fabric next to a pair of scissors. Through endless extenuations of this theme (by 1993 it was a swordfish wearing silk boxing shorts) the fabric was always purple, the colour of the pack. Cigarette packs, which are displayed as a badge of personal identity, are strongly identified with recognisable colours. All cigarette advertising soon became fixated on a single objective: to identify the brand with a colour, or in some cases a number, appearing on the pack. It was a hedge against the future: if tobacco advertising were to be banned, the brand message could still be semaphored, on television and elsewhere, through sponsorship of sporting events and other activities.

The only product claim now permitted was the stark advice of the Chief Medical Officer. Sometimes, in the absence of any other headline, the warning was bizarrely appropriate: a 1995 advertisement showed a very sick-looking multi-coloured frog with its long tongue extended on the ground above the legend "Smoking makes you ill". A 1999 advertisement welcoming readers to "Marlboro Country", now compulsorily voided of cowboys, showed vultures wheeling in a circle, with the headline, "Warning: Picnic Area". A more direct message appeared underneath, "Smoking Causes Cancer". Cigarette advertising had been forced into a flight from meaning, but because of the massive amounts tobacco companies expended on advertising, meaning hardly mattered. The objective was to make their brands, or at least the signalling colours of their brands, ubiquitous. Coca-Cola has followed the same policy all over the world for decades. If brands appear everywhere – in magazines and newspapers, on posters, shop fronts, product displays, the exteriors of buildings, football grounds, discos, and cigarette machines – they cannot be dislodged from the mind. It is the oldest trick in the catechism of advertising: simple repetition. And high visibility implies the endorsement of the society in which these messages appear: anything that is so omnipresent must really be okay.

In 1993 one of Britain's favourite cartoon strip characters kicked the habit. The crumpled fag which had dangled from the lower lip of Andy Capp for 36 years suddenly disappeared. His creator, Reg Smythe, explained, "Too many kids read the cartoon and it was time he set a good example". Too late. Andy Capp's role as a totem of bolshy northern male chauvinism had already been appropriated by another character, and this one was in the employ of a cigarette company. In 1992 posters and newspaper ads began to appear north of the Trent featuring another Reg, a fat middle-aged man of moronic appearance, who promoted Imperial Tobacco's downmarket cigarette brand, Embassy Regal, with the slogan, "I smoke 'em because my name's on 'em". His dirty fingernails clutching the pack obscured the last two letters of the brand name. Reg specialised in gnomic pronouncements of schoolyard wit: "Reg on taxes: too many cabs drive too fast", and "Reg on party politics: If you drop ash on the carpet you won't get invited again".

The ASA determined that the Regal advertisements were not in breach of the voluntary advertising code: because "Reg" was neither young nor attractive, it concluded he could not be taken as a role model by those under 18 years of age. The adjudicators clearly were not readers of *Viz* magazine, the million-selling juvenile comic from which this innovative campaign borrowed its subversive tone. The pages of this comic abound with repulsive characters like "Reg" who flout authority, upholding the appealing virtues of disorder and ignorance . Your parents wouldn't like them, and so kids do. Adults who exercise dominion over you may tell you not to smoke, but Reg says it's all right to cock a snook. While the ASA failed to spot that Reg was an anti-hero fomenting youthful rebellion, *Viz* magazine acknowledged the homage from the world of advertising by running a mock advertisement satirising the campaign, with Reg saying, "I smoke 'em cos I'm chemically addicted to nicotine". Another tribute came from the 1992 Campaign Poster Awards, where the Reg campaign garnered a fistful of top awards. Adrian Holmes, chairman of the agency Lowe Howard-Spink, which created the campaign, enthused "Creative restrictions, far from limiting the advertising mind, actually seem to stimulate it".

Within a twelvemonth of the campaign's launch the Health Education Authority discovered that awareness of the Regal campaign was 91 per cent amongst teenagers in the North of England, whereas only 50 per cent of adults had noticed it. It was particularly popular amongst 11-to-15-year-olds, with child smokers saying it gave them a reason to carry on smoking. Within that age group, in those regions, there had been a significant increases in the rate of regular smoking since the previous year. The authority concluded that the campaign was deliberately and effectively aimed at minors. By then Reg had entered the schoolyard argot. In Manchester, kids no longer called someone stupid a "Wally"; they called him a "Reg". In Gateshead 80 per cent of underage smokers smoked Embassy Regal. The ASA was forced to reconsider its decision and the campaign was withdrawn.

Joe Camel, a wise-cracking, cigarette-smoking "cool" cartoon personification of the RJR Reynolds brand, starred for six years in one of the heaviest US advertising campaigns, beginning in 1987. Four years later, a study by the *Journal of the American Medical Association* found that 91 per cent of 6-year-olds were able to recognise Joe Camel, only 5 per cent fewer than knew Mickey Mouse. More than half the children aged 3-6 could match the Joe Camel logo with a photograph of a cigarette. By 1993 Camel's share of the under-18 market had zoomed from 0.5 per cent to 33 per cent. When the Federal Trade Commission moved to ban Joe, the brand switched to a new tack, introducing Camel Mild in 1994 with a list of schoolboy jests which would have made "Reg" reach for his sick bag, such as "The hard of hearing never confuse Camel Mild with Camomile because the former tastes smoother".

In 1991 B J Cunningham, a chain-smoking entrepreneur in his 20s, took the paradox of cigarette smoking to its logical conclusion, launching a cigarette brand called Death. The pack was decorated with a skull and crossbones and in addition to the government health warning carried this additional manufacturers' advice: "Smoking is addictive and debilitating, if you don't smoke don't start, if you smoke, quit". Cunningham claimed he was introducing a new technique to cigarette marketing – blatant honesty: "breaking the taboo about death and smoking is our USP". The brand was supported by advertising in youth media with illustrations such as chest X-rays showing a shadow and the message "Death Kills". Nevertheless, the Death campaign was condemned by the anti-smoking lobby, which, unlike the ASA in the case of Embassy Regal, saw through a cynical effort to influence young people through nihilism and gallows humour. When the major multiples in the tobacco trade refused to stock his brand, Cunningham fell back on a duty-free import scheme. The crude appeal to feckless teenagers was replaced by pious full-page advertisements in national newspapers, complaining of the duplicitous advertising of other cigarettes. In 1994 five poster companies, whose biggest clients were the established tobacco companies, found ads for Death cigarettes too controversial and refused to accept them. (No such ban was imposed on the "Reg" campaign.) Death was killed when the Imperial Tobacco Company challenged Cunningham's import scheme in the High Court and won.

The tobacco industry also advertised to solicit political support. A "light-hearted" but heavy-handed campaign offered as a guide to civilised social behaviour appeared in the American press in 1995. The advertisement cited eight "amusing" cartoon situations, only two of which had anything to do with smoking. Under the slogan "Together, we can work it out", the sponsor was identified: "in the interest of an informed debate by R.J. Reynolds Tobacco Company. We believe that most smoking issues can be resolved through dialogue and that discussion will help solve the issues without further government intervention".

In Britain the Tobacco Advisory Council, the pro-smoking group financed by the cigarette manufacturers, used press advertising to lobby against a 1992 Department of Health Report which linked smoking with cigarette advertising. It reprised an ancient ad agency joke by showing a fat slob asking a chemist for "a box of tampons so I can ski, surf and ride horses, like they do in the adverts". The copy argued, "Do you believe that an advertisement can make you buy something you don't want? Because the anti-tobacco lobby does...." Nevertheless, in 1994 the Smee Report, commissioned by the government's Health Select Committee and the European Union, affirmed the obvious: cigarette advertising induces people to buy cigarettes. In four countries where bans had been implemented, the number of smokers dropped by between 5 and 9 per cent. The British government banned tobacco advertising, but not yet sponsorship, at the end of 1999. The tobacco companies threw more lawyers at the problem and won an injunction giving them the right to appeal to the House of Lords on the technicality that the ruling pre-empted forthcoming EC legislation.

Anti-tobacco interests are gathering strength throughout the Western world. As part of the "master settlement" with the tobacco companies the colossal Marlboro man billboard bestriding Sunset Boulevard like an urban monument was ceded to the California Health and Education Department for its own campaign. The cowboy's fag now drooped over the word "Impotent", and the tobacco companies had to pay for it. Philip Morris sought to purchase legitimacy in the US. by establishing a department called "Youth Smoking Prevention", and curiously, in view of its conviction that advertising cannot encourage youth to start smoking, launched a $100 million campaign to discourage them from starting. This was another diversionary stalling tactic; Philip Morris did not agree to respect the advertising restrictions aimed at youth which had been demanded by the state attorneys-general in 1997, such as eliminating all human images, including the Marlboro man.

The tobacco industry laid plans long ago to protect its vast worldwide revenues from cigarette marketing through "trademark diversification". In 1990, the fourth largest advertiser in all of Malaysia was a small travel agency specialising in tours to mountain regions. On television, a 60-second spot ran at least once a night, extolling destinations such as the Alps, with their "clean mountain air". The number of Malaysians vacationing in the Alps would appear unlikely to justify such expenditure, but the account was handled by the same advertising agency entrusted with the R J Reynolds business, and that tobacco company paid for all the TV advertising. The travel agency, Salem High Country Holidays, was named after one of their brands. BAT advertised the Benson & Hedges Bistro, a coffee shop in Kuala Lumpur. In Taiwan each tobacco company was limited to 120 magazine ads per year, but 1992 advertising promoting a Virginia Slims fashion show featuring young Western women in the brand's colours at a Taipei disco was not counted against Philip Morris's quota, because it made no mention of cigarettes.

In China, American cigarettes are available only in exchange for hard currency at specified locations convenient for foreigners. Direct cigarette advertising is outlawed. Yet the Philip Morris trademark, the Marlboro cowboy, is one of China's best-known icons. By 1987 Marlboro was China's fourth largest advertiser. Cigarettes were never shown, but the red-and-white Marlboro logo and cowboy appeared everywhere, even on Shanghai street furniture. To the Chinese, cowboys are workers, not heroes. But the horse represents health, success, and vitality. So the cowboy was transmogrified into a leader. In Shanghai in 1993 Marlboro sponsored an hour-long radio programme of American music regularly punctuated by the Marlboro theme song taken from the film *The Magnificent Seven*. Over thundering hooves and the shouts of the round-up, the Chinese voice-over enthused: "Jump and fly a thousand miles ... Ride through the rivers and mountains with courage. Be called a hero throughout the thousand miles. This is the world of Marlboro". Within a decade the sales of Philip Morris quadrupled in China.

Similar tactics are deployed in the west. In the mid-1970s BAT purchased Bucktrout, a centuries-old chandler's in the Channel Islands, with the intention of launching a cigarette of that name, thus enabling it to back into a brand name with romantic associations which might legitimately continue to advertise indefinitely. While these plans never materialised, in the same decade Sotheby's, virtually synonymous with fine taste, was persuaded to lend its august name to a packet of upmarket fags. Dunhill was one of the first to diversify its trademark, stretching it over a successful luxury goods empire. The Marlboro Country Store advertises a worldwide range of goods designed to recall the brand's rugged image. It revived the addictive practice of collecting cigarette coupons, with its own Air Miles redemption scheme. It is rivalled by the Camel Collection, first launched in 1977, and the Lucky Strike Originals Collection. In none of these undertakings is there a whiff of smoke, but there are plenty of associations with macho endeavours of high romance, e.g. expeditions to search for Amazons in the interior of Venezuela.

Tobacco companies have also registered their brands as beer, whisky, financial services, credit cards, electrical goods, footwear, stationery, coffee, model cars, perfumes, cosmetics and Internet-based travel and information services. According to the EC directive, a tobacco company's brand name or branding features may be used on any of these, "but only if the presentation and the advertising of the non-tobacco product are clearly distinct from those of the tobacco product". How this distinction might be made is a conundrum to delight the minds and fatten the pockets of lawyers for years to come.

WHEREVER IN THE WORLD it is still permitted, cigarette advertising concentrates on brand recognition, often reduced to its essentials: the colours of the pack, which require no explanation, no international translation. Where advertising is banned, brand names are nevertheless omnipresent: free sampling in discos, sponsorship of glamorous rock concerts and other events where the price of admission is sometimes an empty cigarette pack. In Kenya free mobile cinemas show cigarette advertisements without health warnings. In the Dominican Republic, the Marlboro name and colours appear on road signs. In Bucharest the amber filters of many of the city's traffic lights advertise the Camel brand. In devising alternative strategies to influence youth markets, the ingenuity of advertising agents who work for tobacco companies seems as limitless as the capacity of their clients' pockets. As the comedian and heavy smoker the late Peter Cook pointed out when he was asked whether cigarette advertising should be banned:

> It's a daft idea. It took me years to work out those Silk Cut ads, so advertising doesn't really hit me. How far could they take this? Remove all cigarettes from Humphrey Bogart movies?[2]

[2] *The Independent on Sunday,* 16 February 1992.

CHAPTER 21
SINGING FROM THE SONGSHEET

Corporate

In the late 1970s the giant German chemical company Hoechst decided it needed a corporate advertising campaign in Britain. It drew up a list of four London agencies and asked them to make speculative presentations. One agency, a JWT team, produced two campaigns. Its favourite showed how chemistry alleviates the problems of humanity: old age, famine, overpopulation. This would stretch minds, but harsh reality was a high-risk strategy. So the agency hedged its bet by also presenting a second campaign, a commonplace effort reciting the company's capabilities. More than a dozen Hoechst managers assembled to judge each agency's ideas, and with Teutonic efficiency, they graded them on a list of twenty-five points. When the results were tabulated, the good news for the JWT team was that their realistic "humanity" campaign was overwhelmingly the first choice, while their alternative had come in third. The bad news, the client explained, was that although as people the Hoechst team loved the controversial proposal, as a company they found it too risky. So the account was awarded to a rival agency, which produced a television commercial personifying the various activities of the company, ending with a shot of a group of people dressed in symbolic costumes standing on a surfboard – to represent the plastics division – together with a pig, signifying agricultural chemicals.

IN MOST COUNTRIES the law recognises a corporation as a "legal person". It is an entity which has "property rights". These can create conflicts with the rights of other individuals – humans – who also recognise another kind of law: morality. Everything a board of directors does, is justified ultimately by the claim that it is acting to defend or increase value for its shareholders, the directors being merely responsible stewards. Leaving aside the contradiction that the dominant shareholders are almost invariably financial institutions and therefore "legal persons" too, and ignoring also the moral question as to whether their enhancement should be the over-riding objective (it is increasingly recognised that companies have other responsibilities – to their managers and workers, to the communities in which they operate, to the environment), it is in any case a Big Lie. Public companies are run for the benefit of the people who run them –

the top managers. In extreme cases, they are run like robber baronies. In the era of the leveraged buy-outs of the 1980s there were plenty of these, the rape of the R. J. Reynolds Tobacco Company, described in *Barbarians at the Gate*[1] being the most notorious. Managers of public companies are constrained in the pursuit of their personal objectives only by considerations which may diminish the public valuation of the company, and hence arouse the shareholders to replace them.

Successful companies outlive the people who start them, yet, to paraphrase a durable 1980s European advertising campaign for Citicorp Venture Capital, anyone would rather be an owner than a manager. Daniel Bell describes the origin of the manager's dilemma in his book, *The Cultural Contradictions of Capitalism*[2]:

> The first deep, internal structural change in capitalism was the divorce of family and property from managerial power and the loss of continuity through the chain of elites. Economic power today lies in *institutions* whose chiefs cannot pass along their power to their heirs and who, increasingly – since property is not private (but corporate), and technical skill, not property, is the basis of managerial positions – no longer have the traditional natural rights, justifications and legitimacy in the exercise of that power and feel it keenly.

Typically a corporation perpetuates the traditions of a family enterprise by creating its own *Weltanschauung* to bond family members, its employees, with a creed of shared values, from profit maximisation to expressions of social concern. Compliance is encouraged by elaborate rituals ranging from salesmen's competitions to dress-down Fridays. As every church has a "mission", so now does every business. The belief system is hallowed in a "mission statement", an earnest compilation of anodyne, irreproachable, and immeasurable Americanised "motherhood and apple pie" aspirations such as "quality", "dedication", "optimisation", and "excellence". Its antecedents are the political party speech and the sermon. The advertising agency is charged with the Alice in Wonderland task of encapsulating this pious pap in a short, distinctive, memorable, and impactful slogan. The result, for major multinational companies, is almost inevitably vacuous: "Your world of financial service", "For the journey ahead", "No one protects more". When commercial realities confound these ideals, the corporations speak their

---

[1] Bryan Burrough and John Helyar, HarperCollins, 1991.
[2] BasicBooks, 1978.

own language of evasion. Depriving someone of his or her livelihood is "right-sizing", dismembering companies is "unlocking shareholder value".

Like a religious cult, the corporation creates its own reality which its members must avow to an alien and sometimes hostile real world. To external audiences, customers, suppliers, governments and media, corporations have always sought to express an image of solidity, respectability, and, increasingly, social concern. American Telephone and Telegraph (AT&T) virtually invented the art of corporate public relations when it began to track public attitudes towards the company in the 1920s. With that came the recognition that the sale of products could be enhanced by selling the company which made them, and so began the great flood of "corporate communications" – brochures, informational films, press advertisements, and eventually television commercials – designed to provide the "legal person" with widespread recognition and accepted status.

In the early 1970s the great mass of UK television viewers was mystified when a commercial extolling an unfamiliar engineering company called Glynwed appeared on its screens. Few would have worked out that it was an eleventh-hour attempt by the company to rally popular support, and boost its share value in a corporate takeover battle. It was not until then that major companies in the UK began to understand that, to many of their "target publics", not least the City, they too were brands, which could add value through advertising. To the delight of time and space salesmen, companies such as Lyons Bakeries began to use popular media as a weapon of corporate defence against hostile bids. Such campaigns were hasty and forced initiatives, and though rarely too little, almost invariably too late. The approach was simplistic and company-oriented – "we need to explain to people what we do" – and the result usually was the formula "parade of products" presentation. A mid-1970s commercial for Dunlop twisted the formula slightly to show what the world would be like without Dunlop's range of products. It raised eyebrows and earned creative acclaim by including a shot of a woman on a tennis court who lost her skirt; Dunlop nevertheless was shortly afterwards forced into a disastrous corporate merger.

The City boom and the cycle of mergers of the 1980s brought a new appreciation of the value of well-known brands. Companies were urged to assert corporate ownership of their individual brands as a tool to drive up the company's share price. However, companies with diversified product portfolios find it difficult to synchronise distinctive brand positionings with the overall corporate image. Allied Lyons, the bakery group, a likely takeover target, slapped its corporate logo on everything it advertised, appropriately enough in a homely Lyons cake commercial, but awkwardly in the case of a sardonic pitch for Castlemaine XXXX aimed at lager louts. In the public mind both Procter & Gamble and Lever Brothers are identified with heavily advertised soap products, but this is hardly representative of the vast scope of their commercial activities. The two companies have different corporate branding policies: Lever Brothers, looking for a cross-product rub-off, does put the corporate logo on its washing powders; Procter & Gamble, taking the view that its brands such as Ariel, Daz, and Bold are in direct competition, does not. When the Swiss company Nestlé bought Rowntree, it acquired the UK's leading confectionery brand, Kit-Kat. A sure way to anglicise the Continental company was to apply its logo prominently to this household name. However, it was felt less appropriate to After Eight, which has always cultivated an association with upper-class "Englishness", and the parent company therefore has only a token presence on the packaging of that brand. Johnson & Johnson similarly restricts its endorsement to those baby and family products which reinforce its cosy, hygienic image, and thus escaped fall-out from a disaster created by the damaging side-effects of one of its pharmaceutical brands, Tylenol, in the US. Reckitt & Colman sensibly did not attempt to gain synergy from the marketing of liquids as disparate as Veuve du Vernay, Brasso, and Dettol.

In theory the brand, too, can benefit reciprocally from identification with a respected company. Thus, while cashing in on the friendly domestic image established for Dulux paint by years of advertising characterised by an endearing sheepdog, ICI lends the technical authority of a giant international chemical company to the brand. But huge, amorphous reputations like this are no substitute for pin-sharp brand marketing and presentation; in the DIY chemical filling and fixing field, where its name had obvious strengths, ICI signally failed in the late 1980s with a range designed to break the stranglehold of Polycell, a relative pipsqueak.

Most corporate communications fail to engage because instead of engaging a consumer need the companies are talking about themselves. Corporate appeals are often much clumsier than advertising for consumer products, and about as convincing as fairy tales. One of the obstacles is that "creatives" have little experience of business and how it works, and, digging into their usual bag of consumer-oriented tricks, produce an irrelevant oversimplification. So the services of international accountant Arthur Andersen were presented to senior executives of major companies in a fifteen-second television commercial by transmuting a snail into a frog. Primarily, though, the client is to blame. It is notoriously difficult to gain client approval for any piece of corporate communications, even a brochure which few people will read, because the task compels top management, often for the first time, to consider what its company is really about. This navel-examining exercise brings to the surface lurking divisions and disagreements which are suppressed in the day-to-day running of the business. Because they derive their personal identity from the corporate culture in which they dwell, executives are much more twitchy about such pronouncements than they are about product advertising. To define a company defines the businessmen who make it their life; corporate advertising touches the *amour propre* of the key executives themselves. As it brings the internal culture into confrontation with the real world, the effect of straining to produce a corporate description can be as devastating and divisive as introducing a firm of management consultants to trawl through operating procedures. The resulting piece of communication is often a stilted defence mechanism, invoking conventions as phoney as those of the archaic "business letter". It's a compromise which none of the managers finds offensive, and none of the intended target audience finds of interest – "a pig on a surfboard".

An advertising agency corporate presentation once included a chart that described the opportunity awaiting the client to become a world leader by playing upon "the rarest ingredient in advertising . . . Truth". Truth is rare because corporate mythology is a hothouse plant which shrivels in the chill air of reality. In 1986, shortly after the world's worst industrial disaster, the Union Carbide gas leak at Bhopal which killed an estimated 5,000 people and disabled tens of thousands, the Chemical Industry Association in the UK commissioned a corporate film designed to allay fears about chemical hazards. The producers persuaded the client that rather than the usual bluster about progress, a frank audience discussion voicing *both sides* of the arguments about controversial issues would show that the industry was concerned and listening. The film was made, but never shown, because the industry refused to admit that issues such as the greenhouse effect might be a reality.

Viewed from the perspective of the world the rest of us inhabit, much corporate advertising is incompetent, irrelevant, or insulting. It cannot reflect well on the quality of the management which sponsors it. Companies eventually realised that if functional distinctions were less important than the brand values attached to a product, so too was it advisable not just to communicate what a company does, but to endow the "legal person" with appealing emotional characteristics. Today most corporations aspire to project benign personalities. How would you describe a person who presented himself as the following firms do?

A 3M newspaper campaign picturing everyday objects with the claim,

"You can hardly go through a single day without touching something a 3M abrasive hasn't touched first". Self-absorbed?

A 1990s press advertisement showing a skyscape with a cloud shaped vaguely like a winged aeroplane. It is the Lufthansa logo and the copy burbles: "Of course we're glad 28 million of you have chosen to fly with us this year. It must mean you like us. More than that, you trust us". Pretentious?

A series of British Telecom press advertisements, each featuring a full-page portrait of a wide-eyed child, for example a small black kid with a football, captioned: "Joe Tear, England manager. On July 19th 2026, he'll want to videophone his Dad from Canada, to celebrate England's first World Cup win since 1966". Customers were urged to regard a serious inconvenience, yet another change of dialling codes following the disruption caused by a previous miscalculation, as a contribution to a better world, because "In the future more people will need more numbers". Disingenuous?

A 12-year-old child was taken by her parents to watch a corporate video. Her verdict: "The only thing that I found remotely fun was counting how many times they said they were 'world-class'. It was fifteen – at least once a minute". Fatuous?

A 1990s newspaper campaign for an association of nuclear power companies calling itself the US Council for Energy Awareness picturing "Foreign Oil" as a nasty cobra rearing to strike, and arguing this competition will "poison America's economy and our national security". A scoundrel wrapped in a flag?

The humorist Bill Bryson enjoys skewering the corporate mindset:

> ... an official of Delta Airlines, one Cindy Reeds, is quoted as saying: "The public asked us to eliminate the food". Excuse me? The customers asked not to be fed? Frankly, I find that a little hard to, uh, swallow. A little further on in the article, Ms Reeds explains the airline's line of reasoning: "About a year and a half ago", she says, "we took a survey of a thousand passengers ... and they said they wanted lower fares, so we got rid of the meals".[3]

While corporations continue to pump out unrealistic drivel, their audiences have grown less credulous, more aware of the difference between corporate image and activity, and more militant when displeased. By organising into single-issue groups, aggravated consumers

---

[3] *Notes from a Big Country*, Doubleday, 1998.

can give corporations a very public bloody nose. The fur industry was driven to the verge of extinction in the UK by the activities, including advertising, of animal rights campaigners. Barclays Bank was forced out of South Africa in the mid-1980s by student boycotts in the US and UK. Hoover sold off its European subsidiary in 1995 after the fiasco of a miscalculated holiday competition. In the same year Shell's determination to dispose of its Brent Spar oil rig in the North Atlantic caused sales to plummet in Germany and it was forced to change its mind. Body Shop had to defend itself vigorously against an orchestrated campaign which sought to discredit its ethical stance. These are only the tips of icebergs. A company under public pressure will haemorrhage from silent defections. In a marketplace where consumers are spoiled for choice between identical products, it doesn't take much to blunt brand loyalties. Even a motorist who is not particularly environmentally conscious may pass up a Shell station for the next brand simply out of a vague feeling of unease.

Yet where audiences believe a company genuinely shares their concerns, and acts on them, the corporate personality is seen to have a soul. Corporate personalities are seen as most genuine and human when they derive from the personality of a living person, like the family companies of old. However, here the advertisement abandons the protective smoke and mirrors of advertising convention for the real world. There's a venerable advertising agency ditty which goes:

> Should the client prove refractory,
> Show a picture of the factory,
> Only in the worst of cases,
> Ever show the clients' faces.

This is sound advice. A prized and fundamental human skill is forming judgements, rightly or wrongly, about one's fellow man, and few company chairmen are photogenic or skilled as actors. The Prudential Insurance Company took the dubious step of employing its chairman as its spokesperson in a 1998 revival of its venerable "man from the Pru" campaign. Doubtless the company saw it as a way of personalising an impersonal institution, but in the resentful climate produced by the exposure of industry "fat cats", today's consumer is unlikely to perceive the "man from the Pru" as disinterested. In those rare cases, however, where the individual has considerable personal flair, it's a gift for the publicity machine. Even in the days before instant international hype, high-profile publicity-seeking entrepreneurs were closely identified with the success of the companies they founded, such as Lever Brothers, Thomas Cook, and Marks & Spencer. In 1868, Alfred Bird, inventor of Bird's custard, prefigured Richard Branson's ballooning escapades when he took to a tricycle to set the world record for the fastest journey from Land's End to John o'Groat's.

When there is a genuine organic connection, the company takes on the personality of its founder and its influence can approach omnipotence. Ben Cohen and Jerry Greenfield founded Ben & Jerry's ice-cream in Vermont on the faux-naïf image of a couple of ageing hippies. The spur to their amazing transformation into a multinational company came when the nationally distributed Häagen-Dazs brand, the ersatz creation of the mammoth Pillsbury company, applied pressure to distributors to freeze out the tiny firm. Ben & Jerry replied by targeting Pillsbury's cherished logo, the Pillsbury Doughboy, with a publicity campaign with an air of artless grassroots improvisation, "What's the Doughboy afraid of?" The campaign won allegiance for the underdog all over America and, after their legal victory, swept Ben & Jerry to national prominence. The company's positioning is anti-corporate and displays an ethos of social concern: 7.5 per cent of its profits are devoted to charity, and suppliers are selected from areas of social need – cookie-bakers in the ghettos of New York, coffee-growing co-operatives in Mexico. The folksy personalisation of the founders encourages consumers to feel – even though they know better – that this product is somehow not cranked out of huge vats by a multinational corporation, but is made specially for you by the pleasant yokel who appears on the label wearing a T-shirt. Your shared concern about injustice provides a rationale for self-indulgence at a premium price: while gulping down this ice-cream you are also helping to save the world. Inevitably, like all proper revolutionaries, Ben & Jerry fell out, and in 2000 their righteous anti-capitalistic enterprise with its social mission of commitment to community values was acquired by that arch-capitalist icon, Unilever. Their hip flavours such as Rainforest Crunch and Cherry Garcia (named after the late leader of the Grateful Dead) were gobbled up by the Evil Empire.

Anita Roddick sells a moral philosophy, too. Through a topical obsession with animal rights and the environment, she grew a small shop in Sussex into a multinational cosmetics manufacturer and retailer, Body Shop International. Although she was removed as chief executive when the company ran into the sand in 1992, she remains the messianic embodiment of the corporate belief. In-store posters, company videos, an in-house magazine and her autobiographical manifesto, *Body and Soul,* ingratiate customers and motivate staff by picturing her with Amazon tribesmen and other saintly associations. "How can you be wrong", she preaches, "when you borrow ideas from Mahatma Ghandi, from Martin Luther King?"

In the past twenty years only one new internationally recognised corporate brand has emerged from Britain: the Virgin phenomenon. That, too, is the brain child of an entrepreneur who linked his personality to a philosophical attitude under an evocative brand name. The package of values which Richard Branson represents springs from his youthful creation, Virgin Records, and his personal exploits as a daredevil balloonist and all-round socially responsible Jim'll-Fix-It. Like Freddie Laker before him and Stelios Haji-Ioannou, founder of Easyjet, afterwards, Richard Branson saw the opportunity to cloak himself as a maverick people's champion and challenge the oligopoly of the international air carriers by founding Virgin Atlantic. The company's interests soon spread over a disparate agglomeration unified only by the charisma of its founder: railway franchises, megastores, a film and entertainment division, a cinema chain, colas, vodka, financial services, and mobile phones. In 1998 his fashion business took on the designer labels with the disarming reassurance, "Not to worry, Richard doesn't design them".

Although middle-aged and one of the ten wealthiest men in Britain, Richard Branson continues to play the role of the youthful underdog. He happily mixes moral issues with business; he supports the legalisation of marijuana, criticises homophobia (he started the biggest gay disco in Europe), and launched Mates condoms to raise awareness of safe sex. He successfully sued "the world's favourite airline" for unfair business practices. More powerful than any image-building advertising campaign was his offer to run the National Lottery, donating all profits to charity. Branson's persona capitalises on consumer disaffection with the insensitivity of large companies: a spunky British schoolboy could do it better. His values are iconoclastic, and when he grows up he wants to be Robin Hood. A 1995 survey of teenagers conducted by MORI for City and Guilds, the vocational awards body, found that young women aspired to be Naomi Campbell or Anita Roddick, while the leading role models for young men were Andy Cole, the footballer, and Richard Branson. Another MORI poll the previous year for BBC Radio 1 asked young people which celebrity they thought would be the most appropriate to draw up a revised list of Ten Commandments. After Mother Teresa, the Pope, and the Archbishop of Canterbury came Richard Branson. And his customers have grown up with him; an NOP poll showed that the brand rates highly across the generations. Knighted for his "services to entrepreneurship" (sic) in 1999, Richard Branson himself is the mainspring of the company's publicity, and is usually personally associated with the advertising. His Midas touch is not infallible: Virgin Cinemas, and the short-haul airline Virgin Express both disappointed, Virgin pulled out of the clothing market in 2000, just two years after its launch, and the performance record of Virgin Rail has sorely tried public patience. Yet Virgin would be worth a great deal less without his physical presence. It is the world's most convincing illustration of how companies can bond emotionally with consumers.

ADVERTISERS SOMETIMES FEAR that really effective direct advertising for their products is inconsistent with projecting an image. The reverse is true: an ad that effectively touches consumer motivations creates the right feeling for the company *automatically*. In 1960s America AT&T's advertising programme was rigidly compartmentalised by objective: there were commercials to promote long-distance calling, others to sell extension telephones, and others to promote the corporate image. Separate batteries of attitudinal questions were devised for each category to measure effectiveness in quantitative tests. When, experimentally, the corporate image battery of questions was applied to commercials in other categories, the company was chagrined to discover that some of its most effective image-building commercials were those designed to sell products and services. On reflection, how could it be otherwise, unless the company is striving to "project an image" that does not relate to consumer needs?

Alas, that is frequently the objective. Corporate advertising has been pungently described as like peeing down your trouser-leg: it gives you a nice, warm feeling and nobody else notices. The reason most of us are not interested is that the companies are using an external medium to reinforce, or reinvent, their own internal mythology, which is not how they are seen by the external world. They deceive themselves. This neurosis, of course, infects not only corporate advertising, but also judgements about advertising the company's brands, too, which helps explain why so much of advertising of all kinds seems so removed from reality.

CHAPTER 22

I LAUGHED ALL THE WAY TO THE OFFICIAL RECEIVER

Banking

Italy's most renowned film director was persuaded to make a series of television commercials for the Banca di Roma in 1992. As he told it, "They censored the most entertaining idea. My little film started with two well-dressed robbers who go down into the bank vaults. They open a big safe, but there's nothing inside, not a penny. Then a voice-over says, 'There's not a single lira left. We spent everything to pay Fellini'. The managers of the bank were aghast: 'A bank without money? In times like these ... I'm sorry, Maestro, but this isn't good enough. You may be The Great Fellini, but we've invested 25 billion lira. Think of something serious, and don't play around with our money'".

ONE WINTER DAY in 1994 an unlikely group of protesters took to the London streets. They wore sober business suits. One, carried aloft on the shoulders of the others, hung with a rope around his neck from a placard which read: "Small Business Crucified by Barclays Bank ... as the Bank of England washes it's [sic] hands". Advertising artistry was in evidence: the placard displayed a logo, $A£E, which stood for Struggle Against Financial Exploitation, whose members maintained that Barclays had ruined their lives by "mistakes and malpractices". Barclay's Chairman, Andrew Buxton, said that $A£E represented a minority, but that he had "made efforts to sort out their problems".

In the recession of the early 1990s Britain's banks had squeezed their customers hard. Newspapers recounted harrowing tales of indifference, incompetence, and extortion. One customer was charged £66 for having an unauthorised overdraft of 72p for two weeks. Another was billed an hourly rate when he invited his bank manager to lunch. In 1991 a letter by an aggrieved small businessman to the *Sunday Times* stimulated the newspaper to launch a campaign which resulted in the Chancellor of the Exchequer, Norman Lamont, calling in the heads of the big four clearing banks for a dressing-down.

The major clearing banks, Barclays, NatWest, Midland and Lloyds-TSB, had created a cosy oligopoly offering parity services at parity prices, and with a generous dollop of arrogance. Despite public obeisance to customer focus, bankers' ecclesiastical language revealed where their hearts lay. Loans were "granted", yet one "applied" for a deposit account. It was tedious to switch one's account – banks were inefficient at this – and they were all the same anyway. Customer retention was no problem; experience proved that a customer at 18 was theirs for life and so the banks focused their advertising on youth. They found it difficult to address this market except in the language of parody, such as a NatWest campaign which attempted to borrow street cred from the uncouth antics of the forehead-studded punk rocker characters from the cult television programme *The Young Ones*.

When a crazy easy credit spiral collapsed in 1992, British banks faced £6 billion in domestic bad debts on top of a previous provision of £9 billion for unwise Third World loans. They reacted by shedding thousands of jobs. There was also a rash of bad publicity about other financial institutions. Household names such as Guardian Insurance, Save & Prosper, and Commercial Union were accused of mis-selling pensions and overcharging, and were forced to offload their self-employed direct sales forces. A 1995 survey conducted by the Henley Centre for the re-insurance company Swiss Re reported that only 29 per cent of adults retained a respectful opinion of the staff of banks and building societies, independent financial advisers were endorsed by 12 per cent, while life insurance salespeople, at 7 per cent, ranked with the traditionally most despised profession, estate agents. Everywhere in Britain traditional trust in financial institutions was haemorrhaging away and the major banks were deeply unpopular.

One of the contributing factors was their advertising. By the 1980s financial services had replaced Lux and Wonderloaf as the big spenders. Banks had discovered marketing. Advertising for the Midland Bank, for example, was obsessed with establishing a confusing range of sub-brands with unlikely names, such as the Orchard Account. Consumers were infuriated, because while squeezing their customers with extra charges, the banks were lashing out vast sums on television advertising. This was exacerbated by the content of the commercials, which merely confirmed the banks' complacency and drift from reality. They were squandering millions on a confabulated world. There was a listening bank, an action bank, a bank that liked to say yes . . . it didn't wash. Unlike most corporations, which are remote from most people's lives, banks are familiar. You go into them. Their customers could easily compare the corporate posture with the reality; they knew that their banks were deaf, listless, and negative. While the advertising strove to create meaningful distinctions within a homogeneous group of institutions, the gap between the image of the industry at large and everyday experience was unbridgeable. So the advertisements seemed unrealistic, condescending, absurd.

The Barclays campaign of 1986, based on Terry Gilliams's cult film *Brazil* and shot by the *Bladerunner* director Ridley Scott, was hailed by the advertising fraternity as breaking new ground for banks. Its bleak Kafka-esque portrayal of the hostile bureaucracy encountered in "other banks" simply identified and reinforced the problem for consumers. In 1994 the Midland was still reminding consumers of their dissatisfaction in a newspaper campaign presenting a simplistic questionnaire with a choice of two statements to tick: "1. I'm totally fed up with my bank, but it's too much hassle to move. I don't want to fill out all those long, complicated forms. 2. I find long, complicated forms very stimulating". The advertiser's solution was a "user-friendly transfer pack", i.e. a form to fill out.

Belatedly, the banks began to realise that people were what their business was about, rather than a distraction from it. They moved from masticating the problem in their advertising towards trying to personalise themselves or their happy customers. The model was the advertising for the Woolwich Building Society, a small player which had consistently featured a perky young female employee chirping the line, "I'm with the Woolwich" with a genuine, warm smile. Barclays relied on fairy tales to present its bank managers as providers of mortgages and other services. In one mid-1990s television commercial a knight was having trouble keeping a huge troll away from his castle. He ran to his bank manager, who was clad in a medieval jerkin and wielding a quill pen. This figure took a sword to the troll and the knight won his castle. The obligatory final gag suggested more travail might yet be in store. "We can't do anything about the neighbours", shrugged the chummy Barclays voice-over with the arrival of a new threat: his parents, towering over the castle, revealed that the troll still rattling the castle gates was just a baby. The image of Barclays Bank was also hugely influenced by the persona of the mugging comedian Rowan Atkinson, playing the pompous and hapless fool in the high-profile advertising of Barclaycard throughout the 1990s.

To build up a reputation as a comprehensive financial services retailer, NatWest introduced members of staff and its specialist advisers. A series of television vignettes set out to demonstrate how these people were just like the rest of us, only more likeable: a fat man coyly suggested we probably could not imagine him playing squash; another chap sitting in an office confessed his father was just a tradesman. For what it's worth, the readers of *TV Quick* magazine, many of whom this campaign would have been designed to please, voted this the second worst advertising on television.

In 1994 the Midland Bank introduced one of its employees, "Britain's least-known pension adviser", under the headline "I am Mike Lindup and I'm real. Not a photographic model". After revealing some ingratiating personal details, Mike smooth-talked his audience, "But don't worry, I don't want to sell you a pension or anything. Not now, anyway. I believe you have to get to know each other before you start to talk about pensions, which are very personal things". He promised to see us again soon in subsequent advertisements. True to his word, Mike reappeared frequently, though revealing himself as an accident-prone clown. A following advertisement showed him entangled in a tennis net, with the headline "I am Mike Lindup and I'd like to talk to you about safety nets". In another he was in bed, with a thermometer in his mouth, though still wearing a suit. "I am Mike Lindup and I'm a little indisposed, but if you call (0800 etc.) one of my colleagues will be in touch". After only a brief acquaintance, our new chum inexplicably disappeared from our lives forever.

Starting in 1995 the Co-operative Bank promoted a policy of ethical investment as its USP, using a series of commercials delivered by weird, threatening close-ups of flat-voiced people photographed through a distorting lens. These unsettling images were intended to represent its concerned customers, interspersed with photographs of dying fish, sewage, and other consequences of indiscriminate commercial investment. They clearly positioned the Co-operative Bank on the leading edge of eccentricity.

Apart from Scottish Widows, with its appealing young woman shrouded in black, the insurance companies, particularly, suffered from lack of brand distinction. Prudential won advertising awards for its simple "I want to be" campaign portraying generic aspirations (e.g. a photograph of a penguin captioned "I want to fly somewhere warm for the winter", plus a logo). Yet, according to the 1995 Henley survey of pension providers, this prominent campaign achieved only a 10 per cent correct brand attribution. "There isn't much difference between brands", the report concluded: "they all begin with Scottish and end with Life. Whenever a Scottish Amicable advertisement was shown, the recall for Scottish Widows shot up".

Towards the end of the 1990s, the institutions began turning the screw of emotional blackmail. A 1997 Midland Bank press ad shows a photograph of a toy car in a suburban back garden with the headline: "This is not an ad about mortgages. It's about children, apple trees and memories". A 1998 Pearl Insurance television commercial featured a young Dad who had to borrow £1 from his son to pay for his fish and chips treat. The kid chastised his father, "You never think about when you're going to need money". Few advertisements in the financial services sector bother to involve Mum, although it's often the woman who has the most influence in the family's key financial decisions. Standard Life found a way of doing it in 1998 by lifting from a highly regarded Safeway campaign the technique of putting wisecracking adult wisdom into infants' mouths. These heart-warming pitches, showing an everyday couple, joined the obligations of parental and financial responsibility. The Scottish Widows campaign of the same year showed an executive leaving his office building for the last time. Carrying his presentation golf clubs, he descended a staircase to meet a dark, cowled figure. The Grim Reaper? No, it was the Scottish Widow herself, ready to escort our hero not into the next world, but towards a happy retirement. Representations of business life were universally simplistic, suggesting that the high street banks had little understanding of business realities and offered only cosmetic solutions, frequently presenting businessmen as innocent chumps. "Then I just had to get the van" summarised the business plan of a loan-bingeing electrician (setting up in business during a housing slump) in a NatWest television campaign.

By the end of the century, NatWest was instructing people how to live their lives. Over the slogan "You only live once" the bank tempted consumers to extend their personal debt in 1998 press advertisements showing blue plaques on London houses bearing inscriptions such as: "Sarah Ellingworth lived here 1968-1998. But never bought that Poggenpohl kitchen she always hankered after". In 1999, its television campaign encouraged people to leave their jobs. An animated commercial in the simplistic style of a safety manual showed figures escaping from offices: clambering into the air conditioning duct, mounting filing cabinets to reach the window, as aircraft slides unfurled from office windows and ejector seats sent managers off on parachutes. While the voice-over advanced the argument that NatWest helped 67,000 people to set up their own businesses in the past year, the monolithic office environment in this piece of whimsy shrieked "banking", and in particular that City landmark, the NatWest tower.

It the banks had acquired personalities, they were schizoid. Amusing embroidery such as this was reserved for consumer messages. When the institutions had something really important to say about themselves, they abandoned their user-friendly advertising personae and spoke like the same old stuffy bankers, in advertisements covering a whole page with copy, and no silly pictures, with po-faced headlines: "Important information for members on the Halifax/Leeds merger".

Yet, starting in the mid-1980s, the face of retail banking had begun to change forever. One bank invested in technology and high standards of customer service and also got the advertising formula right – after a disastrous start. Midland, saddled with high costs and low-yielding assets, began looking at ways of attracting more affluent and upmarket customers. The result, in 1987, was "Project Raincloud", a twenty-four-hour banking system available 365 days of the year, with no branches but staffed by real people on the end of the phone who would perform all of the functions of a traditional bank, apart from business banking. The decision was taken not to identify the new bank with its provenance. Ostensibly this was to avoid eroding the Midland's existing customer base, but more importantly it gave the fledgeling a fresh start, unencumbered by the tattered reputation of its parent. An advertising agency with a reputation for controversial work, Howell Henry Chaldecott Lury, was appointed to launch the new concept and in 1989 the first television commercial appeared. It was a kind of time warp simulation which broke into the middle of an Audi commercial on ITV (with the permission of Audi and the Independent Television Commission). It showed office staff apparently celebrating the twenty-fifth anniversary of an organisation called First Direct, with no indication of what it was. According to agency principal Rupert Howell, "It was a sort of *War of the Worlds* thing", intended to make people sit up and ask "what was that all about?" Four hundred people rang the TV stations to ask precisely that. This jape was followed by a television campaign costing £2.5 million in which actress Charlotte Rampling spoke gnomically about a radical new form of banking, advising viewers to turn off if they were not interested. Howell claimed that First Direct was flooded with calls, about 10,000 over the three months. If the bank had recruited all of these it would have been at a cost of about £600 each. In any event, it was not achieving its target of attracting 100,000 new customers in the first fifteen months.

The First Direct executive responsible for the launch explained what happened next:

> You can't expect customers to buy a product if they don't know what it's all about, so we had to concentrate on building the brand. We made 74 10-second TV commercials explaining the concept of a twenty-four-hour bank without any branches and used really unusual visuals: Wellington boots, laundry baskets, buckets and fish – virtually anything not connected with financial services.

This sounds a bit muddled, and it was. The television commercials, and the mystifying series of small ads which kept appearing on the front pages of national newspapers in 1990, gave no hint of what kind of services were offered by First Direct. Apart from the eclectic objects mentioned, there was no copy, only a phone number to call.

> We bombarded people with images – 70 different ads in all, and made icons out of extraordinary images. The ads were powerful and the point was to reflect the difference of the brand, but I think it might have helped if at the beginning it had been explained that First Direct was a bank, because some of it just passed people by.

Some of her colleagues at the bank were mystified as well:

> I didn't realise there had been a communications breakdown within the company until the day we demonstrated the advertising campaign to the management team. People didn't understand how we could advertise financial services without showing cheque books and credit cards. No one understood the purpose of the commercials. They were concentrating on the product without appreciating that a brand has to be built before customers come in. We changed the strategy. Instead of concentrating on building the brand, we came off television and pushed the product through the press . . . but it took longer to build the brand and get the customers than I had envisaged.

It is a testimony to the strength of the First Direct business concept that it managed to survive this muddled brandspeak claptrap. The bank changed agencies. What eventually pulled in the customers was a no-nonsense direct marketing campaign and a straightforward series of explanatory newspaper advertisements with old-fashioned coupons prepared by the Chiat/Day advertising agency. Logical argument replaced the "branding" bamboozle. Lengthy copy developed themes such as "Shrewd: branches cost money. If you hardly ever visit your branch, you're wasting money". Product advantages were emphasised: higher interest rates on savings, lower charges, automatic bill payment service, subsidised telephone calls, open all the time. First Direct was soon attracting its target of 10,000 customers each month. And backing it up with performance. A survey carried out by NOP found that 89 per cent of its customers were actually recommending First Direct to their friends, *without being asked.* Other banks flocked behind: NatWest, the Co-op, and others cloned direct banking services which flagrantly copied the austere, informative First Direct advertising style.

But, after a wrong-footed launch First Direct had regained its balance and opened up a long lead on its rivals in technology and service. Its reputation was secure enough to legitimise in consumer's eyes an extremely aggressive 1996 press and TV campaign, "Name one good thing about your bank". The reactive campaigns of competitors such as Barclays failed to mount a serious challenge: "If your current bank infuriates you, it only takes a second to change to Barclays. Well usually". Over a pen signing a "funny" long name: A. Ziborrowabanoskavid.

In 1995 the same thing happened in the life insurance industry when a red phone on wheels hurtled over a hill on television screens. This was the launch of Direct Line life insurance, which challenged the consumer to cut out the middleman and pick up the phone to find a better deal. Advertising professionals turned up their noses at this primitive presentation, while life insurance brokerages swiftly became virtually obsolete.

ALL BANKS had recognised the poor image of the industry throughout the 1980s and 1990s; they and their advertising agencies had access to the same depressing results of large-scale consumer attitudinal research. But the corporate culture was in denial. In each bank it was always *the other banks* which were uncaring and inefficient. Their attempts to discriminate between advertising trumpery and service, between corporate culture and reality, cost them dearly. By the end of the century there was real competition in banking. Apart from the direct banking services, other retailers with a big customer base and stainless reputations muscled in. Marks & Spencer started selling pensions and life insurance over the phone in 1995. Virgin Direct broke into financial services, too, when it introduced a low-margin PEP product. Sainsbury's launched a banking service in 1997, and can afford to treat it as a loss-leader to attract customers into its shops. Free banking is the norm and profit margins have been squeezed.

In 2000 Barclays created another PR disaster. In the wake of a Parliamentary investigation which reported that British banks were massively overcharging their customers Barclays made a series of poorly timed announcements: it imposed an unpopular surcharge on cash machine withdrawals, reported fat profits, quadrupled the salary of its chairman, and then closed 171 unprofitable branch offices, mostly in rural areas. *At the same time* it launched a breast-beating campaign on press and television, featuring Welsh film star Anthony Hopkins to extol the virtues of big organisations. This insensitivity redounded on both the bank and the actor; another Parliamentary committee was convened to investigate bank branch closures, while aroused Welshmen called for Anthony Hopkins's recently achieved knighthood to be revoked.

With the single exception of First Direct, which was belatedly able to harmonise its professed values and its performance, as a category, advertising for banks over the past few decades, condescending and out-of-touch with their customers, would seem to have been largely counterproductive. Like airlines, which are permitted to withdraw from television and press commitments whenever there is a major air crash, financial institutions would be advised not to advertise at all at times of disaster.

CHAPTER 23
WHERE THERE'S MUCK, THERE'S MUCK-SLINGERS

Politics

Political language – and with variations this is true of all political parties, from Conservatives to Anarchists – is designed to make lies sound truthful and murder respectable, and to give an appearance of solidity to pure wind.

George Orwell

ON THE BLACK AND WHITE television screen the patrician, balding man stood uneasily on the front porch of a modest clapboard house somewhere in Middle America. He was wearing a rumpled suit and clutching a paper bag full of groceries, awkwardly, like a new father holding a baby for the first time. The man's name was Adlai Stevenson, the civilised, intelligent Democratic candidate for President of the United States, and he was telling us something about the economy. It was 1956. Politics had taken its first clumsy step into show business.

Fast forward to the 1994 elections for the American Senate. Another man – younger, taller, more athletic, and better groomed – bounds across a field holding hands with an attractive woman and two little girls, backlit by the rays of the sun. Dissolve from the happy family to a framed portrait of one of the charming daughters and then to the father standing by an old stone wall amidst wildflowers. This picture, resonating with nature and tradition, is a soothing contrast from the footage of a few seconds ago, when scenes of horrific disasters had flashed across the screen. The voice-over is magisterial: "With fires, earthquakes and a terrible recession, recent years have tested the people of California. Nearly a million moved away, but Mike Huffington and his wife came back to the state that educated him and is the birthplace of their two daughters". Huffington then adds his own insight: "This election isn't just about who you will send to Washington next year. It's about our children and their future". As the music swells to a climax, the family group reassembles. Mr Huffington confides something to his spouse, who smiles radiantly. As she strokes the hair of one of her daughters sitting in her father's lap, this slogan appear on the screen: "Finally. A reason to believe". Spurred by his new wife, Arianna Stassinopoulos, a Cambridge-educated new age mystic, Michael Huffington, the previously little known Republican congressman from California, was trying to "buy a face" and win a seat in the Senate chamber. He spent one-third of his personal wealth on his campaign, an unprecedented $25m (£15.5m). The scale of this investment and the hints dropped by his aspirant wife suggested that he saw the Senate as a staging post for the White House. Huffington was no flesh-presser, and made only a few carefully managed public appearances. He was perhaps the first "virtual candidate", visible almost exclusively on television. His political platform was sparsely furnished, too. Like Hollywood's anti-heroes, *Forrest Gump* and Chance the gardener, the protagonist of *Being There*, he was tapping into voter alienation. His credo: "I want a government that does nothing".

Meanwhile, on the East Coast of America, the enterprising facilitator of the Iranian arms for hostages scandal, erstwhile Marine Colonel Oliver North, recently convicted of lying to Congress, was campaigning for a Senate seat too. His television commercial featured the cover of *Playboy* magazine, showing the nude figure of a former Miss Virginia. She had claimed to have had an affair with his Democratic opponent, whose lame defence was that it had only been a nude massage in a hotel room. "Only a massage?" asked the advertisement.

Political appeals have always been emotional and often dirty. Neither Mike Huffington nor Colonel North was elected to the US Senate, but successful politicians, from Mahatma Ghandi to Adolf Hitler, have always sold simplicities, not complexities. The television medium, with its dramatic compression, its emphasis on personality, and its short memory, is a gift to their successors. By bringing electioneering off the public soapbox and out of the dense small print of the broadsheets to intrude into voter's living-rooms, it has changed the electoral process forever. But does political *advertising*, on television or elsewhere, with its obvious bias, influence your vote?

The British like to believe that traditions of fair play mean that they are too gentlemanly to be swayed by hard-sell advertising. The Saatchi & Saatchi advertising agency, widely credited with having engineered three Tory election victories in a row, swept away that illusion when it started selling a political party like a brand, the way American politicians did. The positive message was a coy picture of Margaret Thatcher embracing a calf. But the chief weapon her team imported was "knocking copy": overt attacks on the opposition. In 1979 the agency assembled volunteers from the Hendon Young Conservatives to pose as a lugubrious, snaking queue of the unemployed in a memorable aggressive poster with the clever *double entendre* "Labour Isn't Working".

The old Left view was that advertising was the handmaiden of capitalism and the work of the Devil. The epiphany on the Walworth Road occurred in 1984 when the Labour head of the Greater London Council, Ken Livingstone, dipped into the taxpayers' pockets to fund his campaign on bus sides and posters to protest the Tory government's decision to abolish London's governing body. His populist plea, "If you want me out, you should have the right to vote me out", did not deflect the government, but it attracted great sympathy, rage, and publicity, confirmed "Red Ken" as a popular media figure, and severely embarrassed the Thatcher government. By the next election, Labour was playing the Devil's tunes, too, with its red rose symbol and the epic film of candidate Neil Kinnock, *The Life of Neil*.

In the British election of 1992, posters were the weapon of choice. These rarely appeared anywhere outside central London, and sometimes there was only one, a mobile poster manoeuvred into place for a photocall, a cynical tactic designed only to stimulate photographic coverage by the news media. The politicians were heeding the advice of Robert Worcester, chairman of the research company MORI. A mountain of research evidence had led him to declare, "The main message that TV news gets across in an election is visual. The things that stick in people's minds are what they saw, and not what they heard".

The poster is a shorthand medium which does not lend itself to the positive exposition of policies, but negatives are easy to dramatise, so it is a suitable surface for smearing tactics in the venerable tradition of the political cartoon. Both parties were influenced by American experience, in which the "Willie Horton" commercial had been credited with helping George Bush win the 1988 presidential contest against Michael Dukakis. This repellent film reminded voters that during the liberal governor's administration in Massachusetts, Horton, a convicted killer, had raped a woman and beaten her fiancé while on furlough from prison.

While party election broadcasts and a sentimental film directed by John Schlesinger, *Major, the Movie* took a softer, more positive line, the key 1992 Tory theme, "You can't trust Labour", was cruder than previously. The American phrase "the double whammy" was introduced to the language over the figure of a small man wearing huge boxing-gloves labelled "More taxes" and "Higher prices". Another poster showed a ball and chain captioned "Five years' hard Labour".

Labour retaliated with an emotional film exploiting the sentimental case of a 5-year-old girl, Jennifer Bennett, to criticise hospital waiting lists. It backfired when investigation revealed a heavy application of advertising gloss: the consultant involved said the operating delay had nothing to do with underfunding of the NHS, while Jennifer's mother claimed she didn't recognise her "story". Labour also demonised members of the Tory Cabinet. William Waldegrave, the Secretary of Health, was pictured on a poster wearing a surgical mask and brandishing a scalpel. The legend underneath: "Tory health policy: Your money or your life". Chancellor of the Exchequer Norman Lamont appeared wearing a sinister expression and a Batman costume, labelled "Vatman". The message was that the Tories had broken electoral promises by imposing additional value added taxes.

Do such tactics work? Like all negative appeals, they run the risk of creating impressions other than those the advertiser intends. The young Mr Waldegrave, for example, scion of a noble family, was an attractive-looking man in a languid, upper-class sort of way, particularly when his weak mouth was covered by a surgeon's mask. Could not this portrayal suggest that the Minister for Health was a doctor? Surely, no bad thing? A survey of 100 undecided London voters quoted in *The Times* reported that few had recognised Mr Lamont as the "Vatman", and those who did thought it was a Tory poster promoting him as a heroic figure. Nearly half of the respondents thought the posters they saw, for both parties, were advertising *the rival party*. In another survey, cited by the *Guardian*, 82 per cent misidentified the party behind the ad.

Nevertheless, political consultants insist that negative attacks work. Yet the apparent success of mud-slinging in politics may trace less to its negative slant than to its choice of battlefield. While run-of-the-mill politicians focus on policies, parroting the party line, voters focus on personalities. By focusing on human character negative advertising arouses interest and secures attention to the message. However, a positive branding of a personality can also achieve impressive results. The most successful politicians are those blessed with "the human touch"; they win hearts and minds not through consistent policies, but by projecting themselves as the solution to disgruntlement with the political system. A second-rank Hollywood actor, Ronald Reagan, became the leader of the Free World by identifying with voter dissatisfaction about "big government"; at the other end of the political spectrum, but for much the same reason, the renegade "Red Ken" Livingstone, standing as a populist independent, prevailed against the applied resources of a hostile New Labour government, to become the first elected mayor of London in 2000.

Developing a positive communications strategy for a political party, rather than a charismatic individual, however, is incredibly difficult.

There are many one-issue interest groups to appeal to, often holding diametrically opposed views. In his book *All's Fair,* James Carville, who ran Bill Clinton's first presidential campaign, recounts that in the late spring of 1992, when he had already hired staff, spent millions of dollars, and won lots of committed delegates, he still needed a rationale. "It took almost three months, but finally our thinking began to crystallize", he wrote. What the team came up with was the somewhat threadbare phrase "Putting People First". It is surely true that negative impressions, being more dramatic, are more memorable. A stinging ad smearing an opponent's character defines him far more sharply than an assault on his policies. Yet what is it that is remembered? During American elections, across the television screen stalk a series of candidates described by their opponents as allies of child-molesters and murderers, hypocrites or crooks. So many viewers may draw the obvious conclusion: if all politicians are scoundrels, and all government is pernicious, why bother voting?

NOT ALL POLITICAL ADVERTISING takes place during elections. Throughout the 1980s and early 1990s, a strange new kind of corporate advertising took over British television screens. Actor Anthony Hopkins became the generic voice of British energy. His orotund Welsh articulation was recruited to underscore scenes of an England forever green in bombastic commercials for British Gas, British Nuclear Fuels, and the renaissance of the Central Electricity Generating Board as National Power. In a shot of a lightning-shattered sky, the latter's new twin, PowerGen, smugly conceded that its cost-efficient power generation could be surpassed only by the Almighty. Televiewers were mystified by the millions of pounds being spent informing them that telephones were a useful way to communicate, that electricity keeps homes alight and factories turning, and that everybody needs water. Most of these national utilities were iron-clad monopolies, with no need to seek new customers or to reassure existing ones. Why advertise?

In addition to the usual Central Office of Information campaigns urging Her Majesty's subjects to wrap up warmly, eat wisely, and not to drink and drive, the Tory Party was using advertising as an instrument to effect fundamental social change by selling off nationalised industries. As the bills were footed by the companies themselves, the government could claim that the aim was not political. But waves of advertising on such a massive scale were not politically neutral. The privatisation issues – for essential services, for the railways and the nuclear industry – were not just selling the prospectus, they were selling Thatcherism.

Agencies are not usually comfortable addressing business issues, which "creatives" scarcely comprehend. Fortunately for them, the aim of the privatisation programme, in addition to replenishing the government's coffers, was to create a share-owning (hence Conservative-voting) consumer society. Moreover, the rules governing pre-privatisation flotation advertising were stringent. The brief was simply to raise a company's profile prior to the official decision to take it public. Stock Exchange rules meant that you could not refer to profitability. You could not even reveal that the company was about to be offered for sale. The pre-privatisation brief was simply to repackage essential public services as trendy lifestyle choices, and so the "creatives" were able to reach into their bag of tricks for the usual visual hyperbole, outrageous puns, and silly send-ups. The subsequent hard-sell flotation advertising was another piece of cake: a simple appeal to greed. The early British Telecom sell-off campaign, "Tell Sid", set the pattern: the man in the street shouldn't miss out on this get-rich-quick scheme. The sell-off of the final £5 billion tranche of government shares in British Telecommunications some years later was promoted by a man in a badly fitting white wig, comedian Mel Smith pretending to be television detective Inspector Morse. A 1994 Spielbergian television pastiche showed, suspended over a moody Cityscape like spectral visitors from outer space, three floating eyes. One City gent asked another what's going on. The answer: "Three eyes floating". This was the flotation of Britain's government-owned venture capital business, Investment in Industry, or 3i.

The sorts of people who write letters to the editors of national newspapers thought the campaigns were banal, wasteful, and silly. Nevertheless the privatisations were a tremendous success. There was no shortage of takers for blue-chip monopolies sold at give-away prices in a rising market, and most of the issues were oversubscribed. In less favourable circumstances, the feckless advertising hoopla was impotent, as in the case of a teaser campaign which appeared on billboards, bus sides and full-page advertisements in the national press in the late 1980s. All this space was devoted to the letters BG, in various lurid colours. Beneath each large letter appeared a word in tiny type, revealing that this acronym stood for ideals such as "Bridging Gaps", "Bolder Goals", "Backing Gumption", "Brilliant Gizmos", and "Beautiful Globe". This hubristic display on behalf of British Gas signalled the imminent deregulation of the gas industry, but the privatisation of the company flopped; it had the misfortune to be timed for Black Monday in October 1987.

In 1989 the government became the advertising industry's biggest customer, outstripping consumer goods companies such as Unilever. The Water Authorities Association alone spent almost £22 million to raise the industry's public profile for privatisation, a figure swelled by individual campaigns by the ten regional water authority boards. It was estimated that the total expenditure amounted to 50p on every householder's water bill. At the time of this splurge, UK sales of bottled water had been booming for more than a decade because of alarm about the quality of drinking water, while the industry claimed it did not have the funds to cope with droughts, replace decrepit Victorian sewage systems, or meet EC standards of pollution. Against this background, the pre-privatisation campaign, aimed at reassuring consumers about water quality, and a follow-up corporate awareness campaign were deeply unpopular. The "colossal scale" of this exercise was condemned by Labour's environment spokesman John Cunningham as a "fruitless and dishonest public relations exercise". His contention that the campaign's undeclared "true aim was to promote water privatisation" was swiftly verified by the sell-off campaign, with a deluge of ads on the themes "Water floats" and "Be an H2-Owner". The result was the usual over-subscribed share issue, plus press coverage which ensured a permanent legacy of public hostility about the poor state of Britain's water supply.

Almost all the privatisation issues were gobbled up hungrily, but did the government succeed in its long-term objective of encouraging widespread share ownership by individuals? The question is clouded by the rise of the pension funds and other institutional investors which have come to dominate the market. In terms of value, in the early 1970s private investors accounted for nearly 40 per cent of the shares traded in London. In 1999, despite a buoyant market, less than 16 per cent were in private hands. But there were many more pairs of hands. In 1979, when the Tories took office, there were only about three million private shareholders. By the end of 1993, there were ten million. Not just "Sid", hanging on to the handful of British Telecom shares he had bought in the first big round of privatisation issues. Britain had entered a new phase of mass share ownership, with an explosive growth of employee share schemes and investment clubs, plus untold numbers of unregistered shareholders who bought PEPs, the government's highly popular tax-efficient Personal Equity Plans. This may be attributable at least in part to the massive privatisation campaigns. The record £104 million COI expenditure under Maggie Thatcher's administration in fiscal year 1987-8 was not matched again until 1998-9, when, under Labour, the government once again became the nation's largest advertiser, topping British Telecom and Procter & Gamble with £105.5 million.

Political advertising may play an important role in America, with its widespread electorate, unserved by popular national newspapers. Yet in all countries, who owns the channels of communication may be a far more influential factor than the advertising which appears on them. In Italy's 1994 national elections, candidate Silvio Berlusconi owned Italy's most popular television stations. He packaged a party called Forza Italia! (Go Italy!), presenting himself as a persona to lead it. His media empire provided him with free and constant access to "news coverage" by TV stations, newspapers, and magazines. His party won a comfortable majority in the Italian parliament.

WE DEMAND that our politicians trade in lies. The Korean state was founded in 2333 BC by a god-man called Tangan, son of a bear-woman, born on the sacred Mount Paekdu. In North Korea, governmental propaganda presents this legend as fact. It also asserts that Kim Jong-il, son of the late "Great Leader" Kim Il-Sung, was born there, too. He was in fact born in Khabarovsk in the far east of Russia. This lie is necessary to defend the assumption of divine right. In Western politics there are other myths which must be defended. No American politician can speechify without invoking the blessing of the Almighty, any more than any Middle Eastern despot can suggest any event has occurred other than through the will of Allah. No American foreign policy is implemented except in the name of democracy, even when it is shoring up a dictator in a country with no tradition of populism. No British political party can admit that full employment is an impossible goal. When the Liberal Democrats tried to launch a serious political debate about the legalisation of cannabis, merely acknowledging a national conversation that had been going on for years, they were derided in the popular press as irresponsible. While the House of Lords is being dismantled, no party may yet suggest it's also time for the Queen to pack her bags. These cynical lies and evasions are the ritual offerings laid by the unbelieving power-seeker prostrating himself before the graven image of Public Opinion.

There is inevitably a cultural lag between what people believe and the policies their leaders propound. The able politician has to keep abreast of the common experience. Political parties, like corporations, have to continually test their dogma against people's notions of reality. In 1994, research amongst voters who had defected showed that while they were strongly right-wing on law and order, they were much less so on education and the National Health Service. This may have been because they had more personal familiarity with the latter (presumably they knew few criminals) and were thus in a better position to compare dogma with personal experience.

At the same time, the electorate has become more impatient of argument. Fast-cutting commercials have shortened its attention span. There is no time for balance or qualification in a soundbite. It is a mandate to conceal, distort or trample on the truth. And it's getting shorter. The average bloc of uninterrupted speech by presidential candidates in the US was forty-two seconds in 1968. In 1988 it was ten seconds. While the candidates were on screen on the major networks in 1968, the time they were actually heard speaking was 84 per cent. In 1988 this had fallen to 37 per cent. No comparable research is available in Britain, but the British politician seems still to get more than ten seconds' exposure, although the venerable five-minute party political broadcast was halved in length for the 1997 British elections.

These three tendencies – the belief in cultural mythology, the perceived contradictions between dogma and personal conceptions of reality, and the demand for a quick and easy fix – mean that it is impossible to fairly communicate abstract concepts, such as political policies. Mass public interest is aroused only when personalities are involved – such as the dethroning of Margaret Thatcher in 1990, the stuff of Shakespeare. Political advertising is the ultimate expression of the "personality testimonial" approach. It's not surprising. If you can't understand the issues, you vote for someone who you think shares your values. Sean Connery, for example, brought both local credibility and the heroic image of his film personality to bear when he campaigned for the SNP in the cause of Scottish nationalism in the elections for the new Scottish parliament in 1999. Yet curiously, politicians have been slow to recruit the support of celebrities – actors, comedians, pop singers, sports stars – in their advertising, perhaps because of a natural reluctance to share the limelight with a rival for popular affection who has a superior stage presence. After all, Ronald Reagan was an actor first. And he was following in the footsteps of Gary Cooper, who was proposed for President of the United States in 1936 by the Gary Cooper Fan Club of San Antonio: they claimed he had demonstrated his political credentials in the film *Mr Deeds Goes to Town*.

FASHION spurs us to achieve individuality through conformity. Cigarettes evade severe restrictions in Western societies through a cynical minimalism which survives even outright bans on advertising. Advertising for banks is usually counterproductive because the boast is so easily denied by the reality of experience. Most "corporate advertising" is as convincing as fairy tales, because it is actually directed at its own management. In the political arena, since abstract concepts, such as policies, are too woolly or too complex for effective compression by the techniques of mass communications, advertising is the ultimate expression of the empty "celebrity testimonial". The distortion of truth through advertising is the engine which drives these and many other sectors. Inevitably, advertising's Big Lies have social consequences too; these are examined in the next section.

PART V

Beyond the bottom line

"We're shopping around for a new agency, and we thought you people might be interested in making a pitch."

CHAPTER 24

THE WONDERFUL FOLK WHO BROUGHT YOU 'TIRED BLOOD'

Admen

It is a great responsibility to mould the daily lives of millions of our fellow men, and I am persuaded that we are second only to statesmen and editors in power for good.
James Wallen, American copywriter, 1925

In 1999 an American judge gave leave for a disgruntled client to sue the British company, Saatchi and Saatchi, perhaps the world's best-known advertising agency, for creating a countereffective television commercial. A chain of sportswear shops claimed that, after just one showing, its sales went into steep decline and the company's valuation on the stock market slumped by two-thirds. That single airing of the $7 million campaign was in the premier American viewing slot, the football Superbowl. The commercial showed a barefoot black runner being hunted down by white men in a military-type vehicle. They caught him, drugged him, and forced a pair of Nike trainers onto his feet. Waking up, he saw the trainers and ran away wildly trying to shake them from his feet. The idea was to demonstrate the intense dedication of the company to its mission of supplying people with sports shoes. Instead, it provoked a furore of racist allegations. The client complained that the agency's creative team had browbeaten him into accepting the advertisement. The agency's legal defence was that it could not be sued for lack of competence in a profession which requires none: "The imposition of a punitive damage award in the absence of guidelines and standards is highly unfair".

ADFOLK are different from ordinary business people. The very brightest university graduates do not go into advertising – they become scientists or academics. But of those who enter the business world, advertising attracts some of the cleverest, particularly those who can think on their feet and relish diversity. There are also plenty of successful ad people who have come straight from art school, or in off the street, armed with a degree only of *chutzpah*. Advertising has no recognised training system, demands no qualifications. By and large people just drift into it. Apart from researchers, who are at the periphery of the process and never make advertising decisions, few advertising practitioners have an instinct for the scientific method, any training in the principles of psychology or an understanding of mathematical concepts such as probability. Their strengths tend to be intuitive and people-based. The emphasis is on persuasive skills – not mass communications expertise, but person-to-person persuasion – because they have to persuade each other.

Admen and women are versatile. Like management consultants and merchant bankers, they are exposed to a wide range of businesses and must adapt to many different corporate cultures. Typically, they are self-absorbed and intensely competitive. In his book *How to Capture the Advertising High Ground*, Winston Fletcher, an advertising agency chairman and a past chairman of the Advertising Association, lists fifteen qualities needed to excel in the black art of advertising: "arrogance, charm, confidence, contacts, creativity, diligence, energy, enthusiasm, literacy, looks, oratory, resilience, self-criticism, self-publicity, and wit". That seems a promising genetic code for success in any business, but to create successful advertisements requires something else: an innate understanding of what makes people tick, plus the ability to reach out and touch those feelings vividly in words and pictures – the instincts of a demagogue.

Advertising was one of the first industries to welcome women into important jobs, as researchers, copywriters and art directors. As more women began to appear in client marketing organisations, they moved into agency management, too, as account handlers and planners. Still, in Britain in 1999, according to the IPA, although half of the people working in ad agencies were women, only 7 per cent of senior managers and just 16 per cent of "creatives" were female. Barbara Nokes, of Grey Advertising, is one of the few women to have reached the level of creative director. She believes, "Creative departments... are very aggressive environments. The trouble is that even now women are brought up to please people, to be accommodating. With creative work you are putting your taste, experience and attitude on the line. And that requires a huge ego". In an industry where it is important that the "face fits" the client, not many representatives of ethnic minorities are agency high fliers either. Most of all, adfolk are young. Ninety per cent of the work force quits advertising before they are 40, according to the 1998 IPA survey; over half of all advertising agency staff are still in their twenties or teens.

Good salesmen always like being sold to. And advertising people are themselves swayed by glamorous images, because it is the basis of their craft to know what's "in". A whole swathe of London's service industries – restaurants, bars, clothes shops, decorative arts – depends on advertising people, who are quick to jump on the bandwagon as soon as something becomes "cool". Most of all, good advertising people love their work and work at it all the time. The pressures are enormous, clients are frequently infuriating, colleagues may be cantankerous, deadlines are always imminent. The best admen and women believe in the integrity of their work and will not yield to the easy temptation to simply give the client what he wants without a vigorous struggle. Unlike business professionals – accountants and lawyers – they often lose clients because of a matter of principle.

And they are anxiety-prone. In a 1996 survey by the Institute of Practitioners in Advertising and the marketing consultancy firm KPMG, company finance directors cited advertising and marketing budgets as the first place to cut costs when business falters. In 1989 nearly 16,000 people worked in the London advertising industry. Then recession bit. Saatchi & Saatchi London shed 250 of its 750 London staff. By 1993 only 11,600 people were working in the centre of British advertising. The industry had lost 18 per cent of its revenue and a quarter of its work force. In good times or bad, clients change agencies frequently, often without justification. Firing the agency is a favourite ploy of the newly appointed marketing supremo. At a single stroke it cuts off links with the policies of the past, and the ensuing chaos buys at least a year's time in which the new policies cannot be evaluated. With every major account change, people in agencies lose their jobs. And so the entire advertising business is chronically insecure.

Most operational systems, from the production processes pioneered by Henry Ford to retailing or air traffic control, aim to eliminate human whim and variability. The product of an advertising agency, creativity, depends on these eccentricities. It springs from a healthy tension between the creative impulse and the businesslike objective. In the ubiquitous statements of "agency philosophy", advertising agents tend to locate themselves in one camp or the other: either creatively inspired "hot shops", or marketing-savvy business advisers. The pendulum swings this way and that. In good times agency people can get carried away with the crest of their own hyperbole, producing wasteful, self-indulgent advertising. When recession bites, clients lose their nerve and insist on banal product-oriented "messages". John Hegley wrote a poem about the eternal conflict:

The Art of Advertising[1]

Ladies and businessmen,
it is unlikely
that any reference
to your bank or beer
or whatever
will appear
in the finished commercial.
Not even by clever implication.
Your product is merely a starting point
providing finance
for fine art.
Let this be your reward.
Art cannot afford
to set its purpose
to the increase of corporate profile or profit.
Indeed the artist may see fit
to advertise a rival product
on your account
to suit some compositional need.
Yes – we guarantee to induce no increase in your sales
because the way the work is done
there will be no way of telling
which product it is you're selling
no logo, no catch phrase
no process of suggestion.
No glorification of consumerism
or the market economy, whatsoever
Art has higher things in mind,
to be doing well
it must be ill-defined
in ambiguity.
Let the artist choose.
You have nothing to lose
but your money.

Like poetry, the best advertising ideas usually spring from a single brain, but the route to market is an involved team process. Agencies

---

[1] Reprinted by permission of PFD on behalf of: John Hegley. ©: as printed in the original volume.

have devised a system for producing ideas which is universal in the business. It convenes a triumvirate of interests: the account executive represents the aims of the client; the account planners use research to interpret consumer desires; the "creatives" are expected to supply the spark that leaps the gap between the two. In practice many people are involved in these functions at various hierarchical levels, and are assisted by specialists such as researchers, media planners and buyers, television producers, typographers and print experts. In a large advertising agency, a major account may involve fifty or more people who may influence the creation of an advertisement, plus a large variety of outside suppliers. Like the group of blind gurus trying to describe an elephant by grasping different parts of it, each of these contributors tends to have a different personal agenda, hence a different idea of how advertising works and what it is supposed to achieve.

The star turn is the originator of the idea , almost always a duo nominally consisting of a wordsmith or "ideas man" and an "art director", although these days both tend to be visually-minded (albeit rarely able to draw). The general assumption is that creative genius is innate:

> In every department other than the creative department, people are taken on from the best colleges, they are trained to the hilt on the job and spend at least a year trailing others. Only in the creative department are people taken on and expected to hit the ground running from day one. Training and recruitment of creatives is all about recreating the norm.[2]

These craftsmen live literally by their wits; above all they want to demonstrate personal brilliance, in order to reinforce and increase the value of their creative reputations. (When they change jobs, they usually go as a team, like a successful stage act.) This aura, reinforced perhaps by exotic dress and behaviour, is the main support for their arguments, which are likely to be presented in aesthetic terms. Many "creatives" are attracted into advertising because of their interest in art, literature, films, or design. It is from this quarter that the notion of advertising as an art form emerges.

The term account planning was coined by Stephen King at JWT London in 1968, although the system was first introduced by the late Stanley Pollitt when he helped form the agency Boase Massimi Pollitt

---

[2] Larry Barker, creative director of the Boase Massimi Pollitt agency and president of the Design and Art Directors' Association, in a speech to D&AD in 2000.

three years earlier. The account planner has the job of providing the strategic platform for the creative leap and the intellectual rationale for the result; he will construct these in terms of the market situation and consumer psychology. Like all apologists, planners can lose the view of the forest while grinding up trees to produce their documentation. Dave Trott, creative director of Bainsfair Sharkey Trott, famously asked his planners for "one word and a thousand facts" – rather than the other way around – and for the sake of concision also prodded them to conceive their briefings in the form of advertising posters.

The role of the account executive (or account handler or manager or director) is a balancing act: he wants to retain the regard of his colleagues, but ultimately he has to please the client, who is the source of his power base. He is the point man of the platoon, and when this team has resolved on an approach, he will lead the presentation to a legion of critics in the client organisation. Because an advertisement is a highly visible exposure of executive judgement a great many people may become involved, not just marketing men, but others: salesmen, the PR department, the board of directors, the chairman. All are anxious to cover their backsides. The chairman, recognising that his position may put him "out of touch", normally consults his wife. Many other executives, prompted by the same feeling, submit the ad, particularly those directed at women, to the dreaded "secretary test".

So, before it is ever seen by the public, every advertisement must satisfy an internal audience, within the agency and at the client. It is here that the process often falls apart. These individuals are disparate in temperament and taste, and also different from the target purchaser. As there is no evidential measure of effectiveness, the decision is a hierarchical one, deferred to the top dog. The task of the creative person, if he wants to keep both the approval of his colleagues and the client's business, often degenerates into pleasing the internal audience. The external audience is marginal to this agenda, which is why so much advertising seems so off-key to those it is intended to influence.

Advertisements also often seem to be very much like each other. This is for the same reason that so many magazine covers look alike. Both are produced by a small group of people trying to impress each other. People create advertising to advertise themselves. They must be *au courant* – hip, cool – and that means following fashionable trends. Their paymasters are keen to avoid personal risk, too, and are really comfortable only when they are doing what everyone else is doing. The client brief is reduced to a request for an imitative style, nowadays often a few modish clichés such as "in-your-face", "off-the-wall", or "edgy". The iconoclastic talent that is responsible for the genuine breakthroughs in commerce, science, and the arts is rare in advertising. In advertising there are no creators like the scientist Richard Feynman, who go back to reason from first principles. Without fashionable provenance, originality would be the very devil to sell, so "creatives" simply recycle the latest pop artefact from the entertainment world.

Many "creatives" disdain the work they do, and almost all of them nurse loftier ambitions: to become a novelist, an artist, or, most glamorous of all, a film director. Production of commercials is invariably contracted out to independent film companies, which have a roster of talented directors and cameramen. Most of these have their eyes on Hollywood. Famous feature film directors such as Ridley Scott (*Blade Runner*), Alan Parker (*Bugsy Malone* and *Angela's Ashes*), and Hugh Hudson (*Chariots of Fire*) began by directing commercials. Young film-obsessed advertising "creatives" vie to work with cult directors who will authenticate the advertising idea with their charisma: David Lynch, the maker of the enigmatic *Eraserhead, Blue Velvet*, and the *Twin Peaks* television series, drew a fee of close to $1 million to make an offbeat film for Adidas focusing on the pain barrier of long-distance running, with no product story whatsoever. Riding the coat-tails of such superstars, the agency "creative" frequently becomes an acolyte. Junior agency and client "suits", even if they attend the shoot, are clearly one-upped. The film director takes over the thinking, and so the entire burden of advertising thought – the weighty, strategic deliberations of the agency-client team – devolves upon an individual who is not advertising-trained and who there is no reason to believe knows anything whatsoever about how advertising works.

One man bears a great deal of responsibility for this turn of events. John Lloyd was a producer for BBC radio who in the early 1980s launched a comedy spoof called *The Hitch-Hiker's Guide to the Galaxy*, which attained classic status. After reproducing its success on television, he went on to create a series of enormously popular TV parodies: *Blackadder, Spitting Image,* and *Not the Nine O'clock News.* Standard fare on the last-named was send-ups of advertising. These sardonic programmes were meat and drink for advertising "creatives", who paid homage by reproducing these conceits in their own humorous advertising efforts. Lloyd reckoned that if imitators could make advertisements out of his ideas, so could he, and beginning in 1994, without any background in advertising, he swiftly produced a series of parodies of advertising genres or specific advertisements which are still revered within the industry, for example, his commercial for Castlemaine XXXX lager which showed a princess turning a frog into a hunky Australian, who then abandoned her for the beer. Lloyd believes programmes like his own have rendered straightforward advertising claims obsolete. His theory of advertising is entertainment-based: to make a brand relevant through humour. He cites alcohol: "You can't say anything good about it really, except in the vaguest terms. You can't say 'This stuff gets you pissed really quickly, and it's not too bad'. So what you're selling is image: 'This is the lager for people like you and me'".

Is advertising merely entertainment? Or is it, as many believe, an art form? Only in the sense that, say fly-fishing or woodworking is an art – that is, it is based on skill or craft and permits self-expression. If it were to fulfil the purposes of art – to free and enlighten the human condition – it would fail in its purpose, which is to proselytise. A more intriguing question is: is advertising a business or an indulgence? On the one hand advertising is dominated by multi-million-pound multinational organisations. But many advertising practitioners act as though their purpose is simply to entertain, or to create artistic effects. Agency staff often behave more like butterflies than businessmen, and agency fortunes are notoriously mercurial.

Advertising is a personality business on a Hollywood scale, as the names agencies give themselves betray. One was called, for a while, Boase Massimi Pollitt Doyle Dane Bernbach Needham Worldwide, though most of these personalities were dead. It's a *virtual* people business. Everything depends on the people *who have the reputation* of being a creative genius, or of having the clients in their pocket. Just as a bit of side, some contacts and a run of good fortune can give a kid on a trading floor a reputation for the Midas touch. Like investment banks, advertising agencies pay such legends legendary salaries. Advertising agencies are always taking each other over as fortunes wax and wane. They don't buy physical assets, but temperamental talent which can flounce out of the door at any minute. To keep them at their desks, earn-out schemes were devised, whereby part of the purchase price of an agency is deferred and linked to future performance, laced with lavish top-ups for achieving targets. The effect of these "golden handcuff" schemes means that when the agency's key people descend the lift-shaft each night, they are taking not just the assets of the business with them, but also the future profits.

The crucifix on which the business hangs is the speculative creative pitch. All advertising agencies need new business all the time: to grow, to replace the constant turnover in disaffected clients, to boost their self-esteem. It's so fiercely competitive that it's customary for advertising agencies to actually deliver the goods – both creative strategy and prototypes – before being appointed and receiving payment. Agency staff thrive on the competitive new business pitch, a crucible in which exciting new ideas must be produced in record time. Adrenaline surges, imagination runs free, staff are pulled off existing accounts, and budgets fly out of the window as the presentation gathers all of the tension, and some of the dazzle, of a Broadway first night. Although a strong agency contender might persuade the potential client to pay a nominal rejection fee, this never approaches the astonishing level of investment involved. Sometimes there's no winner, because the client elects to stay with his incumbent agency. Occasionally, clients go off with the idea without appointing the agency. It's a business strategy the Soho prostitutes who walk the same streets would laugh at.

It's little wonder that the business community at large finds it difficult to accept advertising agencies as grown-up businesses.[3] Indeed, ad agencies are quite spectacularly inept at projecting themselves credibly to their own target audiences. Consider this advertisement, placed by a newly formed advertising agency, in a brochure produced by the Marketing Society (its membership would constitute the core of the agency's potential clientele) for its annual conference. The advertisement consisted entirely of four quotations spread boldly across a full page, above an injunction to call for "a free quote":

Advertising is the rattling of a stick inside a swill bucket.	George Orwell
Advertising is legalised lying.	H. G. Wells
Advertising is the art of making whole lies out of half truths.	Edgar A. Shoaff
Advertising is a racket.	F. Scott Fitzgerald

It is impossible to imagine a similar advertisement placed, say, by a firm of solicitors in the annual conference programme of the Law Society. Nor was it seen as an aberration. On the contrary, this advertisement was singled out for special commendation in the pages of the advertising industry's trade weekly, *Campaign*, for its "creative irreverence". Advertising agencies like to be cute, at all costs – including that of projecting themselves as lightweight, not to say light-headed, dilettantes in the business community.

---

[3] It was a famously successful American creative director and agency founder, Howard Gossage, who said "Advertising is no business for a grown man".

Yet whatever excesses and self-indulgences agencies may be guilty of, it is the client who must carry the can for what appears on your television screen, in print, or on the hoardings you pass. The client sets the agenda, approves the process every step of the way, pays for it all, and has ultimate authority. Every client also likes to contribute to the creative process, and the clever account handler ensures they feel some ownership of the idea. Everyone can write a letter, many clients can write documents, so most of them feel that they can write advertising. Clients are less confident with graphics and film, where agencies can easily outwit them. Clients may be supposed to have better marketing skills, and the successful agency-client partnership is one in which both parties cooperate while respecting each other's superior abilities. Yet personnel turnover in client marketing organisations is high; young people on the make don't stay in one job long. Eighteen months seems to be about average. Agency personnel change frequently, too, but because they have established the discipline of account planning, the preservation of long-term brand vision is often the inheritance of the agency.

ADVERTISING AGENCIES and their clients are usually pretty skilful at developing strategies – i.e. agreeing what they're trying to achieve – and research techniques are available to assist them. More elusive is the vital creative spark which translates plan into persuasion. Because there are few objective criteria of performance, adfolk quickly become jaded and cynical, and so do their ideas: a self-fulfilling vicious circle. Even the very best advertising minds are frequently confounded by the group system and advertising illiterates in positions of power in agencies and client organisations. Like the idealistic writer who takes the Hollywood dollar, or the fictional private eye, admen and women like to portray themselves as cynical, hard-bitten professionals who have sold out truth and genius to clients for money. Like most of us, they use "the Nuremberg defence" to evade big moral issues, by separating the things they have to do to earn a living from real life and genuine personal relationships. Tony Brignull wrote this when he was a copywriter at Abbott Mead Vickers BBDO:

> "Are we a profession?" I asked an account director. "No", he replied. "We're a bunch of tarts".... Some agencies do, in fact, ask employees if they're prepared to work on cigarette accounts or the armed forces or for one political party or another. There hovers a question of your commitment. Are you inboard (a member of the team) or outboard (and soon to be overboard)? In matters of conscience the individual in

advertising gets little help from the industry because we lack a collective conscience. The accepted wisdom is "if we don't do it – fag ads, booze ads, junk ads - someone else will".[4]

There is, in any case, little prospect of reward for the high-principled. When, as a condition of the "master settlement" with the tobacco companies in the US, health authorities were awarded funds and poster sites to conduct anti-tobacco advertising, most did not scruple against employing the same well-known advertising agencies which had served tobacco clients on the grounds that they, too, should have access to the best available talent.

---

[4] *The Guardian,* 21 December 1992.

CHAPTER 25

MEANWHILE, BACK IN THE REAL WORLD

Unreality

"You may fool all of the people some of the time; you can even fool some of the people all the time; but you can't fool all of the people all of the time". Lincoln's appealing slogan rests on two elementary assumptions. First, that there is a clear and visible distinction between sham and reality, between the lies a demagogue would have us believe and the truths which are there all the time. Second, that the people tend to prefer reality to sham, that if offered a choice between a simple truth and a contrived image, they will prefer the truth. Neither of these any longer fits the facts.

Daniel J. Boorstin, *The Image: A Guide to Pseudo-events in America*, 1961

IN 1991 the magazine *Vanity Fair* featured a nude woman on its cover. It caused an uproar of outrage in the media. Not because the woman was nude. Not because the nude woman was the well-known film star Demi Moore. But because the nude film star was plumply pregnant. Five years later another nude figure outraged the public. This was a photograph on a poster of a naked baby, innocent as the day it was born. It was, in fact, shown on the day it was born, wailing, its umbilical cord still attached, smeared with blood and vernix. In the US a parenting magazine, *Child*, refused to print the press version of this advertisement. In Britain the poster provoked a storm of complaints and the ASA ordered it to come down, on the grounds that it was obscene.

The newborn baby was the latest image in a campaign which Benetton, an international chain retailing undistinguished casual clothing for youth in more than 7,000 shops and 100 countries, had developed around controversial social and moral issues. The images were confrontational, always shocking somebody. None of them had anything to do with Benetton's products, nor indeed any public posture adopted by the company. Usually no text was included, apart from the Benetton logo. The questions these advertisements raised were left hanging. The aim of the campaign was simply that, by associating itself with provocative themes, the company would create an affinity with rebellious youth. The

Benetton logo would become a global badge identifying the young people who wore clothing emblazoned with it as right-minded: selflessly interested in social issues, rather than venal acquisitiveness, and hence themselves interesting. A good reason to acquire a new wardrobe. Benetton advertising aroused widespread indignation, disgust, envy and admiration. None of it would ever have survived test by focus group.

Proprietor Luciano Benetton did not use an advertising agency; traditional advertising, he felt, was worthless. Like a Renaissance prince, in 1983 he commissioned a fashion photographer to wander the world searching for emotional images on the general theme of the universality of Man. To harmonise with this advertising approach, at first centred on racial harmony, he even changed the names of his shops: to United Colors of Benetton. The photographer, Oliviero Toscani, had no pretensions about advertising theory. He said his simple objective was "to make people look at the ads. Selling jumpers is the company's problem, not mine". He began by exploiting racial and sexual stereotypes. When a 1989 image of a black woman suckling a white baby had to be withdrawn because of protests in the US, it was followed by a picture of a black man and a white woman holding an oriental baby. A 1991 photo of a priest kissing a nun on the lips created uproar in Italy. A picture of the Queen, regenerated by computer as a black woman, achieved the same result in Britain. The images were sometimes ambiguous. One which showed two children, a cherubic, blue-eyed blond hugging a black child with his hair twisted into horns, caused an avalanche of criticism in the US from civil rights and religious groups. Toscani claimed he was promoting racial understanding: "Black people have been demonised. We're reflecting what already exists". American blacks also misinterpreted a picture which showed black and white hands cuffed together. Toscani had meant: "We're in this together" but overlooked chain gang associations.

Undeterred, Benetton expanded its agenda to public health issues. One image was constructed of hundreds of snapshots of young people, the colours forming a pattern which read "AIDS". Did it mean that all these people had the disease? Or just that it should be on their minds? The ASA ruled against another advertisement which showed a dying AIDS patient surrounded by his family. The British advertising trade press condemned Benetton advertisements and some magazines and owners of poster sites refused to carry them. The advertising community in general had no qualms about revoking freedom of expression for a company which had the cheek to appropriate real issues, moreover without the guidance of an advertising agency:

While the ASA impotently waves the red card and assorted magazine editors vie with the Health Education Authority in the vigour of their denunciation, two youth magazines are reported to be keen on running the ad to stimulate circulation ... Far from denying the ad the oxygen of publicity, the act of banning it actually contributes remarkably to public awareness of its existence ... What they are capitalising on is bad advertising which will eventually backfire on Benetton. This is no criticism of the art direction (the campaign has won numerous creative citations) nor of the indisputably high awareness achieved. The problem lies in the message. Either it is ludicrously pretentious or it is breathtakingly cynical. We are invited to believe that Benetton outlets are a haven for the ethically correct consumer of the Nineties. Yet there seems nothing remarkable in Benetton's products or corporate policy to distinguish it from its competitors in this respect... *American Vogue* is still right to accept the ads and those who ban it over here are wrong. The campaign should stand or fall on its own merits.[1]

Other Benetton advertisements showed topical photo-reportage, pictures which might appear in any newspaper, or in the annual report of a respected charity: an oil-slicked bird, South American children slaving in a factory making mud bricks, economic migrants from Albania crowding onto a ship trying to get to Italy, a war cemetery, a blazing car bombed by terrorists, a Mafia killing. Nevertheless, the ASA banned most of these, and applied pressure through the Committee of Advertising Practice and directly on Benetton to force it to abandon the controversial campaign.

In 1993 the Obscene Publications squad sought to bar British distribution of a leading French newspaper, *Libération*, because it contained a double-page colour Benetton advertisement showing 56 sets of male and female genitalia including those of children. By mid-afternoon the issue was a sell-out in France, where there were only ten calls of complaint. One of them was from the country's advertising trade body which told other publishers it would not tolerate further publication of the ad. Pascal Somarriba, Benetton's head of international advertising, claimed it was not sexual exploitation, because photographer Oliviero Toscani had used his own children. He questioned the different valuations attached to advertising: "It is a study of sexuality and races. It is also about what is tolerated in one arena but not in another. Lots of things like nudity have been tolerated in art down the centuries but are

---

[1] *Marketing Week*, 1992.

not tolerated in advertising". There was another agenda as well: the photograph had been placed in *Libération* in order to qualify for acceptance in the avant-garde section of the Venice Biennale arts festival.

That same year another advertisement attracted the Vatican to the ranks of Benetton critics. Its official newspaper, *L'Osservatore Romano*, denounced the company for "image terrorism" and "making a mockery even of death". The offending images were a bloodied white T-shirt with a bullet hole and the camouflage combat trousers of a soldier killed in Bosnia. A Benetton press release explained that these clothes had been worn by a Croatian soldier killed in 1993, and had been given to the company by his parents. A typewritten message across the advertisement was from his father, saying that he wished his son's name to be used in the cause of peace. A Benetton spokeswoman feigned pious astonishment:

> It is absolutely amazing the Vatican should condemn people who are trying to get important issues debated. The church does not have a monopoly on social issues. If we were trying to sell T-shirts, there probably would not be a worse way of doing it. We are not that naive. It's meant to question the notion of institutionalised violence and the role of advertising . . . in a commercial fairyland which pretends war doesn't exist.

While this image was among the Benetton ads on permanent exhibition in the Frankfurt Museum of Modern Art, the *Frankfurter Allgemeine Zeitung* refused to carry this advertisement. A handful of disgruntled Benetton store owners in Germany used the provocative ads as a pretext for a rebellion against the parent company, though there was no apparent harm to Benetton sales, which, in spite of the 1994 recession, grew 12 per cent to record highs. In Britain, the ASA received only a handful of complaints about the dead soldier advertisement, possibly because the message was in Serbo-Croat.

The commonest complaint about the Benetton campaign was that it was exploitative. A letter to the *Guardian* was typical:

> Using this banner [the United Colors of Benetton] as if it were any of the world's true charities is gross arrogance. The objective here is the pursuit of sales and profit. Certainly profit has a place but not as shown in subterfuge. Human suffering should have no place as a vehicle for merchandise. The company is crassly dishonest to pretend otherwise. Bosnia is a bloodbath now, with very real daily torture and death. How

sick can capitalism get to use this fact to sell "designer" clothing?

By this letter-writer's logic, had Benetton endeavoured to contribute to a solution of any of the questions it aired, or even taken some policy standpoint about them in the way that Anita Roddick claimed to do for the Third World and animal testing with her chain of Body Shops, there would be no grounds for offence. Yet the intensity and flavour of the public reaction suggest otherwise. Benetton was offending a long-standing convention: advertising has nothing to do with real life. Its role is to tell fairy stories. The consumer shies from confronting the truths of birth, ageing, and death. Benetton, in any case, remained unrepentant. With the high-minded justification of "challenging assumptions of beauty", the campaign continued in 1998 with a group photograph of Down's syndrome children, and Benetton ushered in the new millennium in the US and Europe by featuring the photographs of Death Row inmates of America's prisons. Opposing capital punishment was now a fashion statement. As photographer Toscani explained, "I'm not here to judge whether people in this campaign are guilty or innocent and I'm not saying they should be free. I'm just trying to raise awareness of the issue". The American campaign provoked outrage from state governments and the powerful retailer Sears Roebuck reneged on a franchising contract it had just signed. Jerry Della Femina, founder of the American agency Della Femina/Jeary, was one of those offended: "If the death sentence were handed out to those who are guilty of producing excruciatingly tasteless, ineffective advertising and inflicting it on the masses, Oliviero Toscani, the self-proclaimed genius behind Benetton advertising, would be appearing in his own anti-capital punishment ads".

Despite the widespread antipathy within the advertising industry, advertising people recognised that by trading in human emotion, the (however false) Colors of Benetton campaign was accumulating considerable image capital. Where Benetton led, others followed. A worthy three-minute travelogue, ranging from Botswana to the Cotswolds, appeared in the commercial breaks in 1994, with a voice-over offering concerned comment about issues such as elephant conservation, the flight from the land, and the effects of tourism. The reason for the appearance of expensive personalities such as cricketer David Gower and military hero Sir Peter de la Billière, plus a fleet of off-track vehicles, was deferred until midway, when it was revealed that this was a commercial launching a new Range Rover.

Nike appropriated feminist issues in a long-standing (1989-94) press campaign targeting the beauty myths promoted in women's magazines.

The inspirational copy ran:

> A woman is often measured by the things she cannot control . . . by 36-24-36 and inches and ages and numbers, by all the outside things that don't ever add up to who she is on the inside . . . let her be measured by the things she can control, by who she is and who she is trying to become, because as every woman knows, measurements are only statistics. And STATISTICS LIE.

The candid photograph nevertheless showed an attractive woman.

A 1991 television commercial showed a mentally handicapped man stacking the shelves of a supermarket. Shoppers averted their eyes as they swept past him. The man smiled, and the film froze on what now appeared as a perfectly normal happy face. A public service announcement? No, an advertisement for Fuji film. Another commercial in the series played the racial card: an Asian woman waiting by the school gate was shunned by a group of white mothers. When she hugged her daughter the film froze on a smiling white child. These images exerted the power of cognitive dissonance: the real world has intruded into the world of advertising. But unlike the Benetton ads, they resolved the dissonance with a conventional aspirational solution, and hence aroused little controversy.

Does the end unjustify the means? Using death, disability, racial prejudice, and human tragedies as a kind of product claim may seem in dubious taste. But by breaking into people's private lives through advertising, rather than confining the rhetoric to the conventional and more avoidable channels, such advertising can create involvement in social issues. Advertising is by its nature exploitative. In the consumer world, where the avoidance of painful reality is paramount, images which serve to promote an awareness of the real world we live in – that new babies are bloodied with slime, that war is hell – seem a useful counterbalance. By cynically identifying themselves with issues in order to curry favour with certain target groups such opportunistic advertisers are nevertheless at least telling it how it is. By default, they fill an awareness gap created by the failure of conventional public service advertising (see next chapter).

In 1961, when television was still in its infancy, Daniel J. Boorstin foresaw that the increasing powers of mass communications technology, far from sharpening our perceptions of reality, would blunt them:

> The images themselves become shadowy mirror reflections of one

another: one interview comments on another; one television show spoofs another; novel, television show, radio program, movie, comic book, and the way we think of ourselves, all become merged into mutual reflections. At home we begin to try to live according to the script of television programs of happy families, which are themselves nothing but amusing quintessences of us...While we have given others great power to deceive us, to create pseudo-events, celebrities, and images, they could not have done so without our collaboration...We refuse to believe that advertising men are at most our collaborators, helping us to make illusions for ourselves. In our moral indignation, our eagerness to find the villains who have created and frustrated our exaggerated expectations, we have underestimated the effect of the rise of advertising. We think it has meant an increase of untruthfulness. In fact it has meant a reshaping of our very concept of truth.[2]

A sense of unreality permeates the process of developing an advertisement from the outset. Advertising conceptions spring from the assumption that the product, service, or company on offer is the optimum. *No other choice is tolerable.* As these brands function in a competitive environment, the claims of competitors are mutually exclusive, an unreality which the consumer recognises, though the advertisers do not. A communications strategy is then devised which develops this unreality in terms of wish-fulfilment: what the advertiser wants the consumer to know, believe and feel about the brand. It's a wish list which requires an unrealistic degree of involvement from the intended target. At its least imaginative, this hope is simply translated into a dream world sanitised in the advertiser's desired image. The advertiser simply denies reality, and asserts that the opposite is true. *Woman* magazine launched a television campaign in 1994 to correct its dated homemaker image simply by claiming it had changed in some intrinsic though unspecified manner. The only evidence offered for its transformation was the style of the advertising: attractive young downmarket housewives hurtled about in frenetic lifestyle situations: driving cars, refereeing a football game, and chatting in restaurants, a 1990s gloss on the traditional cosy homemaker's world, with no man in sight, nor any working wives. Advertisements like these, which admit the need for change without demonstrably changing the product, simply remind people of their existing convictions. The people they target understand that the world shown in advertising is remote from real experience. Blinkered by their "communications

[2] *The Image.*

strategy", advertisers may not always appreciate the width of the gap, but consumers recognise advertising hyperbole and make allowances for it.

Effective advertising cannot ignore the consumer's prior experience. On the contrary, it takes care to reconfirm preconceptions, before extending them to a new idea. Advertising thus has considerable power to reinforce what people already believe. Couple this with the physiological phenomenon that our senses are always attuned to what's different: the sudden noise or the sudden silence, the leaf that stirs, the red frog, the woman standing in a group of men, the man wearing the beret, the monocle, or the ten-gallon hat. We are conditioned to notice and suspect the nonconformist, the member of another tribe, and exaggerate his different qualities. In this way, minorities become associated with behavioural ticks. Because advertising is based on dramatic simplification, it trades in these visual clichés, shorthand symbols which everyone will instantly recognise: the lascivious Frenchman, the swaggering German, the naive American. Advertising preaches the same popular parables as the tabloid newspapers.

A 1998 full-page press ad, lobbying on behalf of the Multiple Sclerosis Society to press for more extensive prescriptions of an expensive drug, Beta Interferon, and other services for MS sufferers, used an unflattering caricature of an uncaring doctor to represent the National Health Service. The image this charity chose was an intimidating middle-aged man wearing a white coat and a bow tie, with a stethoscope round his neck. While this character may still inhabit Harley Street and the senior staff of major teaching hospitals, 50 per cent of all doctors are now female, and GPs, who are in the front line of prescribing, have not worn white coats for decades.

Sloppy thinking confuses and further degrades these stereotypes. Advertising agencies are not great sticklers for detail, and it's not a great step from dramatic simplification to dumbing down. When the 1995 UK campaign for Peugeot introduced two new models called Inca and Aztec with the headline "Mexican Faves", it provoked an official protest from the Peruvian diplomatic office in London. There were also complaints from people who had allegedly bought package holidays to Mexico as a result of seeing the commercial, and were disappointed not to find Inca as well as Aztec ruins there. "We thought it was just a bit of fun", explained a member of the agency board. "It's all in the right part of the world". An imported beer called Steinlager displayed a similar disdain for detail when it introduced itself to London on tube posters. The label on the bottle showed a traditional German stein. The headline read, "Of course you're whinging poms. Up 'til now you've only had Aussie lager". This ostensibly more authentic lager was in fact from New Zealand.

In 1922 in his book *Public Opinion*, Walter Lippman pointed out the useful role played by stereotypes in distinguishing between "the world outside and the pictures in our heads". These clichés, he explained, "help us defend our prejudices by seeming to give definiteness and consistency to our turbulent and disorderly daily experience . . . they are closer to propaganda. For they simplify rather than complicate. Stereotypes narrow and limit experience in an emotionally satisfying way . . .". In advertising you can use any type of idea, as long as it's a stereotype. It is thus a powerful conservative force, reinforcing prejudices against out-groups and blocking cultural maturity.

Advertising will not embrace a new idea until there exists an identifiable economic group which endorses it. As minority classes get wealthier, sociological shifts create new consumer marketing opportunities which are flagged by the news and entertainment media. And so, after a certain cultural lag which is necessary for businessmen to recognise and accept change, new images appear in advertisements. In 1994 the Swedish retailer Ikea featured the first homosexual couple in a mass consumer advertising campaign in the US, a recognition that this out-group had moved from being some kind of moral or social problem into an economic opportunity. The same year the Dutch tourist authority ran a magazine campaign welcoming homosexual couples: "Sincere greetings from people who respect your choices".

ADVERTISING INHABITS a parallel universe. In this *Truman's World* it cocoons us against reality by trivialising events which occur outside, in the real world. In 1999 the commercial television news provider ITV finally achieved its ambition of moving the traditional "News at Ten" to 6.30 p.m., (a proposal regarded as so threatening to Britain's cultural life that it had been vetoed by former Prime Minister John Major), so that films could be shown in prime viewing time undistracted by a half-hour of reality. Concerns expressed in the broadsheet editorial columns about "dumbing down" were verified in the advertising campaign announcing the change, which paired cataclysmic headlines, such as "World on Brink of Recession?", with shots from favourite films and the soothing reassurance that "with the news moving from 10pm you'll be able to enjoy movies without interruption".

David Remnick, a journalist who lived in Russia during the collapse of communism, observed the subversive influence of frivolous advertising imagery in less comfortable cultures:

> There is something profoundly irritating and American about ads for investment funds or "premium" cat food in a country where the vast majority live in poverty. A year or two of exposure to American-style commercials has produced what decades of communist propaganda could not: genuine indignation on the part of honest people against the excesses of capitalism.[3]

The unemployed youth of the world, slumped in front of television receivers or gathered on street corners under advertising hoardings, with empty pockets and hearts full of anger, do not have the emotional stability to distinguish between advertising conceits and the realities of post-industrial society. Are the ceaseless fantasies of advertising a siren call to revolution? Oliviero Toscani, responsible for the intrusive Benetton images, believes so:

> Advertising will be put on trial, it will have its Nuremberg. Real men all feel inadequate; real mothers are rushed off their feet while the ones in adverts never have a damn thing to do; fictional families are happy, real ones are a mess. Do you remember Pietro Maso, the guy who killed his parents? He is the product of the negative influence which advertising has on feelings. Young people look at a world which they don't have at home.

The rest of us, who are equipped to distinguish between aspiration and actuality, must be on constant guard against manipulation. The denizens of advertising's Lotus Land, a citizenry of consumption which must never be offended, which must be ceaselessly entertained, holding beliefs which must be constantly reinforced and impulses which must be indulged rather than challenged, inhabits a factory farm, not a democracy.

---

[3] *Lenin's Tomb*, Penguin

CHAPTER 26
THE DO-GOODERS

Commonweal

In a 1960s television debate, the erstwhile editor of Punch *magazine and self-appointed defender of public morality Malcolm Muggeridge inveighed against the widespread advertising of chocolate, because it was ruining the teeth, diet and moral fibre of the British public. Yet his opposition to censorship put him in a cleft stick. "I don't think advertising of chocolates should be banned", he concluded, "but they should not be allowed to do it so effectively".*

CAN ADVERTISING EFFECT social change? Various institutions spend a great deal of money trying to: governments, charities and special advocacy groups of all kinds. You might expect that governments, managed by politicians well versed in the skills of projecting false images, should be expert manipulators of advertising. In fact they are very bad at it, because governments operate on the policy of institutional truth. To the politically committed, failure is not an option. If a policy to solve a problem has been arrived at, explicated in a leaflet, and perhaps even flagged on television, they believe the problem has been resolved. All advertising by government departments to promote their policies, whether to convey specific information, such as a change to the tax assessment system, or to encourage a change in attitudes, such as the Department of Transport's drink-driving initiatives, is politically rather than practically driven. Ministers need to be seen to be doing something, and advertising is a highly public way of achieving this. What matters is that an initiative is launched and publicised, not its effect.

Measurement of results is usually omitted, but where it has been undertaken, the fallacy is often clearly exposed. A 1998 article in the *British Medical Journal*, naively entitled "Public Campaigns do not always work",[1] reported on a campaign run by the Doctor-Patient Partnership, an initiative launched in 1996 by the Department of Health and the British Medical Association to try to influence patients to reduce excessive demands made on general practitioners. In a series of nine waves, a million posters and leaflets were distributed to surgeries and pharmacies

---

[1] *British Medical Journal,* 10 October 1998, p. 970.

throughout Britain. Research with ten focus groups amplified by seventy individual depth interviews unearthed not a single person who had heard of the DPP, though when they were told about it, they were sympathetic to its objectives. Shown specific posters from the campaign, patients thought that an "Enjoying Easter" subject was wishing them a happy holiday, rather than pointing out that routine GP services would be closed over the Easter period, while the use of a rabbit as a mascot led many to believe the messages were intended only for children.

In 1995 the British Medical Association proposed that manufacturers should be required to add folic acid to flour to ensure that all women of child-bearing age consumed enough to reduce their risk of bearing a baby afflicted with spina bifida or hydrocephalus. Flour is already fortified with other vitamins – calcium, iron, niacin, and thiamine – yet the Conservative government opted for a less interventionist policy. It mounted a £2.3 million publicity campaign to raise awareness and encourage use of dietary supplements, ignoring the fact that half of all pregnancies are unplanned and it is too late to start taking a supplement after a positive pregnancy test. This initiative won an international prize from the World Health Organisation. At its conclusion in 1998 there was no evidence that it had significantly reduced the number of affected pregnancies. The women most at risk are the poor, who eat a diet lacking in natural vitamins, and these are the same women who were the least likely to have heard of the campaign.

The odds in any case are stacked against government health initiatives. During the 1990s an average of £460 million was invested annually in advertising high-fat and high-sugar foods, mostly to children, while £1 million was being expended by the government promoting health and dental care. Pressure groups which have protested against hyperbolic nutritional themes in advertising have received little joy from the regulatory authorities. According to a 1994 MORI survey commissioned by the National Food Alliance, an umbrella group of fifty-two organisations ranging from the National Farmers' Union to the British Heart Foundation, two out of three parents wanted tougher controls on food and drink advertising aimed at their children. The Advertising Association denies that advertising can influence children to demand products their parents don't want them to have – any more than it encourages adults to smoke, drink, or drive too fast. Against their arguments must be weighed the homely experience of the mother who sees her child jabbing a finger at the television screen. Four in ten said "pester power" evoked by advertising forced them frequently to buy food and drinks. The alliance wanted to restrict meaningless claims such as "full of goodness", "wholesome", and "energy-restoring" unless backed up by sound medical evidence. Such initiatives have been deflected by the pedantry of the self-regulating advertising bodies. In 1994 the pressure group Action and Information on Sugars, supported by the Health Education Authority, complained that Milky Way advertising encouraged children to eat sweets between meals and that ITC guidelines were "out of step with expert nutritional advice". The ITC rejected the complaint on the grounds that the Milky Way advertisements did not literally suggest it be eaten between every meal. The concept of "literal", of course, derives from verbal or written communication; the regulatory authorities find it difficult to interpret the visual metaphors in which the real power of advertising resides. The NFA also complained about the instant reinvigoration implied by a Lucozade commercial in which an exhausted relay runner was passed a bottle of this sugary pick-me-up instead of a baton, and went on to win the race. The ITC rejected this complaint on the basis that a dissolve indicated a time lapse; thus, it might conceivably have been some other race which the runner was shown winning.

Like all advertising, government information campaigns, which are intended to help people cope with reality, shy away from hard truths, because of fears about voter sensibilities. A 1994 road safety television commercial could deal with death only by denying it, in typical Hollywood terms. A young male car driver ran over a teenage girl. Realistic and jolting. Until viewers were reassured that it's only Adland after all, as the light relief arose, literally: a ghost rose up from the corpse to berate the driver. This advertisement appeared in a medium in which entertainment programmes maintain a high body count. Nevertheless, the shock of showing death in advertising was sufficient to arouse a protest which forced it to be broadcast after the 9 p.m. watershed, when youngsters who might receive a salutary impression about the consequences of dangerous driving would be less likely to see it. Bereavement was still a taboo subject before bedtime in 1998, when the same action was taken because viewers complained to the ITC about a powerful Department of the Environment commercial in which a teenage boy riding in a back seat without a seat belt was catapulted forward by a crash, fatally injuring his mother.

In less comfortable times, governments did not flinch at dealing in home truths. The great wartime posters shamed the individual: "Is Your Journey Really Necessary?" and "Loose Lips Sink Ships". That loathsome insect the "Squanderbug" urged people not to buy on the black market in postwar austerity Britain. The Ministry of Information's early postwar road safety posters were frightening: a chilling figure stood on the verge, a cut-out of a waxen-faced widow with the legend, "Keep Death Off the Road".

When a crisis suddenly arises, the government, like any manufacturer with a product recall problem, reverts to the straightforward style of wartime injunctions: sober, lengthy newspaper announcements unalloyed by puns or pictures. To allay public concern during the salmonella scare in 1988, the government offered the advice of the Chief Medical Officer under the spartan headline: "Eggs. The Facts". But the biggest health scare, the threat of AIDS, developed more slowly; the decision to respond to it was debated at length, giving time to develop more sophisticated advertising. For once there was no leadership from Prime Minister Margaret Thatcher, who found the issue distasteful. Vocal opposition came from the Conservative Family Campaign, which included several influential backbenchers. The political masters of the government's Central Information Office were divided. Something had to be done, without causing a panic, or heaping stigma on AIDS victims, or antagonising religious groups. The emphasis, as usual, was to be seen to be doing something, rather than doing something effectively. Thus, the massive AIDS campaign funded by the government between 1986 and 1988 floundered into the credibility gap between advertising dreamworks and the harsh reality of a modern plague. Prudery was its watchword. Condoms could not be advertised in broadcast media, and so the early advertisements could not even mention the C-word. The divergence between advertising conventions and reality was never so marked, and no other public service campaign ever caused such controversy.

The enduring impressions of the initial £20m campaign to raise awareness of AIDS were portentous television images of an exploding volcano, looming icebergs, and a monolithic tombstone inscribed AIDS accompanied by the doom-laden voice of John Hurt warning "Don't die of ignorance". They didn't tell you much, other than that something terrible was going to happen and it was coming through your letterbox. The information leaflet which plopped on the nation's thresholds in January 1987 was a shabby compromise. An earlier, more explicit version had been scrapped after sufficient copies had already been printed to send to every household in the land. The new version made no mention of the words "penis", "anus", or "back passage", nor of any sexual activity which might cause skin trauma. Notwithstanding these coy omissions, the campaign aroused the ire of the Catholic Church, which disapproved of condom promotion, the Church of England, which bemoaned the lack of any accompanying moral guidance, and the Chief Rabbi who thought the campaign "encourages promiscuity by advertising it".

The campaign registered the highest recall ever for advertising aimed at social persuasion, eventually reaching 95 per cent awareness. The creative work, involving stars such as the feature film director Nicholas Roeg, won awards from many creative juries. Though some people complained that the commercials gave their children nightmares, in general it caused little public offence. In a Gallup poll for the Department of Health and Social Security, 95 per cent of those polled agreed that the government was right to be running the campaign. However, it seemed to be quite innocuous. In a Marplan survey for the *Guardian*, only 2 per cent of respondents found the leaflets too explicit, and under 20 per cent thought they would have much effect. A later DHSS survey confirmed this view, showing that the campaign had failed to dispel some of the popular myths about the disease: 43 per cent of people still wrongly believed it could be caught by giving blood, 15 per cent by sharing a glass, and 9 per cent from toilet seats. Only one-fifth of interviewees said that they used a condom. Another survey, conducted by doctors at Southampton General Hospital, found that 44 per cent of respondents could not name one symptom of the disease.

A tidal change occurred in the last week of February 1987, but it had nothing to do with advertising. Sir Donald Acheson, Chief Medical Officer at the Department of Health, became the first person to discuss anal intercourse on television. It was part a television AIDS awareness week, a joint campaign sponsored by all four channels. For a week, whichever programme you switched on, everyone seemed to be slipping condoms onto fingers, cucumbers, or bananas. The Minister for Health and Social Security, Norman Fowler, was one of a host of celebrities who were lined up to say the word "condom" straight out to camera. The absurdity was that condoms could still be seen only during programmes, not in the commercial breaks. As a result, the IBA finally lifted its ban on TV and radio advertising for branded contraceptives, thus eliminating the social stigma of buying them. However, it retained its ban on the use of broadcast media to warn about heart disease, cancer and alcohol-related diseases, on the basis that these were "non-epidemic". In the view of the IBA, apparently, a disease had to reach epidemic proportions before arguments for prophylactic action could be presented on television.

After that moral epiphany, a much more explicit AIDS advertising campaign aroused much less controversy. The poster subjects included a young girl saying, "I didn't want to carry condoms because I'd look easy", and another proclaiming, "It only takes one prick to give you AIDS". A 1988 advertisement featured four phases of seduction – dancing, taxi, necking on the sofa, in bed – with the headline, "How far will you go before you mention condoms?" By 1991 the scare seemed remote enough to joke about; in television commercials a worker urged viewers to "keep Mrs Dawson busy" in the condom factory, and a priapic OAP demonstrated his reusable condom. The greatest health education campaign of all time eventually petered out with radio advertisements and posters offering travellers an information pack about the dangers of having unprotected sex with strangers abroad. According to Liberal Democrat MP Matthew Taylor, speaking in Parliament, so few people applied for it that each response cost thousands of pounds. This chimed with the consistent finding of research throughout the campaign: while awareness and understanding of AIDS climbed, people did not see themselves as personally at risk. The advertising failed to involve them.

It may have been impossible to do so without offending great swathes of society. Public service advertising – by governments, charities, or single-issue political groups – often seems to set itself impossible tasks of behavioural change. Such efforts are often absurdly naive. A series of radio commercials urged Londoners to use the underground more often – an underfunded, overused service stretched beyond the limits of civilised comfort at rush hour – with a series of humorously intended monologues summarised with the injunction, "Don't be boring. Go out on the tube". In 1994 the Spastics Society, recognising that the word "spastic" had long been synonymous with "nerd", "moron", and "pillock", used draconian steps to stop the abuse. It launched a campaign announcing that it had changed its name to SCOPE "for people with cerebral palsy". Fortunately there is no indication as yet that the school-age set has taken to calling their clumsy peers "scopes". An award-winning 1995 campaign for the Commission for Racial Equality aimed to reform entrenched racist attitudes simply by depicting turds, rats, and a firebomb coming through a letterbox over the clever headline "Junk Mail". Socially responsible advertising by governments – or opportunistic brands – without an effective mechanism for effecting social change is like advertising without effective distribution: there's no product on sale. When the mechanism exists, such advertising can be effective. A 1994 American campaign for the Humane Society, which seeks to find homes for abandoned dogs and cats, parodied matchmaking ads in the personal columns. Snapshots of pets carried copy such as: "I'm big, bad and full of energy. If you're into the prissy, bow-on-the-head poodle type, you're barking up the wrong tree. But if you're looking for a howling good time, let's get together and watch the fur fly". These were placed as individual classified advertisements inviting direct response.

While pressure groups advertise to arouse public concern about an issue and thereby influence government policies, the government itself is technically limited to "informing" the public. However, when Minister for Health Kenneth Clarke revealed his controversial plans for reforming the public health service in 1989, without consultation with the medical profession and adamantly refusing to negotiate any fundamental change, he did so with advocacy advertising in another guise: a £1.4 million publicity campaign including leaflets, conferences, and road shows, and a pious slogan, "Putting Patients First". When the British Medical Association responded with full-page press ads, e.g. one headlined "A complete list of the medical bodies who support the government plan for the NHS", over a page blank except for the logo of the NHS, Clarke accused the profession of trying to frighten patients.

In the US, television advertising is a favourite weapon of single-issue political groups. Freedom of choice is a common theme, from the NRA campaign opposing gun laws to the National Abortion Rights Action League (NARAL), which in 1994 equated the freedom to have an abortion with freedom of religion or choice of a hairstyle. The latter was a response to an emotional campaign funded by the anti-abortion interests on the theme "Life. What a beautiful choice". In the UK, advertising which is deemed to have political content is banned in broadcast media except for political parties. So issues are flagged on posters or in full-page ads in the quality newspapers. Advocacy advertising is a modern version of 18th-century political pamphleteering, confronting the consumer with sometimes perplexing advertisements by unlikely advertisers with a vested interest.

An advertising campaign in praise of public houses might seem a pointless exercise in preaching to the converted. The injunction "Be Vocal – It's Your Local" was a rallying cry sponsored by the Brewers' Society, which was contesting a proposal by Lord Young, the Secretary for Trade and Industry, to limit the number of pubs any brewing company could own. Under pictures of cosy pubs which might disappear, the brewers compared this legislation to the dissolution of the monasteries under Henry VIII, and after intensive parliamentary lobbying Young was eventually forced into a climbdown. The headline "300 years after the Bill of Rights, a Bill of Wrongs" referred to a less populist theme. The Bar Council was challenging the Lord Chancellor's proposal to abolish the barristers' monopoly by granting new powers to solicitors. The reforms went ahead.

ADVERTISING AGENCIES love charity accounts, because there's no brand competition and they are a soft touch at award competitions. As they often deal with emotional subjects, the advertisements can be powerful and controversial. A poster with the headline "No one screws more prostitutes than the government" added, in smaller print, "In 1990 prostitutes were fined half a million pounds". Coming just before the Tory government's "Back to Basics" morality campaign, it won a creative award, but failed to change the law on soliciting. The Royal Society for the Prevention of Cruelty to animals was forced to withdraw an advertisement showing the carcass of a horse slung from a hook in a Spanish abattoir, which was judged to be too unsettling. Another, arguing for the reintroduction of dog licensing, showed a towering pile of dead dogs with the headline, "When the government killed the dog licence they left us to kill the dogs". The campaign stimulated over 20,000 people to write letters of support to their MPs. In the ensuing Commons debate thirty-seven rebellious Conservative MPs deserted their party whip to vote, unsuccessfully, in favour of dog-licensing and the Tory government's majority slumped to just seven – its narrowest since the 1992 election.

Blatant political advertising runs the risk of demagoguery, losing sight of its real audience, the movers and shakers, in playing to the gallery. The charity Christian Aid pandered to disaffected youth in its 1999 newspaper campaign showing painful close-up photographs of a pierced tongue and a nipple, from which dangled a little chain. The aim was to win support for the cancellation of Third World debt, and readers were abjured to order and wear this chain as a public token of support for this proposal. The text finally conceded: "We're not asking you to pierce your body with it (after all it's not hypo-allergenic)" – to the undoubted relief of the establishment bankers and politicians whose sympathy would be essential to the achievement of this objective, and of the wealthy greying population which is every charity's target group.

Advertising has also attempted to sell God. In the US various fundamentalist cults have built vast empires through advertising, but broadcasting restrictions muffled religious appeals in the UK until recently. God is an ideal brand with a strong emotional appeal unrestricted by the Trade Descriptions Act; no one can prove that unsupported claims such as life after death are untrue. In the 1980s advertising copywriters amused themselves in a competition writing advertising headlines for a notional Church of England campaign, providing the usual display of irrelevant japery:

- Party at God's House – wine-music-singsongs-virgins.
- If you normally put CofE on official forms fill in this one. Please list the

Ten Commandments in the correct order. No conferring. Call yourself a Christian? Come to Church.
- Visit the British aisles this summer.
- Jesus Wept!

In 1993 God was advertising for real on UK television. The Revd Robert Ellis spent £7,000 of church funds on a brief television campaign on Central TV for the Diocese of Birmingham and Lichfield. His objective was suitably vague: "It was not about bums on pews. Our aim was to keep alive the rumour of God". By 1998 an organisation called the Churches Advertising Network was running a Christmas commercial in the Central TV area aiming to get bums on pews through soap opera themes. A series of people were shown with captions such as "He's on his third marriage", "She had an abortion when she was 14", "She's struggling with a drink problem". These were intercut with shots of a congregation and a vicar preaching from a pulpit, with a voice-over by the actress who played the troubled Debbie Aldridge in the venerable BBC radio series, *The Archers*. "They're not hypocrites", she said, "they're human. You don't have to be perfect to go to church this Christmas".

The storyline of *The Archers* itself was originally conceived by the BBC as a handy means of disseminating government agricultural policies to farmers, and later a much broader range of public information to a wider circle of listeners. In effecting social change, the icons of entertainment, from soap operas to celebrities, are perhaps more influential than direct advertising by governments and organisations. The qualities they represent are more human, hence more comprehensible and convincing, than policy argument. Governments are, in any case, so circumscribed by the need to please all factions that the social education role is perhaps best expressed by single-issue advocates, even conventional advertisers whose focus is selling a product. When Papua New Guinea became an independent nation in 1975 its citizens, separated by mountain barriers and trackless forest, spoke 400 languages. Given the scarcity of government resources, the job of creating national consensus fell by default and chance to the local importer of Isuzu trucks. A cartoon strip advertisement appearing weekly in the *Port Moresby Post-Courier* featuring the adventures of citizen Isuzu Lu became immensely popular. The new nation did not have the political maturity to indulge in political correctness: all of the characters in the strip, black and white, were tribal caricatures. The text was in pidgin, the lingua franca of PNG, and while selling Isuzu trucks, incidentally acquainted the various ethnic groups with the customs of their fellow citizens. In one strip the driver of a ramshackle vehicle, a Westernised Port Moresbyite wearing a rugby strip, has run over a pig. Flailing handfuls of cash, he is trying to appease a Highlander, clad only in a breech-cloth, who holds the point of a drawn arrow at his neck. Isuzu Lu, parked nearby in his truck, observes: *"Breks bilong dispela Isuzu ol i gutpela tru, na mi amamas tru . . . mi no laik painim birua olsem wantok hia"*. Broadly translated, "Thanks to my Isuzu brakes I'm not going to make an enemy here, like this man from my own district has". It was a useful reminder that to a Highlander a pig represents not only his entire wealth running about on four legs, but his totem, his manhood, his status. The weekly adventures of Isuzu Lu offered the most informative popular guide to New Guinea society since Margaret Mead's anthropological studies of the 1920s, and was probably a good deal more reliable.

CHAPTER 27
MATTERS OF TASTE

Morality

If we were to say that "bad taste" is indefensible, then we would have no Impressionist painting, no jazz music, no modern art, nor hundreds of things now deemed worthy of cultural admiration.
              Michael Winner, director of the films *Death Wish*, *Death Wish 2*, and *Death Wish 3*

REGULATORY AUTHORITIES look at what goes into an advertisement, while any good "creative" focuses on what impression is taken out of it. So, the J. Walter Thompson account team was nonplussed when one of its sacrificial stalking-horses for the 1983 Winston poster campaign was approved by the innocents of the Advertising Standards Authority without demur. The picture of a garden gnome standing by a rooster carried the headline "We're not allowed to tell you anything about Winston cigarettes, so here's a little man with a big red cock". (The agency chickened out.)

The advertising industry has always tried to ward off the imposition of government censorship by regulating itself, whilst reserving the right to challenge the rules continually. Almost all radio and television commercials have to be vetted in advance by the Broadcast Advertising Clearance Centre, funded by the Independent Television Commission. For other media, the ASA takes a more passive role; generally it will review an advertisement only when it judges that it has caused "widespread" offence. Thus, while the ITC can prevent the appearance of offending commercials, the harshest recourse of the ASA is to insist that publication not be repeated. Given the length of its procedures and the timing of production processes, this means that the offending poster or press advertisements may remain on view for weeks or months – which is often the intended length of the campaign in any case. The ITC also may react to public complaints by proscribing the appearance of a television commercial before 9 p.m., on the assumption that small children will therefore not see it. The British Board of Film Classification certifies cinema commercials for exposure with appropriate films.

These organisations deny that they are moral arbiters. Their role, as they see it, is to strike a balance between commercial freedom and what the public consider to be offensive, without determining what public taste should be. This is, of course, a deception. In determining their judgements the censors, like everyone else, have to rely on an inner moral compass. However, in their political role as defenders of the probity of the advertising industry, they must also be seen to react to overtly expressed public concerns.

It's a difficult job. For example, one of the judgements the people who work for the regulatory bodies arrogate to themselves is deciding what is funny. On the basis of a single complaint the ASA banned an advertisement by a paper-sack manufacturer in *Farming News* because it contained a photograph of a smiling woman wearing a bikini. At the same time it considered another complaint about an advertisement appearing in the *North Devon Journal*. This featured several photographs of men in jockstraps with the headline: "Climax! Coming Soon! Kaos opens its door for a night of ladies-only safe sex". The ASA found this smutty innuendo unobjectionable on the grounds that it was "humorous".

Sometimes it appears that advertisements are written by a gang of giggling schoolboys obsessed with naughty words. In 1997 some bright spark worked out that the acronym for the retail clothing chain French Connection UK is FCUK.[1] This gave rise to posters emblazoned "FCUK Advertising" and "FCUK Christmas". The ASA found these slogans offensive, but reckoned they would be okay so long as a comma were inserted; it couldn't do anything about the thousands of T-shirts sold. The estimated value of the PR coverage which the chain received was £4 million, ten times its annual advertising expenditure. The company nearly doubled its profits in the first half of 1999, a rise attributed by its founder, Stephen Marks, almost exclusively to its advertising. *Campaign* magazine chose French Connection as its advertiser of the year for 1999, which prompted this response from David Abbott, a highly respected creative director and founder of Britain's now largest agency, Abbott Mead Vickers BBDO :

> Fcuk me, what a brilliant choice for advertiser of the year. Fcuking great idea to put fcuking four-letter words on fcuking big posters, where every fcuking eight-year-old can see them. What a fcuking cool way to get up the noses of those fcuking parents and teacher tossers who are trying to bring their kids up as fcuking goody-goodies. That's the way

---

[1] Trevor Beattie, creative director of the advertising agency TBWA GGT Simons Palmer, has been publicly credited with this insight.

to sell a youth brand, though haven't I seen it fcuking before on the lav walls? Anyhow, great to see the industry magazine behaving in such a fcuking great way – makes me fcuking nostalgic, it does.

An advertisement publicising a mid-1990s art exhibition called *The Naked Shit Pictures* by the ageing mavericks Gilbert and George featured a montage entitled *Bum Holes,* which exposed the eponymous assholes to camera. The ASA rejected complaints, explaining: "The advertisers believed that nudity, a recurrent theme in artistic expression throughout the history of art, was not generally thought offensive". Soon afterwards the ASA denounced the Benetton poster of a newly born baby as "obscene".

Menstruation is a powerful male taboo in many cultures; in Britain it's the women who find it embarrassing. It was not until the mid-1990s that television viewers were permitted to see a demonstration of sanitary towel function. When agony aunt Clare Rayner explained the special absorbency of Vespré Silhouettes Plus, she provoked 300 complaints, mostly from older women, and the ITC decreed "not in front of the children". In *The Image: A Guide to Pseudo-events in America,* Daniel J. Boorstin calls such squeamishness "The New Expurgation . . . aimed less to expunge offensive doctrine than to hide offensive facts of life".

The British tradition of sexual innuendo flourishes in advertising, as copywriters engage in a continual game of cat-and-mouse to elude the veto of monitors. A 1997 poster for Jacob's king-size Club chocolate bar which promised to give men "an extra one-and-a-half inches in their lunch-box department" was banned by the ASA. However, when a 1996 poster for UltraBra showed a semi-dressed woman in a provocative pose with the headline "Who says a woman can't get pleasure out of something soft?", the ASA believed that most people would think the reference was to the softness of the brassiere she was wearing.

British advertisers will often calculatingly exploit the delay in the ASA adjudication process. A 1995 poster campaign for the travel firm Club 18-30 won an award at the Design and Art Direction Awards (DADA) competition, the advertising world's equivalent of the Oscars, for its crude promises of lewd rewards. One poster transliterated the popular holiday song "Viva España" as "Beaver España", a reference to female pudenda; another was headlined "The summer of 69". This campaign was produced by Saatchi & Saatchi, a global agency which does not usually handle advertisers with small budgets. The account manager explained, "Big agencies sometimes take on small accounts on the basis of doing what we would call "breakthrough" advertising – stuff that gets not only them noticed but that gets us noticed too". Both agency and client were well aware that their work could be found indecent and in contravention of ASA guidelines. They also knew that the ASA would not review these ads until it had received a considerable body of complaints. And the campaign would not attract controversial notice in the London-rooted national press until it appeared under its nose, and so the poster campaign was scheduled to begin in the provinces and did not reach London until near its end. After booking some 400 complaints, the ASA duly ruled against it. The ban took effect on the day the last poster contract expired, at the end of the holiday booking season.

Some of the most notorious advertisements are produced by institutions using easy shock effects to pursue good intentions. To promote Easter 1999, a conclave of marketing-minded clerics called the Churches Advertising Network compared the image of the Cuban revolutionary Che Guevara to Jesus, with the slogan, "Meek, Mild. As if. Discover the real Jesus. April 4". A sponsoring vicar from the diocese of Ely, admitted, "There is a danger that people will see the poster and expect something radical from their local church, which might not be what they will actually get. We cannot control the product. Christianity is not a tin of beans". He failed to draw the conclusion that it should therefore perhaps not be sold like a tin of beans, but others did. Harry Greenway, a former Tory MP active in the Conservative Christian Fellowship condemned it as "grossly sacrilegious", and suggested that "those who are in any way responsible should be excommunicated".

In 1995 the British Safety Council managed to offend taboos against both religious and sexual matters with a poster depicting the Pope wearing a hard hat with the headline, "Eleventh Commandment: Thou shalt always wear a condom". It was dropped after protests. Undeterred, in its campaign the next year, the Council took on royalists by showing a fresh-faced Prince Charles kissing his blushing bride, Diana, with the headline, "Appearances can be deceptive . . . use a Johnny Condom". This was after the revelation of Diana's indiscretions, but shortly before the emotional hysteria aroused by her death, fortunately for the members of the Council, who might otherwise have been wheeled away in tumbrils.

In 1998 three posters appeared which appeared to exploit racial prejudice. For example, over the headline "Born to be agile", a brand of sports footwear paired a black man jumping at a basketball hoop with an orang-utan stretching for a tree branch. These primitive advertisements provoked little attention – only thirty complaints, including those from racial organisations, were received by the ASA – until it was revealed that the brand names were bogus; the advertiser was the Commission for Racial Equality, which had deemed it appropriate to spend £250,000 of public money to reinforce racial stereotypes. The campaign was in two stages – the "teaser" posters were later pasted over with the logo of the CRE and the message: "What was worse? This ad, or your failure to complain?" The breathtakingly naive belief that racial prejudices could be moderated by escalation into the public arena was apparently born of desperation. "We have been hitting our heads against a brick wall when trying to get British society to pay attention", said chairman Sir Herman Ouseley. One who took notice was Tory MP Sir Teddy Taylor, who said the Commission should be closed. Another condemnation of this twisted logic came from the ASA, which awarded the CRE the dubious distinction of becoming the first non-tobacco advertiser forced to have its material vetted in advance.

Commercials are often criticised for touching upon themes which are routine in the dramatic programmes with which they appear. In a 1995 Pepe jeans cinema commercial a teenage suicide filmed his own death, glamorising the act as a rebellion against materialistic values with the suicide note, "I used to be a target market". A spokesman for the company argued, "The people we are trying to target are nihilistic, narcissistic and hedonistic – unlike those who might be offended by the ad". Tim Delaney, the creative director of the agency responsible for the commercial, complained, "You cannot exhibit a film like *Natural Born Killers* and then not put this out".

At the end of the 1990s a wave of commercials for products ingested by young people – soft drinks and ice-creams – manipulated sinister images to imply the effects of taking drugs. Thumping music, acid colours, and quick cuts between unrelated images, techniques lifted from the druggy film *Trainspotting*, conveyed the message that narcotics are cool to streetwise teenagers, though not to the regulatory bodies. The ASA did respond, however, to an obvious verbal message by criticising an advertisement for a snowboarding computer game which used drug jargon: "Powder: My body yells, aches for powder: I need the rush, the buzz, I have to get higher than the last time".

Fashion designer Calvin Klein built a brand empire on sexual images of vulnerable youngsters, starting in 1980 with the 15-year-old movie star Brooke Shields. In 1993 he draped the emaciated model Kate Moss over a sofa, an image of full-frontal pre-pubescent nudity to advertise his Obsession fragrance. In 1995 he launched a poster and fashion magazine campaign in America showing young male and female models with stoned, sensuous expressions, sprawling partly undressed in vulnerable poses, legs splayed, knickers showing, crotch thrust forward. On television a male stripling stood before camera while a man's voice-over intoned chat-up lines: "How old are you? . . . That's a nice body. You work out? I can tell". When Klein was accused by the American Family Association of promoting child pornography and NBC television refused to carry the commercials, sales at the fashionable Bloomingdale's department store allegedly rocketed. But it was not just moral activists who expressed concern. The US Justice Department ordered the FBI to investigate a possible violation of Federal decency laws. The models were of uncertain age; he might be charged with sexual exploitation of minors. Mr Klein claimed artistic immunity; his advertising had been "misunderstood". Nevertheless, faced with the prospect of a stiff gaol sentence, he withdrew it. The publicity his brand had received – reinforcing its degenerate, subversive image – was, of course, phenomenal.

IF WE BELIEVE advertising debases the human values which our society treasures, is there a case for demanding good taste in advertising? The first line of defence for advertising agencies is that they are simply doing their job well for their clients. They have to speak the language and express the feelings of real people, not some politically correct idealisation of how people should behave. In their highly competitive environment few agencies can afford social scruples. This argument simply passes the responsibility from servant to paymaster.

Another defence is that if advertisements are acceptable to the target market, the rest of society has no reason to complain. The rebuttal of this is twofold: first, in a multicultural democracy no single group has the right to set standards of public morality, and secondly, although publication in special-interest media may diminish the problem, few media are so focused that they don't have significant overspill outside the intended target group, which may well include children.

Advertising agencies will also claim that the manner in which a sentiment is expressed makes all the difference. Crudity and sexist language are acceptable, they say, if presented with subtlety, wit, irony, and warmth. Thus, the cartoon nymphet on the 1999 Virgin Cola poster who says "Open your mouth, I'm coming" is just good fun because she's not real. Subtlety, wit, irony, and warmth, in any case, are highly judgemental qualities. A joke about women, Jews, Irishmen, or blacks is perceived differently if you are a woman, Jewish, Irish, or black.

The ultimate excuse is that advertisers do not impose new patterns of behaviour; they only reflect what is already acceptable. This is sophistry. Advertising's self-appointed role is to guide our aspirations. For dramatic effect advertising seeks out and promotes exceptional activities at or beyond the margins of social acceptability, presenting them as normative behaviour. Though it is not a root cause of social dysfunction, British advertising at the extremes can fairly be charged with aiding and abetting antisocial activities such as indecent language, obscenity, moral turpitude, youthful promiscuity, sacrilege, cruelty to animals, dangerous behaviour, sedition, racism, sexism and xenophobia, fraud, theft, pimping, runaway children, teenage suicide, violence as a means of resolving conflict, drug-taking, paedophilia, and general public indelicacy.

Of course, the same could be said of books, newspapers, magazines, films, and television programmes, which commonly treat subjects, show images, and use language denied to advertisers. And, like advertisers, they do it for commercial gain. Yet there are at least three important distinctions. With information and entertainment media, there is always an element of self-selection. One knows more or less what to expect. But we don't select advertisements; they are thrust upon us. Secondly, while art and entertainment are loosely regulated in our society, companies which produce goods and services are subject to close control, legally enforced, in matters of health, product quality, employee relations, and trade descriptions. If they fail in these responsibilities they can be sued for redress. We therefore expect these organisations also to accept civic responsibilities – indeed, most corporations boast of them. Their advertising messages thus carry the implied weight of civil sanction. Just as we expect that Tesco sausages are safe to eat, and really do contain meat, so we assume that the attitudes expressed by a recognised company in reputable media have also met with civic approval. Finally, and crucially, though entertainment media provide powerful role models, we are not consciously exhorted to imitate the behaviour of pop stars and characters in soap operas. Such influences are incidental, while the *purpose* of advertising is emulation. With the declining influence of church, school, and family in shaping public morality, advertisements are our daily sermons.

THE MORAL CONSENSUS evolves continually; the past is a foreign culture. The arrogance of imposing the individual taste of self-appointed monitors is obvious, but the complaint system and the dialectics of the review procedures are equally undemocratic. The processing of individual complaints is an acceptable procedure for the purposes for which it was designed: the expression of a personal grievance, say, about police misconduct. It is not a reliable barometer of commonly held public opinion. In 1998 the BACC authorised 24,100 different television commercials and, according to the ASA, 25 million different advertisements appeared in the UK press and other media. In 1997 the Henley Centre estimated that, on average, each British adult views 52,000 commercials, posters, and press advertisements per year. The number of people in Britain aged 15 or older is 47.3 million. That works out to a total of almost 2.5 billion adult advertising impressions. In this context, the number of complaints received by the self-regulatory bodies is infinitesimally small. The single most criticised poster of 1998 showed a lugubrious Jersey cow saying, "When I'm a burger, I want to be washed down with Irn-Bru". It attracted 589 complaints to the ASA. The most controversial television commercial that year was for Levi's jeans; 519 people contacted the ITC to lament the death of Kevin the hamster. In 1998 the ASA received its highest total of complaints: 12,217. That's 0.000005 per cent of total viewer/reader advertising impressions. Assuming the unlikely, that nobody claimed more than once, for every individual who was offended by one of the 52,000 advertisements they saw throughout the year, about four million people were not bothered, or were insufficiently exercised to voice a protest.

The regulatory bodies are frequently exploited as a trampoline to heighten the views of any special interest group – animal lovers, religious faiths, or competitive advertisers – which can mobilise even a few dozen apparently independent complaints. The reaction of the regulatory bodies depends on how well organised the opposition is. Over the past decades the ASA has agreed with many complaints about allegedly sexist portrayals of women. However, in 1998, when Lee Jeans showed a provocative poster of a man's vulnerable naked bottom with a woman's stiletto heel poised above it, the ASA did not ban it. On the basis of its past policy decisions it is inconceivable that it would not have done so had the sexual roles been reversed.

What about the "silent majority" who let other people complain for them? First, it's not a majority. In a 1996 survey by the ASA only a quarter of respondents claimed to have seen any misleading or offensive advertising over the previous year. About a third claimed they "sometimes felt offended by" by press advertisements or posters, although just 2 per cent said they had complained. (This is an overestimate, typical of test respondent declarations of action or intent. As indicated above, total annual complaints received by the ASA have never exceeded 0.03 per cent of the adult population.)

Clearly, inertia conceals a great deal of discontent. The problem is not that there is no consensus of taste, but simply that no mechanism exists for constantly sampling it. Instead of inventing magisterial decrees of conduct and reacting to a complaint system which invites manipulation, the regulatory bodies should actively and continually monitor public opinion to guide their decisions.

In 1998 the ASA uncharacteristically took a tentative step in this direction. It asked a large sample of the public what it thought about a number of controversial advertisements. Bad language offended over 80 per cent. Sixty per cent objected to the French Connection's use of FCUK and F**K. Even mild worlds like "pillock", "git", "bloody" and "damn" were offensive to a majority. More than 70 per cent objected to the portrayal of women as sex objects, many being disturbed by a Katherine Hamnett fashion advertisement which included a glimpse of pubic hair. Half of the sample objected to the druggy imagery in the poster for the snowboarding computer game. Only 10 per cent were opposed to showing homosexuals or lesbians. However, two-thirds of the sample also objected to conventional advertising hyperbole: the portrayal of women as always slim and attractive. Clearly there's a lot to learn about the shifting tides of public taste, and research methodology needs to distinguish between general dissatisfaction with materialistic values and active indignation aroused by offending public morality. Nevertheless, even from this raw experiment, specific lessons could be drawn to guide the decisions of regulatory bodies. Regular dipstick studies on large representative samples would provide reasonable justification for their decisions.

The adjudication process employed by the regulatory authorities is another trap. The monitors focus on literal verbal meaning; gratuitous images fraught with messages easily glide past them. Their deliberations often degenerate into semantic gymnastics, having little relation to the impact of the message on the man in the street. The legally trained US President Bill Clinton defended himself in his impeachment hearings by expounding on the precise meanings of the present tense and of the words "alone", "cause", and, notoriously, "sex". In real life, as opposed to the Inns of Court, people work around the limitations of language by tacitly agreeing on how to use it. As Stephen Pinker, the author of *How the Mind Works*, puts it:

> The sketchiness of language gives the listener considerable leeway in pinning an interpretation to an utterance. That is fine when the interlocutors are co-operative but not when they are adversaries and the interpretation can send someone to gaol. The law requires language to do something for which it is badly designed: to leave nothing to the imagination. Lawmakers and lawyers do their best to co-opt language

for this unnatural job. But at some point we have to fall back on the principle of co-operation and judge the truthfulness of a statement by what a co-operative speaker would expect his listeners to infer.

The same sensible operating principle can be extended to the meaning of visual images. What always matters in advertising is not the intention of the advertiser, but the effect upon the consumer. Effective advertising is often unconventional, disturbing, and vulgar, particularly to those at whom it is not aimed. But surly teenagers, too, have their codes of morality, shielded from outsiders, and advertisers frequently misread the signs. And even when appropriate amongst its own target group, anti-social advertising has effects in a wider realm. A gross 1999 Virgin Airlines newspaper advertisement showing alluring portraits of eight women and suggesting that, apart from "your wife", you might want to consider using a free companion ticket for "your best friend's wife", or assorted pick-ups such as "the florist with nice tulips" or "the French waitress (minus hairy armpits)", offended on many levels, and might easily create distaste for any Virgin enterprise. The game is not worth the candle if a public presentation degrades the reputation of the sponsoring organisation, as Time Warner, the world's largest media group, decided when it sold off its highly profitable but controversial record subsidiary specialising in rap artists because of its crude violent and sex trash output. Corporate citizens are not exempt from the responsibilities of the social contract. Over the long term, wilful offence of public morality can only debase those who practise it. If value can be added to a brand, it can also be subtracted.

CHAPTER 28

MONKEY SEE, MONKEY DO

Behaviour

In 1992 a television station in a small American city was sued for failing to run a spot which a cosmetics firm had booked. The advertiser claimed damages for the loss of profits incurred by the failure of the commercial to appear. The television station was in a double-bind. An award for the plaintiff would require the court to determine an index of financial effectiveness for advertising, thereby setting an unwelcome precedent for American television contractors and advertising agents with disgruntled clients. The defence could only win by denying the influence of the television medium.

PEOPLE ABHOR CHANGE. The older they are, the more difficult they find it. Not unreasonably. Because it means giving up "tried and true" habits which have got them this far. Concepts which require people to change their behaviour are notoriously difficult to sell. And their appeal cannot be predicted by research. As anyone who has tried to introduce an intrinsically new product, not just a new brand, should be aware:

> In 1981 the largest producer of wine in the world (Gallo) decided to market a wine-based product packaged into individual servings ... We took it to our in-house market research department which set up focus groups in nine cities over 14 days at a cost of more than $100,000 ... I've never seen such a negative impression of a new product. First, they assumed we would use the worst wine we had in the product. Then they asked: "Why should you tell us what proportions to mix it in?" and "Why should you tell us what to mix it with?" The list of criticisms went on and on ... I came home, absolutely hammered, saying that it was ... a complete failure and we shouldn't do it. At the same time, about 100 miles away, there were two guys making a product in their garage called California Cooler. Four years later they sold out to Brown Foreman, a big US distiller, for £150 million and the "wine cooler" became a phenomenon. After I left Gallo, it came out with its own product, which became No 1 in the market.[1]

This is why the pioneer in a new field often fails to reap the rewards which fall to those who follow. The successive waves of new technology in the spectacular explosion of telecommunications over the past couple of decades have left a lot of corpses on the beach. Remember the one-way cordless phone systems – Zonephone, Phonepoint, Callpoint, Rabbit? They were licensed by the government in 1989, but failed to impress consumers and were superseded by two-way analogue and later digital systems (Cellnet, Vodafone, Mercury's One2One) which could receive as well as make calls. To avoid monopolies the new networks were prevented from selling direct to the public. The product field was beset by different technologies, spotty coverage, constant technological change, enterprising dealers to whom sellers of airtime paid money for connecting people to their network, and deceptive marketing practice, which virtually gave away handsets while concealing the true cost of the system. The result was a nightmare of consumer confusion. Lots of money was poured into two types of advertising: expensive image-building television campaigns to establish the major networks as brands, and hard-sell retailers' ads cluttered with equipment models and prices. It was a decade before any serious effort was undertaken to explain any of this to the consumer in terms he could understand. This was finally assumed by one of the most successful retailers, the Carphone Warehouse ("carphone" itself by now a misnomer for what had become known as the mobile phone).

Some institutions, such as British Telecom, the Post Office, and the Central Office of Information, spend a great deal of money trying to change people's behaviour: to get them to use the phone more, write more letters, or fasten their seat belts. Anyone who has tried to get one's life partner to modify behaviour, say by remembering to screw the tops of condiment bottles on tightly, put the toilet seat down, or pick the towels up off the floor, knows this is an uphill task. The advertiser also risks attracting the opprobrium directed at any busybody who tries to tell us what to do. A 1994 British Telecom press campaign showed a man and his son on opposite pages, facing away from each other. Both were saying "I'd love to talk to him but he never calls me". It was expecting a lot for the lengthy copy to resolve the generation gap. Another whimsical ad in the series showed a tot using a play phone, with the headline "Is it fair to blame Fisher-Price for the size of your phone bill?" The intention was to persuade people that "the urge to talk is part of growing up", but

---

[1] Harry Drnec, CEO of Maison Caurette, the beer distributor, *The Independent on Sunday*, 1992.

the self-interest of the advertiser would be evident to any parents already concerned about the size of the phone bills generated by older children.

An opportunity to directly measure telephone behavioural change came about on Easter Sunday, 16 April, 1995. British Telecom had designated this as "Phone Day" in Britain. Every phone number in the country was to receive an extra digit. This was preceded for several weeks by a barrage of TV and newspaper ads on the theme "It's 1 to remember". The intended meaning of "remember"– to bear in mind – was confused in the campaign with a second meaning, which was altogether more fun to illustrate – nostalgia. Old photographs were used to liken the forthcoming event to landmark moments of the 1960s (i.e. the formative years of your average ad-person at the time) such as England winning the World Cup and man landing on the moon. British Telecom spent £16 million to get across this simple message. In fact the simplicity was deceptive. You had to drop 1 from overseas calls, and five major cities had completely rejigged numbers. This information never emerged until "Phone Day" itself, when it was simply stated in a classic all-type announcement. British Telecom later reported that by "Phone Day", only one-third of businesses had changed their phone and fax systems to accommodate the new numbers.

The most difficult task in advertising is to get people to try something new. Yet there is one curious corner of the business where advertising people face this challenge all the time: the promotion of new films, usually on posters. Every movie is a new product introduction. The advertising formula is extremely consistent: brand authority is created by featuring the stars or (less often) the director, and the USP – the essential theme or story conflict – is summarised in a few dramatic words and a compelling visual illustration. A whole new brand has been created, which, if ephemeral, has an emotional imagery which is clearly expressed. Sometimes too clearly – the familiar genre and the predictable conflict is so well evoked that it hardly seems necessary to see the film as well.

BECAUSE OF the conventions through which it is expressed, advertising is only a simulacrum of the real world, and we all recognise that. The same is true of art forms – each has its own conventions, and often they are trite. But occasionally art – and more rarely advertising – transcends these conventions and reaches through and grabs us by the heart or by the throat, or strikes us in the gut. We are certainly affected, we may be outraged, but do we actually change the way we feel and think? Can the cultural images presented in films and television and adapted so freely by advertising affect social behaviour?

In the film *Falling Down,* a man driven round the bend by the frustrations of modern life turned a machine-gun on objects and people he found irritating. In some American cinemas, audiences whooped and stamped their feet in approval. After the film *The Deerhunter* was shown on US television, twenty-six suicides from Russian roulette were recorded, thought to be related to a scene in the film. Shortly after viewing a video of the film *Natural Born Killers,* which showed two teenagers getting their kicks by going on a killing spree, two teenage runaways held up a Louisiana convenience store, and shot and paralysed the woman who owned it. Her family sued the film-maker, Oliver Stone. In 1999 the United States Supreme Court ruled that his claim of the right to free artistic expression was no defence, thus opening the gates to a possible flood of litigation. A lawsuit was promptly launched against the producers of the 1995 film The *Basketball Diaries,* in which Leonardo DiCaprio played a teenage heroin addict who gunned down his teachers and classmates, by the parents of three children who died in a schoolyard massacre in Kentucky in 1997.

Director Laurence Gordon was delighted when long queues formed at American cinemas for his 1979 exploitation film about urban violence, *The Warriors.* In the first week three street gang killings were linked to the movie. "People went out and pretended they were warriors", Gordon said. The film was recalled by Paramount. Gordon later produced other films noted for brutal violence, *Die Hard, Predator,* and *48 Hours.* "I'd be lying if I said people don't imitate what they see on the screen" he has admitted. "Look how dress styles change. We have people who want to look like Julia Roberts and Michelle Pfeiffer and Madonna. Of course we imitate". Sir Richard Attenborough, one of Britain's most distinguished film directors, says,

> I do deplore the pornography of gratuitous violence. Precisely what effect that has on the social scene is open to enormous conjecture. But I would find it impossible to dismiss the contention that it has a bearing. Years ago a ghastly piece of violence shocked one – *Psycho* and *A Clockwork Orange* – but now we are inured and young people no longer react in that way to something extraordinary like that.

The director of *A Clockwork Orange,* the late Stanley Kubrick, had second thoughts as well, and withdrew his film from circulation in the UK.

When it comes to influencing what people see, believe, and think, few people in the world have more power than media mogul Rupert Murdoch. *The Economist* has accused the newspapers he controls through

News Corporation, such as the *Sun*, as contributing to "a coarsening of British public life". His American film company, Fox, produces many films notorious for casual violence, and his television channel, BSkyB, broadcasts them in Britain. Murdoch has declared that he is opposed to extremes of violence, but is unsure about the effect of his own productions, and, in any case, is powerless to do much about it:

> We would never do the violence such as you see in a Nintendo game. When I see kids playing Nintendo, and they're able to actually get their character on the screen to bite his opponent in the face, that's pretty sick violence. And you watch the kids doing this to each other and they're yelling and laughing for hours on end. Is it all fantasy, and is it all harmless fantasy? I don't know. There has been violence in movies that we put out. Some of it I dislike ... But is violence justified? Is the violence of *Lethal Weapon* OK? I think so. If it involves personal cruelty, sadism – obviously you would never do that. The trouble is, of course, that you run a studio, and how free are you to make these rules? The creative people give you a script and are given last cut on a movie. The next thing, you have a thirty-million-dollar movie in the can which you may disapprove of.

Violence is omnipresent in TV programmes and advertisements. By the age of 12 the average American child, watching around three hours of television a day, has witnessed 8,000 murders and more than 100,000 other acts of violence, according to the American Psychological Association. Will these children not assume that violence is a normal means of resolving disputes and achieving what they want? The classic rebuttal is that from an early age viewers can tell the difference between fiction and reality. The evidence is not totally convincing. According to British research conducted by the Independent Television Commission 55 per cent of 8-year-olds do not fully grasp that the characters of soap operas such as *Grange Hill*, *Neighbours*, and *East Enders* are fictions created by actors. At the age of 12, that figure is still 35 per cent. (Viewers of voting age were not interviewed.)

In terms of the power images have to shape opinion, whether people can distinguish between fantasy and fact hardly matters. In these days of recycled "library" news footage, "dramatic reconstructions", "docu-soaps", and rigged audience participation, the line is hard to draw in any case. But it is unnecessary to make a distinction. Fact is one method of persuasion; parable is another. The purpose of fictive devices is to allow people to experience new things at secondhand. They have always been invoked as a means of instruction and edification, from the plays of Sophocles, through the Bible, to playlets performed in the African bush to teach people the elements of hygiene or political theory. Thus even the exaggerated mayhem of cartoon characters may legitimately provoke concern. A 1994 commercial for Tango soft drink in which a football fan's head spun across the pitch was banished beyond the 9 p.m. watershed by the ITC on the grounds that the action might be imitated in the school playground. (Another, featuring an exploding granny, was allowed, without reported repercussion.) Nevertheless, many of the anxieties expressed by those who complain seem frivolous. Would a commercial showing an animated Pepperami sausage rubbing its head against a grater really lead children to try the same stunt? If so, what more challenging problems might such a vulnerable child have to engage?

A significant body of social scientists and commentators, plus most of those who have a vested interest, argue that films and television do not affect social behaviour in this crude mechanistic sense. They claim that no causal link has been demonstrated between events shown on film and television screens and real-life behaviour, such as the imitation of violent acts. In his 1995 book published by the Institute of Communications Studies at Leeds University, Professor David Gauntlet avowed: "The search for direct "effects" of television on behaviour is over. Every effort has been made and they simply cannot be found".[2]

Against such academic pronouncements must be laid the common sense testimony of parents, teachers, and other professionals who observe the everyday behaviour of children. Teachers reported an alarming increase in incidents of kicking in the playground whenever the kick-fighting Power Rangers appeared on children's television. The first Tango television commercial, aired in 1992, featured a spherical orange genie who danced down the street to slap a Tango drinker around the cheeks, with the slogan "You know when you've been Tango'd". Viewers complained that this stunt had become a playground craze, while doctors reported that children were coming in with ear injuries, and the commercial was eventually suspended.

The social sciences have failed to find direct proof of a causal relationship, just as the tobacco industry has failed to satisfy itself that their advertising directly causes youngsters to start smoking, in the face of a wealth of coincidental evidence. A 1993 study identified 1,752 Californian adolescents aged from 12 to 17. None had ever smoked, they

[2] *Moving Experiences: Understanding Television's Influences and Effects.*

said, and never would – even if a friend offered them a cigarette. Three years later, half had changed their minds. Thirty per cent had experimented with smoking. Seventeen per cent were now willing to smoke, and 4 per cent were already smoking. Those who had been able to name a favourite cigarette advertisement in 1993 – usually Camel or Marlboro – were by 1996 twice as likely to have started smoking or be willing to start as those who could not. Those who owned a cigarette promotional item or were willing to use one in 1993 were nearly three times as likely to progress towards smoking as the others. The researchers concluded that 34 per cent of teenager experimentation was the result of tobacco advertising and promotion.[3] Many people might agree that this study demonstrates that advertising can overcome a teenager's determination not to start smoking. Yet others would argue that, because of the many influences which any teenager is exposed to during the process of growing up, no *causal* link has been established.

With this kind of defence advertisers put themselves in a double-bind. If advertising is to be effective it must change attitudes and, in some way or other, behaviour: the way we shop, or vote, or deal with others. And yet advertisers deny that their efforts can influence social behaviour such as violence, smoking, and drinking. Spokesmen for tobacco manufacturers and distillers and media owners consistently claim that the barrage of cigarette and booze advertising does not cause people to start smoking or drinking, or to smoke or drink more. Those who produce films glamorising antisocial behaviour crouch behind the same shield, and sometimes the media support them on their leader pages:

> There is also that sturdy perennial – the advertising argument. TV can influence millions of people to buy soap powder; therefore it is powerful and able to influence millions of people to behave against a host of other influences and follow its dictates. To sell a product, however, is not an attempt to change fundamental behaviour. Simply to switch from one brand to another, or be reminded to buy something more of something you want, does not go against a complicatedly implanted moral code. There is no theory that links screen violence to real-life violence in the way you can link advertising a product to selling a product. The analogy does not hold.[4]

---

[3] John Pierce of the University of California, San Diego, *Journal of the American Medical Association*, 1996.

[4] *The Independent*, 3 August 1995.

Until social Darwinists discover that consumers have developed a circuitry in their brains exclusively devoted to brand choice, and unaffected by any other experience, reasoning, example, or emotion, this inspired model of how persuasion works must be rejected as a piece of Jesuitical speculation. Advertisers and film-makers command the most powerful communications means of communication the world has ever known. They massage our senses with sights and sounds beyond our life experience. They summon powerful personalities from all over the world to corroborate their claims. They can even bring them back from the dead. Television and films can show anything the mind can imagine. And show it as reality. Of course these media influence our opinions and behaviour. As do newspapers, novels, parents, peers, and pals. Only more so.

In the last decade of the 20th century purveyors of branded goods have gradually come to realise that advertising, specifically, works by trying to create an emotional bond with the consumer. A brand aims to become his friend, someone who shares his viewpoint and will take his advice. Like the other content of the media in which it appears, advertising influences attitudes, creates value systems and affects behaviour. The church, schools, parental guidance – all of the traditional sources of authority in the community have been replaced by the authority of the media. Advertising, because it deals in aspirations, has become the new formulator of moral imperatives: "Just Do It!" exhorts Nike. Adidas replies with a reference to the three stripes on its shoes: "Earn Them".

The academics who find no demonstrable link between the power of the visual media and social behaviour are in the same position as advertisers who can't reliably predict whether their ads will shift goods. They simply do not have the right techniques for measuring these effects with any degree of certainty. But do we require copper-bottomed proof? It's what we believe that matters. Do we really believe that what we see on the screen cannot influence human behaviour? It so, why do we act as if it can? Why does every newspaper, quality or tabloid, habitually chose to illuminate printed arguments on every topic, trivial or grave, with a scene from a film or television programme or commercial? If an anti-social action shown on the screen has no influence whatsoever on those who see it, how does an improving social message? Why does the government plough millions into advertising designed to change our social behaviour? Why, in 1999, did governments pressure tobacco companies worldwide to collaborate in developing major advertising campaigns aimed at *discouraging* under-age smoking?

Since we behave as if we believe in the suggestive power of media imagery, we should form our judgements according to what we practise rather than what we can conclusively prove. We cannot *prove* that "honesty is the best policy", nor any of the other maxims by which we regulate our lives. Yet many societies acknowledge such concepts as a principle of behaviour. Those advertisers who insist on direct evidence of advertising causing unsocial behaviour may be swayed by the emerging syndrome of "ad rage". Quite apart from the usual sources – anomie, deprivation, poverty, and the rest – the lad who set fire to the carpet warehouse on the Ordsall estate in Salford reported to his counsellor from the Salford Urban Mission that he did it because he was "sick of seeing the ads for Carpet World on television".

MOST PEOPLE, in Britain at least, are tolerant of advertising, because it adds colour to life and is often entertaining. A 1998 survey claimed that 80 per cent of Britons "like" advertising. Because of this tolerance, advertising's powerful effects on shaping society – the way we think and the way we act – are often underrated. Advertisers and their agencies, who can succeed only by changing consumer beliefs and behaviour, pay little heed, except to deny that they can influence social behaviour – smoking, drinking, and violence. They are dissembling, of course. Real people know that the world of advertising is unreal and make allowances for it. But do advertising professionals? The advertising industry has achieved no consensus on quality and behaves more like a branch of show business than of real business. When it comes to real social issues, the people who create advertising are essentially frivolous, and those who authorise it generally irresponsible. It is impossible to ignore the public presence of advertising; whether one agrees with its values or not, it expresses and helps to shape the national character. Just as unrestrained industry destroys the ecology, the excesses of advertising pollute the social environment.

THE FINAL SECTION considers how the new technologies will accelerate both the commercial and social effects of advertising.

PART VI

Beyond Y2K

"Hi, this is Bill Gates. Time to buy some new software."

CHAPTER 29
THE DAY AFTER DOOMSDAY

Technology

The grassroots Canadian consumer watchdog called "Adbusters" expresses its opposition to the materialistic values of consumerism by subversive escapades such as defacing advertising posters. In 1999 it promoted a nationwide "Buy Nothing Day" – by printing that message on T-shirts and selling them.

ON 2 APRIL 1993, which swiftly became known as "Marlboro Friday", the bell seemed to toll for the end of the fat years of advertising. Because tobacco taxes are low in the US, Philip Morris and other companies had been able to milk margins of 40 per cent or more from their premium brands for years. Then discount retailers started selling unadvertised brands at half the price, and in an economy mired in recession smokers stampeded to them. Early in 1993 these off-brands shot up from 30 to 40 per cent of the market. Philip Morris panicked, and instead of toughing it out by defending brand value at all costs as the marketing textbooks counsel, the company slashed prices on its leading brands by 20 per cent.

Philip Morris had let down the side. Not only did its own profits and share value fall sharply, but BAT also lost 15 per cent of its market valuation. The shock-waves spilled out of the tobacco sector, spreading a global price war to nappies, motor cars, condoms, pullovers, newspapers, and perfumes. Even robust brands like Benetton and VW had to slash prices. All over the world sales fell and stock market valuations shrank for brand-rich companies such as Kellogg's, Procter & Gamble, and Heinz. Tomkins, the conglomerate that had just taken over Rank Hovis McDougall, was constrained to write off the £600 million at which the RHM brands were valued.

To marketing men and women it looked like Doomsday. Virtually unassailable global reputations had been built on the premise that brands are worth more, but now it looked as though advertising had overexploited brand equity. Despite all the smoke and mirrors of illusion, was genuine brand value perhaps something more intrinsic to the product? In 1994, when the advertising agency Young & Rubicam asked consumers to identify Britain's twenty most distinctive brands, the names they volunteered were not products in the Unilever or Procter & Gamble stables, but those with a mythic content: Rolls-Royce and Porsche motor cars, Irn Bru soft drink, and Le Creuset cookware. Few were massive advertising spenders, perhaps because their markets were small, or perhaps because established brands which are really different don't need to advertise. Amongst the big, popular brands of goods and services, there was a decreasing perception of intrinsic difference, as the supermarkets demonstrated by undercutting major brands with own-label imitations.

The supermarkets themselves were under threat. The UK retailer which increased floor space most quickly in 1994 was not a high-quality advertiser like Sainsbury's or Tesco, but the discount retailer Kwik Save. US-style warehouse discount stores and "category killers" pioneered by Wal-Mart and Costco moved into Britain that year. The supermarkets responded with a vicious price war spearheaded by their own lines of cheap products, such as Tesco's "New Deal" pricing line and Sainsbury's "Essentials". They too had chosen to sacrifice their expensively purchased brand identities on the cut-price altar. In the High Street consumers became accustomed to virtually continuous sales, even pre-Christmas. There had long been a profit shift from manufacturing to retail; now it seemed to be feeding through to the consumer. As the economic noose choked growth in the nations of the West, the suspicion dawned that the hard-up consumer might finally have figured out how the advertising shell game works and was starting to buy on price rather than promise.

At the same time mass media, with their mass economies of scale, were fragmenting. They were returning to an earlier model. The last great technological paradigm shift affecting advertising had been television. When TV advertising began in the US fifty years ago there was no national coverage and major advertisers were sceptical of the new medium. In its early days television was tarnished by the downmarket image of the Veg-O-Matic vendor. Huge chunks of airtime were dispensed cheaply to small sales promotion companies which sold kitchen gadgets, wonder cleaners, magic polishes, and other gimmicks – the kind of thing you see demonstrated in the upper balconies at the Ideal Home Exhibition. The market stall was their provenance, and these hucksters recognised the demonstration power of the new medium. Taking advantage of cheap rates and slack regulation, they filled the off-peak hours with hard-sell commercials which mesmerised audiences for ten or fifteen minutes – all produced live on camera, of course.

These pioneers had a singularly uncluttered view about the purpose of advertising: it was expected to sell goods then and there – and it worked. Until rates stiffened, driving the early pitchmen out of the TV temple. Yet the hard-sell tradition is alive and well today, and living in the ghettos of cable and satellite and morning and late night terrestrial television, wherever airtime is sold at distress prices. Measured in terms of "minutage", that is the sheer amount of time bought rather than its cost or the size of the total audience reached, during the 1990s the world's largest advertiser was not Coca-Cola, nor P&G. This laurel was claimed by a small international company called Interwood, which marketed the latest versions of the gadgets, wonder cleaners, and magic polishes of the 1950s. Companies like this specialise in "As-Seen-on-TV" marketing, often supported by direct response ads in the press. They always know exactly how effective their advertising is. Their business model is simple and immediate. Did the advertisement bring in enough orders to pay for itself, and a bit more? If it did, run it again.

Cable and satellite television created a proliferation of viewing channels, which began to mount a serious challenge to the dominance of the traditional telecasting networks. In the US, new channels reduced the audience share commanded by the traditional networks by almost half between 1980 and 1998. At the start of the 1999/2000 televiewing season, advertising-supported cable television accounted for 39 per cent of all viewing, versus 54 per cent for the four networks. Cable offers a much wider selection of channels; fibre optics could extend the choice to as many as 500. In Britain, when two competitive satellite television operations were launched at the end of the 1980s to viewers who were already paying a TV licence fee, many observers thought both were doomed. Yet in 1994 the survivor, Rupert Murdoch's upstart British Sky Broadcasting, went public in an offering which valued the business at some £5 billion, substantially more than the entire ITV network. Cable television developed more slowly, but by 1998 these new alternatives accounted for more than a fifth of all the hours Britons spent watching commercial channels.

The new technology revived television's market trader roots. In the fragmented media world there was always time and space going cheap. Lengthy "infomercials" appeared on European television, while in the US and the UK entire channels on cable TV were devoted to shopping, with credit card orders placed by phone. The two main players were Home Shopping Network, an unreconstructed pavement hawker, and QVC, which, using a softer sell, by the mid-1990s claimed to have built a constituency of repeat purchasers in 47 million American homes. What did they buy? A lot of junk like food dehydrators and zircon jewellery. But the medium also set out stalls to sell ladies' fashion, and not at distress prices. The preferred creative strategy is a straightforward pitch delivered by a well-known personality, mixing sales patter with "entertainment" in the time-honoured tradition of the pavement peddler. Often these celebrities bring a powerful authority to their role, because they are selling designs which bear their own name. And, true pitchmen, they have no inhibitions about boring their audience. Their "infomercials" are programme-length shows. On QVC the American icon Diane Von Furstenberg launched a range of silk clothing purportedly designed by herself, and chatted to viewers who called in. In less than two hours she sold 29,000 items to 19,000 customers for a total of $1,200,000. Joan Rivers peddled jewellery, and that queen of conspicuous consumption Ivana Trump flogged $220 suits in volume. "In the department store", she said, "you sell a couple of dresses. When you go on television you sell hundreds of dresses in a couple of hours".

Consumer durables advertise on shopping TV too. In 1994 Volvo aired half-hour commercials to entice customers into their showrooms, and claimed to have sold 100 cars. Kodak showcased its compact disc visual technology, Photo CD, while Sharp introduced a new camcorder on cable TV. The TV shopping channels claim that the core group of purchasers are not couch potatoes but professional people and managers who have little time to shop and are disenchanted with the crowds at department stores. By 1993 cable television was selling $2.2 billion worth of goods annually in the US. That was tiny fragment of total retail turnover, but sales had grown sixfold over the previous six years.

Advertising agencies were rattled. In 1994, the world's best-known brand, Coca-Cola, abandoned the traditional advertising agency relationship in favour of specialised project groups. It replaced the blockbuster "one-world" approach with as many as forty different commercials playing riffs on a generalised theme, "Always". These were aimed at the discrete audiences attracted by new TV outlets such as MTV and sports channels. Because of the great inroads made by cable pay-TV, mighty P&G, which put 90 per cent of its budgets into the medium, began questioning the future of advertising-funded television in the US. Harking back to the heyday of radio broadcasting in the 1930s and 1940s, when American advertising agencies also produced the network programmes in which their commercials appeared, P&G began once again to make its own show, the comedy series *Northern Exposure.* In the UK the liberalisation of broadcasting regulations had also encouraged a trend towards programme sponsorship, which replaces commercials and largely eliminates the need for advertising creativity. With these portents in the breeze, agencies were contemplating their navels and struggling to reinvent themselves by integrating various other marketing functions within their services.

Proliferating television channels were just one of a number of structural changes sweeping brands, retailers, and advertising agencies into the 21st century on a technological tsunami. In all media technological advances were creating more efficient opportunities to address special interest groups, even individuals. The dynamic between the brand and the consumer began to splinter into many pieces, and fault-lines opened up. There were more radio stations, more newspapers and magazines. There were more cross-media connections: when the home shopping television channel QVC launched in the UK in 1993, the satellite TV channel Sky Television bought a minority share in it. And – horrors – the floodgates opened to direct marketing media: telephone selling, direct mail and leaflet drops, which could be more precisely targeted than ever before, and where there was no traditional percentage pay-off for advertising agencies, and often no perceived need for their services. Non-traditional media started to eat into advertising budgets.

Direct marketing grew about 40 per cent in the UK in the early 1990s. Traditionally, this technique used the post or telephone to sell expensive products people don't buy very often, such as cars or insurance polices. However, in 1992 British Airways spent more than £500 million on an advertising campaign offering free flights. Its purpose was to build up a vast database on air travellers which it could then use to target specific mailings to key customers, rather than trying to influence them through wasteful mass media advertising. In 1994 Heinz, which markets more than 300 food products in the UK, sent tremors through the advertising industry by abandoning conventional advertising for individual products. Instead of long-familiar campaigns like "Beanz meanz Heinz" on TV, posters, and magazines, a lavish colour leaflet dropped through your letterbox, but only if you lived in the right neighbourhood. It offered money-off coupons to try various products, plus a £10,000 prize competition which you could enter free, provided you completed a lengthy questionnaire which pried into personal details and your shopping and media habits. Heinz and other companies had long used techniques like this for more specialised products, such as baby foods, where it would be wasteful to try to reach young mothers by mass media. What was new was the application to mass products of broad appeal, low value, and high frequency of purchase – the natural constituency of mass media advertising.

There's no such thing as a free lunch, even beans. Because you could buy a can of beans bearing a supermarket label for half the price of its brand, Heinz was building a database which could be used to target buyers of Tesco or Sainsbury's own-brands and entice them back to its brand with special inducements. Unlike broad-scale "theme" advertising, direct marketing can be precisely aimed at the most productive customers and its effectiveness can be measured by results. Heinz still spent large sums on television, but switched the emphasis to overall brand values embracing the entire range, to nourish the belief that all Heinz products taste better and are more wholesome. It's an approach which General Foods espoused thirty years ago, but now supported by much more efficient direct marketing initiatives for individual products.

Direct selling of insurance and banking by phone became the most exciting growth areas for consumer financial services in the 1990s. In a 1995 survey of 100 large British companies, conducted by the Manchester Business School, more than half said that database marketing would be their main promotional tool by the start of the new millennium. With the development of computer technology, visionaries predicted the end of mass marketing itself and urged companies to focus on "one-to-one marketing" which aims to exploit the maximum potential from the small fraction of a company's best customers, rather than increasing their share of all potential customers. It's an instinct door-knocking home improvement salesmen have followed for generations: first selling replacement windows, perhaps, then returning over the years to double-glaze all the windows in the house, clad the exterior with new siding, add patio doors, then a conservatory – and by then probably it's time to replace the replacement windows. Over the years, mass media advertising had gradually shifted the goalposts away from *selling* to individuals to simply aiming to sustain *awareness*. According to the advocates of direct marketing, that's because mass media are not much good at doing anything else.

Until recently the only way you could address a sales message to a single individual was extremely remote and inefficient: by post. New media have now opened up opportunities for quick and convenient *two-way* communication with individual consumers. Computers now enable companies to build durable personal relationships with great multitudes of people through frequency marketing programmes. Airline frequent flyer schemes owe their success to a crafty combination of personal rewards designed to build customer loyalty:

> In 1980 . . . the average business traveler had a half-hour tolerance for delay before changing airlines. Booked on American from O'Hare to LaGuardia, you'd walk next door to United if your plane was more than 30 minutes late. By the late eighties, this tolerance had increased to 3 ½ hours.[1]

It's not just the free travel that achieves this astonishing influence on behaviour. The airline has extended the hand of friendship to the business traveller. He has been assured that the airline knows who he is and what his needs are likely to be. The airline has told him that it thinks he is important and values his worth. The airline provides him with an individual record of his purchases and recognises that he is a high-volume purchaser of the company's products. It's the nostalgic relationship you used to have with the corner butcher or fishmonger, who would save you scraps for your pet. That's what every customer wants, and it's a policy that holds out the reward of lifelong loyalty.

Supermarkets responded to manufacturers' direct marketing attempts to win the loyalty of individual customers by launching their own schemes. Tesco was the first in Britain to offer supermarket loyalty cards, and this scheme was credited with bringing it level with the market leader, Sainsbury's, by early 1995, and then outstripping all its rivals. All airlines now have frequent-flier programmes. Most supermarket chains promote club cards. So what happens when all competitors offer the same kind of bribes? Will loyalty schemes become the victims of their own ubiquity, like Green Shield trading stamps? Probably not, because as well as providing important databases for one-to-one marketing, they ultimately depend on quality of service, which can create an emotional preference for a particular brand or company. Retailers such as Tesco are close to their publics and obsessive about ensuring that the reality of their store operations has some resemblance to the images portrayed in their advertising.

THERE WAS LIFE after Doomsday. "Marlboro Friday" was forgotten as the American economy revived and the Dow index of stock market prices began its record-breaking sprint to the end of the millennium. But, like the minor tremors that precede an earthquake, this slippage between the value of brands and economic cost was a cautionary reminder that when times are hard, reason begins to prevail over self-indulgence. At the end of the 1990s British retailers such as Asprey & Garrard and Hamleys, which had built flourishing businesses as brand names specialising in frivolous goods, were still acutely suffering the consequences of the setback to Far East economies in 1997.

There were still more turbulent times ahead for advertisers and their agencies. The recession had coincided with fundamental technological changes which fragmented advertising media and disrupted traditional

---

[1] Don Peppers and Martha Rogers, The *One to One Future*, Currency Doubleday, 1993.

ways of marketing: new printing processes, direct marketing, satellite and cable television were changing the rules forever. A staggering proliferation of media was now available, making both advertisers and agencies work harder for less return.

Then along came the Internet.

CHAPTER 30
THE GARDEN OF EDEN

Internet

The money is to be made in traditional businesses which happen to use the Net for distribution. Soon we'll no longer think of the Net as anything but a distribution medium, an incredible telephone.

Michael Wolff, *Burn Rate*

As generations of householders have done, you've decided to use the long winter nights to plan your garden. However, you have not sent away for nursery catalogues, you have not kept newspaper cuttings of gardening articles, you own no gardening books, you take up neither pad nor pencil. Instead you slip the "Garden Planner" disk into your CD-ROM player. Using the simple graphic program, you draw the outline of your garden on your screen in exact proportion. You key in the vital statistics: its geographical location, soil type, orientation to the sun and the location of surrounding walls and buildings. A click on the smiling sun icon and your garden is overlaid with a grid representing half-meter squares shown in three different tones corresponding to areas of sun, deep shade, and partial shade. Now you click on the garden encyclopedia icon to select your trees, shrubs and plants. Each variety is shown in full colour, and you click on buttons to see how high and wide it will grow, how it changes through the seasons, what soil and sunlight conditions it needs to thrive, and what maintenance it requires. As you make your selections you drag them to squares on your garden plot. The program will refuse to plant specimens too close together and will bleep to warn you when sunlight or soil conditions are inappropriate. As you build your garden, you can use your mouse to view the display from any angle. A click on the calendar icon will show how the floral display will change month by month.

Switching to the annual calendar, you can see how your garden will mature in five years or ten years time. You adjust the colours and sizes of your groupings by replacing some of your original selections. You can alter the angle of view, too. Clicking on the garden fork icon will reveal what your garden maintenance programme should be month by month. The insect-shaped icon will tell you which pests to be on guard against and how to deal with them. When your garden is exactly right, you print out a hard copy of your design plus a list of the plants you've selected and the compost, fertilisers and other products you'll need.

At this stage, previous generations of householders would have started writing or telephoning to nurseries or making the rounds of the garden centres to try to locate the chosen plants. A tedious task, and if you had chosen unusual varieties, usually you'd have to settle for something else, which could disrupt your entire plan. Instead, you now click on the shop icon to summon up a list of retailers who claim to stock the goods you require. You may choose to check their advertisements, too, before selecting a few suppliers which you find appealing, and sending them your plant and product list by modem. You use the standard stock query form which asks them to respond with availability and prices. When they do, you place your orders by credit card or cash transfer, arranging for delivery to be made to your home or, to save carriage costs, your nearest collection centre. You retain a detailed plan, which you can amend over the years, and a complete record of your purchases. So do the suppliers whom you have contacted. Because they can now predict your pattern of behaviour, the means to retain your loyalty are in their hands. They can offer you a contract to supply the consumable products they know you will need regularly – compost, fertilisers and pesticides – and advise you at the right season of plants which they know will be of particular interest to you.

Gardening is the most popular active leisure pursuit in Britain. More than 80 per cent of adults have access to a garden, and over two-thirds visit a garden centre at least once a year. At the start of the new millennium it was a £3.5 billion industry spending around £33 million annually in classic advertising media, plus lavish amounts on catalogues and direct marketing. It's one of those pastimes, like DIY and cooking, which anyone can try, but which requires a great deal of expertise to do well. Simply to acquire the necessary understanding in these pursuits traditionally demanded a long apprenticeship and experience gleaned from a great deal of trial and error. Novices would often turn to a professional, a retailer, or an experienced enthusiast for specific advice. However, the boom in leisure activities and the development of modern self-service retailing methods created new high-volume information channels. Sources of personal advice were overwhelmed by the mass media: newspapers, magazines and books, radio and television programmes, and printed literature provided by branded products or retailers. The demand was so strong that information itself has become a product. The best-selling author in Britain today is the enterprising Dr D. G. Hessayon, who as proprietor of PBI, a leading manufacturer of garden fertilisers, recognised the need early on and virtually cornered the gardening information submarket with a series of popular easy-does-it booklets. He has sold forty million of them worldwide.

Today the problem for consumers, overfed from a variety of self-interested sources, is information indigestion. Consumers must rely on their advice. Yet apart from the privileged questioners of the *Gardener's Question Time* panel, the flood of information is aimed at mass audiences. The individual amateur gardener still has to dig very hard to find the solution to his very parochial concern: what will look good and thrive in that particular corner of my garden?

In the new age of technology the balance of information power shifts to the consumer. The unique promise of the computerised "Garden Planner" concept is that it will enable you to apply comprehensive knowledge expertly to a very precise area: your garden. You will know exactly what you want to buy to put in it, what products you require to nurture it, and where to get them most conveniently and cheaply. After that, a little hands-on experience will swiftly turn you into the world's leading expert on your garden.

In many markets such as this the Internet means that suddenly there is a whole new way of doing business. Yet the "Garden Planner" does not yet exist, except in rudimentary form, such as Geoff Hamilton's Garden Designer introduced by GSP in 1996. Because it requires a total reorientation of the way companies traditionally do business, the "Garden Planner" model – developing new planning and delivery systems to satisfy individual needs – has not yet been widely exploited on the Internet. Companies open virtual shops instead, because that is how they sell now. Yet there are no technological barriers to perfecting the capabilities described above in many consumer sectors. What is missing is the distribution link, and that is simply a matter of commercial enterprise, an effective alliance between a CD-ROM publisher and a horticultural supplier, for example.

According to a Guardian/ICM survey 37 per cent of British adults had online access at home or at work by the end of 1999. People in Britain now do their banking and make financial investments from home over the Internet; they buy computer gear, books, CDs, videos, and fine wines, download music, plan their leisure activities, make travel arrangements, do the weekly grocery shopping and apply for divorces. These activities amounted to well below 1 per cent of all retail sales in 1999, a figure predicted to reach 3 per cent by 2004, according to the retailing research firm Verdict, or 7.5 per cent by 2005, according to the US consultancy

Forrester Research. In the US the cable television operators dedicated to home shopping, QVC, Home Shopping Network, and ValueVision, had seen the future and struck deals with portal companies to sell their wares via e-shopping. Nevertheless, at the start of the new millennium selling via the Internet was still in its infancy.

So what was holding e-commerce back? Fraudulent trading was already being effectively addressed. Accessing online service providers was still unnecessarily complicated, but a few cogent exceptions such as Amazon had already pointed the way forward. Physical distribution was still a key problem; systems for the home delivery of grocery shopping were being re-invented, with massive and costly infrastructure. However, the major obstacle to the growth of e-commerce remains the mindset of the companies which try to use it. Most of the big companies which could benefit hugely from the Internet are in a state of denial about it. The railways did not start airlines, Hollywood tried to ignore television, IBM did not spawn Microsoft. None of the big communications companies cashed in on the Internet: why didn't Disney create Yahoo, AT&T start America Online, and Time Warner develop Excite? Because these organisations have a substantial financial and cultural investment in the business they know, resulting in the phenomenon known as "leadership resistance". All companies have a vested interest in maintaining the status quo. The short term governs: they are fearful of cannibalising their existing trade.

For these companies, the Internet is not yet *essential,* so they pay only lip service to the new medium. The way they operate *now* conditions the way they approach e-commerce. An early model was the idea that e-retailing would be enhanced in the same way that physical shopping is, by grouping online shops together in cyberspace shopping malls, with the big names pulling traffic to all the sites. This ignored the obvious: that customers don't have to get back into their cars to visit another site. Virtual shopping malls such as Barclays Bank's disastrous Barclaysquare, which ran on CompuServe, also suffered from not being taken seriously by the big names which tenanted them. W.H. Smith failed to grasp the point of e-retailing by offering only 100 bestsellers.

Retailers view their website as merely another shop and set out their wares in the same way. The "Garden Planner" model, which requires a new dynamic of discovering and resolving individual consumer needs by direct interaction, is still embryonic: in 2000 a new horticultural dot.com company, crocus.co.uk, was offering to deliver from a nursery stock of 6,000 varieties, plus advice on planting, or even to put plants into the ground, but had not made the connection to self-planning. Only a handful of estate agents and car retailers were beginning to develop extra services which contribute to the consumer purchase decision.

Even dot.com companies created exclusively to trade online are still learning how to do it. Websites are almost invariably badly produced and have considerable capacity for generating ill will. The companies which sponsor them make the same mistakes they do in their paper communications; they design their website pages in the leaden style of a corporate brochure. You have to click through a lot of guff to find what you're looking for. It's like going into a shop to buy a sandwich and being given a cookbook. Others think the Internet is a shop window: their pages are stuffed with displays designed to dazzle and entice. That's like going into a department store to buy a pair of knickers and being directed to the fashion show in progress on the fourth floor. An online sales site is neither a brochure nor a shop window. It is a sales counter. The customer is already in the store. The reason he's there is that he has already reached the second behavioural stage. He is not in pre-contemplation mode; he is contemplating action. He probably knows more or less what he wants. At the sales counter he must be able to ask for it immediately and receive an appropriate response. Too many online sellers decorate their counter, the home page, with promotional displays designed to attract the attention of the aimless browser. The genuine customer can't see the sales assistant behind the counter for all the clutter.

THE BIG LIE about the Internet is the contention that it is an advertising medium. It seems logical to put advertising on the Internet. Without any of the heavy costs and tiresome proscriptions which regulate other media, the high traffic sites on the World Wide Web can invent advertising devices of all kinds. By 1999 technology had developed to the extent that the lingerie firm Victoria's Secret was able to run a 21-minute commercial on the net, a full-length catwalk show with a cast of scantily clad supermodels. And the Internet can encompass the whole marketing process: from attracting initial interest, to demonstrating or even sampling the product or service, to taking the money. Surely an ideal advertising medium?

In this role the World Wide Web has so far failed to deliver on its promise. Many new dot.com companies based their hopeful business model on attracting income from on-line advertising. They were fishing in a tiny pond. Even the best-known sites, such as Time Warner's Pathfinder have not generated substantial advertising revenues. In the UK, according to the self-promoting Internet Advertising Bureau, online advertising accounted for only 0.6 per cent of all advertising revenue in 1999, and the majority flowed to just ten websites, most of them in the information technology sector, such as IBM, Microsoft, and British Telecom, or online retailers such as Amazon and the auctioneer QXL.

The primary technique used by the online advertising sector, accounting for more than 80 per cent of all revenues, was the flash or banner flickering like a neon sign on the Reeperbahn inviting an incautious visit. Despite the irritation factor for surfers, these devices are popular with advertisers, because they know immediately how many people are attracted to their messages, and whether they generate enquiries or sales. Yet, results are poor. According to a 1997 survey conducted by Forrester Research and reported by Internet World, only 2 per cent of these devices had *ever* been clicked upon. In 1999 the click rate had slipped below 0.5 per cent. These are the sort of inefficient response figures expected for untargeted mass mailings. By tracking eye movements, a 1999 study by the Poynter Project at Stanford University discovered that while 45 per cent of site visitors do actually look at banner ads, it's only a flicker of attraction, on average lasting just 1 second. And they don't follow through; the study confirmed a click rate of less than 0.4 per cent. For every 1,000 who clicked, only 18 placed an order. As an average charge for an advertising site banner is £25 per thousand visitors, that works out to an advertising cost of nearly £700 per sale – insupportable for any product likely to be sold online.

For all the hype, in essence Internet advertising is nothing more than a merchandising display, like a retail shop which dangles signs from its ceiling, festoons its aisles with shelf-talkers, puts brochures on the counters, or flags offers on instore television. Like these distractions Internet advertisements will usually be ignored, and for the same reason. The shopper is already in the shop, and has usually come there for a purpose. The effective role of an advertisement on an Internet site is the same as a small ad or a boldface entry in the Yellow Pages – to assist someone to find what he is looking for. Cyperspace man is not prepared to endure irrelevant advertising blather at the cost of his own time and money. The consumer who has entered an Internet site, like someone who has picked up the telephone, is at the point of planning and decision, and in that context there is little opportunity for embellishment. He may be curious enough to trigger an advertisement or two, but is likely to find the process frustrating. He is now in search mode, intently foraging for information in the same way that he scans a catalogue or the classified advertising pages.

The advertising which has found acceptance on online services is that which people want to see: classified ads – and some of them allow subscribers to place standing instructions to automatically receive all ads offering, say, a collie dog, or a three-bedroom flat. The true commercial future of the Internet does not lie in theme advertising. It is shopping from home, by touch instead of telephone.

All service providers are trying hard to control the crowds flocking through their free Internet gateways by diverting them to branded virtual shops. The retailer Boots, for example, established www.handbag.com, offering free internet access and information on women's issues as a lure. But it's impossible to control the Internet. Very little initiative is required to wander out of the virtual car park into the limitless trails of cyberspace. Those who do will have access to what manufacturers and retailers have always feared – comprehensive competitive pricing information.

Today companies can get away with selling inferior products at inflated prices because consumers are too ignorant, too lazy, or too busy to comparison shop. The life insurance industry is notorious for selling poor-quality products for premium prices. Consumers can't be bothered to learn the detail of life insurance investments, so they are swayed by well-targeted marketing and a "trustworthy" brand name. In 1996 the Prudential, which had recently relaunched itself with a new advertising image, achieved a dramatic sales increase in its long-term life insurance products, at a time when, because it was burdened with the cost of a large sales force, it languished near the bottom of many of the industry's performance measures. Its neighbours at the tail end of the league tables included other household names such as Royal Insurance, Sun Life, Friends Provident, Britannia Life, and AXA Equity and Law. But the Internet now permits the consumer to take over the product search and selection function, electronically interrogating retailers or direct suppliers and in doing so, comparing terms and prices. Those who can't puzzle it out for themselves will work through information brokers who can.

John Lewis has traded successfully on its "never knowingly undersold" promise because most customers most of the time can't be bothered to hunt for a better offer. In the future its customers can make John Lewis a lot more "knowing". You should be able to select your goods in the shop, dial up a customised search engine on your mobile phone to find a better price, and tell the staff to match it.

Broad-band technology, allowing consumers to access the Web at faster speeds through the PC, interactive television and mobile phones is imminent. It will unlock the staggering mass market potential of e-commerce, by shifting the entry gate from the computer, which requires skill, intelligence, and a degree of determination to operate, to television, which everyone knows how to work.

"Going to the shops" will become a more specialised activity. And when they are in real shops people may do a lot more touching and feeling than purchasing. Because they will be better informed about products and prices. Dozens of specialist magazines with titles such as *What Hi-Fi?*, *What Cellphone?*, *What Camera?*, or *What Laptop?* have sprung up in recent years to fill this knowledge gap; now they offer websites. Today an informed and determined British consumer will test drive a new model of car at a local dealer, but he will save himself thousands of pounds by purchasing it abroad. Dot.com companies are now moving in to service that demand.

The Internet will create a world of comparison shoppers. Seated at the controls of the information machine, the consumer thrusts the gears of marketing communication into reverse. Those providing goods and services will now have to react to his brief. Retailers, who have already largely foregone the advantages of personal service, on the Internet also relinquish advantages of location and shop design. Information, price, service, and delivery become paramount. E-tailing, as it inevitably became known, has granted start-ups an advantage over bigger companies, which were unable to give their dot.com activities undivided attention. The newcomers achieve faster delivery because they invest heavily in back-office and fulfilment operations, and have developed marketing targeted at individual customers.

ADVERTISING WILL CHANGE, too. It has already acquired a new informational role: because there is no handy directory of website addresses, in 1999 a gold rush of fledgling dot.com companies aiming simply to publicise their website address began to pour into the media. Newspapers, magazines and television welcomed these naive cash-rich start-ups by hardening their advertising rates. Apart from this initial publicity function, the Internet will usurp the traditional informational role of advertising. Most newspapers are heavily supported by income from classified advertising for jobs, houses, cars, auctioneers, and second-hand goods. Virtual traders such as autobytel and e-Bay are supplanting them; speciality shopping magazines such as *Loot, Exchange & Mart,* and *AutoTrader* have already converted to the Internet. In America classified revenues have begun decline. In Silicon Valley, in a growth economy, recruitment advertising in the *Los Angeles Times* fell by 8 per cent in the last quarter of 1998 compared to the previous year; for the

San Jose Mercury News all classified advertising was down by this amount.

On the Internet, the advertising practitioners of the 21st century have to reinvent their craft. Their inventory of antics aimed at snatching the consumer's attention, the communications skills of a drowning man, are worthless in this context. The marketing man's concept of a remote, bovine mass audience somewhere out there in Adland dissolves into a montage of individual faces, very close at hand. The opportunities to target customers precisely is immense, using intelligent agent technology which determines the individual characteristics and preferences of the potential customer, and then lets him know about specific products or services. In mass advertising, even the most persuasive argument is by nature vastly inefficient because that argument must reach the right person at the right time: when he or she is at a vulnerable (contemplation) stage. If not, it's ignored. The Internet is much more precise, as it involves pro-activity: the consumer seeks out the advertiser.

Nevertheless, in a competitive marketplace the consumer is unlikely to make a purchase unless the information sought is presented by a trusted name – the retailer, the manufacturer, the dot.com company, or perhaps one of a new breed of specialist distribution agents. So, the essential purpose of mainstream media advertising will remain: to enhance the reputation of the supplier. But now the advertisers will have to manipulate their image-making mirrors not in the distant make-believe Adworld of mass marketing but in the new reality, where because the consumer can so easily initiate contact with the manufacturer or the retailer, he will be able to test corporate imagery against actual performance.

In his 1994 book *The Glittering Haze,* advertising agency chairman Winston Fletcher trotted out the timeworn "informational" defence of the social contribution of advertising:

- Advertising introduces people to useful new products and reminds them of old products they had almost forgotten.
- Advertising tells people where they can buy goods at low prices and where they can invest their savings at advantageous rates.
- Advertising informs people where they can go to be entertained and what they can do to alleviate their pains and sufferings.
- Advertising lets people know how to use products in ways they had not previously thought of and how to improve themselves in ways they had not previously dreamed of.

- Advertising warns people against behaving dangerously and encourages them to behave responsibly.

- Advertising adds extra dimensions – of consistency, glamour, quality, reassurance, value – to the things people buy.

- Advertising saves people time, by providing neatly encapsulated, easily absorbed information.

This catechism is an evasion. While all of these tenets may have applied in the early days of advertising, its informational role has long since atrophied, and persists today largely in the classified sector. Most of the advertising created over the past fifty years has been devoted to the penultimate benefit listed above: the creation of brand imagery. All of the others, which are based on the provision of information, have now become the province of the Internet. Consumer will use them to arm themselves *against* the blandishments of advertising.

CHAPTER 31
ROUND THE BEND DOWN THE YELLOW BRICK ROAD

Future

When Christopher Columbus sailed east across the Atlantic Ocean looking for China, he could not know that sea-going Chinese junks were already crossing the Indian Ocean behind him to trade along the east coast of Africa. For his 1492 expedition, Columbus had to beg Philip II to provide him with three ships. In 1391, in the province of Nanking, the Chinese had planted fifty million trees, to provide wood for the fleets of the future.

LONG-TERM THINKING is no longer fashionable, either in government or in commerce. It is almost undetectable in the advertising industry, where clients, campaigns, and the people who create them all have short-term goals. Thirty years ago, campaigns used to run, with minor variation, year after year, drumming the same message into the public consciousness: "Nothing Works Faster than Anadin", "Drinka Pinta Milka Day", "A Mars a Day Helps You Work, Rest and Play". Now, messages have largely been abandoned for impressions; the cultural models they imitate and the business cycles they aim to steer accelerate faster and faster. Campaigns change with the seasons.

Yet the establishment of a brand personality is a long-term project. Global brands have now swollen beyond Jeremy Bullmore's representation of a modest "bundle of values" (Chapter 4). Like Hollywood films, which export American sentiments, they carry all the elements of a belief system. Just as successful religions do, successful brands must embody values which satisfy enduring emotional yearnings, yet adapt to new social habits as they evolve. What new trends are emerging which will affect how people react to advertising messages over the long term?

The couch potatoes are sprouting
Throughout the second half of the twentieth century television was the dominant leisure activity. For the great mass of consumers, personal and social activities of all kinds were replaced by passive hours spent before the flickering gogglebox. Towards the back end of the 20th century, with

PCs outselling television sets and Internet access provided free, that trend began to reverse. Digital television is the gateway to interactive services, and by 2000, one in ten UK households had signed up for it. Its golden promise for advertisers is that it brings measurable direct response techniques to television. The viewer can call up a split-screen panel to apply for more information or make an immediate purchase. The home shopping channels such as QVC have read the future and have begun to convert to an electronic network platform using interactive TV technology such as the satellite TV company Sky Television's Open TV interactive channel, launched in 1999.

The PC will soon be as omnipresent as the TV in the home, and will eventually merge with it. But a keyboard demands input. The viewer has to *do something*: send an e-mail, play a game, or surf the Internet on a shopping expedition or a quest for information. That means less time available to watch television. In households which have computers, television viewing is in decline; where there is Internet access it's falling faster. However, the most common means of advertising on interactive TV remains that dubious legacy of the Internet model, banner advertising. The Internet cannot replace traditional image-building advertising media. Thus, the more time people spend fingering the keyboard, or the remote control television monitor input device, the less they will be exposed to meaningful advertising *themes*. Those most likely to be excluded are the choicest advertising targets: the better-off, better-educated consumers.

Introducing the amazing new, improved bullshit detector
Once upon a time people used to settle points of fact in pub arguments by ringing up the information desk of the *Daily Telegraph*. Now anyone can be an expert. Access to high-quality knowledge has been thoroughly democratised. As consumers find it increasingly easy to compare the performance and costs of one brand with another, they will become much harder to deceive. Though not everyone has the will, the skill and the intelligence to find out how the world really works, the opinion-formers we all harken to are much better informed today. Everyman's natural bullshit detector has been upgraded, and this will severely inhibit the scope of deceptive practice for all advertisers, including politicians. The early experience of Internet traders suggests that if on the high street the customer is king, in the virtual world he can be a tyrant. Advertisers receive lots of complaints and demands for straightforward answers. In a dialogue conducted by e-mail or voice mail there's little scope for adspeak and PR waffle.

Technology empowers consumer resistance, too. If we are to be able to construct virtual television channels reflecting our own interests, will we also be able to blank out advertisements? A technique for obliterating those pesky website banners is already on the market.

"Lonely Hearts" rule
With the consumer in command of the information process, the role of advertising focuses on the essentials: announcements of what's new, and the forging of a long-term emotional bond, to create a brand preference which will override opposing rational appeals such as product distinctions and temporary price reductions. Much of today's advertising fashion, crudely aimed at gaining awareness at whatever cost to the brand personality, is self-destructive. The effective advertiser will have to behave less like a shill and more like a friend.

What is a friend? A friend is someone who is usually glad to see you. A friend trusts you. A friend will say nice things about you to other people. A friend will make excuses for you when you fail. In developing interpersonal skills most people discover it's usually a good policy to treat other people as though they were friends – even strangers. Particularly if you want something from them. As in any friendship, that means penetrating through the masks they present to the world to stroke that conflictive contraption of creativity and pathology which drives the inner spirit – what Arthur Koestler called "the ghost in the machine".

This is what's at the bottom of the glib phrase "relationship marketing". Friendship is not a natural role for corporations, and they will find it awkward to simulate. Smaller, more flexible operators will find it easier to project sincerity: "We try harder". Larger organisations may find that effective "relationship marketing" is beyond their natural grasp.

The rebel's paradox
Who am I? What is the purpose of my life? A world driven by freewheeling technology heightens our philosophical anxieties. In the past, comfortable answers were provided, sufficient to endure for one's lifetime at least, by church or state. These institutions do not control the new technology. Many people are attracted to new belief systems which urge them to find their identity and social purpose inside themselves. But these definitions seem real only to those who share the same belief system. So people withdraw within closed communities, either physically, in security-gated housing estates or communal squats, or spiritually, subscribing to "isms" of every description. Symbolic fragments are freighted with heavy meanings: iconoclastic posters on the walls of

teenagers' bedrooms in the leafy suburbs, the homilies of self-help books, the inarticulate grumblings of pop songs.

In industrial societies, there is a craving for self-identity through "independent expression". The hymns of the new secular religion exult in the integrity of the individual spirit: the favourite karaoke performance of the Japanese corporate "salaryman" is "I Did It My Way"; in the domed cathedral erected for the British millennium celebrations a showbiz rendition of the lyrics "When you walk through a storm keep your head up high", as emotionally stylised as a kabuki performance, nudges aside "Jerusalem" and "God Save the Queen" as the expression of national purpose. To demonstrate that they are unique individuals, not part of the herd, wannabe rebels join a peer group – a herd. Otherwise, who would be able to appreciate the particular character of their unique identity? In his novel, *The Idiot*, Fyodor Dostoevsky described the 19th-century bourgeois urge to make a social impression as "a commonplaceness desirous above all things of being independent and original without the faintest possibility of becoming so". By the middle of the 20th century, the search for differentiation turned inwards: "doing your own thing" was elevated into an ethical principle. But by then individuals were no longer just workers or citizens; they had become consumers dependent on a lifestyle determined by the market. Individual self-expression now takes the form of novel fashion choices, trends which the market is poised to identify and mimic, quickly converting each new quirky gesture into normative behaviour.

Thus, much of the marketing strategy of the late 20th century was based on the paradox of the faint-hearted rebel. This motor car, or beer, or perfume, or newspaper will allow you to express your own individual personality, but it is the preference of so many other people like you that no one can laugh at you for purchasing it. The mission of advertising was to pretend there was a plausible balance between those antithetical concepts.

As free-market enthusiasts are keen to point out, Adam Smith's invisible hand of competition ensures that there is plenty of room for consumer self-expression in the global hypermarket. There are hundreds of different brands of shampoos, cornucopias of vegetables – often grown to organic specification and flown in from all over the world – a constant cascade of "bestselling" books, while the neighbouring multiplex vomits forth an endless shimmering stream of new films and hundreds of new channels may be summoned on your home television set. But these are options, not choices. The choices have been made by those who control the means of distribution: the manufacturers, the major multiple retailers, and the behemoths of the entertainment industry. The power of selection is concentrated into fewer and fewer minds, and from Tesco to the BBC, they are motivated primarily by mass market considerations of brand share and profit. If you're into the simple life, there's infinitely more choice in a street market in Rajasthan than in your local supermarket, and you'll find what you want a lot more quickly.

The global hypermarket does not innovate, it monitors emerging trends in consumption and copies them. The packaged expressions of autonomy it offers are losing credibility. It is becoming increasingly difficult to maintain with a straight face that the selection of a car or a cosmetic is an expression of rugged individualism. The Internet, however, offers genuine alternatives. Because of its low start-up costs and worldwide reach, small companies, even 13-year-old HTML hackers, can service quite specialised interests. And not just in commercial terms. If you're planning a walking holiday in Corsica, for example, you don't have to rely just on the generalised handouts you can get from a travel agent or the state tourist authority. You can page through the diary of someone who has made the walk and published it on the net for no other reason than, perhaps, egoism or altruism. The Internet provides an authentic means of expressing personal autonomy: some day everyone will have their own website, the ultimate badge of personal identity.

The 30-second sermon
If some corporations have more resources than most governments, and more global distribution centres than nations have consulates, it is inevitable that brand names will be drawn into political and ideological confrontation. Non-governmental organisations such as Greenpeace were able to mobilise the weapon of consumer boycott to win victories over adversaries as powerful as Shell Oil, on the issue of waste disposal, and the French government, about Polynesian nuclear testing. Companies are far more vulnerable to consumer boycotts than are countries; they feel the pain and they can react more quickly. Consumers get worked up about a great many issues. In 1995 alone, Texaco was the subject of three national protests: because of alleged exploitation of tribal lands, for refusal to hire people with HIV, and for investment in Burma. In a Gallup survey that year, of 30,000 consumers for the Co-operative Wholesale Society, a third said they had boycotted stores or products on at least one occasion. In America at that time, according to other surveys, three-quarters of households were boycotting at least one product, usually because of concern about company practices. Today, comparatively under-resourced pressure groups can use the Internet to

rally a worldwide protest within minutes. A number of ideologically incompatible fringe groups fused briefly to ignite a highly visible protest at the 1999 World Trade Organisation conference in Seattle. The increasingly interlinked dependencies of global trade make advertisers equally vulnerable.

Companies were swift to reflect consumers' growing concern with social issues in advertising's ingratiating mirror. Mainstream companies routinely extol wholesome themes such as family values, the protection of the environment, the rights of the disabled, international understanding, and racial integration. The kaleidoscope of impressions crowding your television screen during the commercial break – the joyful ethnic wedding party, the small boy listening to his pregnant mum's tummy, the Masai warriors squinting into the sun, the choir of gospel singers – were they promoting British Telecom, British Airways, the Midland Bank, or the Hanson industrial conglomerate?

In pursuing these strategies, mainstream advertisers have to be mindful of the pernicious contrary. For each special interest which is favoured, there is a danger of arousing the prejudice of another. It's not just pre-schoolers who harbour mutually incompatible desires. German motorists boycotted Shell because of the environmental effects of its operations but demand petrol-guzzling cars. British consumers oversubscribed privatisation issues but were outraged by the remuneration of the "fat cats" who ran the new companies. They demand cheap meat, but deplore factory farming. The political system finds it increasingly difficult to bridge these gaps, and brands which take sides on an issue can be caught in the squeeze.

Who needs creativity?
In the last twenty years creativity in advertising has come to rely more and more on borrowed values: associating the brand with a celebrity, an issue, an interest, a stance, something that people empathise with. In encouraging this trend advertising agencies have run out of road. The road ends at a cliff called sponsorship. Nike paid £250m over ten years for the privilege of sponsoring the Brazilian football team. A Hollywood blockbuster can expect to rake in $10 million in product placement, at around $30,000 a shot. Children's collecting crazes, such as the late 1990s Beanie Babies, don't result from advertising, but from clever marketing tactics. The Y2K version of this phenomenon, Pokémon, has its own television show, thus exempting it from both advertising expenditure and regulation. Advertising has burst the bounds of classic media, where there is some possibility of measuring effect, and from which advertising

agencies traditionally gain their remuneration. Today, much of our world, and particularly leisure activities, is a stage for sponsorship. And there's no real place here for the musings of advertising agency copywriters and art directors.

The fragmentation of globalisation
Globalisation became the buzzword of business just as nationalism was renewing ancient political schisms amongst ethnic groups all over the world. How can these two powerful cross-currents be reconciled?

Coca-Cola is the universal cliché of global marketing. It is the second best-known word in the world, after OK. Its logo is the third most recognised symbol in the world, after the Christian cross and the Muslim crescent. It built this monolithic global franchise through marketing imperialism, exporting the American dream unadulterated by any sensitivity to cultural differences. Yet any advertising professional who has worked in more than one country knows that it is notoriously difficult to export a sharply focused advertising concept devised for one country into another, just by translation. At the simplest level, there is the problem of homonyms. The British contingent of Unilever management insisted on retaining the name Gibbs in Germany, where it is pronounced like the German word "gyps", and so launched its toothpaste in that market in 1964 by advising consumers to brush their teeth with plaster. In Cantonese, "Coke adds life", literally translates as "Coke brings your ancestors back from the dead". Cultural signals vary, too. The French don't react well to commands, so the Nike slogan "Just do it" became the rather more timid "La vie est à toi", or "Your life is your own". Ad people in foreign markets are easily misled by their own cultural assumptions, before learning elementary codes: for example, that in India, white does not stand for purity, but for death. And advertising history is replete with anecdotes such as the slogan, proposed by an American copywriter to launch a range of Dunlop adhesives in Britain, for use "at home and on the job".

The trick is to respect national differences without degrading the global aspiration. It's a lesson British Airways learned the hard and expensive way. On a wave of hubris engendered by its belief in its own advertising claim, "The World's Favourite Airline", it introduced a diversity of multicultural design on the tail fins of its aircraft in 1997. By 1999, BA had replaced the Union Jack on two-thirds of its fleet with exotic ethnic impressions ranging from Chinese calligraphy to a Polish design of a cockerel. This composite imagery flew in the face of the major tenet of branding theory: that branding must be singular and consistent in every manifestation. It also abandoned the basic motivational strategy which lies behind all advertising for international airlines: the appeal to national stereotypes, such as Teutonic thoroughness, the submissive charm of the Oriental hostess, American technological skill, or, perhaps the most reassuring reputation of all to airline passengers: unflappable British reliability. BA persevered in its folly for a few years, against the fulminations of Lady Thatcher, air traffic controllers, and large sections of the British public, coming back down to earth only when archcompetitor Richard Branson cheekily dressed his Virgin aircraft in the discarded cloak of British nationalism. In 1999 BA began repainting half of its fleet of 308 aircraft with a redesigned Union Jack logo. After reputedly expending £60 million on its "one world" image, the company was left with the worst of two worlds: a schizoid brand personality.

If its basic promise satisfies universal emotional longings, a globalised brand can sit comfortably with emerging nationalism because it represents the aspirations of that society. Whether they end up as part of India or Pakistan, kids in Jammu and Kashmir want to ride on Hondas, not oxcarts. They want to wear designer sunglasses and drink Coca-Cola or maybe Seven-Up, not Thumbs-Up, just as people do in films and on television. In the 1990s Coca-Cola's global advertising strategy was the emotional ambition to "teach the world to sing". The clothing retailer Gap entered the new millennium with a wordless television campaign promoting a global lifestyle disguised as freedom of choice. So long as they communicate effectively across cultural obstacles to universal yearnings, multinational advertisers create their own virtual culture.

The Holy Grail discovered
The technological developments in communications which have democratised access to knowledge have the potential to empower the advertiser as well as the consumer. It is now technically possible and economically viable to apply the measurement disciplines of the direct response art to general image-building advertising on a large scale, with virtually instantaneous results. The systems for exposing pre-test advertisements to highly selective samples exist, and so do the interactive response mechanisms. All that is lacking is appropriate methodology, some verifiable simulated action, such as Horace Schwerin's fifty-year-old "competitive preference" measurement, or even actual sales. A web "currency" called Beenz already exists, which can be exchanged for free goods, discounts, and special offers. Samples of householders are now induced to scan all their regular purchases so that research companies can monitor them by computer. For those who do their shopping on the

Internet, comprehensive data on purchase behaviour will be available without any extra input. Realistic quantitative measurements of the effects of advertising are for the first time within the grasp of the advertising industry. These will free motivational research from the ignorant tyranny of the self-serving focus group and educate the people who create and judge advertising in the techniques of psychological persuasion.

Official: good taste defined
The same techniques – informed selection of mass research samples, downloading test materials, and interactive response mechanisms – permit regulatory bodies, and anyone else who is interested, to constantly monitor public reaction to existing or proposed advertisements or any other presentations in the public arena. A broadly based instant sampling of opinion will provide a more credible basis to support decisions on what is – or is not – deemed to be in acceptable public taste.

Happy ever after?
The assumption of free-market philosophers is that economic growth is the key to human happiness. On the other hand, songwriters, who perhaps are in closer communion with the human spirit, say that the best things in life are free. Folk wisdom agrees that money can't buy happiness. What's the point of owning a shiny new car if London's streets are so clogged with immobile metal that you can't drive it without losing a wing mirror? Economic prosperity, as measured by Gross Domestic Product, has doubled in the UK and the US over the past thirty years. Yet in 1995 a MORI survey reported that one in five Britons subscribed to life values which could be categorised as "post-materialist". In 1970 only one in twenty held such convictions. Some observers believe that increasing affluence only creates increasing dissatisfaction, and in the end people will reject the values of materialism. They contend that status-seeking through conspicuous consumption, and the structures which enable it, such as advertising, will melt in the new dawn of a post-materialist society.

Yet, as income rises, so do expectations. Many Britons now aspire to holiday in the Seychelles rather than Blackpool. The suspicion remains that ambition always outstrips achievement; the drive for self-actualisation explains why people like Rupert Murdoch and Bill Gates go on working. The carrot is always in front of the donkey. It's the challenge that motivates, not the prize; outstripping others is the allure of the race; the reward is merely symbolic, of no more intrinsic value than a laurel wreath. Until society succeeds in channelling the competitive impulse in other directions, it will continue to be focused on the achievement of economic power and the baubles – trophy wives and badged brands – which display success to rivals.

ADVERTISING has been an intrinsic part of our lives for only about 150 years. The graphic revolution of the first half of the 20th century developed it into the most powerful instrument of mass persuasion the world has yet known. In the second half of the century, its focus has been dissipated by a proliferation of new media with fragmented audiences, and there is evidence of consumer resistance to intangible "added brand values" in hard times. The new technologies have created an escalating race in which consumer perception quickly evolves to master each new trick: attention span adapts to jump-cut filming, imagination resolves the oxymoron of virtual reality, shopping habits adjust to the Internet.

Consumers soon learn to interpret each new deceitful advertising gesture and take what they want from it. Paid advertising in classic media is, after all, the most transparent and attributable form of propaganda. More insidious – as the lines smudge between independence and sponsorship, documentary and entertainment, editorial and handout, policy and sound-bite – are the techniques of mass persuasion we don't even recognise as self-interested.

In the Depression years in America, an enterprising man could get rich by placing a classified advertisement in small-town papers which read in its entirety: "Hurry! Send $1 now!" plus a postal address. Until the postal authorities clapped him in gaol. Today he operates a website or international direct marketing scam, and the authorities dispute who has jurisdiction. Techniques change, but the Big Lie continues to exploit the same source of human vulnerability. An early, flawed axiom of advertising was that it should aim at people with a mental age of 12. The truth is, successful propagandists have always aimed not at our heads, but at our emotions, and in our hearts we are all 12-year-olds. Our insecurity is cradle-to-grave.

BIBLIOGRAPHY

Bell, Daniel, *The Cultural Contradictions of Capitalism,* Basic Books, 1976

Boorstin, Daniel J., *The Image: A Guide to Pseudo-events in America,* Atheneum, 1961

Bullmore, Jeremy, *Behind the Scenes in Advertising,* NTC, 1991

De Groot, Gerald, *The Persuaders Exposed. Advertising and Marketing: The Derivative Arts,* Associated Business Press, 1980

Fletcher, Winston, *A Glittering Haze,* NTC, 1992
 – *How to Capture the Advertising High Ground,* NTC, 1994

Franzen, Giep, *Advertising Effectiveness: Findings from Empirical Research,* NTC, 1994

Hamilton, Carl, *Absolut: Biography of a Bottle,* Texere, 2000.

Hopkins, Claude C., *My Life in Advertising/Scientific Advertising,* NTC, 1998

Institute of Practitioners in Advertising, *Advertising Works: Papers from the IPA Advertising Effectiveness Awards,* NTC (biannually since 1981)

Koestler, Arthur, *The Act of Creation*, Hutchinson Danube, 1964

Lewis, Richard W., *Absolut Book: The Absolut Vodka Advertising Story,* Journey Editions, 1996

Ogilvy, David, *Confessions of an Advertising Man,* Atheneum, 1962
 – *Ogilvy on Advertising,* Crown Publishers, 1983

Packard, Vance, *The Hidden Persuaders,* David McKay, 1957

Peppers, Don, and Rogers, Martha, *The One to One Future,* Doubleday, 1993.

Sutherland, Stuart, *Irrationality: The Enemy Within,* Constable, 1992

INDEX

ABB 28
Abbey National Building Society 128
Abbot ale 92
Abbott, David 19, 243-4
Abbott Mead Vickers BBDO 19, 220, 243
Absolut vodka 111-12, 134, 136, 141
Acheson, Sir Donald 236
Action and Information on Sugars 234
Activewear 166
Adbusters (Canada) 263
Adidas 113, 124, 146, 217, 259
Advertising Association 95, 212, 233
Advertising Standards Authority (ASA) 58, 124, 174, 222, 223-4, 225, 242, 243, 244, 245, 246, 249-50
Advil 31
Aero 33
After Eights mints 122, 182
Age Concern 137
Ahmed, Shami 35
AIDA (linear sequential model) 20
AIDS 235-7
Aignier, Ladislas (Lucien) 97
Air Miles 85, 103, 177
Aitchison, Jean 55, 98
Alien 62
Allied Dunbar 128
Allied Lyons 181-2
Alpacino 35
Altman, Robert 165
Amazon 276

Ambre lacquer 110
American Express 60, 70
American Family Association 247
American Telephone and Telegraph (AT&T) 181, 188
American Tobacco Company 95
Amis, Martin 149
Amnesty International 130
Anadin 281
Andersen, Arthur 182
Andrews toilet tissue 154
'Andy Capp' 173
Angela's Ashes 217
Apple Macintosh 59, 62, 102, 147
Aquascutum mackintoshes 157
Archers, The 67, 240
Ariel 16, 31, 124, 182
Ariston washing-machines 105
Aristotle 37, 39
Armani, Giorgio 163
ASA *see* Advertising Standards Association
Asda 167
Asprey & Garrard 134, 269
AT&T *see* American Telephone and Telegraph
Atkinson, Rowan 117, 191
Attenborough, Sir Richard 255
Audi 81, 194
'Aunt Jemima' 119-20
Australia Advertising Standards Council 57
autobytel 278
AutoTrader 278
Avenir 68
AXA Equity & Loan 63, 277

BA *see* British Airways
Babylon Zoo 147
BACC 248-9
Bacon, Sir Francis 51
Bailey, David 87
Bailey's Irish Cream 31
Bainsfair Sharkey Trott 216
Baker, Danny 154
Banana Republic 163
Bar Council 238
Barclaycard 117, 125, 126-7, 191
Barclays Bank 125, 185, 189, 191, 196, 274
Barclaysquare 274
Barker, Larry 59, 215
Barnett, Bernard 17
Barnum, P. T. 55, 56
Bartle Bogle Hegarty 12, 164
Basketball Diaries 255
BAT *see* British American Tobacco
Bates (Ted) & Co 170
Bauer, Eddie 60
Bayer 33
  Bayer aspirin 33
BBC 8, 50, 148, 217, 240
Beanie Babies 286
Beatles 150
Beckett, Samuel 91
Beecham's Pills 27
Beenz 288
Bell, Daniel 150*n*, 180
Bellow, Saul 66
Ben & Jerry ice-cream 186
Benetton 38, 136, 148, 222-6, 231, 244, 263
Benetton, Luciano 223
Bennett, Jennifer 200-1
Benny, Jack 153
Benson, Richard 155
Benson & Hedges 137, 172
Bistro, Kuala Lumpur 177

Berlusconi, Silvio 205
Best, George 113
Bic company 30
Bierce, Ambrose 150
Bird, Alfred 186
Bisto 33
Blackadder 117, 217
Blackmores Active Woman Formula vitamins 57
Blade Runner 62
Blue Velvet 217
BMP.DDB 59
BMW 13, 31
Boase Massimi Pollitt 215, 218
Bob & Ray 152
Boddington's beer 13, 112-13
Body Shop, The 75, 185, 186, 226
Bold 182
Bon Marché (Paris) 166
Boorstin, Daniel J. 27, 76, 114-15, 121, 222, 227-8, 244
Boots 59, 60, 277
Borg, Bjorn 118
Bottomley, Virginia 23
Bow, Clara 162
Braathens airline 92
Branson, Richard 186, 187-8, 288
Brasso 182
Brazil 191
Brewers' Society 238
Brignull, Tony 22-3, 220-1
Britannia Life 277
British Accounting Standards Board 33
British Airways (BA) 13, 58, 61, 109, 132, 138, 145, 267, 287-8
British American Tobacco (BAT) 170, 177, 263
British Board of Film Classification 242
British Gas 84-5, 100, 147-8, 202,

INDEX

203
British Heart Foundation 93, 233
British Market Research Society 22
British Meat 108
British Medical Association 232, 233, 238
British Medical Journal 136, 232
British Nuclear Fuels 202
British Rail 57, 154
British Safety Council 245
British School of Motoring 57
British Sky Broadcasting 256, 265
British Telecom (BT) 61, 65, 119, 184, 203, 204, 253-4, 276
Britvic 9-10
Broadcast Advertising Clearance Centre 50, 242
Brown & Williamson 170
Brown Foreman 252
Brylcreem 116
Bryson, Bill 184
BSkyB television 256, 265
BT *see* British Telecom
Bugsy Malone 217
Bullmore, Jeremy 30-1, 281
Burke (research company) 18
Bush, George 116, 200
Buxton, Andrew 189

Cable television 265
Cadbury 30, 33, 34-5, 69
   Cadbury's Flake 94
Camel cigarettes 174-5, 177, 178, 258
"Camel News Caravan" 169
Campaign (magazine) 16, 17, 41, 174, 219, 243
Campbell, Naomi 187
Campbell Soup Company 3

Cardin, Pierre 34
Carling, Will 117
Carling Black Label 16, 124, 143, 154
Carlsberg 151
Carlton & Smith 42
Carpet World 260
Carphone Warehouse 253
Carville, James 202
Castlemaine XXXX lager 101, 124, 143, 144, 182, 217-18
Castro, Bernadette 108
Castro Convertible sofa beds 108
Caterpillar 34
Céline 166
Cellnet 253
Central Office of Information 202, 253
Central Television 240
Cerullo, Morris 45
CGI *see* Computer Generated Imagery
Chanel 133
   Chanel No. 5 121
Channel 4 News 93
Chaplin, Charlie 116
Chariots of Fire 217
Charities Aid Foundation 117
Charles, Prince 118, 149, 245
"Charles Atlas" 80
Charlton, Bobby 113
Chemical Industry Association, UK 183
Cher 118
Chesterfield cigarettes 115, 169
Chevrolet 80
Chiat/Day advertising agency 195
Child (magazine) 222
'Cholmondley-Warner' 153, 154
Christian Aid 239
Church of Scientology 79

Churches Advertising Network 240, 245
Churchill, Winston 101, 169
Cinzano 16, 118
Citicorp Venture Capital 180
Citizen Kane 152
Citroën cars 117, 154
Clairol 167-8
Clancy, Kevin J. 22
Clarke, Kenneth 238
Claymation 167
Cleese, John 13
Clinton, Bill 64, 86, 117, 202, 250
Clockwork Orange, A 255
Club 18-30 244-5
Club Med 80
Co-operative Bank 192, 195
Co-operative Wholesale Society 285
Coca-Cola 4, 10, 29, 31, 34, 61-2, 97, 116, 118, 121, 123, 143, 144, 173, 266, 287, 288
Cohen, Ben 186
Cole, Andy 187
Cole, George 117-18
Collins, Joan 16, 118
Columbus, Christopher 281
Comme Des Garçons 165
Commercial Union 102, 190
Commission for Racial Equality 237, 246
Committee of Advertising Practice 224
Compton, Denis 116
Computer Generated Imagery (CGI) 63-4
Concord 110
Connery, Sean 206
Conqueror letter paper 93
Conservative Christian Fellowship 245

Conservative Family Campaign 235
Conservative Party, British 136-7, 199, 200, 202, 204, 239, 246
Consumer Research Centre 57
Cook, Thomas 185
Cooke, Peter 178
Cooper, Gary 206
Coors Brewing Company 34
Corby trouser press 69-70
Costco 264
Courage beer 136
Covent Garden Soup Company 113
Coward, Noël 142
Crawford, Joan 162
CRE *see* Commission for Racial Equality
Creutzfeldt-Jakob disease 49
Crisp, Quentin 161
Cristall vodka 110-11
'Crocker, Betty' 6, 120
Croft Port 139
Crowther, Leslie 16
Cunningham, B. J. 175
Cunningham, John 204

DADA *see* Design and Art Direction Awards
DAGMAR (linear sequential model) 20
Daily Mirror 110
Daily Telegraph 137, 171, 282
Daks of London 80
D'Arcy, Masius, Benton & Bowles 22
Datewise Worldwise 38
Dawkins, Richard 45-6, 74
Daz 31, 154, 182
Dean, James 52, 172

INDEX

Dean cigarettes 172
Death cigarettes 175
Dee, Jack 153
Deerhunter, The 255
de Groot, Gerald 22
de La Billière, Sir Peter 226
Delaney, Tim 246
Delicatessen 106
Della Femina/Jeary 226
Delta Airlines 58
DeMille, Cecil B. 62
Department of the Environment 234
Department of Health and Social Security 232, 236
Department of Trade and Industry 167
Department of Transport 232
Design and Art Direction Awards 15, 244
Dettol 182
Diana, Princess 245
DiCaprio, Leonardo 255
Dichter, Ernst 47, 142
Diet Coke 116, 121
Dietrich, Marlene 79, 162
Dior, Christian 166
Direct Line 92, 196
Dirt Devil vacuum cleaners 121
Disney, Walt 50
Docker's trousers 164
Doctor-Patient Partnership (DPP) 233
Dole, Bob 117
Don't Look Now 152
Doritos crisps 15
Dostoevsky, Fyodor 284
DPP *see* Doctor-Patient Partnership
Dr Collis Brown's tonic 27
Drambuie 145

Dukakis, Michael 200
Dulux paints 182
Dunbar, Robin 53
Dunhill 177
Dunlop 34, 37-8, 142, 146, 181, 287
Dutch (magazine) 165

e-Bay 278
Easy Rider 122
Easyjet 187
Economist, The 76, 137, 255
Edward Scissorhands 152
Egg (Prudential Insurance banking division) 100
    Egg credit card 156-7
Eggsvertising 65
Einstein, Albert 18, 98, 99
Ekman, Paul 48
Elizabeth II 223
Ellesse 166-7
Ellis, Reverend Robert 240
Embassy Regal 148, 174
Emporio Armani 163
Enfield, Harry 153, 154
Eraserhead 217
Ericsson 35
Esquire 13
European Commission 133
Eurostar 105
Evans, Chris 121
Everest double-glazing 96
Everlast jeans 166
Exchange & Mart 278

Face (magazine) 102, 155
Fairy Liquid 96
Falling Down 255
Falun Gong movement 45
Family Planning Association 87

Farming News 243
Federal Communications Commission 8
Federal Trade Commission 175
Fellini, Federico 189
Fendi 161-2, 165
Ferrari 32
Ferrero Rocher 156
Feynman, Richard 14, 217
Financial Times 76, 137
Findus Lean Cuisine 152
First Direct Bank 103, 194, 194-6, 197
Fishbein, Martin 20
Fisherman's Friend 120-1
Fitzgerald, F. Scott 219
Fletcher, Winston 10, 212, 279
Flintstones, The 110
Ford, Mrs Gerald (Betty) 49
Ford cars 30, 32, 121, 122, 152
Forrester Research 273-4, 276
Forza Italia! 205
Fosters 143, 154
Fowler, Norman 236
Fox, James 117
Fox, Michael J. 116
Fox film company 256
Frankfurter Allgemeine Zeitung 225
Freberg, Stan 137-8
French Connection UK 243, 250
Friends Provident 277
Fry, Stephen 121-2
Fuji film 227
Fussell, Paul 62*n*

Gable, Clark 162
Gallo 252
Gap 121, 147, 163, 165, 288
Garbo, Greta 162
Gates, Bill 289
Gaultier, Jean-Paul 148, 165
Gauntlet, David 257
Geest 28
General Electric Company 115
General Foods 268
General Mills Company 120
'George the Bear' 143
Georgia State University 73-4
German Christian Democratic Party 101
Gibbs toothpaste 287
Giggs, Ryan 113
Gilbert and George 244
Gilliam, Terry 191
Ginsberg, Allen 147
Givenchy perfumes 133
Glenmorangie whisky 65
Glenn, John 69
Glynwed engineering company 181
God 239-40
Goddard, Paulette 162
Goldblum, Jeff 151
Goleman, Daniel 48
Golubkov, Lyonya 10, 11
Gorbachev, Mikhail 115
Gordon, Laurence 255
Gossage, Howard 219*n*
Gould, Philip 28
Gower, David 226
GQ magazine 13
Grand Met 33
Great Escape, The 152
Greenfield, Jerry 186
Greenpeace 285
Greenway, Harry 245
Grey Advertising 212
Grolsch beer 105
Gruenfeld, Deborah 62-3
GSP 273
Guardian 171, 201, 236, 273

INDEX

Guardian Health 126
Guardian Insurance 190
Gucci handbags 157
Guerlain 166
Guinness 30, 95, 148, 149, 151-2

Häagen-Dazs 33, 81, 86, 134, 138, 154, 186
Haitai gum 154
Haji-Ioannou, Stelios 187
Halford's 92
Halifax Building Society 62, 110, 156
Hall, Jerry 116
Hamilton, Geoff: Garden Designer 273
Hamlet cigars 138, 154
Hamleys 269
Hammer, M. C. 123
Hammer Films 33
Hamnett, Katherine 250
'Hannibal Lector' 152
Hanson 152
Haring, Keith 141
Harlow, Jean 162
Harp lager 111
Harris paintbrushes 70
Harrods 75
'Hartley, J. R.' 9
Hauer, Rutger 152
Head and Shoulders 108
Healey, Denis 116
Health Authority, British 173
Health Education Authority 174, 234
Hegarty, John 12-13
Hegley, John 213-14
Heineken beer 13, 19
Heinz 30, 34, 263, 267-8
Hell's Angels 162

Helmsley Hotels 119
Hemingway, Ernest 121
Hendon Young Conservatives 199
Henley Centre 66, 190, 192, 249
Henry, Steve 12
Her Majesty's Theatre 78
Hessayon, D. G. 272-3
Heublein 33
Hirst, Damien 142
Hitch-Hiker's Guide to the Galaxy, The 217
Hitchcock, Alfred 33
Hoechst 179
Hofmeister beer 143
Holiday Inns 27
Holmes, Adrian 174
Holsten Pils 16, 101, 143, 151, 155
Home Shopping Network 265, 274
Honda 32, 133
Hoover 185
Hope, Bob 152
Hopkins, Anthony 196-7, 202
Hopkins, Claude C. 3, 9, 14
Hopper, Dennis 122
Hopper, Edward 139
Horton, Willie 200
Hovis 33, 138
Howell, Rupert 88, 194
Howell Henry Chaldecott Lury 12, 194
HSA: health insurance plan 116
HSBC financial services 93
Hudson, Hugh 217
Huffington, Mike 198-9
Humane Society (US) 237
Hunt, Gareth 96
Hurt, John 235
Hutchison Telecom 137
Huxley, T. H. 69
Hyundai 145

IBA *see* Independent Broadcasting Authority
IBM 62, 70, 276
Iceland Stores 86
ICI 182
Iglesias, Julio 118
Ikea 230
Imperial Tobacco Company 174, 175
Independent, The 19, 96, 103
Independent Broadcasting Authority (IBA) 236
Independent Television Commission (ITC) 58, 86, 87, 194, 234, 242, 244, 249, 256, 257
Inland Revenue 60-1
Institute of Practitioners in Advertising 212, 213
  Advertising Effectiveness Awards 15-16, 17, 41, 86
Interbrand (consultancy) 34
Interflora 87
Internet Advertising Bureau 275
Internet World 276
Interwood 265
Investment in Industry (3i) 203
IPA *see* Institute of Practitioners in Advertising
Irn Bru 249, 264
ITC *see* Independent Television Commission
ITV 265
Ivaran Lines 125

Jackson, Jesse 63
Jackson, Michael 116, 118
Jacob Club biscuits 244
Jaguar 32
Jamón Jamón 99
Jansson, Mikael 165

Jaws 48, 128
'Joe Camel' 175
John, Elton 116, 121
Johnson & Johnson 182
Jones, "Reverend" Jim 45
Jones, Steve 121
Joplin, Janis 146
Jordan, Michael 118
Journal of the American Medical Association 175
JWT *see* Thompson, J. Walter – Agency

Kahneman, Daniel 47
Kaufmann, George S. 157
Kaye, Tony 142, 146
Keeler, Christine 94
Kellogg's 29, 47, 65, 263
Kennedy, Jackie 114
Kiam, Victor 121
Kim Jong-il 205
King, Stephen 215
Kinnersley, Paul 83
Kinnock, Neil 200
Kit-Kat 33, 182
Kitchener, Lord 44, 136
Klein, Calvin 167, 246-7
Knight, Gladys 120
Kodak 266
Koestler, Arthur 39-40, 42, 43, 44, 78, 109, 283
Koss, Kate 246
KPMG 213
Krugman, H. E. 20
Kubrick, Stanley 255
Kwik Save 264

Labour Party, British 19, 28, 200-1, 204

INDEX

Lacroix, Christian 166
Ladies' Home Journal 120
Lady Clairol 168
Laker, Freddy 187
Lamont, Norman 189, 201
Lancaster, Burt 105
Land, Edwin 40
Lane, Kenneth Jay 114
Lanvin 165
Law, Denis 113
Lawson, Nigel 116
Leary, Denis 155
Leary, Timothy 163
Le Bon, Gustave 82
Le Creuset 94, 264
Lee, Spike 33
Lee Jeans 164, 249
Leeds Building Society 118
Legendary Joe Bloggs Inc. Co. 35
Leibowitz, Annie 163
Leicester Polytechnic 101
Lennon, John 121
Lever Brothers 9, 88, 124, 182, 185
Leverhulme, Lord 9
Levi's Jeans 16, 71, 87, 101, 105, 133, 147, 154, 164, 167, 249
Levi Strauss 164
Lewis, John 277
Le Witt, Sol 142
Liberal Democrat Party 205, 237
Libération 224, 225
Ligget Group 170
Lincoln automobiles 60
Lindup, Mike 192
Lintas 22
Lipman, Maureen 119
Lippman, Walter 230
Livingstone, Ken 116, 200, 201
Lloyd, John 156, 217-18
Lloyds-TSB 189
LMVH *see* Louis Vuitton Moët Hennessy
Lock, James and George 99
London buses 85
London Zoo 70
Loot 278
L'Oréal Preference hair colourant 168
Loren, Sophia 118
Los Angeles Times 278
Louis Vuitton Moët Hennessy 166
Lowe Howard-Spink 174
Luckies 169
Lucky Strike 0riginals Collection 177
Lucozade 234
Lufthansa 184
Lux 190
Lynch, David 217
Lynx (animal rights group) 87
Lyons Bakeries 181

McCollum Spielman Worldwide 7
McDonalds 118
McEwan's lager 144
McKern, Leo 139
McLennan, Bill 23
McQueen, Steve 152
Madonna 162
Mailer, Norman 32, 146, 147
Major, John 38, 230
Major, the Movie 200
Maker's Mark bourbon 112
Manchester Business School: survey 268
Manchester United 113, 124
Marcuse, Herbert 147
Marinetti, Emilio Filippo Tommaso 140
Marketing magazine 88
Marketing Society 219

Marks, Stephen 243
Marks & Spencer 30, 35, 113, 186, 196
Marlboro 172, 173, 176, 177, 178, 258, 263, 269
Mars Bars 281
Martini 13, 155
Mask, The 63
Maslow, Abraham 74
Mates condoms 187
Matthews, Bernard 16-17, 96
Maugham, William Somerset 49
Mavrodi, Sergei 10-11
Maxwell House Coffee 81
Mazda cars 103
Mazza, Samuel 109-10
Meat and Livestock Commission 142
Mercedes-Benz 31, 146
Mercer, Johnny 123
Mercury 125, 153-4, 253
Metropolis 106
Michelob 112
Microsoft 80, 276
Midland Bank 68, 189, 190, 191, 192, 194
Milk Marketing Board 281
Milky Way 234
Miller beer 105-6
Mills & Boon 32
Minder 117-18
Mini cars 32
Miss Clairol 167-8
Missoni 165
Misty cigarettes 172
Mitsubishi Carisma 132
MMM 10-11
Moët & Chandon 91
Monkhouse, Bob 153
Monopolies and Mergers Commission 30, 133

Monroe, Marilyn 64, 162
Monty Python 70
Moore, Demi 222
MORI polls 187, 200, 233, 288, 289
Morris, Philip 176, 177, 263
Moschino, Franco 165
Moult, Ted 96
'Mr Bean' 117
Mr Deeds Goes to Town 206
'Mr Grayson' 153, 154
Mr Kipling Cakes 33
Mrs Merton and Malcolm 148
MTV 105, 266
Muggeridge, Malcolm 232
Muji 35-6
Multiple Sclerosis Society 229
Murdoch, Rupert 255-6, 265, 289

Naked Shit Pictures, The (exhibition) 244
National Abortion Rights Action League (US) 238
National Broadcasting Company, US 169
National Dairy Council 128
National Food Alliance (NFA) 233, 234
National Health Service 19, 201, 238
National Lottery 11, 47-8, 187
National Newspaper Campaign awards (1995) 91
National Power 100-1, 202
National Savings 126
Nationwide Building Society 127-8
Natural Born Killers 255
NatWest Bank 92, 189, 190, 193, 195
Nescafé 96
  Gold Blend 16

Nestlé 33, 34, 182
New London Theatre 78
New York Times 114
New Yorker 75, 76, 136
Newman, Nanette 96
Newman, Paul 118
News Corporation 256
News of the World 152
Newspaper Publishers' Association 59, 106
Next 165
NFA *see* National Food Alliance
Nice 'n Easy hair colourant 168
Nielsen, Leslie 117
Nike 101, 133, 146, 155, 164, 211, 226-7, 259, 286, 287
Nikko hotels 139
Nin, Anaïs 73
9 1/2 Weeks 152
Nissan cars 109, 110, 152
Nixon, Richard 77-8
Nokes, Barbara 212
Nokia 35
North, Oliver 199
North Devon Journal 243
Northern Exposure 266
Norwich Union 53
Not the Nine O'clock News 217
NPA *see* Newspaper Publishers' Association

Obsession fragrance 246
Ofili, Chris 141
Ogilvy, David 43, 69, 106
Ogilvy & Mather 88
OK 10
Old Spice 154
One2One mobile phones 121, 127
Ono, Yoko 121
Orange 137

Ortiz, Cristina 165
Orwell, George 198, 219
Osborne Veterano Brandy 98-9
Osservatore Romano, L' 225
Ouseley, Sir Herman 246
Oxo 29

Paciott, Cesare 165
Papua New Guinea 240-1
Parker, Alan 217
Parker Sonnet (pen) 110
Parkinson, Norman 113
Pascal, Blaise 48
Pavlov, Ivan 3
PBI 273
Pearl Insurance 193
Pepe jeans 164, 165, 246
Pepsi-Cola 95, 101, 110, 116, 123, 133, 143, 144
    Maxwear fashion range 34
Pernod 94
Perrier 31, 68
Persil 31, 124
Peterman, J.: catalogue 106
Peugeot cars 32, 152, 154, 229, 306
Pfizer pharmaceutical company 117
Phileas Fogg snacks 153
Photo CD 266
Picasso, Pablo 109
Pierce, John 258
Pillsbury 33, 186
Pinker, Stephen 250-1
Pirelli tyres 127
Playboy 199
Pokémon 286
Polaroid 40, 141
Pollitt, Stanley 215
Polo mints 68
Polycell 182

Polykoff, Shirley 167-8
Ponzi, Charles: scam 11
Porsche 32, 264
Post Office 57, 253
Power Rangers 257
PowerGen 202
Poynter Project, Stanford University 276
Pret à Porter 165
Pretty Polly stockings 85
Prince of Wales Duchy Originals 118
Pringle sweaters 167
Procter & Gamble 18-19, 31, 124, 182, 204, 263, 266
Prudential Insurance Company 53, 185, 182, 277
    Egg (division) 100
    Egg credit card 156-7
Psycho 48, 255
Publicis 100*n*
Punch magazine 232

Quaker Oats 119-20
QVC 265, 266, 267, 274, 282
QXL 276

Radion 88
Rampling, Charlotte 194
Range Rover 226
Rank Hovis McDougall 33, 263
Ratner, Gerald 56-7
Ratner Group 56-7
Rawle, Graham 94
Rayner, Clare 244
Reagan, Ronald 115, 169, 201, 206
Reckitt & Colman 182
Red Rock cider 117
Redgrave, Steve 116

Rediffusion 95
Reebok 113, 124
Reeves, Rosser 110
Refugee Council 129
'Reg' 174, 175
Reith lectures (1966) 55, 98
Remington company 121
Remnick, David 230-1
Rémy Martin 31
Renault cars 32, 94, 96, 154
Reservoir Dogs 152
Reynolds, Burt 118
Reynolds (R. J.) Tobacco Company 175, 176, 177, 180
Rhys-Jones, Griff 16, 143
Ricci, Nina 142
Rivers, Joan 266
Road Safety Campaign, UK 136
Rockefeller, Mrs Nelson 49
Roddick, Anita 186, 187, 226
Roeg, Nicholas 152, 236
Rogers, Sir Frank 171
Rollnick, Stephen 83
Rolls-Royce 31, 106, 264
Ronson 121
Roosevelt, Eleanor 115
Roosevelt, Franklin D. 38
Rossiter, Leonard 16, 118
Rover cars 32, 94
Rowan and Martin's Laugh-In 150
Rowntree 33, 182
Royal Bank of Scotland 127
Royal Insurance 80, 125-6, 277
Royal Marines 79
Royal Society for the Prevention of Cruelty to Animals (RSPCA) 239
Ruddles County beer 112
Rumpole of the Bailey 139
Russell, Jane 162

INDEX

SAA *see* South African Airways
Saab 32
Saatchi, Charles 142, 173
Saatchi & Saatchi 87, 142, 199, 211, 213, 244
Saga Home Insurance 79
Sainsbury's 13, 29, 59, 196, 264, 268, 269
St Laurent, Yves 133
Salem High Country Holidays 177
San Jose Mercury News 279
Sanders, Gwenda 171
Save & Prosper 190
Sayers, Dorothy 97
Schiffer, Claudia 117
Schlesinger, John 200
Schwerin, Horace 3, 4-7, 8, 22, 87, 288
   Schwerin Research Corporation 7, 82, 95
SCOPE 237
Scott, Ridley 62, 191, 217
Scottish Amicable 192
Scottish National Party 206
Scottish Widows 86, 192, 193
Scrumpy Jack cider 126
Sears Roebuck 226
Securicor 57
Sekonda Watches 153
Sephora cosmetics 166
Sewell, Brian 139
Sex Pistols 147
Shake and Vac 156
Sharp 266
   Sharp SD-3076 85
Shell Oil 185, 285, 286
Shields, Brooke 246
Shirley Valentine 152
Shoaff, Edgar A. 219
Siemens 148
Silence of the Lambs 152

Silk Cut 137, 173, 178
Singing Detective, The 128
Skol Lager 143
Sky Television 267, 282
Smarties 33
Smee Report 176
Smirnoff vodka 33
Smith, Mel 203
Smith, W. H. 274
Smythe, Reg 173
SNP *see* Scottish National Party
Solid Fuel Advisory Council 61
Somarriba, Pascal 224-5
Sony 118, 146
   mobile phones 108
Sotheby's 114, 177
South African Airways 69
South Carolina Federal Bank 101
Spastics Society 237
Specht, Ilon 168
Spice Girls 118
Spitting Image 217
Sprite 155
Standard Life 193
Starch (linear sequential model) 20
Stassinopoulos, Arianna 199
Steeplechase amusement park, Coney Island 56
Steinlager 229-30
Stephanie, Princess, of Monaco 118
Sterling Products 33
Stevenson, Adlai 198
Stewart Ivory and Company 126
Stilton cheese 132
Stoli vodka 111
Stone, Oliver 255
Stones Bitter 61
Stork SB margarine 16
Storr, Anthony 45, 88
Stott, Nigel 83
Strand cigarettes 52

Streep, Meryl 63
Struggle Against Financial Exploitation 189
Stuart, Paul 163
Sun Life 277
Superdrug 59, 133
Sutherland, Stuart 48-50, 51, 53, 54
Swayze, John Cameron 169
Swimmer, The 105

Talleyrand-Périgord, Charles Maurice 55
Tango 9-10, 101, 146, 257
Tarantino, Quentin 33
Taylor, Elizabeth 119
Taylor, Matthew 237
Taylor Sir Teddy 246
Teletubbies 50
Tennent's Pilsner 151
Tesco 30, 60, 133, 167, 248, 264, 268, 269
Tesla, Nikola 40
Tetley Tea 87
Texaco 285
Thatcher, Margaret 199, 202, 204, 206, 235, 288
Thelma and Louise 152
Thompson, James Walter 42
  Agency (JWT) 29, 30, 41-2, 156, 179, 215, 242
3i 203
3M 183-4
Timberland shoes 105
Time Warner 251
  Pathfinder 275
Times, The 201
Tio Pepe sherry 92
Tobacco Advisory Council 176
Tomkins 263
Toscani, Oliviero 223, 224, 226, 231

Toshiba 128
Toyota 133
Toys 'R' Us 70
Trade Marks Act (1994) 123
Trott, Dave 216
Trump, Ivana 266
Turner, Tina 116
TV Quick magazine 191-2
TV-Link 101
TWA 103
Twain, Mark 131, 150
Twilight Zone, The 152
Twin Peaks 217
Tylenol 182

UBI 69
UltraBra 244
'Uncle Ben' 120
'Uncle Sam' 44, 136
Unilever 7, 22, 31, 186, 287
Union Carbide 183
US Army 4-5, 8
U.S. Classic Inc. 166
US Council for Energy Awareness 184

Valentine, Tim 100
ValueVision 274
Vanity Fair 222
Vatican, the 225
Vauxhall cars 32, 68, 109, 154
Veblen, Thorstein 75
Velvet Underground 146
Verdict 273
Vespré Silhouettes Plus 244
Veuve du Vernay 182
Viagra 117
Vicary, James 4, 8
Viceroy cigarettes 170

INDEX

Vico, Giambattista 49
Victoria & Albert Museum 139
Victoria's Secret 275
Vidal, Gore 73
Viktor & Rolf 166
Virgin 35, 58, 187
Virgin Airlines 109, 251, 288
Virgin Atlantic 187
Virgin Cinemas 188
Virgin Cola 247
Virgin Direct 196
Virgin Express 188
Virgin Rail 188
Virgin Records 187
Virginia Slims 177
Virtual Vineyards 76
Visa Delta 94
Viz magazine 174
Vladivar Vodka 153
Vodafone 127, 253
Vogue 136, 166
Volkswagen cars 32, 70-1, 81, 129, 145, 263
Volvo cars 31, 32, 125, 145-6, 157, 266
Von Furstenberg, Diana 266
Vriens, Matthias 165

Wal-Mart 264
Waldegrave, William 201
Wallace and Gromit films 167
Wallen, James 211
Walls ice cream 86
Wanamaker, John 9
Warhol, Andy 141
Warner Brothers 50
Warriors, The 255
Water Authorities Association 204
Waugh, Auberon 149
Wayne, John 114

Wearing, Gillian 70
Wedgwood 92
Weight Watchers 34
Welles, Orson 136, 152
Wells, H. G. 101, 136, 149, 219
West, Mae 116
Which? magazine 33
White Diamonds 119
Windsor, Duchess of 114
Winner, Michael 242
Winston cigarettes 172
Wispa 68-9
Wolff, Michael 271
Woman magazine 228
Women's Wear Daily 165
Wonderbra 13, 85
Wonderloaf 190
Woolwich Building Society 191
Worcester, Robert 200
World Health Organization 233
World Trade Organisation 286
Wranglers 164
Wright, Robert 74
Wrigley's chewing-gum 96, 154
Wyer, Robert, Jr. 62-3

Yankelovich, Clancy, Shulman 22
Yellow Pages 9
Yellowhammer agency 87
York, Duchess of 115
Young, Dr Brian 50
Young, Jimmy 16
Young, Lord 238
Young & Rubicam 263
Young Ones, The 190

Zanussi dishwashers 107